"*Liturgy in Migration* offers solid scholarship that is not satisfied with fine analytical surveys but also asks critical questions and sees future challenges. One finds chapters on diverse Western Christian traditions and Eastern ones, and the overall picture ranges from Pentecostalism to Oriental Orthodoxy. This is particularly praiseworthy, because there exist hardly any scholarly studies that compare specific Eastern and Western liturgical traditions with each other. Here is one! It is a most valuable study, most warmly recommended to scholars, policy makers, and anyone interested in the most relevant subject of migrations!"

—Basilius J. Groen
University of Graz, Austria

"The history of worship is often told using relatively fixed, settled, and static categories to describe very dynamic practices and communities. This volume offers a needed corrective, pointing to the significance of boundary crossings, pilgrimage, cross-cultural and inter-faith encounters in shaping worship practices. It serves to chasten sweeping summaries of historical experience that ignore these movements, to highlight the limits and value of our fragmentary knowledge, and to inspire a renewed sense of wonder of what it means to belong to the body of Christ."

—John D. Witvliet
Calvin Institute of Christian Worship
Grand Rapids, Michigan

Liturgy in Migration

From the Upper Room to Cyberspace

Edited by Teresa Berger

A PUEBLO BOOK

LITURGICAL PRESS
Collegeville, Minnesota
www.litpress.org

A Pueblo Book published by Liturgical Press

Cover design by David Manahan, OSB. Cover image: Thinkstock.

© 2012 by Order of Saint Benedict, Collegeville, Minnesota. All rights reserved. No part of this book may be reproduced in any form, by print, microfilm, microfiche, mechanical recording, photocopying, translation, or by any other means, known or yet unknown, for any purpose except brief quotations in reviews, without the previous written permission of Liturgical Press, Saint John's Abbey, PO Box 7500, Collegeville, Minnesota 56321-7500. Printed in the United States of America.

Library of Congress Cataloging-in-Publication Data

Liturgy in migration : from the upper room to cyberspace / edited by Teresa Berger.
    p.   cm.
  "A Pueblo Book."
  Includes index.
  ISBN 978-0-8146-6275-5 — ISBN 978-0-8146-6276-2 (e-book)
    1. Liturgics—Congresses.   2. Emigration and immigration—Religious aspects—Christianity—Congresses.   I. Berger, Teresa.

BV169.5.L59   2012
264—dc23   2012031716

Contents

Foreword   vii
  Martin D. Jean

Acknowledgments   ix

Introduction   xi
  Teresa Berger

1. Belonging to the Church   1
  Graham Ward

Part 1: Historical Moments of Liturgical Migration

2. Ritual Practices on the Move between Jews and Christians: Theories and Case Studies in Late Antique Migration   19
  Clemens Leonhard

3. A Shared Prayer over Water in the Eastern Christian Traditions   43
  Mary K. Farag

4. Migrating Nuns—Migrating Liturgy: The Context of Reform in Female Convents of the Late Middle Ages   83
  Gisela Muschiol

5. "From Many Different Sources":
  The Formation of the Polish and Lithuanian Reformed Liturgy   101
  Kazimierz Bem

6. Methodism's "World Parish": Liturgical and Hymnological Migrations in Three Ecclesiastical Generations   131
  Karen B. Westerfield Tucker

7. An Immigrant Liturgy: Greek Orthodox Worship and
Architecture in America   155
Kostis Kourelis and Vasileios Marinis

Part 2: Contemporary Liturgical Migrations

8. Eastern Christian Insights and Western Liturgical Reforms:
Travelers, Texts, and Liturgical Luggage   179
Anne McGowan

9. Hispanic Migrations: Connections between Mozarabic and Hispanic
Devotions to the Cross   209
Raúl Gómez-Ruiz, SDS

10. Sounding the Challenges of Forced Migration:
Musical Lessons from the Ethiopian Orthodox Christian Diaspora   229
Kay Kaufman Shelemay

11. Asian American Catholics and Contemporary Liturgical Migrations:
From Tradition-Maintenance to Traditioning   243
Jonathan Y. Tan

12. Soundings from the Liturgical Ecumene:
Liturgical Migration, Christian Mission, and Mutual Conversions   259
Charles E. Farhadian

13. Liturgical Migrations into Cyberspace: Theological Reflections   279
Stefan Böntert

List of Contributors   297

Index   301

Foreword

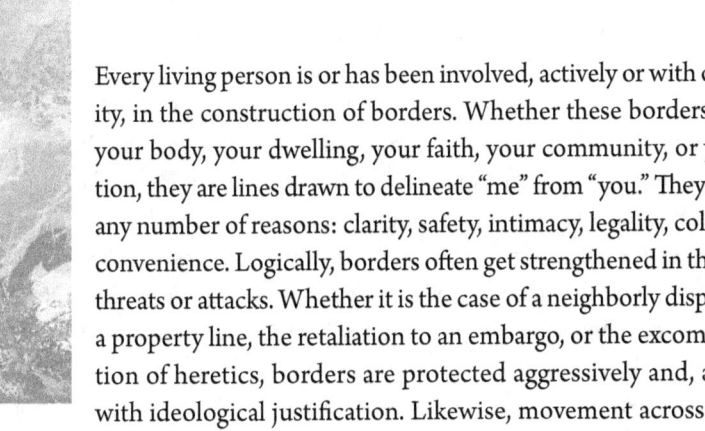

Every living person is or has been involved, actively or with complicity, in the construction of borders. Whether these borders outline your body, your dwelling, your faith, your community, or your nation, they are lines drawn to delineate "me" from "you." They arise for any number of reasons: clarity, safety, intimacy, legality, collegiality, convenience. Logically, borders often get strengthened in the face of threats or attacks. Whether it is the case of a neighborly dispute over a property line, the retaliation to an embargo, or the excommunication of heretics, borders are protected aggressively and, at times, with ideological justification. Likewise, movement across borders is inspired by equally strong motivations: by desire for new knowledge or experiences, by coveting of neighbors' possessions, by eruptions in nature, by ethnic cleansing, by the need to strengthen one's own communal identity, by the desire to enlarge oneself, by love.

If the liturgical renewal movement of the mid to late twentieth century was meant to reclaim atrophied and lost practices of earlier times for the sake of strengthening religious identity and enlivening worshiping communities, then of equal interest to us must surely be the reasons why these readaptations did *not* take root. It is revealing to observe liturgy being formed "on the ground" as a result of local human circumstance, as opposed to the regrafting of historical practices to contemporary ones. These rites are windows into the beliefs, demarcations of power, and personal piety of those who practice them. They shift, inevitably, because we shift in our geographical circumstances, in our relationships, and in our reactions to the changing culture outside our door and on our iPad.

I am gladdened and proud that this volume on the crossing of borders comes out of the Yale Institute of Sacred Music, because it is our core mission to move across the hallowed realms of academic disciplinary boundaries. Rather than view liturgy as a list of rubrics and texts on a page, we are asked to consider the host of forces that come into play in its construction and performance: music, art, space, ethnic identity, global media, the internet, and so much more. Worship is the domain not of the liturgical scholar alone, but equally of the ethnomusicologist, the anthropologist, the art historian, the ethicist, the theologian, the cultural critic. It seems to take as large a group of people to understand a community's worship as it does to engage in the worship itself.

Virtually all Christian communities confess that God calls them into prayer and that these patterns of prayer are central to their life and mission in the world. Our hope is that this volume will heighten interest in this central area of Christian studies and that, in some small way, the call to prayer will extend itself to those who wish to know more about how Christians live out their lives. Indeed, not only will students of worship find new knowledge here, but those who form and engage in liturgy will be inspired by the grandeur and diversity in Christian experience. Understanding this will hopefully lead us to welcome more openly the "migrations" that enter our worship on a weekly basis.

As I commend this magnificent volume to you, I also honor its architects. Professor Teresa Berger, the book's editor, who, with our colleague Professor Bryan Spinks, invited to Yale a host of scholars and leaders in the spring of 2011 to our triennial conference on liturgical studies. No two people spoke the same disciplinary or ecclesial language, but they shared the interest that produced the essays before you. I thank all who were involved and hope that their labors bring much fruit to the consideration of our own border constructions and crossings.

                                          Martin D. Jean
                                          Director
                                          Yale Institute of Sacred Music

Acknowledgments

Excerpts from the English translation of *The Roman Missal* © 2010, International Commission on English in the Liturgy Corporation. All rights reserved.

Reproduction of "Still for Thy Loving Kindness": text, Charles Wesley (from *Hymns and Sacred Poems*, 1740); music, Swee Hong Lim; music © 1988 General Board of Global Ministries, GBGMusik, 475 Riverside Dr., New York, NY 10115. All rights reserved. Used with permission.

Reproduction of "O mnus oeuy Preah bahn bong-hagn [For the Lord Has Shown to All of Us]": Micah 6:8 paraphrase and music, Sarin Sam; English paraphrase, S T Kimbrough Jr.; words and music © 1999 General Board of Global Ministries, GBGMusik, 475 Riverside Dr., New York, NY 10115. All rights reserved. Used with permission.

Reproduction of "Bari sot, bari sot, bari sot [Holy, Holy, Holy]": words and music, Sarin Sam; English, S T Kimbrough Jr.; words and music © 2000 General Board of Global Ministries, GBGMusik, 475 Riverside Dr., New York, NY 10115. All rights reserved. Used with permission.

The translation of the Armenian text of the Epiphany rite, found in the appendix to chapter 4, is taken from *Rituale Armenorum*, ed. Frederick Conybeare, trans. Arthur John Maclean, originally published by Clarendon Press in 1905. © Oxford University Press. Used with permission.

The translation of the Greek text of the Epiphany rite, found in the appendix to chapter 4, is adapted from *The Great Book of Needs*, vol. 1, © 1998 St. Tikhon's Seminary Press. Used with permission.

Introduction

Teresa Berger

Migrations are writ large into our contemporary world. The International Organization for Migration estimates that close to one billion people are migrants, owing to economic reasons, political unrest, humanitarian crises, natural disasters, environmental displacement, human trafficking, and individual choice (and these are only a few of the complex causes for the startling number of migrants worldwide).[1] Processes of migration are not a new fact in history; the last hundred years of rapid globalization have simply made such processes a dominant feature of contemporary life. In the last quarter century, the number of people on the move worldwide has doubled, from one hundred million to nearly two hundred million people,[2] and processes of migration are expected to intensify in years to come, leading some to think of our times as the "age of migration."[3] Faiths too are crisscrossing the globe: Islam has grown in Europe, African-originated churches in North America, and a Japanese Buddhist group in Brazil. Moreover, it is not only people who are increasingly on the move, but also other living beings. Beyond the age-old, long-distance animal migrations, we now encounter African fish on North American dinner plates,

---

1. See the *World Migration Report 2011*, p. 49, available online at http://publications.iom.int/bookstore/index.php?main_page=product_info&cPath=37&products_id=752&zenid=f838c3201667ef014e1754354073f6b5. Last accessed 30 March 2012.

2. These numbers are given by Daniel G. Groody, a theologian who has written extensively on migration; see his essay "Crossing the Divide: Foundations of a Theology of Migration and Refugees," *Theological Studies* 70 (2009): 638–67, here 638f, and his publications listed in footnotes 9 and 11 of this chapter.

3. See *The Age of Migration: International Population Movements in the Modern World*, ed. Stephen Castles and Mark J. Miller, 4th ed., rev. and updated (New York: Guilford Press, 2009).

Brazilian killer bees in the southern United States, and Asian carp in the Great Lakes region. A host of contemporary phenomena also circulates globally, from cultural trends, technological advances, and diverse knowledges to most material goods, whether raw, finished, discarded, or inadvertently released. Among those materials are endangered woods like mahogany, international electronic waste dumped in Africa and India, and radioactive materials—for example, from the 2011 nuclear disaster in Japan—traceable in other parts of the world. Finally, there is the large-scale migration, especially of youth, deeper and deeper into cyberspace and constant connectivity. Indeed, there seems to be little in the contemporary world that is not on the move. *Liturgy in Migration* will show this to be true also of liturgical practices—both in the contemporary context of globalizing flows and in the manifold migrations of liturgical history—which might be said to stretch from the entryway of the Upper Room to the edges of cyberspace.

Migration Studies

In making use of the category of migration as an interpretive lens for the study of liturgy, the present volume is part of a larger discursive map on which migration has surfaced as an important marker. This is true of contemporary debates not only in the media or among policy makers (including those in the ecclesial realm[4]) but also in the world of scholarly reflection and analysis.[5] Migration studies continue to multiply, with migrations of religious traditions

---

4. The Vatican, for example, has an office, the Pontifical Council for the Pastoral Care of Migrants and Itinerants, that attends to the spiritual needs of a broad range of people on the move, among them "migrants, exiles, refugees, displaced people, fishermen and seafarers, air transport personnel, nomads, circus and fairground people, those who go on trips for reasons of piety, study or recreation, land transport workers and other similar categories." See the council's self-description on the Vatican web site: http://www.vatican.va/roman_curia/pontifical_councils/migrants/documents/rc_pc_migrants_doc_19960520_profile_en.html. Last accessed 11 April 2012.

5. The literature continues to grow: A good introduction to the interdisciplinary nature of migration studies is provided in *Migration Theory: Talking across Disciplines*, ed. Caroline B. Brettell and James F. Hollifield, 2nd ed. (New York: Routledge, 2008). Deeper attention to religious traditions on the move can be found, for example, in *Immigration and Religion in America: Comparative and Historical Perspectives*, ed. Richard Alba et al. (New York: New York University Press, 2009), and in *Immigrant Faiths: Transforming Religious Life in America*, ed. Karen I. Leonhard et al. (Walnut Creek, CA: Altamira Press, 2005).

Introduction xiii

of growing interest, especially in the sociology of religion[6] and in ethnographic research.[7] In theological circles too, the theme of migration has been of growing interest, especially in the last five years. The journal *Concilium* in 2008 dedicated a volume to exploring *Migration in a Global World*;[8] the same year saw the publication of a collection of essays that offered "theological perspectives on migration."[9] Two years later, Gemma Tulud Cruz published *An Intercultural Theology of Migration*, which seeks to provide a theological interpretation of a particular contemporary migration, namely, that of Filipina domestic workers.[10] In 2011 the cover of a leading Catholic magazine promised its readers "A Theology of Migration."[11] Elaine Padilla and Peter Phan have just edited *Theology of Migration in the Abrahamic Religions*,[12] and William T. Cavanaugh's recent book, critiquing a modern transfer of devotion from the church to the nation-state, appeared as *Migrations of the Holy*.[13] Scholarly research and conferences dedicated to religion and migration also are on the rise.[14]

---

6. See, for example, Caroline Plüss, "Migration and the Globalization of Religion," in *The Oxford Handbook of the Sociology of Religion*, ed. Peter B. Clarke (New York: Oxford University Press, 2009), 491–506.

7. See, for example, the essays in *Mobile Bodies, Mobile Souls: Family, Religion and Migration in a Global World*, ed. Mikkel Rytter and Karen Fog Olwig, Proceedings of the Danish Institute in Damascus 7 (Aarhus: Aarhus University Press, 2011).

8. *Migration in a Global World*, ed. Solange Levebvre and Luiz Carlos Susin, Concilium 2008:5 (London: SCM Press, 2008).

9. *A Promised Land, a Perilous Journey: Theological Perspectives on Migration*, ed. Daniel G. Groody and Gioacchino Campese (Notre Dame, IN: University of Notre Dame Press, 2008). The volume, which focuses on undocumented Hispanic migrants coming to the United States, had roots in a 2002 conference in Tijuana, Mexico, on Migration, Religious Experience, and Globalization. An earlier volume directly related to the 2002 conference was edited by Gioacchino Campese and Pietro Ciallella: *Migration, Religious Experience, and Globalization* (New York: Center for Migration Studies, 2003).

10. Gemma Tulud Cruz, *An Intercultural Theology of Migration: Pilgrims in the Wilderness*, Studies in Systematic Theology 5 (Leiden: Brill, 2010).

11. *America* 204:3 (2011). The cover took up the title of an essay by Daniel G. Groody in that issue: "A Theology of Migration: A New Method for Understanding a God on the Move," pp. 18–20.

12. *Theology of Migration in the Abrahamic Religions*, ed. Elaine Padilla and Peter Phan, Christianities of the World (New York: Palgrave Macmillan, 2012).

13. William T. Cavanaugh, *Migrations of the Holy: God, State, and the Political Meaning of the Church* (Grand Rapids, MI: Eerdmans, 2011).

14. The following are three examples apart from the 2011 ISM conference, Liturgy in Migration. In 2005 a conference at the Yale Institute of Sacred Music, titled Sex and Religion in Migration, examined how religious and gender identities arise and develop in relation to

Liturgy in Migration: The 2011 Conference

The developments sketched above provide the larger context within which the conference on Liturgy in Migration was conceived. Organized by the Yale Institute of Sacred Music (ISM) and its program in liturgical studies, the conference took place 24–27 February 2011 at Sterling Divinity Quadrangle in New Haven, Connecticut. The present volume began as a collection of papers presented at that conference and has grown to include other research related to the theme of liturgy in migration. The ISM conference already offered a richly diverse set of case studies of liturgical migrations, past and present. Rooted in an expansive view of the field of liturgical studies—a view fostered by the interdisciplinary character of the ISM—the conference not only highlighted traditional liturgical topics but also paid attention to material and visual culture and to musical traditions, all key dimensions of liturgical life. At the same time, no attempt was made to represent all, or even most, major migratory flows in the history and practice of liturgy. Any attempt at such representation would be doomed to failure, not least because so many details of the historical migration of liturgical materials continue to remain invisible to us today. Rather, the task envisioned was more modest and also more specific—namely, to examine a select number of liturgical migrations, past and present, across a variety of boundaries, among them geographic, ethnic, ecclesial, and chronological ones. The larger hope was that these case studies, when taken together, would yield insights into the characteristics, patterns, and directions of liturgical migrations and flows. Put differently, the aim of the conference was to display, through quite specific examples, what this particular interpretive lens—that is, the optic of migration—enables us to see. This aim also informs the present volume, born out of the 2011 conference.

Migration as an Interpretive Lens for the Study of Liturgy

At the heart of both the 2011 conference and the present volume lies the conviction that the category of migration constitutes an intriguing contemporary lens with which to pursue the study of liturgy. The category of migration,

---

one another in the context of globalization. In May 2011, Erfurt University's Theologisches Forschungskolleg hosted a conference on Liturgy and Its Contribution to the Integration of Migrants. In April of 2012, a conference hosted by the University of Salzburg's Centre for Intercultural Theology and Studies of Religion focused on Migration as a Sign of the Times, bringing into conversation critical analyses from both the social sciences and theology.

to begin with, offers a new optic for rethinking liturgical developments in history. The importance of such a new lens or optic should not be underestimated, as Nathan Mitchell has recently emphasized in his volume on liturgy in the Theology in Global Perspective Series. Mitchell describes in particular the importance of a shift of lenses in the twentieth century with regard to how cultural change happens: from a prevalent understanding of such change through the image of trees—that is, growth originates in a root, is vertical, and expands by branching out—much cultural theorizing has moved to the image of crabgrass or a rhizome, where growth happens through multiple, horizontal, nonlinear, and quite random circulations.[15]

The lens of migration for the study of liturgical history in many ways privileges a rhizomic over an arboreal optic. This rhizomic optic provides an alternative to other lenses such as those of an "organic development" or an "evolution" of liturgical rites, predicated as these lenses are on images from evolutionary biology and their popularization. In liturgical historiography, the influence of these models remains quite pronounced—for example, when liturgical development is described as a "selective evolution," with "the weaker variants of the species" dying out as "the fittist" survive.[16] Conceiving liturgical history in such evolutionist terms has had an effect of naturalizing power: a historical narrative is imagined whose unfolding requires the identification of root elements from which later elements are understood to have branched out. At the same time, contemporary understandings of liturgical development have also begun to embrace a more rhizomic optic, even as this embrace has not been explicitly theorized as such. An example can be found in the work of Paul Bradshaw, who has substantially rewritten the history of early Christian worship as we knew it. Leaving behind both previous certainties and the need for a historiographic master narrative, Bradshaw, in the introductory chapter to the 2002 edition of his *The Search for the Origins of Christian Worship*, outlines the development of his own interpretative strategies by mapping his move away from a narrative of neatly linear development toward an acknowledgment of the starkly fragmentary,

15. See Nathan D. Mitchell, *Meeting Mystery: Liturgy, Worship, Sacraments*, Theology in Global Perspective Series (Maryknoll, NY: Orbis Books, 2006), esp. 3–47. Mitchell draws on the influential thinking of Gilles Deleuze and Félix Guattari, as well as its theological reception in the work of, for example, Graham Ward—see esp. 8–19.

16. The example is from Robert F. Taft, "How Liturgies Grow: The Evolution of the Byzantine 'Divine Liturgy,'" first published in *Orientalia Christiana Periodica* 43 (1977): 355–78, here 356. In a later version of the essay in Taft's *Beyond East and West: Problems in Liturgical Understanding*, 2nd ed., rev. and expanded (Rome: Edizioni Orientalia Christiana, Pontifical Oriental Institute, 1997), 203f, this wording is softened.

disparate, and localized nature of the extant evidence.[17] Bradshaw stresses the silences, absences, and aporias the historian encounters in these sources. With such methodological principles, Bradshaw finds himself in the midst of what drives postmodern historical analyses: an emphasis on fragmentariness, the mediations of textual representations, discontinuity, and difference.[18]

Liturgy in Migration chooses to foreground—critically and self-critically—a particular contemporary lens, all the while acknowledging that this lens owes its interpretive allure to the kinship with postmodern rhizomic sensibilities and their interest in circular and random movements, flows, and changes. That said, it would be all too facile to dismiss *Liturgy in Migration* as being in conversation merely with a currently fashionable theory that, in a few decades, will have exhausted its appeal. For one thing, liturgical studies has always been in conversation with contemporary intellectual trends and theorizing (we have but to think of the influence of models of evolution in twentieth-century liturgical historiography, mentioned above). Liturgical studies, in other words, is always shaped by the intellectual conversations of its own time. The best we can do is to enter into these conversations critically and self-critically; the alternative would be to let these conversations shape our thinking unbeknownst to us. Moreover, the reality of multiple migrations is easily discernible as written deeply into the Christian tradition itself.[19] Not only are the "migration stories of the Hebrew Scriptures . . . often the sites where God's revelation takes place,"[20] the gospels themselves stand as a witness to a linguistic migration, as they capture the words of Jesus in another language from the one he spoke. The early Christian centuries are filled with multiple migrations,[21] be they missionary travels, journeys into exile (e.g., Athanasius to Trier, Hilary of Poitiers to Asia Minor), pilgrimages (e.g., Egeria's travel to the Holy Land), or even professional moves (e.g., Augustine's relocation to Milan, with its profound

---

17. Paul F. Bradshaw, *The Search for the Origins of Christian Worship: Sources and Methods for the Study of Early Liturgy*, 2nd ed. (New York: Oxford University Press, 2002), 1–20. The chapter was substantially rewritten from the first edition.

18. Such a reading of Bradshaw's methodological principles does not negate his findings but simply suggests how these emerge under the conditions of the author's own times.

19. One could say that analogously with the category "gender," migration is an ancient reality seen through the lens of a contemporary theory.

20. Robert Schreiter, "Catholicity as a Framework for Addressing Migration," in *Migration in a Global World*, ed. Levebvre and Susin, 32–46, here 34.

21. More on this in Donald Senior, "'Beloved Aliens and Exiles': New Testament Perspectives on Migration," and Peter C. Phan, "Migration in the Patristic Era," both in *A Promised Land, a Perilous Journey*, ed. Groody and Campese, 20–34, 35–61.

consequences for the history of Western Christianity). Liturgical practices and texts also migrated. Two well-known examples are the fourth-century cross-fertilization and osmosis that took place in eucharistic praying, and the ninth-century migration of a model Roman liturgical book north across the Alps at the request of Emperor Charlemagne, who sought to promote the Roman liturgy through royal patronage. This migration resulted in a hybrid Frankish/Gallican-Roman Rite that shaped liturgical life in the West.

These and similar historical migrations can be brought into conversation with contemporary globalizing liturgical flows. The latter are legion, from Eastern liturgical elements that have influenced Western liturgical reforms to diasporic Ethiopian churches in North America, from evolving Asian American and Hispanic liturgical practices to the migration of elements of Christian worship into cyberspace—not to mention the global spread of Pentecostalism and US megachurches or even the much smaller international circulation of feminist liturgies. *Liturgy in Migration* obviously can only highlight a few of these migrations.

Overall, the discipline of liturgical studies—with its profound interest in spatial performance, historical processes, material culture, and bodily practices—is well positioned to investigate, in some detail, what a scholarly inquiry that foregrounds the category "migration" might yield for our understanding of liturgical life and practice. And liturgical studies as a scholarly discipline has something to gain from the insights garnered through the optic of migration, especially a clearer understanding of how people, practices, ideas, and materials travel and change. To date, nothing has been published on this subject in the field of liturgical studies.[22]

Liturgy in Migration *at a Glance*

To introduce more concretely the work of the book, a look at the overall structure and individual chapters will prove helpful. The volume is divided into two main parts: one dedicated to historical migrations, the other focused on contemporary migratory flows. These two main parts are prefaced by two essays that, in very different ways, lay the groundwork for the presentations that follow. The present *introduction* sketches the background, context, and contours

---

22. The closest companion to the present volume to date is a collection of essays recently published in Germany, *Religion und Migration: Frömmigkeitsformen und kulturelle Deutungssysteme auf Wanderschaft*, ed. Eberhard Tiefensee und Claudia Kraft, Vorlesungen des interdisziplinären Forums Religion der Universität Erfurt 7 (Münster: Aschendorff, 2011).

of the book's subject matter and offers a first orientation to the essays gathered in this volume. *Graham Ward*'s essay, which follows, addresses a basic question underlying all migratory movements—namely, what does it mean to belong in the first place? The question is becoming increasingly significant today, not least because of intensifying global mobility and advanced technologies of communication. Ward argues that these developments are fostering ways of "believing without belonging," which critique and undermine traditional liturgical givens, such as a sense of sacred space and the importance of the physical copresence of worshipers. New practices of piety, and the manner in which these new "technologies of the self" inform identity and a sense of belonging, challenge core ecclesial convictions of what it means to belong. In the face of such challenges, Ward calls for the church to engage more deeply in formation in what it means to belong ecclesially.

The first main part of the volume highlights six moments of liturgical migration in history. *Clemens Leonhard* opens this section with a sustained inquiry into the relationship between Jewish and early Christian ritual practices. In conversation with recent theories about the relationship between these faith traditions, Leonhard presents case studies that enable a closer look at migrations of ritual elements and practices between Jews and Christians. Among the ritual elements and practices highlighted are the festivals of Pesach and Easter, blessings after meals, and liturgies of the Word. Through these case studies, Leonhard is able to demonstrate the complexities of ritual migratory flows between Jews and Christians in late antiquity.

In the essay that follows, *Mary K. Farag* focuses on a prayer that almost all Eastern Christian traditions have in common in their respective Epiphany rites, the prayer for the sanctification of the waters. Farag probes the various versions of the prayer that circulated in the Eastern traditions, specifically in the Armenian, Byzantine, Coptic, Ethiopic, and Syriac liturgies, with a view to mapping possible migratory movements of the text. She pays particular attention to three aspects of the prayer: its use of Hellenistic terminology, its parallels in the prayers of books 7 and 8 in the *Apostolic Constitutions*, and its significance for the issues of prayers addressed to Christ and of epicleses invoking Christ.

Gisela Muschiol's essay introduces a liturgical migration rooted in reform movements in late medieval convent culture. Reforms in female convents, often entailing liturgical changes (i.e., in language, form, or frequency of the liturgy—of the Hours and also of the Mass), adhered to certain rules, irrespective of the religious order to which the convent belonged. These rules themselves followed a specific pattern of movement: sisters who had left their previous convents and migrated into the convents that were to be reformed brought with them a way of life and a liturgy that were (or were supposed to be) truer to the original monastic rule. Muschiol's essay considers these nuns on the move and the liturgical migrations they instigated and examines their impact on the life of the convents being reformed.

With *Kazimierz Bem*'s essay we move to an example of migratory movements from within the sixteenth-century reformations, in this case the formation of a Reformed liturgy in both Poland and Lithuania. Bem traces this little-known liturgical migration, first visible in 1550, of Reformed worship from its original context in Germany and Switzerland eastward. The author pays particular attention to the struggles, among Calvinists and Brethren, toward a unified Reformed liturgy in Poland and Lithuania.

In the essay that follows, *Karen B. Westerfield Tucker* attends to a specific form of liturgical migration by studying three different generations within the same ecclesial tradition, Methodism. Tucker seeks to identify what "Wesleyan" genetic materials (both liturgical and hymnological) persisted and what materials mutated as the result of geographic, cultural, and generational circumstances. The insights from this case study lead her to pinpoint constituent elements of Methodist/Wesleyan liturgical identity that are particular to context yet also global in scope.

Kostis Kourelis and *Vasileios Marinis* also trace a liturgical migration spanning several generations: in their case the migration from Orthodox liturgical life in Greece to the liturgy of the Greek American community. Greek Orthodox Christians, who left a home country where Orthodoxy was the national church, found themselves in a position of religious minority in North America. At the same time, the cultural and administrative distance from the national church led to an environment of liturgical freedom rarely experienced by Orthodox populations in the Old World. Kourelis and Marinis map the complex developments of Greek Orthodox liturgical life in the New World with particular attention to liturgical language, liturgical practices, and—with the help of a case study—the architecture of Greek American parishes.

The second main part of the volume moves toward six contemporary processes of liturgical migration. An essay by *Anne McGowan* on the impact of Eastern Christian traditions on Western liturgical life opens this particular section. The author's analysis spans several centuries of migrations of Eastern liturgical materials westward: she shows how Eastern liturgies took up residence in the West when they accompanied groups of Eastern Christians who settled in the West, and how Eastern liturgical texts traveled west and were sometimes incorporated into Western devotions and liturgical rites. The last part of McGowan's essay brings us to the twentieth-century liturgical reforms and contemporary Western liturgical practices, both of which continue to be shaped in conversation with the ritual practices and theological ethos of Eastern Christian worship.

Raúl Gómez-Ruiz, SDS, examines Hispanic migrations by analyzing two different sets of Good Friday processions in both the liturgical and popular realms. One set of processions takes place in Toledo, Spain, and is part of the Hispano-Mozarabic liturgy and popular piety practiced by the Mozarab community of Toledo. The second Good Friday procession, in San Antonio, Texas, incorporates both liturgical and popular elements and reveals parallels to the Toledo events. Descriptions of the processions provide the basis for reflections on Hispanic devotion to the cross (of which the processions are an expression) and on how the processions themselves, as a form of "cultural memory" (Jan Assmann), might have migrated between the liturgical and popular realms.

Kay Kaufman Shelemay introduces an example of forced migration with her analysis of the challenges to the performance and transmission of the Ethiopian Orthodox musical liturgy after the 1974 Ethiopian Revolution. The author is able to draw on her research among Ethiopian Christians now resettled in the United States in order to sound the challenges to the transmission and performance of this liturgy in postmigratory settings. Kaufman Shelemay's case study explicates more broadly ways in which liturgical music flows across geographical boundaries, travels through various media, and, in the process, reshapes both itself and other repertories.

Jonathan Y. Tan inquires into what it means to be Asian, American, and Catholic in today's increasingly global and interconnected, yet also fragmented, world. The author argues that the ahistorical essentialism of early theologies of liturgical inculturation emphasized the ideals of cohesive group identity, overarching harmony, and unity, thereby subsuming differences and excluding the particularities, hybridities, and conflicts that are generated by generational shifts, multiple belongings, and repeated border crossings. Tan aims to deconstruct the essentialized categories of racial-ethnic, cultural, and religious identities so as to be able to remix them in new keys. He suggests that in fact Asian American Catholic liturgical ministries are already beginning to move away from classical tradition-maintenance to the creative remix of traditioning. They are thereby also moving away from liturgies that uncritically reinscribe the past to worship as a creative and dynamic endeavor that seeks to encompass the multiplicity of hybridized and conflicting constructions of faith and identity.

Charles Farhadian draws our attention to Christian missionary expansion, which—long before the term "globalization" was fashionable among social scientists and media researchers—carried with it liturgical practices that sought to connect local distinctiveness and worldwide liturgical givens. As the Christian faith crosses cultural and linguistic boundaries and as local people are drawn into a world religion that spans the entire globe, worship also becomes a site of competing claims and orientations. Farhadian suggests that liturgies worldwide appear to mark boundaries and promote crossings between local and spatially remote centers, yet liturgies do so in quite unpredictable ways. The author illustrates his claims with case studies of liturgical practices in various churches around the globe.

Stefan Böntert's essay concludes this volume with an inquiry into a recent migration (already gestured at in the subtitle of this book), namely, that of liturgical elements and celebrations into cyberspace. The author sketches a theological argument for taking seriously online, interactive liturgical gatherings as one possible contemporary form of ecclesial assembly, while also insisting that these online assemblies can only supplement, never replace, liturgical celebrations of participants bodily present to each other in one place. Online assemblies obviously are a far cry from the gathering of the disciples around Jesus in the Upper Room, and yet, when understood as God-sustained sites of ecclesial gathering, they might be seen as part of the larger journey of God with God's people through time.

Liturgy in Migration—Quo Vadis?

At the end of this volume and its diverse essays—and, indeed, in light of them—shared themes and a host of new questions emerge. This, of course, is exactly what a vibrant scholarly conversation should engender. In concluding this introductory essay, I sketch some of the shared themes as well as the new questions, not as a way of suggesting closure but rather as a way of pointing ahead.

First, it is probably fair to say that participants in the conference, as well as readers of *Liturgy in Migration*, will share an initial sense of being overwhelmed by the diversity and complexity of liturgical migrations put on view. Even if we left historical migrations aside for a moment and concentrated on contemporary global liturgical flows alone, the evidence remains overwhelming. Today there are more than two billion Christians worldwide (roughly a third of the world's population), many of whom will be at worship on any given Sunday— whether gathered in an emerging Methodist congregation in Cambodia, a diasporic Ethiopian church in Washington, DC, a megachurch in Brazil, or an online parish in cyberspace. To map the diversity of contemporary worship practices—and the many migratory flows at the heart of them, whether of people, practices, texts, or technologies—is impossible. At the same time, not to acknowledge this diversity and the underlying migratory flows seems equally impossible. Living in an "age of migration" as we do, liturgical practices have to be understood within this framework, not in occlusion or ignorance of it.

A second shared theme involves the key category itself. Migration proves to be a constructive optic through which to view both historical and contemporary processes of liturgical transition. For one thing, the category of migration is flexible enough to allow for different understandings of movement and growth rather than locking us into an evolutionist, linear model alone. With its more rhizomic lens, migration thus creates space for thinking broadly about varieties of liturgical movements, some of them not linear, others—especially in the early centuries—no longer discernible in their directionality. In contradistinction to an arboreal lens (which migration does not supplant but rather supplements), this new lens encourages us to see beyond simply linear developments to circular, even random, movements, profound disruptions, unexpected turns, and aporias.

A third shared theme across *Liturgy in Migration* could be said to be this: there is no liturgical development without migratory flows woven into it (even if the most basic flow were only that of time). Just as there is no Gospel without culture—at least not in a way that would allow us neatly to juxtapose the two—so also there is no liturgy that does not already bear traces of migration, maybe most fundamentally in the fact that the Word of Life already meets us in a migration from the original language in which it was spoken and lived. To put this point differently, there is not something called "liturgy" to which then is added "migration." The two are always intertwined, at least since the doors of the Upper Room opened.

So much for some shared themes emerging in *Liturgy in Migration*. Here are some of the many questions that emerged. First, a critical question about the optic of migration itself. It is certainly worth asking not only what the lens of migration enables us to see but also what it occludes or disables in the viewer. No lens or optic, after all, only fosters clearer sight. In contemporary scholarship, for example, aquatic metaphors have been put to good use, not least in liturgical scholarship.[23] Such aquatic metaphors suggest—even more

---

23. Bryan D. Spinks has made use of aquatic metaphors as the governing principle for his organization of historical stages; see his *Early and Medieval Rituals and Theologies of Baptism from the New Testament to the Council of Trent*, Ashgate Liturgy, Worship and Society series

strongly than the image of migration—the nonlinear, fluid character of movement and flow.

Second, a host of important questions emerged out of the discussions following the presentations at the 2011 conference. These questions included the possibility of distinguishing between authentic and inauthentic migrations; the differences between forced liturgical migrations on one side of the spectrum (e.g., among Ethiopian Christians) and willing or even desired liturgical migrations on the other side of the spectrum (e.g., in missionary movements); the differences in migrations of "heavy" and "light" liturgical materials, such as those of the Armenian Rite versus Pentecostal practices; the question of mapping the broader cultural impact of liturgical migrations; and finally, the question of future migratory patterns, now that globalization has both hyper-differentiated as well as hybridized the ways in which we belong.

Beyond these questions, the nature of scholarly discourse and the knowledge protocols of academia themselves deserve to be noted. These too both enable and constrain. In reflections on liturgical migrations, what these knowledge protocols constrain are faith claims about the movement of God's Spirit deep within (and beyond) the many migratory movements in Christian history. Suffice it to say that the category of migration, when translated into a liturgical practice, might well end up to mean "pilgrimage," a pilgrimage that is ultimately deeper into the heart of God.

In Conclusion: Giving Thanks

It remains for me to thank a number of people at the Yale Institute of Sacred Music and at Yale Divinity School without whose unfailing support and hard work neither the 2011 conference, Liturgy in Migration, nor this editorial project would have been possible. Above all, I am grateful to my colleague Bryan D. Spinks, with whom I planned and coordinated this conference, and to the director of the Yale Institute of Sacred Music, Martin Jean, who generously hosted the 2011 conference and enthusiastically supported the publication of these papers. I thank Melissa Maier, ISM manager of external relations and publications, for her care in overseeing the organization of the conference (especially for "greening" the event) and for managing the publication of this volume. Melissa was ably assisted in these tasks by Albert Agbayani. I owe a depth of gratitude to John Leinenweber, ISM research assistant, without whose

---

(Burlington, VT: Ashgate, 2006). Thomas A. Tweed has used aquatic metaphors in his *Crossing and Dwelling: A Theory of Religion* (Cambridge, MA: Harvard University Press, 2006).

unfailing good will and editorial skills I could not have completed this work. I also thank Stephen McCarthy, who translated Stefan Böntert's essay.

I continue to be grateful to the wonderful ISM staff, without whose dedication the institute's manifold activities could not flourish, especially Jacqueline Campoli, Kristen Forman, Andrea Hart, Trisha Lendroth, and Sachin Ramabhadran.

Finally, it has been a pleasure to work with the editors and staff at Liturgical Press, which has also published the previous two collections of papers from the liturgy conferences at the Yale Institute of Sacred Music.

1
Belonging to the Church
Graham Ward

What is it to belong? I raise this question because belonging is fundamental both to one of the roots of our word "religion"—*religare*, to bind—and to the context from which we gain our word "liturgy"—*leitourgia*, an act of civic service or benevolence. Belonging is also fundamental to our understanding of church, *ekklesia*, which is not just an assembly of citizens, soldiers, or believers in Christ but a corporation of those who have been called out, *ekkaleō*, to function collectively. All three of these words—"religion," "liturgy," and "church"—are political terms; they concern practices that are public, done not just with respect to the organizations they give expression to (pious communities, assemblies, the *polis*) but with respect also to the field of power, authority, and legitimation that structures the public sphere. Central to St. Augustine's argument in *De vere religione* is the fact that acts constituting piety, devotion, and worship are acts in which belonging is exercised, and through that exercise community is constituted.[1]

By my question posed above I wish to get at something more primordial, however, than the exercises of belonging. Theologically, we could of course here move directly to the intratrinitarian *societas*, to human beings created in the image of the triune God, to the opening of the kingdom of God to all believers in Christ, and to the call to discipleship and following. We could develop such a theology with an exploration of the Marian act of original obedience—"Be

---

1. Augustine, *De vere religione*, in *Augustine: Earlier Works*, trans. John H. S. Burleigh (London: SCM, 1953), 218–82.

it done unto me according to thy word"—and the issuing of blood and water from the side of Christ following the crucifixion. Not that tracing this theologic would be mistaken. This, after all, is what the church believes—and we will return to this theological account later. But to understand the difference that marks belonging in Christian worship, I want to explore the anthropological rootedness of exercises in belonging first. What is it that draws people not only to come together—for this can be a temporary phenomenon like students gathering for a protest—but to belong? Belonging is commitment and entails the historical sustainability of a collective. So what draws people to joining, say, a book reading group, a trade union, a political party, or a parish church? I recognize and accept that these forms of belonging are not the same and that they present levels of self-interest, at least to begin with. One can join a reading group out of loneliness; one can join a union for protection against exploitation by an employer. But, I suggest, belonging is more than self-interest. In fact, genuine commitment to a group requires aspects of self-sacrifice for the sustainability of the group to be possible. So I raise the question of whether these belongings are each expressions of a fundamental human condition. What makes us view free association as a human right? It has to be more than a liberal, democratic liberty (which would also claim the right to nonassociation, to privacy) since such liberties have a particular history—and free association is viewed as an ancient, if not natural, right. We are not islands. We *like* to congregate—not always, but with some regularity we meet up as families, and we meet up with friends, and those people who have no family or have no friends are, on the whole, pitied by the rest of us. We are not islands. But why?

I have emphasized "like" in "like to congregate" because I want to get beneath the Christmas parties, the pub lunch, the union meeting, and Sunday Matins to an embodied need, an embodied urge, an embodied drive: a desire in which self-interest plays a part but is certainly not the whole of the story. I am not ready yet, however, to explicate that "liking" or to relate it to anything religious.

Why the Question of Belonging Is Important

I want to begin by providing a context in which the question of belonging becomes important in order better to investigate its connection with ecclesiology and liturgy in our contemporary world. The post–Second World War experience of the West, particularly western Europe, has been dominated by secularization—evidenced in the decline in church attendance and the rise of what Grace Davie once termed and examined as "believing without belonging."[2] We will leave aside here the question of postsecularity and the modifications to, even rejections of, the secularization thesis.[3] For the moment we will focus on the "without belonging" since all analyses suggest this trend has not only continued but is accelerating owing to global migration patterns, the movement of displaced persons, and refugee crises. This "not belonging" that Davie characterizes as evident in the relations between church and society has a far broader trajectory with a far more profound historical basis than just post–Second World War Europe. Its historical roots lie with the rise in the call for greater moral autonomy and the subjective individualism that characterized the Enlightenment. Kant, as one of the first Europeans to write his own anthropology, viewed moral individuals as those mature enough to believe in their own rationality and able to make their own judgments on the basis of evidence and argument.[4] Kant certainly was not advocating social atomism—he had a strong sense of society and one's duties as a citizen toward it. But even coming to the sense of what those judgments were—acting in accordance with what the universalization of that behavior would mean for all other people—puts at the heart of the matter the individual, the Cartesian ego. Kant's ethical commonwealth is a collection of individuals living beyond their own particular inclinations toward a universal good (to be rewarded in an afterlife).

While certain figures, like Hegel and Marx, wanted to correct the subjectivity of that position by emphasizing the collective and communal, still the cult of today's hyperindividualism (creating one's own lifestyle and even one's own identity) lies historically in the continuation of that ideology of moral autonomy, given spiritual depths by romanticism. Only with romanticism was Enlightenment rationalism counterpoised with a new interest in the irrational and with a growing sense that rationality itself was multiple: there was no universal reason, pure or otherwise. This trajectory, fostered by philosophers such as Schopenhauer and Nietzsche, led directly into twentieth-century skepticisms, pluralized epistemologies, the promotion and valuation of difference, and the attention to the other—all key characteristics of the

---

2. Grace Davie, *Religion in Britain since 1945: Believing without Belonging* (Oxford: Blackwell, 1994).

3. For a critical account of "postsecularity," see my *The Politics of Discipleship: Becoming Postmaterial Citizens* (London: SCM Press, 2010), 117–58, and Michael Hoelzl and Graham Ward, eds., *The New Visibility of Religion* (London: Continuum, 2008).

4. Immanuel Kant, *An Answer to the Question: "What Is Enlightenment?"* trans. H. B. Nisbet (Harmondsworth: Penguin Books, 2009).

postmodern condition and also of the deregulation of financial markets.[5] Thus, the question goes, "Whose rationality?" and a point is reached where a person of some enormous power can claim there is no such thing as society, only collections of individual consumer choices; and the liberal (and neoliberal) political and economic agenda, inflated with the logics of laissez-faire, turns upon the extension and maximization of choice as an index of freedom. So there has been a decline not only in belonging but in the values attributed to belonging. Nietzsche famously challenged such values by ridiculing them in terms of a slave morality.[6]

This "not belonging" has probably been most famously examined recently in the work of Robert Putnam as a decline of "social capital."[7] There has been much debate among sociologists about this term and about the quantitative data Putnam employs to arrive at his conclusion that socially we are becoming ever more fragmented and are ever more opting for an opt-out position. We are, to use Putnam's metaphor, increasingly "bowling alone"—evidenced in the decline of various civic associations (from Scout groups to Rotary circles), professional associations, and political engagement. In fact, churches (or mosques, or temples, or synagogues), as well as the liturgies that not only bind the collective but form the mentality that makes a collective, have probably been among some of the most resistant sites to this deterioration of belonging, this erosion of social capital. But as Grace Davie points out, these sites too, with secularization, have succumbed to the gravitational pull of the "free market" in opinions, beliefs, designer lifestyles, knowledges, spiritualities, and brand-name products.[8] To employ a metaphor used by Charles Taylor in his massive volume *A Secular Age*—with reference to the transit and transformation of believing following the demise of Christendom—there has been a "nova effect." In the expanding universe of unbelief, we have entered a phase in postmodernity in

---

5. As Jameson and Harvey both demonstrated in their accounts of postmodernism, the economic climate of the 1980s and 1990s and the rise of neoliberal economics were profound factors in the development of the postmodern condition. See Frederic Jameson, *Postmodernism or the Cultural Logic of Late Capitalism* (Durham, NC: Duke University Press, 1991), and David Harvey, *The Condition of Postmodernity: An Enquiry into the Origins of Cultural Change* (Oxford: Blackwell, 1991).

6. Friedrich Nietzsche, *Beyond Good and Evil*, trans. R. J. Hollingdale (Harmondsworth: Penguin Books, 1973), 122.

7. See Robert D. Putnam, *Bowling Alone: The Collapse and Revival of American Community* (New York: Simon and Schuster, 2000).

8. See Davie, *Religion in Britain since 1945*, 29–44, and more recently, *Europe, the Exceptional Case: Parameters of Faith in the Modern World* (London: Darton, Longman & Todd, 2002).

which possibilities for believing have exploded in millions of fragmented directions, each fabricating a narrative of what Taylor calls "self-authorization."[9] He claims, "The salient feature of Western societies is not so much a decline in religious faith and practice . . . but rather a fragilization of different religious positions, as well as of the outlooks both of belief and unbelief."[10] In the wake of the nova effect and the splintering of the Christian faith, there is an ever-increasing spiritual pluralism fused with a social atomism such that collective life, whether religious or not, begins to disappear.

Virtual Association Capitalism (VAC)

My question is what happens to belonging in such a context. The need to belong, after all, like the need to believe, is written into the structure of what it is to be human. Before examining this question, let me turn to one of the paradoxes of our postmodern condition with respect to the diminishment of collective life. In a sense this diminishment has to be viewed in the context of the exponential rise in telecommunications: notably, Skype, e-mail, online chat rooms, and multiple user domains (blogs, Twitter, Second Life), iPods, mobile phones, and social networking sites like the formidable Facebook. We have never been so much in communication with each other or as involved in the recovery of old associations with whom we had lost contact. The flow of images and tweets is worldwide and unabated. So a social paradox emerges: an increasing sense of "without belonging" and also an increasing sense of virtual association; a rapid decline in social capitalism and a very rapid increase in what might be termed virtual association capitalism (VAC). And VAC is, for all its virtuality, capital, because it has the power to change things in and through mutual association. Witness the way in which defenders and supporters of Wikileaks could vandalize trading (even if only for a short time) among credit card bankers and even on Amazon.com.

The employment of social networks and mobile connections in the recent Arab Spring uprisings is well attested. Text messages relayed across networks intersecting with other networks orchestrate a massive chain reaction, mobilizing thousands and directing them to very specific locations in order to focus and concentrate their political force. Furthermore, this power is seen to have a positive value—it can bring people together for a common cause and harness

---

9. Charles Taylor, *A Secular Age* (Cambridge, MA: Belknap Press of Harvard University Press, 2007), 589.
10. Ibid., 595.

their individual capabilities in lobbying for change. In Tunisia, Bahrain, Egypt, and Libya this lobbying was able to demand greater democratization, increased transparency, and an end to the police state.

I note, however, that the effects of such organized communication can also be easily countermanded by a greater media force. In Britain, for example, students protest, text, and cry against the raising of student fees for university education; the government counters the rhetorical effect of their communications through using newspaper columns, television interviews, multiple web sites, policing, and organizing the way the greater public receives information about both the protests and the new fee regime. In other words, while the students act terrestrially, the government can align the media satellites extraterrestrially. Overall, whether promoting one side or the other, in the rise of virtual association capitalism, it is the media who are in control. At least since the groundbreaking book by the anthropologist Benedict Anderson, we have grown accustomed to understanding the imaginary nature of societies.[11] In France there was also the seminal work by the situationist Guy Debord writing about the spectacle society—that is, a society that is made to appear in and through the spectacular event or the visual dissemination of such events through the media.[12] Postmodern cultural theorists and sociologists gathered these analyses into the work being done on simulacra and simulation by Jean Baudrillard,[13] most famously by Michel de Certeau[14] and Gilles Deleuze.[15] Belonging today, according to such philosophies, is virtual.[16] That is, it is a media

---

11. Benedict Anderson, *Imagined Communities: Reflections on the Origins and Spread of Nationalism*, 2nd ed., rev. and extended (London: Verso, 1991). See also other developments of this notion: Cornelius Castoriadis, *The Imaginary Institution of Society*, trans. Kathleen Blamey (Cambridge, MA: Polity Press, 1987); Charles Taylor, *Modern Social Imaginaries* (Durham, NC: Duke University Press, 2003).

12. Guy Debord, *La société du spectacle* (Paris: Buchet/Chastel, 1967), trans. as *The Society of the Spectacle* (London: Rebel Press and Aim Publications, 1987).

13. See Jean Baudrillard, *Simulacra and Simulation*, trans. Sheila Glaser (Ann Arbor, MI: University of Michigan Press, 1994).

14. See Michel de Certeau, *The Practice of Everyday Life*, trans. Steven Rendall (Berkeley: University of California Press, 1988).

15. Gilles Deleuze, *Difference and Repetition*, trans. Paul Patton (New York: Continuum, 2004).

16. "Virtual," it must be noted here, does not mean "immaterial." Material conditions have an impact on virtual realities and virtual associations on many levels. In terms of the church, as Paul reminds us in his First Letter to the Corinthians, the Body of Christ is made up of flesh-and-blood organs for the life of Christ, its individual members. There are also relations with material objects, from church property to wafers for the Mass. Furthermore, there is an

effect. Certain corollaries follow from this with highly significant consequences for our own examination. In what follows, I highlight five in particular.

To begin with, VAC, as a media effect, is locked into the transience of fashion trends. Media, which had always been technology driven, are financially sustained only by popularity, by creating or tapping into a market. If no one had wanted to buy the books coming off the Gutenberg press, then the press would have folded or turned its technology toward producing something that would be bought. Media technologies are always associated with markets and marketing, and the most important product that it needs to market is itself: its power, its importance, its ability to produce, communicate, and sell information. All forms of virtual belonging have, like all other goods in the market, a shelf life, a sell-by date. All forms of virtual belonging are continually morphing, because to continue to exist they must be ahead of the game; if they don't recruit, if they don't appeal, then the "belongers" in such an association move elsewhere.

And so, secondly, belonging as such becomes nomadic. Belongers now resemble shoppers with loyalty cards for certain stores who, if bargains are on offer in a competitive store, have no hesitation switching their loyalties. An indication of the fragility of postmodern associations is that corporations (large or small, global or local) that desire affiliations sense the need to seal the affiliation with some form of symbolic gesture of belonging: a card, a signed pledge, a regular giving back to customers as a "reward" for their (continuing) custom. Such nomadism is now a worldwide problem, generated by ecological and military crises and also by the ebb and flow of available work. In 2011 a surprising survey among European countries found that, owing to the crisis of the Euro and the savage spending cuts on public services, many Europeans were becoming economic migrants, leaving "from Lisbon to Luanda, Dublin to Perth, Barcelona to Buenos Aires."[17] If one of the characteristics of postmodernity is the space of flows, or space as flow,[18] then one of its consequences is the breakup of traditional forms of belonging.

---

important financial commitment. In virtual reality, and in virtual association more generally, the immateriality or invisibility of the communications themselves is counterbalanced by the materiality of the means for receiving and sending such communications, by the physical reality of people in communication (with homes and property to which bills can be sent), and by the financial outlays needed to maintain the association. There may well be a further "dematerializing" of community itself in its further extension across large social networks, but virtual reality remains totally dependent upon material conditions.

17. *The Guardian*, Thursday, 22 December 2011, 1.

18. For this term and its use, see Manuel Castells, *The Informational City: Information Technology, Economic Restructuring and the Urban Regional Process* (Oxford: Blackwell, 1989).

An observation on these first two corollaries, the one concerning the concept of time (transience) and the other concerning the concept of space (nomadism): both these concepts have moved toward collapse in and through advanced media technologies. They have been redefined by these media technologies and so have our experiences of time and space. Absorbed into media technologies, time and space are fast becoming virtual entities, as omniscience and omnipresence sit in our laps on an iPad or in our pockets on an iPhone. The real is now malleable, liquid, generated by someone, somewhere. This is the age of *The Matrix* and of *Inception*.

Third, belonging that is transient, nomadic, and led by trends leads to forms of association that are eclectic and self-selected. Like so much furniture today, our belonging is self-assembled, and what we belong to reflects such bricolage because all forms of corporation, in order to appeal to as wide a public as possible, diversify what they offer. In the sixteenth and seventeenth centuries the wealthy collected fragments of rock, religious relics, stuffed animals, and exotica from across times and geographies in "cabinets of curiosity." In postmodern times we inhabit such cabinets, and this makes our belonging both bespoke and fragile. The fragility is not necessarily a bad thing, and it does not need to be experienced as mid-twentieth-century existential angst. It can be experienced as the angelic lightness of being—always open to new meadows of interest, new blooms and blossoms. The bricolage approach to belonging has a tendency toward a strong evaluation of aesthetic experience in the wide sense of that term, which is concerned not just with the beautiful but with the senses (*aesthesis*). Bits are assembled with an eye to the intensity of immediate experience, the "feel-good factor," which cannot be disassociated from changes in the temporal that prize the saturated moment, the present, the instant. This approach has an impact upon the effectiveness of the practice of belonging (which strengthens association) being integral to an overall "technology" in the Foucauldian sense of that term.[19] Foucault defines certain "technologies of the self," forms of discipline that instill values and habits in the group that practices such technologies. These technologies socialize participants in distinctive ways, reinforcing the sense of belonging because they constitute ways in which self-identity is formed. To cite the anthropologist Talal Asad, who has employed Foucault's work on technologies to examine the concept of ritual, systematic

---

19. See Michel Foucault, "Technologies of the Self," trans. Robert Hurley et al., in *Michel Foucault: Ethics; The Essential Works of Foucault, 1954–84*, ed. Paul Rabinow (Harmondsworth: Penguin Books, 2000), 223–51.

practices create and control "particular moral dispositions and capacities."[20] The body becomes a site for the inculcation of aptitudes by governing authorities (sacred or secular); the performer is created and perfected in and through the performance. Asad compares this process in the Christian development of moral discipline in the medieval church to modern secular society today, but what I am pointing to here is the way transient and nomadic forms of belonging lack the technological effectiveness for fostering the disciplines needed for strong identification. To use older, more liturgical terminology, they lack the theological discipline and depth that allow for effective formation. Belonging becomes weak and at the surface of the body; identification and identity are weakened proportionally. To put this theologically, if divine, trinitarian *missio* determines human vocation (the call to participate in God's divine plan for salvation), then the question of weak "technologies" and superficial formation invites an examination into whether vocations can be effectively understood today—whether divine pedagogy is being helped, or even hindered, by transient and nomadic forms of belonging.

The reference to Talal Asad, in particular to his important essay on "The Concept of Ritual,"[21] points to a fourth corollary of virtual belonging. The benchmark for technologies of subject formation throughout Asad's essay is the medieval church. In showing the shift in the function of ritual from a situation in which rites were a form of discipline to rites as symbolic of transcendent meaning, medieval Christendom is viewed as the high-water mark of what we might call "technologies of belonging." Although Asad's work is not necessarily an illustration of this, nevertheless imaginary society and virtual sodalities are haunted by the phantoms of nostalgia: a time when there was face-to-face communication, when physical location mattered, and when real time was rich with significance. To some extent virtual belonging creates myths of a past corporation and cooperation, neighborliness, and older forms of commodity exchange.

A fifth and final point: to use a term favored by Charles Taylor, virtual belonging is excarnate. Taylor writes in *A Secular Age*, "Official Christianity has gone through what we can call an 'excarnation,' a transfer out of embodied, 'enfleshed' forms of religious life, to those which are more 'in the head.'"[22] This follows from the last point because *A Secular Age* is profoundly marked

---

20. Talal Asad, *Genealogies of Religion: Discipline and Reasons of Power in Christianity and Islam* (Baltimore: Johns Hopkins University Press, 1993), 65.
21. Ibid., 55–80.
22. Taylor, *A Secular Age*, 554.

by nostalgia for the incarnational culture that modernity has been travelling away from for the past four hundred years, a nostalgia for a lost Christendom. Although Taylor is aware that there has been a revolt against such excarnation in postmodernity,[23] which he views as a continuation of a romantic trajectory (in the work of the neo-Nietzscheans), virtual belonging is a further unfolding of the logic of the Enlightenment and modernity. We will return to this point. For now, I wish to emphasize that embodiment is lost, erased, or forgotten and that avatars and surrogates (there have been two recent films with these words as their titles)[24] are increasingly dominant as the social becomes mobile, motile, and malleable. Rootlessness, a disengagement with concrete location or an inability to root oneself in a single location, increases with waves of migration and the call (particularly in Western professional careers) to be flexible, to move where the job markets are. Globalization, to be managed, to be ridden and used to one's advantage, requires multiple displacements. The specter raised is an old metaphysical one: Gnosticism—and scholars such as Cyril O'Regan have done much to uncover the new forms Gnosticism has taken from the Enlightenment onward.[25] Put like that, contemporary culture announces a certain heresy. I am not concerned here with its heretical possibilities—although in the context of discussing liturgy (which is a religious category), heresy might be worth discussing at some point.

Before returning to our central question about belonging, which is in danger of becoming lost to sight in the complex weave of our present condition, let me highlight another irony thrown up by postmodernity. Excarnation has its sociopsychological reaction, evident increasingly in the kinds of virtual belonging associated with what Pete Ward has called "liquid church"[26] and with the liturgies such network ecclesiologies foster. Postmodernity ushered in a reawakening of desire; the libidinal economy is somehow anthropologically and existentially more profound than instrumental reason. The neo-Nietzscheans, from Bataille, Deleuze, and Lyotard onward, defined a new order of the sacred with respect to such economies. Sacred is more Bataille's language; others speak of a nonmetaphysical but transcendent flow (Deleuze) and the sublime horizons of the "unpresentable" (Lyotard).

With the reawakening of desire there was a new turn to embodiment, witnessed most recently in the turn to affect (and the attention to our emotional

---

23. Ibid., 613–15.
24. James Cameron's *Avatar* (2009) and Jonathan Mostow's *Surrogates* (2009).
25. See Cyril O'Regan, *Gnostic Return in Modernity* (Albany, NY: SUNY Press, 2001).
26. Pete Ward, *Liquid Church* (Norwich: Paternoster Press, 2002).

and sensate life) and the work of cognitive scientists on the relation of body to environment and mind. I am thinking here of the work of the philosophers of the flesh like George Lakoff and Mark Johnson,[27] as well as the more popular work of Antonio Damasio,[28] Joseph LeDoux,[29] and Daniel Goleman.[30] These scientific examinations, these philosophical and moral reflections—on desire, the body, the sensorium, and our emotional life—parallel, endorse, and encourage a cultural emphasis upon experience.

Our contemporary culture is not only saturated with the spectacular (aural, visual, and tactile); it also valorizes the intensification of human experience—whether this is in the cinema's production of special effects, Dolby surround sound, and 3D viewing; the increasing popularity of "extreme sports"; the multiplication of celebrity chefs and programs centering on food; or the increase in binge drinking and vodka eyeballing. On one level these phenomena are commensurate with postmodernity's love of excess, but excess is only the means to an end, the end being the experience of the "pure present" (an analogue of the appeal of "pure wool," "pure water," and "pure soap"). These forms of purification and intensification of experience are major forms of contemporary transcendence, a purely immanent transcendence *through* the body, not *out* of it.

If one of the buzz words at the moment is "interactive," then what we are treating here is a very familiar liturgical (and theological) theme: participation. The role of "participation" in virtual belonging is both to embrace the experience on offer in an intensely subjective manner and to generate a sense of inclusion. Participation here allows both for hyperindividualism and for being a part of a community of such individuals, an audience no longer passively watching but actively engaged in its own production. This is at the heart of contemporary experiences and construals of "intimacy," and it finds its expression as much in online sex as among a group of Christians singing "And his banner over me is love." Intimacy without kinship, like the intense eroticism without

---

27. George Lakoff and Mark Johnson, *Philosophy in the Flesh: The Embodied Mind and Its Challenge to Western Thought* (New York: Basic Books, 1999).

28. Antonio Damasio, *The Feeling of What Happens: Body and Emotion in the Making of Consciousness* (London: Vintage, 2000).

29. Joseph E. LeDoux, *The Emotional Brain: The Mysterious Underpinnings of Emotional Life* (New York: Simon and Schuster, 1996).

30. Daniel Goleman, *Emotional Intelligence: Why It Can Matter More than IQ* (New York: Bantam Doubleday, 1996).

sexual relations in the vampire novels of Stephenie Meyer,[31] is one of the key characteristics of virtual association and another form of "safe sex." The same wish for the pure present, real presence—though it is a simulacrum, even a parody, of what sacramentally is understood by "real presence"—is as evident in bungee jumping as in Graham Kendrick's "Shine Jesus, Shine": a transcendent experience of light without shadow, a supercharge of purely positive emotion, a realized eschatology. I have begun to be more explicit about Christian liturgy and the theology that informs it here not only because I am examining belonging as the foundation, origin, and goal of being liturgical, but also because a trip around Bryan Spinks's recent book, *The Worship Mall*,[32] reveals showcase studies that express each of the corollaries of what I called VAC, though to different degrees. Dozens of examples of liquid and blended liturgies manifest and promulgate the eclectic liquidity of contemporary social relations. If among these studies are examples where communion, community, kinship, participation, belonging, and rootedness come together, among the Amish and Wenger Mennonites they are distinctly and self-consciously countercultural. So an investigation into belonging as it pertains to liturgy becomes significant for at least three reasons: first, because there is a decline in face-to-face belonging (and social capital); second, because there is a momentous acceleration occurring in virtual association capitalism (VAC); and third, because the corollaries of these two trajectories are far reaching not just socially and culturally but also theologically. In the following, final part of my essay, I return to that foundational question, to be approached, in the first instance, philosophically and anthropologically rather than sociologically: What is it to belong?

Belonging as an A Priori

To some extent we are investigating here an a priori condition that must still affect contemporary forms of belonging. That is, we are looking into a human condition that will inevitably change given different historical, cultural, and social contexts or find new modes of manifesting itself. But three questions announce themselves in the context of our present concerns with liturgy and migration: What does that a priori condition tell us about liturgy? How does

---

31. Author of the best-selling four-volume *Twilight* series that began in 2005 with the publication of *Twilight*. By October 2010 over 116 million copies had been sold, with the books translated into thirty-eight languages.

32. Bryan D. Spinks, *The Worship Mall: Contemporary Responses to Contemporary Culture* (London: SCM, 2010).

it enable us to predict possible trajectories for future liturgies given its present manifestations? And how may we better orientate those trajectories such that those future liturgies might counteract some of the negative social, cultural, and theological possibilities they portend? We have space only to sketch answers to these questions rather than to present a detailed examination.

For brevity's sake, let us delineate three forms that belonging takes as an anthropological a priori. First, for evolutionary biologists (and cognitive scientists building upon their presuppositions), belonging is written into the genetics of who human beings are because it is a survival mechanism. We do not necessarily have to accept a Hobbesian picture of each human being fighting all others for the protection of what is his or her own, but pace Nietzsche, without the herd mentality human beings would not have survived at all. We need each other, and in the recognition of that need is the further recognition that we can achieve more by pooling our resources than by self-sufficiency. The collective is stronger in any given environment than the solitary—physically, emotionally, and intellectually. In their different ways, Hobbes and Rawls have, of course, developed notions of the contractual society on this basis, but the contractual society is a formal rather than a natural belonging. In fact, the contractual society is already an imagined community.

The second form of belonging as an anthropological a priori can be related to philosophers like Aristotle who wished to root belonging not in human biology but in a natural disposition among fellow creatures—the mutual recognition of rationality, the development of language systems, the division of labor and eventually of classes. We are social animals and hence will search out the best means by which to organize ourselves for maximal flourishing. The polis develops on this basis.

The third form of belonging as an anthropological a priori can be found among theologians on the basis of a reading of the Scriptures—for example, the book of Genesis. Karl Barth initiated his anthropological inquiries with an understanding that being human is at least two, male and female, for that is how we were made.[33] Other theologians, like Augustine, hold that because human beings are made in the image of God, they are triune not only in their individual natures but in all their relations: they will create societies because the Godhead itself is a triune *societas*.[34] Our belonging then issues in both

---

33. See Karl Barth, *Church Dogmatics* III.1, trans. J. W. Edwards et al. (Edinburgh: T&T Clark, 1958), 308.

34. See Augustine, *The Literal Meaning of Genesis*, trans. John Hammond Taylor, SJ (New York: Paulist Press, 1982), 1:94–97.

friendship and kinship, and these are foundational forms of relating out of which community arises. Barth sails very closely to a biological essentialism, as I have shown elsewhere.[35] But the theological conception of belonging for Augustine, or Aquinas, is a natural inclination, albeit one that differs from the philosophical account of Aristotle insofar as nature here cannot be divorced from creation as it issued from the Word of God. The natural is analogically related to the divine; the world is a theater for the operations of God.

These three forms of belonging as an anthropological a priori foster liturgies as binding social disciplines or rules for coexistence. The evolutionist account of belonging has been developed into contractual responsibilities, some associated with civic ceremonies. Other secular liturgies might include how we apply for and get a job, sign a contract of employment, and are placed on a company's payroll. The second, philosophical and communitarian understanding of belonging also, for Aristotle, issued in civic ceremonies that were religious. He used the word *leitourgia* to describe the service given by wealthy citizens in providing for certain civic festivals.[36] These were occasions when belonging was not only made visible but celebrated frequently as a gift of the gods, one of whom might be the city's founder or patron. The third theological form of belonging issues in the church (for Christians) and the notion of the kingdom of God. The liturgies within the church are earthly participations in the divine *societas*. They too not only manifest a social reciprocity between those on earth and the all-giving triune God; they celebrate such a relation as it has been made possible in and through Jesus Christ.

Ecclesial Belonging

On the basis of the above analysis of belonging, what can we say about liturgies, restricting ourselves to the contemporary church for the moment, in which associations are becoming increasingly virtual? As I mentioned, Charles Taylor opines a movement from the late Middles Ages into modernity that has changed the face of religion as it is experienced and practiced today. He calls this movement the "great disembedding."[37] It is concomitant with another movement identified by Max Weber, the disenchantment of the world. As I also observed, Taylor's book is resonant with nostalgia. It is a nostalgia that he observes is evident also in theological narratives of the "great decline" found in

---

35. See my *Cities of God* (London: Routledge, 2000), 182–201.
36. Aristotle, *Politics* 5.8 (1309a).
37. Taylor, *A Secular Age*, 146–59.

theologians such as Fergus Kerr, Catherine Pickstock, and John Milbank—the decline from orthodoxy into the snake pits of nominalism. I do not accept such a narrative, and nostalgia is a self-indulgence. Yes, a great disembedding has taken place, and the liquid church so extolled by Pete Ward, as well as the liquid liturgies detailed in Bryan Spinks's recent book, are its ecclesial manifestations. But it is no good being Luddite about all this. What is missing and evaporating in all this liquidity is not the sense of belonging but the substance. To belong is rooted in human nature: we need to belong; we seek to belong. But in the weakening of our belonging there is a diminishment in forms and practices of belonging that have a stable identifying core that could give substance to belonging. How might this be rectified in a way that recognizes our increasingly virtual forms of association, and the liquidity of both our churches and liturgies, but offers them a more solid theological basis than they seem to have at the moment?

Beyond a lack of belonging to the church as both a denomination and an institution and the binding of the liturgical in a practice of social and spiritual formation, there is the belonging to a tradition: the Christian tradition. The tradition is not homogenous and monolithic. It is a complex phenomenon whose history shows all the vicissitudes of cultural accommodation and power politics. Nevertheless, the tradition has its source in Christ and bears a history of christological and pneumatological reflection. The tradition is at the heart of what I have called the "eschatological remainder."[38] Our social disembedding is delivering us to a profound forgetting of the Christian tradition.

The emphasis on the experience of God's grace now, the central key to most new forms of worship—which is the theological equivalent of modernity's obsession with *modo*, the "now"—encourages a dangerous ignorance. I juxtapose here "nostalgia" and "tradition," for tradition is not a looking backward to the heaps of rubble that constitute the past—Walter Benjamin's view of history. Tradition is futural in its orientation; it is a bearing of what has been into what is and what will be; it is the wisdom of *memoria*.

Put briefly, in order to inhabit liturgically where we are today in and through and beyond all liquidities and flows of time, space, and peoples, we need better and more informed catechesis. We need the tradition to be taught so that it may become again our teacher. Forms of sociality will always change—few live today in villages, while most live in cities and megacities. Even those living in villages are often commuters. Continually, with the effects of both globalization

---

38. See my *The Politics of Discipleship: Becoming Postmaterial Citizens* (Grand Rapids, MI: Baker Academic, 2009), 167–80.

and global warming, people will have to shift to where conditions for their flourishing are optimal. Informing all our liturgies and church lives has to be an awareness of belonging to the Christian tradition, with its veneration for *memoria* (which is at the heart of thanksgiving) and its eschatological investment in the future. In calling tradition our teacher, we are actually making a profound theological gesture, for it is the Spirit of Christ who leads us into all truth. The tradition, then, is not simply some immanent movement of history but the hidden operations of God through the transits of time. The God of Abraham, Isaac, and Jacob is the God of our fathers and mothers: true worship is not an adrenaline rush in the present; it is a response to God in the recognition that we are the bearers of a heritage in which God has spoken and speaks; it is a witness amid the cloud of witnesses; it is a participation in the hymn of thankfulness offered by the communion of the saints. Our belonging is articulated in the great second-person plural "we," in the exhortation after lifting our hearts: "Let *us* give thanks to the Lord." In brief, the church must educate—toward what it means to belong ecclesially.

PART 1

Historical Moments of Liturgical Migration

2

Ritual Practices on the Move between Jews and Christians: Theories and Case Studies in Late Antique Migration

Clemens Leonhard

Rituals play sophisticated roles in the expression, modification, or maintenance of the identities of the groups that perform them. Yet people, ideas, and rituals move between groups. The movements of rituals influence these identities, while the rituals themselves change during these processes. The following essay discusses examples of rituals that migrated between Judaism and Christianity in late antiquity. The first section presents the two dominant theoretical approaches to the relationship between Jews and Christians, as developed by Israel Yuval and Daniel Boyarin.[1] The second section discusses four specific cases of late antique ritual practices in order to better develop a concept of migration with regard to liturgies.

---

1. Israel Jacob Yuval, *Two Nations in Your Womb: Perspectives of Jews and Christians in Late Antiquity and the Middle Ages*, trans. Barbara Harshav and Jonathan Chipman (Berkeley: University of California Press, 2006 [in Hebrew: 2000]); Daniel Boyarin, *Border Lines: The Partition of Judaeo-Christianity*, Divinations (Philadelphia: University of Pennsylvania Press, 2004). Recently, Peter Schäfer criticized Boyarin's approach (based on earlier articles that led up to Boyarin's *Border Lines*) for studying details of Christian influence upon rabbinic Judaism in certain rabbinic texts without confronting Boyarin's master narrative on a broad scale; see his *Die Geburt des Judentums aus dem Geist des Christentums: Fünf Vorlesungen zur Entstehung des rabbinischen Judentums*, Tria Corda (Tübingen: Mohr Siebeck, 2010).

I. Judaism and Christianity

In his seminal study, *Two Nations in Your Womb*, Israel Yuval refers to a precept in Jewish Halakah that may be taken as a clear example, and hence as a point of departure, for the search for migrations of Christian customs into Judaism. Joseph Yuspa Seligman Hahn Nordlingen (1570–1637) collected norms and instructions, including rules for gestures at the celebration of the Seder Pesach. He explains how one should eat the *afikoman*—a piece of unleavened bread that is consumed at the end of the festive meal at Pesach:

> It is a voluntary [i.e., especially eager fulfillment of a] commandment that the size of the *afikoman* should be of *two* olives, but nobody should [eat] less than [the required minimum of] the size of *one* olive [of the *afikoman*]. And when he eats [the *afikoman*], he should place his hand under his chin and his mouth in order that crumbs of the *afikoman* that fall from his mouth should fall into his hands. Thus, he can eat them again out of esteem for the unleavened bread [of the *afikoman*].[2]

Yuval assumes that Ashkenazi Jews appropriated these customs surrounding the *afikoman* from the Christians' way of handling consecrated hosts. Moreover, the Christian rituals of *depositio* and *elevatio hostiae* on Good Friday and on the morning of Easter Sunday provide a model for the handling of the *afikoman* during the celebration of the Seder. In these Christian liturgies, the simple act of storing consecrated hosts somewhere else than in their normal place in the church (i.e., in the tabernacle) is enriched with mimetic allusions to Jesus' burial, like covering the consecrated host with a piece of cloth.[3] The ritual manipulation of the *afikoman* in Judaism cannot be traced back beyond the Middle Ages and is, therefore, likely to have migrated from Christianity to Judaism. Israel Yuval concludes that

> whenever we find a similarity between Judaism and Christianity, and we do not have grounds to suggest a shared heritage, we may assume that it is indicative of the influence of the Christian milieu on the Jews, and not vice versa, unless it may be proved that the Jewish sources are more ancient. The reason for this

---

2. *Sefer Yosif Omez*, http://www.hebrewbooks.org/14589, accessed 2 February 2007, no. 774, p. 170; see Yuval, *Two Nations*, 242. On this author, see Alexander Tobias, "Hahn (Nordlingen), Joseph Yuspa Ben Pinehas Seligmann," in *Encyclopedia Judaica*, ed. Fred Skolnik, 2nd ed. (Detroit: Macmillan Reference USA, 2007), 8:231.

3. Israel Yuval, *Two Nations*, 244.

assumption is quite simple: minority cultures tend to adopt the agenda of the majority culture.[4]

Yuval thus reverses the burden of proof for the reconstruction of directions of borrowing and migrations of customs and rituals. The claim of Jewish influence upon Christianity must be substantiated, explained, and documented at least as carefully as the assumption of the opposite direction. Yuval's examples from medieval Europe are plausible because Jews lived as minority groups within a Christian environment. This relationship between Jews and Christians cannot simply be read back into earlier stages of the history of the development of both religions, yet we will examine instances from these earlier stages of the history of Judaism and Christianity, taking Yuval's observations as a point of departure.

Texts from antiquity stand at the center of Daniel Boyarin's study *Border Lines*. Boyarin tells the history of early Judaism and Christianity as a process of mutual self-definition by means of the establishment—rather than the detection—of the notion of heretics and heresies. Thus, the borderlines between Jews and Christians are not facts that entice heretics to transgress them but are, on the contrary, murky. The identification and expulsion of heretics increases the exactness of the border. Medieval Christianity is therefore not just the heir of a marginal Jewish sect. With regard to the theological tenets that many scholars during Second Temple times shared, the Christian assumption of a "second power in heaven" is, for example, more conservative than the rabbinic rejection of this idea.[5] As Boyarin shows, binitarian Christology is not a particularly innovative idea of first- and second-century theologians.

Judaism and Christianity emerged as separate religions only in the fourth century, according to Boyarin. Until then we should look, rather, for associations, *collegia*, or clubs that perform certain rituals. A ritual or custom migrates not from an abstract entity of Judaism to a comparably abstract Christianity, but between groups of associations (many of whose members identify themselves as Jews) toward another group of clubs (who meet regularly in order to celebrate a banquet in memory of Jesus Christ). We must assume the presence

---

4. Ibid., 21–22.

5. Boyarin, *Border Lines*, 92: "Reexamining the historical trajectories of Logos theology has consequences for the historiographic representation of the 'parting of the ways.' If anything, this investigation will raise the distinct possibility that Christian theology, far from 'gradually draw[ing] away from Judaic tendencies,' actually maintained a more *conservative* Judaic approach to the doctrine of God than did the Rabbis, and that it is they—if anyone—who drew away from earlier Jewish theology."

of certain such groups in order to be able to observe ritual migrations. It may, however, turn out that we observe moves, migrations, and transitions of ritual elements between groups with clear boundaries—for example, established by the payment of a membership fee in a *collegium*—where it is possible to know who belongs to the group and who does not. Whether a *collegium* must be regarded as Christian or Jewish, and whether or not it would have accepted members who were also active in other, different *collegia*, will in some cases remain unclear. Boyarin shows that we can usefully study the course of differentiation between groups without determining their religious identity a priori but rather by mapping the migrations of rituals and ritual elements of groups who are on the way to shaping late antique Judaism and Christianity.

Furthermore, Yuval's observation that the majority culture influences the customs of minorities can also be applied to late antiquity. In the first centuries of the Christian era, that "majority" was the culture of Rome. This is important in the search for migrations since parallel phenomena, such as similar rituals performed by Jews and Christians, may occur because both are Greeks and Romans, not because they are Jews and Christians. Based on Boyarin's approach, concepts like "syncretism" and "influence" can only be used in a preliminary way. Pure forms of Christian and Jewish religiosity, and Christian and Jewish social behavior that may be contaminated or even mixed, may turn out to be anachronistic constructs. Nevertheless, the ancient discourses about mixture, hybrids, heresy, apostasy, and change reveal rituals on the move between groups and debates about their impact upon the self-definition of these groups. With this, we come to four case studies I wish to highlight.

II. Four Case Studies of Ritual Migrations

Ritual elements migrate from one group to another and from one liturgical setting to another. For antiquity, such blatantly obvious examples as the medieval treatment of the *afikoman* are not as easily found. Yet the ancient sources nevertheless preserve some information about similar phenomena. In what follows, I look at four such phenomena in turn.

1. Publius Aelius Glykon Zeuxianos Aelianus's Tomb Inscription

A theological doctrine may be debated by individual thinkers and enter the literary record in different ways, but a ritual is performed by groups and thus watched and imitated by several people. Its echoes in literature may vary from instructions on how to perform a certain ritual to remarks about practice, observed or imagined. A regularly performed ritual may have a lasting impact on a group of people and their understanding of themselves. As rituals cannot be performed in an individual's mind, we must ask, "What is a group?" The interest in the reconstruction of groups evokes the inscription on the tomb of Publius Aelius Glykon Zeuxianos Aelianus from Hierapolis in the Lycus valley near the biblical towns of Laodikeia and Colossae.[6] Glykon had a tomb built for himself and his family and established endowments intended to insure that his tomb be properly decorated on important festivals after his death. Thus he writes:

> [Names indicating the ownership of the grave.] He left behind 200 Denaria for the grave-crowning ceremony to the most holy presidency of the purple-dyers, so that it would produce from the interest enough for each to take a share on the sixth day of the month during the Festival of Unleavened Bread. Likewise he also left behind 150 Denaria for the grave-crowning ceremony to the association of carpet weavers, so that the revenues from the interest should be distributed, half during the Festival of Kalends on the fourth and seventh of the month and half during the Festival of Pentecost. A copy of this inscription was put into the archives.

The owner of the grave entrusted the funds to the members of two different trade guilds of his city. Philip Harland notes that these are not associations identified as Jewish, which is strange because a Jewish association is attested at Hierapolis. Glykon and his wife probably regarded themselves as Jews but were thoroughly integrated into local Roman society. The inscription does not betray any knowledge of the rabbinic laws of idolatry, some of which contain prohibitions intended to reduce contacts between Jews and other Romans just around the celebration of the Kalends.[7] Apparently, Jews of Hierapolis were used to keeping Pesach and Shavuot; perhaps they celebrated these festivals on movable dates within the solar year as did the rabbinic Jews. Jews of the area may have determined festival dates by systems of intercalation or by astronomical

---

6. Walter Ameling, ed., *Inscriptiones Judaicae Orientis*, vol. 2: *Kleinasien* (Tübingen: Mohr Siebeck, 2004), no. 196, pp. 414–22 = Jean-Baptiste Frey, *Corpus Inscriptionum Iudaicarum: Recueil des inscriptions juives qui vont du IIIe siècle avant Jésus-Christ au VIIe siècle de notre ère*, vol. 2: *Asie, Afrique* (Città del Vaticano: Pontificio Istituto di Archeologia Cristiana, 1952), 777. The translation and explanatory remarks are taken from Philip A. Harland, *Associations, Synagogues, and Congregations: Claiming a Place in Ancient Mediterranean Society* (Minneapolis: Fortress Press, 2003), 207–10.

7. The tractate *Avodah Zarah* of the Mishnah begins with rules intending to restrict certain contacts between Jews and Gentiles. Kalends and Saturnalia are the first Gentile festivals mentioned there.

observations, relying on networks of associations for such information. It is, therefore, astonishing that Glykon's inscription presupposes that associations with pagan or mixed membership would know these dates in advance.[8]

The inscription highlights three aspects of the study of the migration of rituals. First, the associations of purple dyers and carpet weavers can be regarded as forums for the exchange of knowledge about ritual practices of others, if not for the actual performance of such practices. Second, we may assume that customs migrated along with personal contacts; although not necessarily in a technical sense, it is highly probable that Glykon was a member of the two associations mentioned in the inscription.[9] He trusted the associations to continue to oversee the decoration of his tomb on these festivals, which implies that he cannot have been the only conveyor of information about Jewish festivals in those associations. Third, we may ask whether the migration of the Jewish custom of celebrating Pesach and Pentecost into the pagan ritual of adorning the grave transgresses and/or establishes a borderline between Jews and polytheists or pagan Romans. The question cannot be answered if posed in this way, for the migration and amalgamation of the customs blur any preexisting border between Jewish and pagan festivals, allowing the performance of allegedly pagan acts within the celebration of Jewish festivals. Actually, it blurs the borderline between Jews, purple dyers, carpet weavers, Romans, and polytheists.[10]

On the one hand, this inscription is an outstanding instance of the migration of rituals. It suggests the existence of—perhaps hotly debated, perhaps tacit—assumptions about religious identities. Harland observes that the inscription "does not necessarily involve a lack of some distinctive cultural

---

8. See Arye Edrei and Doron Mendels, "A Split Jewish Diaspora: Its Dramatic Consequences," *Journal for the Study of the Pseudepigrapha* 16 (2007): 91–137, esp. 104, n. 20. The authors observe that the Mishnaic description of messengers said to be sent in order to inform Diaspora communities about the correct Jerusalem-based intercalation was not supposed to reach the Lycus valley. The flexibility of intercalation in late antiquity is demonstrated by Sacha Stern, *Calendar and Community: A History of the Jewish Calendar, 2nd Century BCE–10th Century CE* (Oxford: Oxford University Press, 2001).

9. Harland, *Associations*, 207–10, assumes that Glykon belonged to both of the associations mentioned. He may also have been a member of the Jewish association in his town. According to Ameling, *Inscriptiones Judaicae Orientis*, 418, membership in an association was not a prerequisite for the establishment of an endowment. Should Glykon not have been a member of both associations, the inscription requires an even tighter social network between Jews and non-Jews to account for the fact that the trade guilds were reliable.

10. Harland's observations (in *Associations*, 207–10) imply that the club of the purple dyers could have had more social functions than simply gathering the artisans of the trade.

characteristics on the part of the Jews in relation to society at large, or the disintegration of group boundaries,"[11] but on the other hand, the observation of this migration destroys the perception of the borders that should have been passed in the course of this migration.

Glykon's normal and inconspicuous behavior points to the fact that there are borderlines at places where we do not expect them. Conversely, such borders are missing at places where we do expect them. This shows that Glykon's ritual information migrated across borderlines according to contemporary imagination while he actually seems to have abided by ancient ones. Contemporary scholarship did not overcome the urge to explain Glykon's behavior as heresy—in Boyarin's sense. We should not try to find a heresiological category for Glykon and make him a hybrid, a pagan God fearer, or even a Judeo-Christian. On the contrary, adjusting our understanding of Jews and Romans at this point seems more useful.

This example illustrates the hermeneutic difficulty of the search for ritual elements that migrate between Judaism, Christianity, and paganism. Furthermore, it makes reconstructions of belief systems more complex because the performance of a ritual may or may not indicate the performer's belief. Glykon probably believed in the everlasting future of the stock market at Hierapolis (as the precondition for a constant flow of interest from his endowment) and was convinced of the importance of public honor beyond death. It is not evident that he believed in God who gave the Torah to his people and commanded them to celebrate Pentecost. This complements Daniel Boyarin's observations on the differentiation of doctrines. A reviewer of this question says, "The common sense assumption that doctrinal development inevitably re-orders community boundaries is not necessarily so and real life can be far more complex."[12] Groups of people who believed in certain doctrines, and people who performed certain ritualized acts, certainly overlapped. The borderlines between them were not, however, congruent. The study of ritual migrations increases the visibility of this complexity.

2. Pesach and the Migration of a Festival

The New Testament authors John (19:36) and Paul (1 Cor 5:7) compare Jesus with the Passover animal. Paul's use of this image implies that he does not expect the addressees of his letter to the Corinthians to celebrate Pesach.

---

11. Harland, *Associations*, 210.
12. Jonathan Gorsky, "Notes and Comments: The Parting of the Ways—a Review Essay," *The Heythrop Journal* 50 (2009): 996–1005, 996b. Gorsky makes that point frequently.

The image of "Christ our Pesach animal" is designed to increase the plausibility of Paul's ethical argument. Groups that cherished the memory of Jesus Christ did not celebrate Pesach.[13]

The Christian custom of celebrating Easter can be traced back into the middle of the second century. Melito of Sardis (and the very enigmatic document *Epistula Apostolorum*) is the first author who most probably bears witness to a Christian celebration of Easter. His homily *On Pascha* explains Easter on the basis of the Old Testament institution of the first Pesach in Exodus 12. Unfortunately, Melito does not hint at liturgical elements of the celebration of his community. However, some lines indicate how he envisages the Jewish Pesach of Jesus' times, because he contrasts elements of Jesus' death and crucifixion with customs of Greco-Roman symposia:

> So then, you [referring to the Jews] . . . rushed to the slaying of the Lord. You prepared for him sharp nails and false witnesses, and ropes and scourges and vinegar and gall and sword and forceful restraint as against a murderous robber. For you brought both scourges for his body and thorn for his head; and you bound his good hands, which formed you from earth; and that good mouth of his which fed you with life you fed with gall. And you killed your Lord at the great feast.
>
> And you were making merry, while he was starving; you had wine to drink and bread to eat, he had vinegar and gall; your face was bright, his was downcast; you were triumphant, he was afflicted; you were making music, he was being judged; you were giving the beat, he was being nailed up; you were dancing, he was being buried; you were reclining on a soft couch, he in grave and coffin.[14]

Jesus' death is thus said to have occurred at the time that the Jews celebrated the last Pesach ever. According to Melito's ideology, Judaism ceased to exist—or at least lost its right to exist—at the time of Jesus' death. When Melito hints at the way Jews celebrated Pesach a century before his own time, he cannot but describe it with sympotic elements: making merry, drinking wine and eating bread, making music, dancing, reclining on a soft couch. Melito betrays no knowledge of rabbinic Judaism or of the place and time of Jesus' death in

---

13. Clemens Leonhard, *The Jewish Pesach and the Origins of the Christian Easter: Open Questions in Current Research*, Studia Judaica 35 (Berlin/New York: De Gruyter, 2006), 215–16.

14. *Peri Pascha*, nos. 79–80, in Melito of Sardis, *On Pascha and Fragments*, ed. and trans. Stuart George Hall, Oxford Early Christian Texts (Oxford: Clarendon Press, 1979), lines 553–81, pp. 43, 45. Cf. Leonhard, *Jewish Pesach*, 42–55.

Jerusalem. The time of Pesach does not fit the accounts of any of the gospels or any understanding of Jewish customs. The biblical laws in Exodus 12 and Deuteronomy 16 require that the Pesach animals be eaten in the evening. The gospel according to John presupposes that Jesus died in the afternoon, at the time when the Pesach animals were slaughtered in the Temple—not yet eaten. The Synoptic Gospels envisage Jesus' death at another date of the calendar, yet they agree with John on a time during the day. Furthermore, Melito says that Jesus was killed "in the middle of the day"[15] to emphasize the monstrosity of the crime, not to convey a bit of historical memory. Although Melito's knowledge of things that modern interpreters recognize as Jewish is at best minimal, his invectives betray his opinion about the Jews of his time when he pretends to speak about Jesus' coevals.[16] Arye Edrei and Doron Mendels's analysis of a "split" in the Jewish Diaspora supports these observations.[17] They conclude that the Western Diaspora of Judaism had access only to the Greek texts of ancient Jewish tradition, especially the Septuagint. This tradition gradually expanded into the extracanonical books, but these Jews had no access to knowledge about the customs, beliefs, and religious laws developed by the rabbis in Palestine

---

15. Jesus is said to have been murdered "in the middle of Jerusalem" (*Peri Pascha*, no. 93, lines 692 and 694, p. 53) and "in the middle of the street and in the middle of the city, at the middle of the day for all to see" (no. 94, lines 704–5, p. 53). Urban C. von Wahlde, "The References to the Time and Place of the Crucifixion in the Peri Pascha of Melito of Sardis," *Journal of Theological Studies* 60 (2009): 556–69, emphasizes that Melito did not know anything about the place and time of Jesus' crucifixion but wanted to convey theological issues only.

16. Jewish *collegia* in the Diaspora may have held banquets at Pesach. This is presupposed here for Melito's contemporaries (as well as in the Hierapolis inscription—see the first case above—although Ameling, in *Inscriptiones Judaicae Orientis*, rightly emphasizes that the inscription does not refer to a meal held at the festivals). Further studies are required in order to assess the ways in which Roman adherents to oriental cults like that of Jupiter Dolichenus expressed their adherence to the cult in the life of their *collegia* far removed from the central sanctuary of the god. They may have created their own set of festivals or adapted the festivals celebrated at that central sanctuary. Edrei and Mendels, in "A Split Jewish Diaspora," observe that the Jews of the Western Diaspora could have dedicated a banquet to the memory of the biblical obligation to go to Jerusalem and to celebrate Pesach there. See my "'Herod's Days' and the Development of Jewish and Christian Festivals," in *Jewish Identity and Politics between the Maccabees and Bar Kokhba: Groups, Normativiy, and Rituals*, ed. Benedikt Eckhardt, Supplements to the Journal for the Study of Judaism 155 (Leiden/Boston: Brill, 2012), 189–208.

17. See Edrei and Mendels, "A Split Jewish Diaspora," but compare the modification of the thesis about the early development of the Christian Easter I put forward in *Jewish Pesach*. Thus, Melito could have known "biblical" Jews (in Edrei and Mendels's sense) and understood them very well, especially because their customs did not differ much from his own. The notion that Melito was a Jew, a Judeo-Christian, or the like is unwarranted and unnecessary.

and Babylon, which were never translated into Greek.[18] Thus, Melito may have known the Diaspora Judaism of his time and region quite well.

It is plausible that Jewish *collegia* held a symposium honoring the day of Pesach. On the one hand, they would not have performed the sacrificial rituals prescribed in the Torah, because they knew from the Bible that those were restricted to the Temple.[19] On the other hand, they were not aware of the rabbis' innovative suggestion to modify their symposia held on the evening of Pesach. Thus, Jews of the Greek Diaspora need not have begun to celebrate after nightfall; they may well have begun in the afternoon, at the time when people began to hold a banquet, but also at the time when Jesus would have died on the cross—of course not at the time when Jews would have celebrated Pesach in Second Temple Jerusalem.

Few ritual elements of the Christian celebration of Easter can be reconstructed on the basis of Melito's homily. Melito's interpretation of the Christian Easter points to the liturgical setting of his community as Quartodeciman. Later sources that describe the Quartodeciman liturgy of Easter indicate that the Christian celebrations began at the same time as the Jewish ones, but the Christians inverted the mood of the celebration. While the Jews celebrated, the Christians fasted and started to celebrate only when the Jewish Pesach had ended.[20] The Syriac *Didascalia*, which speaks about the Christians' fast, may, of course, presuppose that the Christians had already been fasting for some time when they eventually started their celebration. Nevertheless, the idea of fasting for just a few hours seems farfetched. Thus, it is more likely that the term "fast" indicates a mood and thus the theological meaning attached to the first part of that Christian celebration. The fast parallels the Jewish celebration of the festival in a conspicuous way.

---

18. I do not agree with Edrei and Mendels's assumption of a long and elaborate prehistory of the Mishnah before the destruction of the Second Temple. Yet even with a modification regarding the development and expansion of *halakah* and *aggadah* in Hebrew and Aramaic, the thesis explains many phenomena discussed here.

19. In this context Polycrates's description of the Jews who remove leaven from their houses needs to be revisited; see my *Jewish Pesach*, 271–72. On the one hand, the assumption that Jews removed leaven from their houses remains plausible because the custom could have been observed by people not intimately connected to a Jewish community or to Jewish households. On the other hand, we must ask why Jews of the Western Diaspora should have performed this rite at all. They may have adapted and performed customs of the Bible that did not require the Temple. The removal of leaven remains the most conspicuous instruction for the festival, which did not require the ritual slaughtering of a Pesach animal and other elements of the Temple cult.

20. Leonhard, *Jewish Pesach*, 217–24, 268–85.

This fits perfectly with the lines of Melito's sermon quoted above. Melito hints at a Jewish banquet that took place while Jesus was tortured to death. This corresponds to the liturgical reality of Melito's—not Jesus'—time, for Christians mourn Jesus' death while Jews celebrate Pesach. As soon as the Jews end their celebration, the Christians may celebrate Easter. In this sense, the Christian Easter began as an anti-Pesach in the second century.[21] Later generations would exploit the mimetic potential of this celebration, which was first held against Diaspora Judaism and only on a secondary level at the time of Christ's death.

Easter is, therefore, an instance of migration between Judaism and Christianity. The Pesach of the Jewish Diaspora radically changes its ritual shape and meaning when it crosses the borderline from Jewish groups to congregations like Melito's. The festival establishes that border as the very point where it changed its shape and meaning. Eventually, Christians celebrate Easter and Jews celebrate Pesach. The more the Christian celebration moves toward mimetic correspondences with the New Testament accounts of the passion, the less it becomes anti-Jewish regarding the structure of its rituals.[22] In the fourth century, Easter became an elaborate commemorative liturgy of Christ's passion, death, and resurrection, covered more than a week, and lost its calendrical contact with the Jewish Pesach.

3. Blessings after Meals

The tenth chapter of the oldest extant church order, the so-called teaching of the twelve apostles, the *Didache*, instructs the readers how to pray after meals.[23] On a very superficial level we may detect parallels to the much later attested rabbinic forms of grace after meals, *birkat hamazon*. Substantiating such parallels is difficult because the search for exact verbal parallels in ancient rabbinic prayers is anachronistic. This is borne out by many rabbinic statements concerning the formulation of prayers. Early rabbinic literature emphasizes that the statutory

---

21. The history of the Christian Sunday reflects the same pattern. The Sunday is still unknown to the authors of the New Testament, although they all agree on the fact that the empty tomb of Christ was discovered on a first day of the week. Pliny does not yet refer to the Sunday. His remark that the Christians meet *stato die* can refer to any rhythm of meetings of the Christian *collegia* that are actually troubling him. The *Letter of Barnabas* is the first text that mentions Sunday as an anti-Sabbath; see my *Jewish Pesach*, 122–24, 136–40; for Pliny, see Klaus Thraede's magisterial study, "Noch einmal: Plinius d. J. und die Christen," *Zeitschrift für die Neutestamentliche Wissenschaft und die Kunde der älteren Kirche* 95 (2004): 102–28.

22. Leonhard, *Jewish Pesach*, 273–79.

23. "After you have had your fill"; see Paul F. Bradshaw, *Eucharistic Origins*, An Alcuin Club Publication (Oxford: Oxford University Press, 2004), 24f (translation), 25–42 (commentary).

prayers, as well as mealtime *berakhot*, should not be fully standardized—notwithstanding certain rules for their composition.[24] Prayers had to retain some degree of spontaneity and improvisation and allow the persons praying to adapt them to their situations. Rabbinic texts sometimes suggest alternative formulations or abbreviations of prayer texts. Furthermore, as soon as some degree of standardization becomes visible, liturgical poets compose a whole branch of Jewish literature as replacements of those allegedly standardized forms of prayer. These highly artistic forms of poetry were not invented on the spot or improvised, yet their mere existence indicates that the recitation of a wholly standardized text was not regarded as the only way to fulfill one's religious obligations. In addition, liturgical poetry is normally linked to its liturgical setting by alluding to biblical texts read on the same day in the synagogue, indicating the practical survival of the idea that prayer should not consist only of stereotyped text.

This situation is indirectly supported by the Dura Europos fragment that probably bears witness to a form of mealtime prayer very close to rabbinic terminology and rhetoric, although not a version of the later attested *birkhot hamazon*:

Fragment "A":
(1) Blessed is X king of the world/eternity
(2) apportioned food, provided sustenance
(3) sons of flesh cattle to . . .
(4) created man to eat of . . .
(5) many bodies of . . .
(6) to bless all cattle
(8) . . . prepared . . .

Fragment "B":
(1) for
(2) pure (animals) to (eat?)
(3) provides sustenance
(4) small and large
(5) all the animals of the field . . .
(6) . . . feed their young
(7) and sing and bless[25]

---

24. The question has been discussed in a broad and well-documented context by Allan Bouley, *From Freedom to Formula: The Evolution of the Eucharistic Prayer from Oral Improvisation to Written Texts* (Washington, DC: Catholic University of America Press, 1981).

25. Steven Fine, *Art and Judaism in the Greco-Roman World: Toward a New Jewish Archeology* (Cambridge: Cambridge University Press, 2005), 174–77; text and translation, 175; cf. Bradshaw,

We cannot assess the specific liturgical purpose of the Dura Europos fragment; it is not liturgical poetry. Some bits of its terminology and imagery immediately suggest the ritual context of grace after meals.[26] As written texts, the fragments do not indicate how spontaneous prayer would be improvised in rabbinic circles, but they are of paramount importance because they show that early Jewish prayer was indeed diverse and differed from later coined standards.[27] They also show that the mere act of writing is not necessarily connected with standardization. Thus, the question of whether prayers would be written or transmitted orally is secondary to the more basic requirement of variety and diversity.

The prayer text of *Didache* 10 may also differ markedly from the later standardized forms of *birkat hamazon* while still deriving from the same cultural

---

Eucharistic Origins, 34–35. The two fragments were found in the rubble that was piled up inside the wall and that covered the street and the houses near the wall in order to strengthen the ramparts. It is, therefore, securely dated to the early third century.

26. See the discussion in Fine, *Art and Judaism*, 176–77.

27. Many studies refer to the passage in *Jubilees* 22 as an instance of *birkat hamazon*: "Isaac and Ishmael came from the well of the oath to their father Arbaham to celebrate the festival of weeks (this is the festival of the firstfruits of the harvest). . . . Isaac slaughtered a sacrifice for the offering; he offered (it) on his father's altar which he had made in Hebron. He sacrificed a peace offering and prepared a joyful feast in front of his brother Ishmael. Rebecca made fresh bread out of new wheat. She gave it to her son Jacob to bring to his father Abraham some of the firstfruits of the land so that he would eat (it) and bless the Creator of everything before he died. Isaac, too, sent through Jacob [his] excellent peace offering [and {p. 128} wine to his father] Abraham for him to eat and drink. He ate and drank. Then he blessed the most high God who created the heavens and the earth, who made all the fat things of the earth, and gave them to mankind to eat, drink, and bless the Creator. 'Now I offer humble thanks to you, my God, because you have shown me this day. I am now 175 years of age, old and with (my) time completed. All of my days have proved to be peace for me. The enemy's sword has not subdued me in anything at all which you have given me and my sons during all my lifetime until today. May your kindness and peace rest on your servant and on the descendants of his sons so that they, of all the nations of the earth, may become your {p. 129} chosen people and heritage from now until all the time of the earth's history throughout all ages.' He summoned Jacob and said to him . . ." James C. VanderKam, *The Book of Jubilees: A Critical Text*, 2 vols., Corpus Scriptorum Christianorum Orientalium (CSCO) 511 = CSCO, Scriptores Aethiopici 88 (Louvain: Peeters, 1989), 127–29; parentheses and square brackets are in the original. The text does not give a fixed formula for Abraham's blessing after meals. It does not quote Deuteronomy 8:10. The degree to which this text reflects the normal custom of blessing God in the context of a meal is difficult to assess. Furthermore, the situation may reflect a special custom for Shavuot, the consumption of firstfruits, or the situation of the biblical characters involved in the narrative. We can infer from this text that *Jubilees* does not know the medieval rabbinic *birkat hamazon*.

background as the rabbinic prayers. *Didache* 10 probably predates their traditions by at least several decades. As the prayer mentions "Jesus, your [i.e., God's] servant/child," it is a Christian text in a very broad sense of the term. *Didache* 10 looks like a Jewish prayer made part of a Christian liturgy. Is it an example of a ritual element that migrated from Judaism to Christianity?

Even if *birkat hamazon* influenced Christian customs, it did not have a long-lasting impact on Christian liturgies. This can be attributed to two factors. First, saying grace after meals became unimportant as soon as preprandial prayers were regarded as the crucial element of the Eucharist. After the development of the genre of the anaphora in the fourth century[28] as a hallmark of the Christian Eucharist, prayer formulas for grace after meals were hardly preserved in the record.[29] True, Christians treated the consecrated host with great awe and respect and were supposed to pray after its reception,[30] but such prayers did not reach the same level of importance as the anaphora spoken before eating. The

---

28. Reinhard Meßner suggests that this genre of Christian prayer (the *"Eucharistiegebet"*) evolved in the fourth century; "Über einige Aufgaben bei der Erforschung der Liturgiegeschichte der Frühen Kirche," *Archiv für Liturgiewissenschaft* 50 (2008) = Martin Klöckener and Angelus A. Häußling, ed., *Liturgie verstehen: Ansatz, Ziele und Aufgaben der Liturgiewissenschaft* (Fribourg: Academic Press, 2008), 207–30, esp. 216. *Birkat hamazon* is not a very likely ancestor of eucharistic prayers because it is the point in the meal after which bread can no longer be eaten. Someone who wants to eat bread must again recite the appropriate *qiddush* and continue with at least an abbreviated form of *birkat hamazon* after eating the bread. See my "Blessings over Wine and Bread in Judaism and Christian Eucharistic Prayers: Two Independent Traditions," in *Jewish and Christian Liturgy and Worship: New Insights into Its History and Interaction*, ed. Albert Gerhards and Clemens Leonhard, Jewish and Christian Perspectives 15 (Leiden: Brill, 2007), 309–26. Christian preprandial prayers are by definition recited before eating the bread.

29. A prayer for saying grace after the consumption of the Eucharist survived in the *Barcelona Anaphora*; see the magisterial study by Mikhail Zheltov, "The Anaphora and Thanksgiving Prayer from the Barcelona Papyrus: An Underestimated Testimony to the History of the Anaphora in the Fourth Century," *Vigiliae Christianae* 62 (2008): 467–504. It is difficult to assess the date of the composition of this anaphora, but in any case an anaphora is pronounced over bread and wine together. Justin's testimony does not support the idea of a combination of the blessing of bread and wine at the very beginning of sympotic celebrations of the Eucharist. The *Barcelona Anaphora* rather attests a stage of the development of the Eucharist that postdates its sympotic shape. The prayer after the consumption of the Eucharist could be an adaptation (a highly interesting one) of a pious custom to pray after Communion, and not a survival of *birkat hamazon* in Christianity.

30. *Didache* 9 can be regarded as an effective prayer in this respect because of the rubric in 9:5 with its quotation of Matthew 7:6. This presupposes that the two chapters of *Didache* 9 and 10 reflect a single celebration—an assumption not shared by all its interpreters.

level of importance can be inferred from the fact that they are recommended to individuals as private prayers.[31]

Saying grace after meals in eucharistic contexts lost its importance as soon as—and because—Christian Eucharists stopped being meals. Elaborate forms of grace after meals belong to symposium types of liturgies. As soon as the Eucharist shifted from this sympotic context to other social institutions, it ceased to be perceived even as a symbolic, reduced form of a meal. Consequently, acts that were typical of meals became abbreviated or vanished. In the Didachist's community the communal recitation of grace after meals was still an important custom because the *Didache* reflects a symposium type of eucharistic celebration.

This observation widens the perspective. Jews and Christians are not the only groups who pray after meals. During typical banquets the pagan properties of the event were indicated by typical gestures (libations) and words (songs, toasts to the gods, or toasts calling upon the gods) after the meal and before the beginning of the drinking party. Christians and Jews apparently replaced these ritual elements in the middle of their banquets with comparatively short prayers. In the long run, the custom was preserved and expanded in rabbinic Judaism and marginalized in Christianity.

This complicates the search for—and identification of—migrations of ritual elements. The Christians of the *Didache* (together with other groups[32]) and rabbinic Jews composed, performed, discussed, and sometimes even wrote down prayers for grace after meals. Christians may have inherited this custom from Judaism. Yet Christians and Jews had the same strong motives to replace the pagan performances in the middle of normal banquets. The mere fact that Jews and Christians said grace after meals does not, therefore, indicate that one of them borrowed the custom from the other. A philological approach that tries to reconstruct core traditions or original forms from which the extant examples have derived is bound to fail in this case. Already the Dura Europos fragment suggests that early rabbinic prayers were multifarious and improvised in actual

---

31. See Theodore of Mopsuestia's second catechetical homily on the Mass, nos. 27–28, in Raymond Tonneau and Robert Devreesse, *Les homélies catéchétiques de Théodore de Mopsueste: Reproduction phototypique du Ms. Mingana syr. 561 (Selly Oak Colleges' Library, Birmingham)*, Studi e Testi 145 (Città del Vaticano: Biblioteca Apostolica Vaticana, 1949), fols. 145r–146r = pp. 576–81.

32. 1 Corinthians 11 mentions a cup being drunk *after* the meal. This probably refers to a replacement of the pagan cluster of ritual elements at the end of the meal and at the beginning of the drinking party. The manipulation of wine stood at the center of this ritual.

practice, adhering to certain patterns[33] and using typical words and metaphors. The people could identify a prayer and its function, and ritual experts would have taken their own worn-out paths when they prayed. The wording of such a piece of prayer could have been typical of a person's style and of the customs of a certain *collegium*, but not of abstract entities like Judaism and Christianity.

In comparison with the development of the Christian Easter, the prayers for grace after meals are a much more unreliable example for ritual migrations between Judaism and Christianity. One could classify these developments as an instance of migration of a ritual from the society that kept pagan or polytheist customs to Jewish and Christian *collegia* or houses. Jews, and for some time also Christians, seem to have changed parts of that ritual element with regard to the ritualized acts that were performed, as well as with regard to the words that were spoken. Yet they both adhered to the customs of their society.

4. Liturgies of the Word

Jews and Christians perform solemn readings from the texts of the Holy Scriptures in certain liturgies. During the first millennium, both developed systems of reading for appointed times during the year.[34] Soon ritual elements began to accompany the reading. In what follows, I inquire into possible migrations of the larger liturgical structures between Judaism and Christianity.

Rabbinic texts show that Jews performed reading services on Sabbaths, as well as on Mondays and Thursdays. These services were not connected with a communal meal. Christians also performed mandatory reading services before the celebration of the Eucharist, at least since the fourth century. One may thus wonder whether Jewish liturgies of prayer and reading were taken over into Christianity and combined with the eucharistic meal.[35] Throughout history

---

33. The prayer of *Didache* 10 apparently contains three sections like the ancient form of the rabbinic *birkat hamazon*, perhaps because these prayers replaced three invocations over the three kraters of mixed wine that were customary among their Greek and Roman neighbors.

34. In those ritualized acts both religions differentiate and indicate the canonical status of certain texts. Thus, the reading from the Torah in Judaism differs as markedly from the reading of the *haftarah* as the reading from the gospels differs from that of the New Testament epistles, or the Old Testament, in many Christian traditions. The ritual means of differentiation are not, however, identical in Judaism and Christianity. Many aspects of these rituals require further study.

35. Hans Bernhard Meyer's magisterial handbook on the history of the Mass, *Eucharistie: Geschichte, Theologie, Pastoral; Mit einem Beitrag von Irmgard Pahl*, Gottesdienst der Kirche: Handbuch der Liturgiewissenschaft 4 (Regensburg: Pustet, 1989), 116–19, refers to two groups of theses about the origins of the Liturgy of the Word. (1) It could have been inspired by Jew-

this combination of a Liturgy of the Word with the celebration of the Eucharist remained the norm. Furthermore, churches of the Reformation preferred to drop the Eucharist and keep celebrating independent services centered upon reading and preaching to dispensing with this Liturgy of the Word. Second, why the Liturgy of the Word had to be performed just *before* the Eucharist has to be explained. Since the earliest celebrations of the Eucharist took the shape of Greco-Roman banquets, one would expect any Liturgy of the Word to follow after the meal. Christians and Jews did not differ in this respect. Yet, rabbinic Jews apparently did not only meet in settings of communal meals but also assembled in order to study Torah and to discuss religious laws, as well as for prayer. If Christian and rabbinic community meetings were basically organized as symposia, the congregants would eat first and then engage in learned debates and the discussion of matters pertaining to their *collegium* afterward—preferably over some cups of wine.

By the fourth century, however, the reading and explanation of Scripture in Christian communities always preceded that part of the service in which bread was eaten and wine was drunk. Despite all similarities of the details of the ritual, the Christian Eucharist of late antiquity and the Middle Ages is a vestige neither of a symposium nor of a Jewish Sabbath morning celebration. If the Christian Liturgy of the Word were to be regarded as a ritual element that migrated from Judaism to Christianity or was preserved in both religions as a survival from Second Temple times, Christians must at some time in their history have appended the Eucharist to a Jewish celebration.[36] Yet no sources suggest a reversal of the well-established structure of typical banquets in Christianity. We must therefore look for other possible points of departure of the development of the Liturgy of the Word within the Eucharist than the Greek, Roman, Christian, and Jewish symposium—as well as the rabbinic Sabbath morning service.

---

ish meal customs (e.g., the recitation of the Haggadah at the Seder Pesach) and early Christian customs to remember and proclaim Christ during Christian meals. (2) Early Christianity could have taken over the Jewish synagogue service and appended the Eucharist to it. Meyer rejects the latter thesis. Regarding the first, he does not raise the point that a sympotic structure would normally make people eat first and then remember, proclaim, and debate matters of importance for their group afterward.

36. See Reinhard Meßner, "Die Synode von Seleukeia-Ktesiphon 410 und die Geschichte der ostsyrischen Messe," in *Haec sacrosancta synodus: Konzils- und kirchengeschichtliche Beiträge*, ed. Reinhard Meßner and Rudolf Pranzl (Regensburg: Pustet, 2006), 60–85, esp. 75–77, for another solution to the problem of the emergence of the liturgy of the word.

Dating of developments plays a crucial role in this discussion. Tracing back the Liturgy of the Word beyond the fourth century, we find a few hints in the vast corpus of the writings of Origen. They point to the existence of a precursor of the later Eucharist in Origen's time and region.[37] Other traditions that were composed and/or transmitted in the third century still mention eucharistic celebrations without a shadow of a Liturgy of the Word preceding them. It is evident for Origen's time that Christians engaged in organized as well as ritualized Scripture readings. Origen spent much of his lifetime expounding biblical texts for catechumens and Christians who sought to increase their religious knowledge. Yet such services do not explain the later rule that the Eucharist must be preceded and not followed by a Liturgy of the Word.

At this point, one possible objection must be taken up. Justin Martyr describes two eucharistic services, one of which is preceded by a Liturgy of the Word, in his *First Apology* several decades before Origen's time:[38]

> And on the day called Sunday, all who live in cities or in the country gather together to one place, and the memoirs of the apostles or the writings of the prophets are read, as long as time permits; then, when the reader has ceased, the president verbally instructs, and exhorts to the imitation of these good things. Then we all rise together and pray, and, as we before said,[39] when our prayer is ended, bread and wine[40] and water are brought, and the president in

---

37. See Harald Buchinger, "Early Eucharist in Transition? A Fresh Look at Origen," in *Jewish and Christian Liturgy and Worship: New Insights into Its History and Interaction*, ed. Clemens Leonhard and Albert Gerhards, Jewish and Christian Perspectives 15 (Leiden: Brill, 2007), 207–27.

38. Justin Martyr, *1 Apology* 67.3–6, English translation in Ante-Nicene Fathers (ANF) 1:185f, http://www.ccel.org/ccel/schaff/anf01.toc.html, accessed 15 December 2011.

39. Justin refers back to *1 Apology* 65.1 where the neophytes join the congregation and all pray together before they kiss each other and continue to celebrate the Eucharist. The reference suggests that Justin regards the prayer of the congregation, and the subsequent meals, as a self-contained unit of the ritual sequences of baptism followed by the Eucharist or of a study session followed by the Eucharist.

40. Justin Martyr, *1 Apology* 67.5: "Bread [*artos*] and wine [*oinos*] and water [*hydōr*] are brought." The parallel passage, *1 Apology* 65.3, contains a more awkward text stating that the president receives "bread [*artos*] and a cup of water [*potērion hydatos*] and mixed wine [*kai kramatos*]." See Andrew McGowan, *Ascetic Eucharists: Food and Drink in Early Christian Ritual Meals* (Oxford: Clarendon Press, 1999), 151–55, who argues convincingly that the passages that deal with the Eucharist in Justin's apology were updated to the later standards of Eucharists celebrated with wine. His best arguments do not come from the scarce evidence of manuscript variants but from other passages in Justin's work, which speak about water in eucharistic contexts. Those latter passages escaped the scrutiny of the copyists because the references to the Eucharist were more sublime.

like manner offers prayers and thanksgivings, according to his ability, and the people assent, saying Amen; and there is a distribution to each, and a participation of that over which thanks have been given, and to those who are absent a portion is sent by the deacons.

Justin describes the reading and exposition of certain texts followed by prayer and the celebration of the Eucharist. In the preceding chapter he had already referred to the institution narrative of the Last Supper.[41] Justin therefore understands the communal meal of the congregation as a successor of Jesus' last meal and as a fulfillment of the Lord's commandment to celebrate it. Is the part of the service that precedes this celebration of the Eucharist a precursor of the Liturgy of the Word, and hence is Justin the earliest witness for the basic structure of the medieval Mass? Two aspects of Justin's text support a negative answer to this question. First, Justin describes not only the Sunday liturgy but also the Eucharist that follows the liturgy of baptism. The celebration of the Eucharist is not, therefore, connected with a compulsory Liturgy of the Word. Baptism can take its place.[42] Second, Justin understands his community as a philosophical school. It is true that the postmedieval reader of the *Apology* cannot but think of the ritual of the Mass here. Yet Justin's community—the only one that he knew in Rome, according to the acts of the martyrs—need not have regarded this activity as a Liturgy of the Word in a modern sense, nor even as an integral part of the celebration of the Eucharist. Listening to a reading of the sacred text, and to an exposition of its ethical contents, was likely the normal occupation of the members of this congregation—as a typical philosophical club, not as a typical Christian congregation. Moreover, Justin's *Apology* is not a witness to an inversion of the structure of the symposium. It is not likely a symposium at all. The Eucharist that he describes is a very ascetic event. Andrew McGowan takes up Adolf von Harnack's suggestion that Justin adheres to a movement of Christians who refused the consumption of wine and meat—the two most conspicuous and typical elements of the pagan sacrificial cult and cuisine.[43] Several pagan movements of philosophers shared these tenets and this way of life. Thus, we may take Justin's description of the Eucharist seriously with regard to the sequence of the ritualized acts. Bread and water are brought in front of the president of Justin's congregation. He recites prayers over both, apparently not over the bread and water separately. There

---

41. Justin Martyr, *1 Apology* 66.3.
42. See Bradshaw, *Eucharistic Origins*, 74, and Meßner, "Die Synode," 73–74.
43. McGowan, *Ascetic Eucharists*.

is no indication of a prayer after the meal or of a subsequent drinking party. This does not come as a surprise, because it would be odd to hold a drinking party with water.[44] On the one hand, the shape of Justin's celebration of the Eucharist is determined by several features of his community, such as its self-understanding as a philosophical school and its abstinence from wine. These specific characteristics of Justin's community had no impact on later churches; they were not precursors of the later developments that contributed to fourth-century imperial and mainstream Christianity. On the other hand, Justin's example shows that different challenges could lead to considerable adaptations of the shape of the celebration of the Eucharist. This indirectly supports the following observations about the development of a possible precursor of the fourth-century combined celebration of a Liturgy of the Word together with the Eucharist.

Andrew McGowan and Paul Bradshaw[45] describe the transition from a group of congregations that celebrated symposia to meetings in the morning that were eventually regarded as celebrations of the Eucharist. While Tertullian still emphasizes that the president of the community distributes *apophoreta* (portions of food that are left over from a meal and may be taken home by the guests or distributed to other members of the group)—perhaps from a symposium of the previous evening—Cyprian hints at the fact that many members of the church take part only in these morning assemblies, where they receive consecrated bread and wine.[46] There was just not enough space available for all members of the church to celebrate a symposium in the evening. Furthermore, many members of the church of Carthage were not accustomed to the celebration of lavish symposia in their everyday, modest lives. Especially in those cases where some members of the community continued to hold symposium-like celebrations in the evening, it is clear that such morning celebrations were not symposia.[47] Considering the rising importance and power of the presidents of

---

44. Meßner, "Einige Aufgaben," 220–22, collects further items that cast doubt on the traditional assumption that Justin represents the first stage of what would become the structure of the Mass.

45. Andrew McGowan, "Rethinking Agape and Eucharist in Early North African Christianity," *Studia Liturgica* 34 (2004): 165–76, taken up by Bradshaw, *Eucharistic Origins*, 99–103.

46. Cyprian, *Letter* 63.16. Cyprian rebukes people who prefer to distribute and to drink water in these eucharistic morning celebrations. He instructs them to use wine.

47. Ibid. Cyprian senses the difference. He even risks destroying his own argument about the president's representation of Jesus during the celebration of the Eucharist, adducing a farfetched allegorical explanation of the timing of the Last Supper in order to get rid of any objection against the fact that the Eucharist is celebrated in the morning. Evidently, symposia

these communities, probably the morning celebrations were not even symposia *in nuce*; they were also not intended to be regarded as symbolic meals. One must look for other social institutions that might have functioned as a seed crystal—to use an image from the process of crystallization—for something like a Liturgy of the Word preceding a much more abbreviated form of Eucharist.

The morning celebrations presupposed by Cyprian may have been derived from the Roman custom of holding morning *salutationes*.[48] Groups of clients visited and greeted their wealthy patron in his house each morning. The morning *salutationes* made different levels of the social hierarchy of the participants visible by means of ritualized acts. They thus affirmed the social role of the patron and resulted in support for the clients who would receive gifts in return for their act of bestowing social honor upon the patron. Social hierarchies had long before entered the church and made sympotic equality an experience of only a few of its members. Little more than a century after Cyprian's time, the Eucharist as a symposium had been superseded by the Eucharist as the second part of the Mass, at least in most churches of the ancient Christian world. The Eucharist as a morning *salutatio* of the patron of the local church, or its president, is a plausible point of departure for this development, which opens new ritual space not yet filled with well-established customs. To be sure, this development itself is not attested in the sources. Yet such events differed markedly from a symposium in several respects. They concentrated upon the overarching role of the president of the church. No prophetic speech was expected from any other member of the church. Cyprian's morning celebration became independent of any symposium. Cyprian does not describe the details of its ritualized performance, yet it perfectly corresponds to the later forms of eucharistic celebrations that combine the ritual manipulation of bread and wine into one short act.

---

were still held in the afternoons and evenings, and morning celebrations were Eucharists but not symposia. Eucharists could also be held in prison (*Letters* 5.2.2, 15.1.2).

48. See the recent study by Fabian Goldbeck, *Salutationes: Die Morgenbegrüßungen in Rom in der Republik und der frühen Kaiserzeit*, KLIO: Beiträge zur Alten Geschichte, Beihefte, new series 16 (Berlin: Akademie-Verlag, 2010). Goldbeck discusses *salutationes* in the city of Rome from the late Republic until the early empire. He assumes that *salutationes* were unique with regard to Rome and restricted to the uppermost echelons of society. Several other sources indicate, however, that similar customs were practiced in other cities of the Roman Empire where systems of patronage prevailed. See Richard P. Saller, *Personal Patronage under the Empire* (Cambridge: Cambridge University Press, 1982), and Allen Brent, *Cyprian and Roman Carthage* (Cambridge: Cambridge University Press, 2010), 69–75.

Unlike Justin, who seems to have performed a similar Eucharist but avoided wine, Cyprian's church definitely preferred wine but could also have combined the ritual manipulation of bread and wine because nobody associated it with a symposium. In Cyprian's Eucharists the bishop's clients lined up in order to greet him and to receive spiritual, and especially material, support from him individually.

The later-attested celebrations composed of a Liturgy of the Word followed by the Eucharist may be the result of the adaptation—and thus the migration—of Roman customs into the churches that abandoned the decentralized, smaller, and more egalitarian celebrations of symposia, in *collegia* and houses, in favor of more centralized meetings between church leaders and the people that resembled the morning *salutationes* of wealthy and powerful Romans.

Similarities between Christian and Jewish readings of the sacred texts may or may not be the result of migrations between these two groups. That the early church began to read and expound biblical texts before the celebration of the Eucharist is not plausibly explained as the migration of a Jewish ritual into Christian liturgies, but Justin's and Cyprian's examples show that liturgical practices could converge in certain aspects, even though the reasons for this convergence could vary considerably. While Justin's congregation celebrated a reduced meal in the context of their philosophical meetings, Cyprian distributed the Eucharist to the clients of his sector of the church of Carthage who lined up in the morning in order to greet the bishop as their patron. Justin's Eucharist reflects modes of behavior of the philosophical clubs that migrated into the customs of his group of followers. The elements of the normal meals of associations, which were changed in order to represent basic tenets of Christianity, were condensed into a brief ritual manipulation of bread and water.

Regarding the concept of a migration of ritual elements from one group to another, the morning *salutationes* may have moved into Christianity although Christians did not choose deliberately to imitate a custom of others. Cyprian's morning celebrations functioned within the Roman social system of patronage, using the same codes and modes of behavior, and thus the early medieval Mass emerged from a social institution that nobody ever understood as a meal.

III. Concluding Observations

The four case studies presented above indicate different modes of migration within liturgies. Some customs migrated from one group to another as soon as the people who practiced them moved that way, just trying to behave as they did before. However, Glykon's tomb inscription must be taken as a warning against facile reconstructions of borderlines between groups and against the assumption of doctrines and beliefs as reasons for the course of these borderlines.

Justin and Cyprian entered the historical records as martyrs (and bishop in the case of Cyprian), although they remained a philosopher and a patron especially in their interaction with their pupils and clients respectively. This supports Yuval's observation that the majority culture—Rome—influenced Christian (and Jewish) customs. Jews and Christians continued to practice Greek and Roman customs even though they changed the shape of these customs, making them appear Christian or Jewish. Yet even these adaptations are only visible as such because they differ from typical behavior in certain details, thus referring back to their non-Christian or non-Jewish models.

Especially regarding *birkat hamazon* and grace after meals, Jews of Second Temple times, as well as later Christians and rabbinic Jews, had good reasons to change the normal course of a formal meal at this point. Thus, the performances of customary sets of ritualized acts migrated into Jewish and Christian groups but were adapted to different social situations. The question whether this migration occurred independently in Christianity and Judaism cannot be answered, for Christians and Jews shared the custom of maintaining a high degree of flexibility and improvisation in the performance of mealtime prayers. These factors—adaptations, flexibility, and variety of prayer texts—probably created a forum that facilitated the migration of smaller details of liturgies.

Regarding Pesach and Easter, Jews probably discontinued celebrating Pesach after the destruction of the Temple, which removed its pilgrimage center. The rabbis recreated Pesach, reshaping a normal symposium according to some elements of the ritual and textual repertoire of Pesach. We have almost no data that suggest that Jewish *collegia* in the Western Diaspora would have celebrated Pesach, but it is not implausible that some members of Diaspora Judaism followed customs as the early rabbis did, even if they were not dependent upon them. Melito and the Quartodecimans' celebration of Easter seems to have been created in opposition to Jewish customs. Therefore, the Christian Easter probably began as a ritual that migrated from one group of associations to another. It was turned upside down when it crossed the border between them, migrating by inverted imitation, not as a custom that certain migrants continued to perform in their new social context but as a custom that was taken up in opposition to the practice of another group.

These examples from early Christianity and Judaism suggest that migration of ritual elements is a more useful concept than the categories of "influence" or even "parallel." It causes the researcher to look for specific migrants that carried customs from a specific place to another, or from one group to another.

In cases where customs migrated without a group of people who simply continued elements of their behavior, the process of migration comes to the fore, calling our attention to the changes of customs and rituals. Any reconstruction of ritual migrations between Judaism and Christianity—or rather between Jewish and Christian groups—must take into account the surrounding world of Greeks and Romans.

3

A Shared Prayer over Water in the Eastern Christian Traditions

Mary K. Farag

I. Introduction

With the exception of the Maronite tradition and the so-called Assyrian or Nestorian tradition, all Eastern Christian traditions have one prayer in common in their respective Epiphany rites: the prayer for the sanctification of the waters.[1] These Epiphany rites—namely, those of the Armenian, Byzantine, Coptic, Ethiopic, and Syriac traditions—differ in significant ways, both in lectionary selections and in prayers, but all possess one prayer in common: a prayer referred to by its incipit, "Great Art Thou." Earliest manuscript witnesses to this prayer date to the eighth century in the Byzantine tradition (the Barberini euchologion), the eighth to ninth century in the Syriac tradition (*British Museum, add. 14,494*[2]), and the ninth to tenth

---

The author is grateful to Teresa Berger, Bryan Spinks, and the participants of the conference Looking East, held at the Yale Institute of Sacred Music, New Haven, CT, 10–11 November 2011, for their comments on this paper.

1. For the Maronite Epiphany rite, see J.-M. Sauget, "Bénédiction de l'eau dans la nuit de l'Épiphanie selon l'ancienne tradition de l'église maronite," *L'Orient Syrien* 4 (1959): 319–78. For the so-called Assyrian or Nestorian Epiphany rite, see A. J. McLean's contribution in Frederick C. Conybeare, *Rituale Armenorum* (New York: Georg Olms Verlag, 2004). Conybeare's work was originally published in 1905.

2. A. du Boulay and G. Khouri-Sarkis, "Le bénédiction de l'eau, la nuit de l'Épiphanie, dans le rite syrien d'Antioche," *L'Orient Syrien* 4 (1959): 211–32, here 212.

43

century in the Armenian tradition (Codex A in Conybeare's edition[3]). The earliest manuscript witnesses in the Coptic and Ethiopic rites remain unknown.

The prayer has been variously attributed to Basil of Caesarea, Proclus of Cyprus, and Severus of Antioch.[4] Two codices describing Armenian ritual history claim that Basil of Caesarea composed the entire blessing of the waters rite during a stay at Jerusalem.[5] A twelfth-century Greek euchologion also attributes the rite to "Archbishop Basil" and mentions that he composed it at the request of the Council of Nicaea.[6] Jacob of Edessa specifically attributes the prayer "Great Art Thou" to a certain Proclus "bishop of one of the towns of the island of Cyprus."[7] Finally, an Ethiopic euchologion attributes the prayer to Severus of Antioch.[8] The attributions roughly date the prayer's composition to sometime between the fourth and seventh centuries. Jacob of Edessa's witness offers a *terminus ante quem* of the seventh century.

Importantly, the first half of "Great Art Thou" is found not only in Epiphany rites but also in the Byzantine baptismal water blessing. This fact has shaped much of the scholarship on "Great Art Thou," since it has raised the question of whether the prayer originated in a baptismal rite or an Epiphany rite.[9] Scholar-

---

3. Conybeare, *Rituale Armenorum*, ix.

4. P. de Puniet, "Bénédictions de l'eau," in *Dictionnaire d'archéologie chrétienne et de liturgie*, ed. Fernand Cabrol and Henri Leclercq (Paris: Letouzey et Ané, 1913–53), 2/1:685–713, 704–7.

5. Conybeare, *Rituale Armenorum*, xxix.

6. Ibid., 430. The idea that the Council of Nicaea commissioned Basil of Caesarea to write the prayer is, of course, anachronistic.

7. *The Synodicon in the West Syrian Tradition*, trans. Arthur Vööbus, Corpus Scriptorum Christianorum Orientalium (CSCO) 368 (Louvain: Secrétariat du Corpus Scriptorum Christianorum Orientalium, 1974), 214.

8. Carl von Arnhard, *Liturgie zum Tauf-Fest der aethiopischen Kirche* (München: Akademische Buchdruckerei von F. Straub, 1886), 24.

9. Hubert Scheidt's study of baptismal water blessings argues that the baptismal version of "Great Art Thou" is dependent upon the Epiphany version: Scheidt, *Die Taufwasserweihegebete im Sinne vergleichender Liturgie-Forschung untersucht* (Münster: Aschendorff, 1935), 54. Hieronymus Engberding argues the opposite, namely, that the prayer originated in a baptismal context and later came to be used in the Epiphany rite: Hieronymus Engberding, "Ein übersehenes griechisches Taufwasserweihegebet und seine Bedeutung," *Ostkirchliche Studien* 14 (1965): 281–91, 290–91. Engberding has been followed by Sebastian Brock, Miguel Arranz, and Nicholas Denysenko: see Sebastian Brock, "Studies in the Early History of the Syrian Orthodox Baptismal Liturgy," *Journal of Theological Studies*, n.s. 23 (1972): 16–64, 45n1; Miguel Arranz, "Les sacraments de l'ancien euchologe constantinopolitain, pt. 6: L'Illumination' de la nuit de Pâques," *Orientalia christiana periodica* 51 (1985): 60–86, 71–72; Miguel Arranz, "Les sacraments de l'ancien euchologe constantinopolitain, pt. 7: L'Illumination' de la nuit de Pâques," *Orientalia christiana periodica* 52 (1986): 145–78, 161–62; and Nicholas E. Denysenko, *The*

ship has also posed two other questions about the celebration of Epiphany: How does the origin of the Epiphany feast relate to the origin of Christmas and to Lent?[10] Were existing traditions, such as the Jewish feast of Tabernacles or the Egyptian Nile cult, Christianized to establish the feast of Epiphany?[11]

As the three questions make clear, the history of inquiry has focused on the origins of Epiphany. I do not address this issue of origins in the present study, though the inquiry remains open and important. Instead, I would like to compare and contrast the various versions of the prayer that circulated in the Eastern traditions and to highlight the following three aspects of the prayer: (1) its use of Hellenistic terminology, (2) its parallels in the prayers of books 7 and 8 in the *Apostolic Constitutions*, and (3) its significance for the issues of prayer addressed to Christ and of epicleses invoking Christ.

II. A Comparison of the Various Versions of "Great Art Thou"

A. Editions

Three publications make possible a comparison of the Armenian, Greek, Coptic, Syriac, and Ethiopic versions of "Great Art Thou." Conybeare's *Rituale Armenorum*[12] contains editions of the Armenian and Greek versions. For the Armenian tradition, Conybeare uses a ninth/tenth-century manuscript as his collation base, and he collates it with versions from ten other Armenian manuscripts dating from the eleventh to the seventeenth century. For the Greek tradition, Conybeare collates the baptismal version and the Epiphany versions in the eighth-century Barberini codex with four other manuscripts. Budge's *Blessing of the Waters on the Eve of the Epiphany*[13] contains a Coptic

---

Blessing of Waters and Epiphany: The Eastern Liturgical Tradition, Liturgy, Worship and Society Series (Burlington, VT: Ashgate, 2012), 98.

10. The bibliography on this issue is vast and cannot be reproduced here. Thomas J. Talley's conclusions continue to be followed: see his *The Origins of the Liturgical Year* (New York: Pueblo, 1986), 79–162, and "The Origin of Lent at Alexandria," in *Worship: Reforming Tradition* (Washington, DC: Pastoral Press, 1990), 87–112. For the most recent summary of the issues at stake, see Paul F. Bradshaw and Maxwell E. Johnson, *The Origins of Feasts, Fasts and Seasons in Early Christianity* (Collegeville, MN: Liturgical Press, 2011), 123–57.

11. See especially René-Georges Coquin, "Les origines de l'Épiphanie en Égypte," in *Noël, Épiphanie, Retour du Christ*, Lex Orandi 40 (Paris: 1967), 139–70; and Jean Daniélou, "La Fête des Tabernacles dans l'exégèse patristique," *Studia Patristica* 1 (1957): 262–79.

12. See note 1.

13. E. A. Wallis Budge, *The Blessing of the Waters on the Eve of the Epiphany* (New York: Henry Frowde, 1901).

version of the prayer from Tuki's euchologion, printed in 1761–62 at Rome, and two Syriac versions from manuscripts at the British Museum. Budge dates both Syriac manuscripts to the ninth and tenth centuries. As noted above, du Boulay and Khouri-Sarkis date the first of Budge's Syriac manuscripts to an earlier range: the eighth to ninth centuries. The second manuscript contains an important title that attests to the literary (as opposed to oral) transmission of the prayer. The title mentions that the rite has been "translated recently from the Greek."[14] Finally, Arnhard's *Liturgie zum Tauf-Fest der aethiopischen Kirche*[15] presents a version of the prayer from an Ethiopic paper euchologion together with a German translation of the text. Arnhard unfortunately provides no indication of the manuscript's approximate date. Since the euchologion is a paper codex, it cannot have been written earlier than the thirteenth century.[16] While the Armenian and Greek versions can be studied on the basis of multiple manuscripts, study of the Coptic, Syriac, and Ethiopic versions can only be based on one or two manuscripts (or one printed edition in the case of the Coptic) until further research is conducted on Coptic, Syriac, and Ethiopic liturgical manuscripts.

B. Structural Differences

The Armenian versions of "Great Art Thou" are significantly shorter than the Greek, Coptic, Syriac, and Ethiopic versions. As noted above, the Greek baptismal prayer over water and that of the Epiphany rite are almost identical up to a certain point, namely, passage 22.[17] Likewise, the Armenian version of "Great Art Thou" corresponds closely to the Greek, Coptic, and Syriac versions up to the point of passage 22. The only passage between 1 and 21 that the Armenian version does not share with any other version (including the Greek baptismal prayer) is passage 9, a quotation of Psalm 75:8.[18] From passage 22 onward, the Armenian version loses much of its stable correspondence with all the other versions, especially the Coptic, Syriac, and Ethiopic ones, in the following five ways.

14. Ibid., 81.
15. See note 8.
16. There is also a translation of the Slavonic Epiphany rite available, but the translator makes no mention of the source he used. In any case, it does not differ significantly from the Greek version and is therefore not included in this study or in the appendix. See Alexios von Maltzew, *Bitt-, Dank- und Weihegottesdienste* (Berlin: Karl Siegismund, 1897), 542–49.
17. References to passage numbers refer to the numeration scheme I use in the appendix.
18. All references to the Hebrew Scriptures refer to the Septuagint.

1. A loose rendition of passage 22 (a petition requesting cleansing, healing, and sanctification for those who use the water) in the Greek, Coptic, Syriac, and Ethiopic versions follows the epiclesis of passage 31 in the Armenian version, not the petition of passage 21 in all the other Eastern versions.

2. Out of its three Old Testament anamnetic passages, the Armenian prayer contains only one in common with the four Coptic, Syriac, and Ethiopic pericopes (23–25, 28) that commemorate God's use of water in salvation history. The common pericope concerns Elijah's contest with the prophets of Ba'al in 3 Reigns 18.[19] As for the two other anamnetic pericopes in the Armenian prayer, one is unattested in any of the other Eastern versions and concerns Moses' use of wood to sweeten the bitter waters in Exodus 15. The other is only attested in the Greek version's expansive anamnetic section, which contains seven pericopes and concerns Elisha's use of salt to render the waters wholesome in 4 Reigns 2.

3. The Armenian version does not include passage 32, found in all the other Eastern versions, a petition for the sanctification, blessing, cleansing, and health of those who use the water.

4. Like the Greek version, the Armenian prayer includes a petition for God's servants unattested in the Coptic, Syriac, and Ethiopic versions (passage 33).

5. Finally, the Armenian version does not include passage 35, contained in all the other versions, which specifies the means by which God's name is to be glorified/praised in passage 36 (by means of elements, human beings, angels, things visible, things invisible).

The Armenian prayer is overall shorter than all its other Eastern counterparts. The Coptic and Syriac versions are slightly longer, and the Greek version is even longer than its Coptic and Syriac counterparts. The Coptic and Syriac prayers possess fewer points of similarity with the Armenian prayer than the Greek prayer does—that is, the Greek prayer is more closely related to the Armenian prayer than the Coptic and Syriac ones are.

The Greek prayer also includes two anamnetic passages found in neither the Armenian version nor the Coptic, Syriac, and Ethiopic versions. Passage 27 remembers the waters that flowed from the cloven rock in Exodus 17, and passage 30 closes the Old Testament anamneses with a New Testament one. In Nicene fashion, passage 30 makes remembrance of revelations given at

---

19. I adopt here the titles used by editors Albert Pietersma and Benjamin G. Wright to refer to 1 Kings, 2 Kings, 1 Samuel, and 2 Samuel in *A New English Translation of the Septuagint* (New York: Oxford University Press, 2007).

Christ's baptism: the harmony of the Trinity and the consubstantiality of the Father and the Son.

The Syriac version differs structurally from all its Eastern counterparts in its transposition of passages 4–8 with passage 3. This may be due to a reinterpretation of who the intelligible beings are in passage 10. While all the other prayers specify that the intelligible beings are the celestial luminaries (the sun, moon, and stars), the Syriac version interprets them to be the angelic hosts. Whether or not this implies that the Platonic notion of the celestial luminaries as intelligible beings was forgotten or disregarded at some point in Syriac theology remains uncertain.

The Coptic and Ethiopic versions share the same structure: they both include elements typical of eucharistic prayers, such as the *Sursum corda* and pre-*Sanctus* diaconal responses. They both expand passage 11's description of the angelic hosts so as to introduce the *Sanctus* hymn.

The Ethiopic version, however, differs from all its Eastern counterparts in a number of ways. (The following section will discuss differences in phraseology; here I focus on structural ones.) The Ethiopic version includes two additional epicleses (passages 10 and 13), the first requesting that the Holy Spirit might blow over the water, and the second requesting that the Holy Spirit be sent over the water. The Ethiopic version also transposes two short petitions (18 and 19). Finally, it adds a petition (passage 34), lacking in all the other Eastern versions, that requests that participants' names be written in the book of life and be unified with the saints.

These observations suggest the following hypothesis. The Armenian prayer on the one hand and the Coptic and Syriac prayers on the other attest to two early redactional states of the "Great Art Thou" prayer. These two different redactions of the prayer were at some point coalesced and further expanded, resulting in the prayer as we now know it in the Greek tradition. The fact that the Armenian prayer loses stable correspondence with the Coptic and Syriac versions at exactly the same point that the Greek baptismal version parts ways with the Greek Epiphany version further suggests that the Armenian version reflects a very early stage of the prayer's redaction. The Ethiopic version is probably dependent upon the Coptic version, but it adds two epicleses and one petition and transposes two short petitions. Its phraseology also differs significantly from all the other Eastern versions, as the following section will discuss.

This hypothesis is represented by the following schema, which represents loose relationships, not immediate dependencies.

I do not hypothesize that the two different prayers from which the Armenian versions on the one hand and the Coptic and Syriac versions on the other were translated, derive from a single Ur-prayer so as to leave open the possibility that the earliest phase of the prayer's circulation was not literary but rather oral. The two hypothesized prayers might not have been different literary redactions of *one* initial literary prayer, but the earliest phase of the prayer's literary history may have been quite diverse, stemming from an even more diverse performative history.

The Armenian, Greek, Coptic, Syriac, and Ethiopic versions transmitted in manuscript traditions are literary redactions of Greek *Vorlagen*. The title in one of the Syriac manuscripts, as mentioned above, provides evidence for this, since it describes the Syriac prayer as a translation of a Greek one.

C. Differences in Phraseology

The versions differ not only in structure but also in phraseology. Not all of the phraseological differences can be attributed to choices made in the process of translation. Only the most notable differences will be reviewed here; these concern the themes of creation, God's ineffability and incarnation, and the epicleses. It will be seen that a study of phraseological differences substantiates the hypothesis that was presented in section B.

1. *Creation*. Passage 2 concerns the concepts of creation ex nihilo, God's providence, and the correlation between the four elements of creation and the four seasons of the year. I will discuss the Hellenistic terminology of this pericope in section III; for now, I will highlight differences of phraseology among the various versions. According to the Greek and Armenian versions, God brings everything into being from nonbeing by his *will* (βούλησις), whereas

the Coptic, Syriac, and Ethiopic prayers attribute creation ex nihilo to God's *power* (δύναμις). One Armenian manuscript (assigned siglum D in Conybeare's edition) omits the ex nihilo phrase altogether in addition to the mention of God's providence. The line simply reads, "For by thy volition thou broughtest all creatures into being."

With the exception of Armenian D, the Armenian, Greek, and Coptic prayers then describe God's providence (πρόνοια) as the *dioiketes* (governor) of the creation, using the technical terminology of city governance (διοικέω). One Syriac manuscript provides an interpretive translation of (presumably) the same Greek text: "By Thy care Thou dost direct and provide the world with food." Providence is here interpreted as "care," and providence's role as the *dioiketes* (governor) is explained as providing food for the world. Another Syriac manuscript reads, "By Thy grace Thou dost fill the people with food." Instead of providence, this Syriac prayer speaks of grace; it is grace that provides food. Armenian manuscript F describes providence not as a *dioiketes* (governor) but rather as a chariot director. Whereas most of the Armenian, the Greek, and the Coptic versions employ the metaphor of the cosmos as a city with God's providence at its head, Armenian F employs the metaphor of the cosmos as a chariot, led by providence, the charioteer. The Ethiopic version does not speak of God's providence at all, nor of the cosmos being directed by a governor/charioteer, but rather of God's knowledge providing solace: "Durch die Erkenntniss Deiner [*sic*] hast Du Deinen Geschöpfen Trost gespendet."

The Ethiopic version also differs from its other Eastern counterparts in its line concerning the number four. Whereas the Armenian, Greek, Coptic, and Syriac versions all speak of creation's four elements and the year's four seasons, the Ethiopic version speaks of the world's four corners and the cycle of days: "Du bist's, der die Welt an den vier Winkeln abgeschlossen hat. Du bist es, der die Welt mit einem Kreise von Tagen begrenzt hat." The Ethiopic version's omission of the Hellenistic concept of four elements (earth, air, fire, and water) is not confined to passage 2 alone. The Ethiopic version also omits the concept in passage 35, where the Greek, Coptic, and Syriac versions (the passage is altogether unattested in the Armenian tradition) all mention the elements as one of the means by which God's name might be glorified, along with human beings and angels.

The prayers present a number of notable variants, which I will discuss in detail in section III: God's will or power is credited with creation ex nihilo; God's providence directs the cosmos like a governor or charioteer, or God's knowledge provides solace; and the creation is composed of four elements and four seasons or four corners and a cycle of days.

Though all versions except the Ethiopic list the same members of creation in passages 3–11, they differ in their descriptions of them. After describing how the sun and the moon bless and glorify God, all versions make mention of the stars but attribute to them various roles (passage 5). The stars "magnify" God in the Armenian versions, "meet together" before God in the Greek, "have been set in order" by God in the Coptic, "praise" God in the Syriac, and crown the heavens in the Ethiopic. The Ethiopic version does not make mention of the earth's establishment upon the waters, while the Armenian, Greek, Coptic, and Syriac do (passage 7). In passage 8, whereas air was poured out for the purpose of breathing in the Armenian, Greek, and Coptic versions, air was poured out *like* a breath in the Syriac, and in the Ethiopic version air is not associated with respiration but was simply commanded by God to blow.

As mentioned above, the description of the angelic hosts is somewhat variable across the versions. The Greek, Coptic, and Syriac versions speak of the six-winged Seraphim and many-eyed Cherubim standing and flying, whereas the Armenian speaks of them "mounting upward." The Ethiopic version only mentions the Seraphim, describing them as both winged and full of eyes.

2. *God's ineffability and incarnation.* The versions differ not only in their description of God's creation and providence and in their description of the individual members of creation, but also in their description of God and the incarnation. Whereas most of the Armenian versions and the Greek, Coptic, and Syriac all make mention of God's "unapproachable glory," this phrase is not attested in the Ethiopic or in Armenian F. In those versions that do contain the phrase, God's unapproachability dovetails into a series of apophatic epithets. The Greek and Coptic versions employ the same terms: "incircumscribable" (ἀπερίγραπτος), "unoriginate" (ἄναρχος), and "ineffable" (ἀνέκφραστος).[20] Armenian B also employs these three terms but includes two additional terms as well: "indescribable" and "unattainable." The other Armenian versions do not include the term "unoriginate" but replace it with "indescribable." The Syriac versions complement the "unoriginate" concept with its logical conclusion. If God has no beginning, it follows that he has no end: "Without end and without beginning, and who canst not be comprehended." While the Ethiopic version has the same basic import as all the other versions—namely, that God has no beginning/end and cannot be bounded—it formulates the ideas in quite different terms: "Vollkommen in Deinem Wesen, keine Grenze hat Dein

---

20. The first two are also found in *Apostolic Constitutions* 7.35 and in the Greek and Coptic Anaphora of Gregory. The last is also found in the Anaphora of John Chrysostom.

uranfängliches Sein und kein Aufhören Dein zukünftiges Sein, denn ewig ist es (Dein Sein), übersteigend menschliche Erkenntniss."

In remembrance of God's incarnation, all versions quote Philippians 2:7 in some way. Most of the Armenian versions and the Greek, Coptic, and Syriac quote the verse in full—"taking the form of a servant, being made in the likeness of man"—but Armenian I omits the last phrase. The Ethiopic version rewrites the first phrase so that instead of taking the form of a servant, God takes away the fetters of his servants: "Hast hinweggenommen die Fesseln Deiner Knechte." All versions furthermore describe God's *birth* in passage 15, but Armenian E speaks of God's *emanation*. The incarnation results in the *liberation* of humans in the Armenian and Greek versions and the *blessing* of humans in the Coptic and Syriac. The Ethiopic version speaks of humans being prevented from dying: "Du hast die Menschenkinder dem Tode vorgezogen."

3. *Epicleses.* Finally, there are notable differences in the two epicleses that all versions share. In the first epiclesis, passage 17, the Greek, Coptic, and Syriac versions all request the presence of Christ through the Holy Spirit, but the Armenian and Ethiopic simply request that the Holy Spirit be sent. In the second epiclesis, passage 31, the Greek, Coptic, and Syriac versions all request that the waters be sanctified by the Holy Spirit. This is requested in the form of an epiclesis in the Greek and Coptic versions, but the Syriac simply describes the sanctification as taking place. In the Armenian versions, Christ is requested to draw nigh through his Holy Spirit and bless the water. Unlike any of the other versions, the Ethiopic asks that God's power remember the participants with mercy and that God's name grant blessing and sanctification ("Segensweihe") to the waters.

Because the prayer refers to the addressee's incarnation, it is clear that the epicleses (and indeed the prayers in their entirety) are addressed to Christ. Most of the Armenian versions make this abundantly clear by addressing the "Word God" in passage 15, except for Armenian E and N, which omit "Word." The Coptic version makes the address to Christ unmistakable by twice explicitly addressing "Jesus Christ" (passages 17 and 23) and once addressing "Christ" (passage 36). Though the Greek and Syriac versions do not explicitly address the Word or Jesus or Christ, they do make their address to Christ clear in the final doxology, as the Armenian and Coptic versions do, by speaking of the addressee's name being glorified together with the Father and the Holy Spirit. Though the Ethiopic version does not omit references to the incarnation, its final doxology appears to address the Father, contrary to all the other Eastern versions: "In unserem Herrn Jesus Christus, O Du Herr der ganzen Welt und [auch] Dein heiliger Geist." We will return to the issues of the address to Christ and the epicleses in section V.

These observations of phraseological differences reflect differences in translation and in the reception of "Great Art Thou" in various traditions. A number of the observations substantiate the hypothesis of the previous section. The Armenian and Greek versions pattern together in their attribution of creation to God's will in passage 2 and in their soteriological portrayal of the incarnation as providing liberation in passage 15. This supports the hypothesis that the Greek and Armenian versions share a source. The Greek, Coptic, and Syriac versions pattern together in their inclusion of the elements in passage 35 and in their phraseology of the two epicleses. This supports the hypothesis that the Greek, Coptic, and Syriac have a common source. The discussion of phraseology also provides abundant evidence for the independence of the Ethiopic prayer. Because the Ethiopic tradition is known to have adopted many liturgical prayers via the Coptic tradition, I hypothesized in section II that the Ethiopic prayer is probably related to the Coptic one. If so, the Ethiopic prayer would constitute a relatively free redaction of the Coptic version. It is also possible, however, that the Ethiopic prayer reflects yet a third unknown Greek redaction of the prayer that circulated at some time.

III. Hellenistic Terminology in Passage 2

As noted in section II.C.1, the Greek versions, the Coptic version, and most of the Armenian versions all utilize the metaphor of the cosmos as a city, directed by its governor, the providence of God. The metaphor and language used by these prayers is Stoic in origin and was adopted by several Christian authors.

In doxographic literature,[21] Chrysippus, one of the founding Stoic philosophers, is often credited with the claim that "the cosmos is directed by the gods' providence." This dictum is attributed to Chrysippus in the works of Sextus, Stobaeus, Diogenes Laertius, and Pseudo-Plutarch. For instance, Diogenes Laertius writes, "The cosmos is directed according to mind and providence,

---

21. The following conclusions are based on an analysis of a Thesaurus Linguae Graecae (TLG) search for διοικ-, κοσμ-, and προνοι- within one line of each other. The term "doxography" was invented by Herman Diels in his *Doxographi Graeci* (Berlin: G. Reimer, 1879) to describe literature that compiles opinions of philosophers (without commentary or criticism) and organizes them according to a particular set of themes. See the following multivolume set for a more recent bibliography on doxography and for a reanalysis of Diels's work: J. Mansfeld and D. T. Runia, *Aëtiana: The Method and Intellectual Context of a Doxographer*, 3 vols. (New York: Brill, 1997, 2009, 2010).

as Chrysippus says in the fifth [book of his], *On Providence*."[22] Other authors such as Eusebius of Caesarea ascribe the same claim to the Stoics in general. Two Roman Stoic philosophers, Gaius Musonius Rufus and Marcus Aurelius, make the same claim in their own works. As Silke-Petra Bergjan concludes in her study of the Stoic understanding of providence, while it is possible that the terminology ascribed to the Stoics is proper not to the Stoics themselves but to later descriptions of them, it is more likely that the Stoics themselves used such terms since they are closely tied to Stoic cosmology and physics.[23] By contrast, a number of authors consider that the Epicureans and atomists held the opposite view: that the cosmos is directed not by providence but rather by some irrational nature.

In their own defense of God's providence, two Christian apologists adopted precisely the language attributed to Chrysippus and to the Stoics in general. In his apology *To Autolycus*, Theophilus of Antioch writes, "Now we also confess that God exists, but that He is one, the creator, and maker, and fashioner of this cosmos; and we know that all things are directed by His providence, but by Him alone."[24] Likewise, Eusebius of Caesarea in book 8 of his *Preparation for the Gospel* quotes Philo at length in defense of the notion that God's providence directs the cosmos. One of the urgent questions with which both Christian apologists and their interlocutors were engaged was whether God himself exercises providence, or whether subordinate gods are responsible for this task.[25] In answering this question, the primary issue at stake was God's transcendence and immanence. Arguing that God himself exercises providence maintained a strong notion of divine immanence, whereas arguing that intermediary beings exercise providence insisted on a strong notion of divine transcendence.

What is interesting with regard to "Great Art Thou" is that Eusebius resolves the immanence/transcendence problem by claiming that the Logos is *pronoia*

---

22. *Vitae philosophorum* 7.138. The Greek reads, τὸν δὴ κόσμον διοικεῖσθαι κατὰ νοῦν καὶ πρόνοιαν, καθά φησι Χρύσιππός τ' ἐν τῷ πέμπτῳ περὶ προνοίας. See H. S. Long, *Diogenis Laertii Vitae Philosophorum*, 2 vols. (Oxford: Clarendon Press, 1964); the text is from the Thesaurus Linguae Graecae.

23. Silke-Petra Bergjan, *Der fürsorgende Gott: Der Begriff der Pronoia Gottes in der apologetischen Literatur der Alten Kirche* (New York: Walter de Gruyter, 2002), 48ff.

24. *To Autolycus* 3.9. The translation is adapted from The Ante-Nicene Fathers series (Grand Rapids, MI: Eerdmans, 1977), 2:113. The Greek reads, ἡμεῖς δὲ καὶ θεὸν ὁμολογοῦμεν, ἀλλ' ἕνα, τὸν κτίστην καὶ ποιητὴν καὶ δημιουργὸν τοῦδε τοῦ παντὸς κόσμου, καὶ προνοίᾳ τὰ πάντα διοικεῖσθαι ἐπιστάμεθα, ἀλλ' ὑπ' αὐτοῦ μόνου. See R. M. Grant, *Theophilus of Antioch: Ad Autolycum* (Oxford: Clarendon Press, 1970); the text is from the Thesaurus Linguae Graecae.

25. See Bergjan, *Der fürsorgende Gott*, 5.

(providence), thereby preserving the Father's transcendence while at the same time objecting to the Platonic notion that multiple intermediary beings undertake the task of providence.[26] Bergjan's study of Eusebius's thought on providence argues that it was Eusebius who pushed the philosophical notion of providence into the realm of Christology.[27] This theological move on the part of Eusebius is significant for understanding the coherence of "Great Art Thou." In ways similar to two other prayers addressed entirely to the Son (namely, the Greek and Coptic Anaphora of Gregory and the Anaphora of Thomas), "Great Art Thou" focuses on three acts of providence: creation, sustaining the creation, and the incarnation (i.e., restoring the creation). "Great Art Thou" explicitly speaks of *pronoia* and even uses technical philosophical vocabulary to describe *pronoia*'s work. Eusebius's thought on providence suggests that the association of the Son with providence in prayers addressed to the Son has to do not only with the common notion of the Son as demiurge,[28] but also with the idea that it is the Son's particular prerogative to exercise providence.[29]

As noted in section II.C.1, Armenian F does not employ the same "*dioiketes* : city :: God's providence : cosmos" analogy as the other Armenian versions and the Greek and Coptic versions do. Rather, Armenian F employs the analogy of the cosmos as a chariot, with God's providence as the charioteer. This is one of two central metaphors that Theodoret of Cyrus utilizes in his work *On Divine Providence*.[30] Though attested in a Christian treatise on providence, the chariot metaphor does not have as strong a tradition in Hellenistic philosophy as the city-state metaphor does.

---

26. Ibid., 271.
27. Ibid., 306.
28. The notion of the Son as creator or demiurge is amply attested in ancient and late antique Christian literature. Late antique art also bears testimony to this notion: the illustrations of the Cotton Genesis codex (British Library, Ms. Cotton Otho B VI), depict the creator with a cross-nimbus and cross-staff. See Kurt Weitzmann and Herbert L. Kessler, *The Cotton Genesis* (Princeton, NJ: Princeton University Press, 1986), 37, and Herbert L. Kessler, *Spiritual Seeing: Picturing God's Invisibility in Medieval Art* (Philadelphia: University of Pennsylvania Press, 2000), 6. I am grateful to Linda Safran for calling my attention to this codex.
29. Christianized Stoic terminology of *pronoia* acting as a *dioiketes* is not confined to apologetic literature. It is also found in two of the pseudo-Clementine *Homilies* (2.36 and 11.34) when the apostle Peter preaches to Clement and others that the cosmos is directed by God's providence. It is also found in a commentary on Psalm 105:7 variously attributed to Eusebius of Caesarea, Apollinaris of Laodicea, and John Chrysostom. Finally, it is found in Didymus the Blind's commentary on Zechariah 9:11-12.
30. The other metaphor is that of the cosmos as a ship.

The *dioiketes*-city metaphor is not the only indication that "Great Art Thou" stands firmly in the Hellenistic thought world. The concept of the "four elements" is a well-known Hellenistic notion, but its juxtaposition with the four seasons of the year is also telling. The correlation's context lies in Hellenistic theories of medicine. *On the Nature of Man* in the Pseudo-Hippocratic corpus draws a correlation between the four bodily humors and the four seasons of the year. One of Galen's important contributions to the theory of humors was to further correlate the four humors with the four elements. This second-century influential medical practitioner and theoretician's humoralism came to dominate medical philosophy in the Greek-speaking empire.[31] The prayer's juxtaposition of the four elements with the four seasons does not draw a simple parallel between two sets of four things but more likely bears reference to the guiding theory of medical practice in which the season of the year, and the particular element associated with the season, indicated to physicians which of the four bodily humors was in preponderance and thus disrupting the patient's equilibrium. For instance, in the summer there was likely to be a preponderance of yellow bile in a patient's body, owing to the prevalence of the element of fire during this season.

The language of the Armenian, Greek, Coptic, and Syriac versions of passage 2 in "Great Art Thou" reflect the context of Hellenistic philosophy and medicine. On the one hand, the correlation of the four elements of creation with the four seasons of the year resonates with Galen's important and influential contribution to Hellenistic medicine. On the other hand, the metaphor of the cosmic city under the governance of God's *pronoia* is characteristic of one aspect of Stoic philosophy that was adopted and Christianized among apologists.

IV. Parallels in the Apostolic Constitutions

There is a prayer corpus that, like "Great Art Thou," makes explicit mention of God's *pronoia*. Prayers in books 7 and 8 of the fourth-century church order the *Apostolic Constitutions* (AC) do not contain the peculiarly Stoic formulation identified in the previous section, but they do contain a significant number of parallels to the "Great Art Thou" prayer. The parallels are not sufficient for positing a direct relationship between AC and "Great Art Thou," whether in

---

31. Vivian Nutton, "Humoralism," in *Companion Encyclopedia of the History of Medicine*, ed. W. F. Bynum and Roy Porter (New York: Routledge, 1993), 286–87.

terms of author or milieu, but the parallels do offer a further context in which to interpret the language of "Great Art Thou."

The particular prayers in question are two based upon seven Jewish benedictions,[32] 7.34, 7.35, and the eucharistic prayer of 8.12. The fact that 7.34 (or the prayer of which it is a redaction) constituted one of the sources for 8.12 has long been noted.[33] Those two prayers will therefore be discussed together after the following consideration of 7.35.

A. The Prayer of 7.35

Prayer 7.35 not only begins with the same psalmic incipit as the Epiphany prayer, "Great art Thou, O Lord" (Ps 146:5), but also, and more importantly, shares some of the Epiphany prayer's peculiar creation imagery.

Like "Great Art Thou," AC 7.35 explicitly uses the term *pronoia*. Along with a number of other titles, it calls the Father "the Bestower of providence."[34] In describing (1) the heavens stretched out as an arch, (2) the earth established upon the waters, and (3) the distribution of air for respiration (the themes of "Great Art Thou" 6–8), the prayer names all four Hellenistic elements: "The heaven knows Him who fixed it as a cube of stone, in the form of an arch, upon nothing, who united *earth* and *water* to one another, and scattered the vital *air* all abroad, and conjoined *fire* therewith for warmth" (italics mine). In speaking of vital air being scattered abroad, AC 7.35 further shares the particular imagery of passage 8 in which air is poured out for breathing. Such an image of air being poured out or scattered abroad for the purpose of providing respiration is unattested in Scripture and in apocryphal literature.[35] A further point of comparison in passage 8 lies in its depiction of the sea bounded by sand. Both "Great Art Thou" and AC 7.35 draw on an image in Jeremiah 5:22 of the vast seas assigned a boundary of sand. Passage 8 simply reads, "Thou hast bounded the sea with sand," while AC 7.35 employs more colorful language: "The sea

---

32. See the following study regarding the seven benedictions and *Apostolic Constitutions* 7: David A. Fiensy, *Prayers Alleged to Be Jewish: An Examination of the* Constitutiones Apostolorum (Chico, CA: Scholars Press, 1985).

33. Bousset noted the similarity of the two prayers; see his "Eine jüdische Gebetsammlung im siebenten Buch der apostolischen Konstitutionen," *Nachrichten von der Königlichen Gesellschaft der Wissenschaften zu Göttingen: Philologisch-historische Klasse* (1915): 438–85. See also Fiensy's synopsis of the prayers in *Prayers Alleged to Be Jewish*, 189–97.

34. The Ante-Nicene Fathers series (Grand Rapids, MI: Eerdmans, 1979), 7:473. All translations of AC are taken or adapted from this volume, which will be referred to as ANF 7.

35. The books of Enoch speak of storerooms of winds in the heavens but do not relate them to respiration. See 1 Enoch 18, 76; 2 Enoch 40; and 3 Enoch 14, 23.

raging with waves, and feeding a flock of ten thousand creatures, is bounded with sand, as standing in awe at Thy command."[36] Finally, AC 7.35's lengthy apophatic pericope contains two of the three apophatic terms employed in passage 12: "uncircumscribable" (ἀπερίγραφος) and "unoriginate" (ἄναρχος).

The cluster of similarities between the Epiphany prayer and AC 7.35's portrayal of God's *pronoia*, the four elements, particular creative acts, and apophatic terminology is also found in the prayer of 7.34 and in its lengthier counterpart in 8.12.

B. The Prayers of 7.34 and 8.12

Neither 7.34 nor 8.12 share the Epiphany prayer's incipit, but they do emphasize God's *pronoia*. According to 7.34, God exercises a different sort of providence in different kinds of creatures. Like passage 2 in "Great Art Thou," AC 8.12 specifically attributes both the act of creation and the act of providence (sustaining the creation) to the Logos: "For Thou, O eternal God, didst make all things by Him, and through Him it is that Thou vouchsafest Thy suitable providence over the whole world."[37] AC 8.12 also ascribes the creation ex nihilo to the Son, as passage 2 does: "For Thou art eternal knowledge [. . .] who didst bring all things out of nothing into being by Thy only begotten Son."[38] In AC 7.34, the notion of creation ex nihilo is juxtaposed with creation out of four elements. The pericope describes the human body as created out of the four elements but the human soul as created out of nothing. Like AC 7.35, AC 8.12 mentions the four elements by name when detailing how the heavens were stretched out as a tent (as in passage 6) and how the sun, the moon, and the stars were appointed (passages 4–5). According to 8.12, the element of earth was established upon nothing, and water was made for drinking, air for breathing (as in passage 8), and fire for illumination and warmth.

Not only do the two prayers in AC mention the four Hellenistic elements; they also describe the seasons of the year. Unlike "Great Art Thou," however, they do not draw the correlation between the elements and seasons that was influential in medical literature. The celestial luminaries (the sun, moon, and stars) rise and set according to God's commands in order to form the seasons of the year in 7.34. In 8.12, God appoints the seasons for the purpose of supporting living creatures with fruits.

---

36. ANF 7:473.
37. Ibid., 487.
38. Ibid.

In addition to the concepts of providence; creation ex nihilo; the four elements; the four seasons; the creation of the celestial luminaries, heaven, and earth; and the praise of the angelic hosts, the two prayers also share the Epiphany prayer's image of the sea bound by sand. AC 7.34 depicts the fury of the ocean stopped by the sand at God's command, while AC 8.12 contrasts the vastness of the seas with their obedience to the "smallest sand." Like the Epiphany prayer and AC 7.35, 8.12 also utilizes the apophatic term "unoriginate" (ἄναρχος) as an epithet for God.

Finally, it is significant that 8.12 shares all three major themes of "Great Art Thou." Not only does it illustrate the Logos's acts of creation and providence, as in 7.34 and 7.35, but it also stresses the incarnation of the Logos. Though AC 8.12 does not quote Philippians 2:7 as "Great Art Thou" does, it similarly presents the incarnation as a paradox: "He was pleased by Thy good will to become man, who was man's Creator."[39]

The parallels between the three prayers in AC and "Great Art Thou" are striking. They suggest that "Great Art Thou" is related to AC or to its sources in some way. While many of AC's sources are known, the only sources known for the prayers in books 7 and 8 are the seven Jewish benedictions. David Fiensy's reconstruction of the seven benedictions does not contain any of the Epiphany prayer's similarities to AC.[40] "Great Art Thou," therefore, could be related to an unknown Hellenistic source that AC's redactor employed, or it could be related to AC itself; if the latter, the relationship is not one of direct dependence. Owing to the lack of verbatim correspondence with AC, it is not possible to argue that "Great Art Thou" is directly dependent upon it.

V. The Significance of "Great Art Thou" for Two Issues in the Study of Eucharistic Prayers

Though it is unclear whether 7.34 and 7.35 are eucharistic prayers, we can have no doubt in the case of 8.12, the so-called Clementine Liturgy. The fact that the themes in "Great Art Thou" correspond so closely to those of a eucharistic prayer is significant. "Great Art Thou" is not, strictly speaking, a eucharistic prayer,[41] but it can nevertheless inform two issues in the study of

---

39. Ibid., 489.
40. See Fiensy, *Prayers Alleged to Be Jewish*.
41. The eucharistic prayer structure found in the Coptic and Ethiopic "Great Art Thou" is thought to be a later development.

eucharistic prayers: the issue of prayer addressed to Christ and the issue of epicleses.

A. Prayer Addressed to Christ

The Christology of AC has long been a matter of debate since a number of scholars argue that it is Arian or Eunomian in character.[42] If indeed the prayers of AC reflect a theology of the Son's subordination, it is clear that "Great Art Thou" differs from AC in this regard. By addressing the entire prayer to the Son, including apophatic epithets usually addressed to the Father, "Great Art Thou" reflects a high Christology.[43]

"Great Art Thou" adds one prayer to a small corpus of late antique prayers addressed entirely to Christ. This addition is significant since without it the corpus is only attested in prayers preserved in the Egyptian tradition (the Anaphora of Gregory[44] and the Anaphora of Thomas[45]). "Great Art Thou" constitutes a prayer addressed to Christ that circulated through much broader geographical regions in late antiquity.

The only known controversy regarding prayer addressed to Christ in the late antique East is that of Shenoute of Atripe against the so-called Origenists. In his work *Contra Origenistas*, Shenoute polemicizes against them for refusing to address prayer to Christ, insisting that rejecting such prayer entails the espousal of antitrinitarian theology.[46] Aloys Grillmeier has called attention to a seventh/eighth-century inscription in a hermitage at Kellia that also defends prayer to the

---

42. For studies that argue for AC's Arian and/or Eunomian theology, see C. H. Turner, "Notes on the *Apostolic Constitutions*: The Compiler an Arian," *Journal of Theological Studies* 16 (1914–15): 54–61; Georg Wagner, "Zur Herkunft der Apostolischen Konstitutionen," in *Mélanges liturgiques offerts au R. P. Dom Bernard Botte* (Louvain: Abbaye du Mont César, 1972), 525–37; and Thomas A. Kopecek, "Neo-Arian Religion: The Evidence of the Apostolic Constitutions," in *Arianism: Historical and Theological Reassessments*, ed. Robert C. Gregg (Philadelphia: Philadelphia Patristic Foundation, 1985), 153–79. See also Marcel Metzger, "La théologie des Constitutions Apostoliques par Clément," *Revue des sciences religieuses* 57 (1983): 29–49, 112–22, 169–94, 273–94.

43. Kopecek argues that supporters of Aetius and Eunomius permitted prayer addressed to Christ, but only in a restricted and qualified way. See Kopecek, "Neo-Arian Religion," 170–72.

44. For a study of the address to Christ in the Anaphora of Gregory, see Albert Gerhards, *Die griechische Gregoriusanaphora: Eine Beitrag zur Geschichte des eucharistischen Hochgebets* (Münster: Aschendorff, 1984), 176–242.

45. Mary K. Farag, "The Anaphora of St. Thomas the Apostle: Translation and Commentary," *Le Muséon* 123 (2010): 317–61.

46. See Hans-Joachim Cristea, *Schenute von Atripe: Contra Origenistas* (Tübingen: Mohr Siebeck, 2011).

Son. Whether the inscription can be understood as evidence for the resurgence of the controversy in the seventh or eighth century is unclear. Grillmeier sees in the inscription a summary of Shenoute's argument, which raises the possibility that the inscription is a quotation or paraphrase taken from a literary text.[47]

It is possible that the late antique dispute arose in response to prayers addressed to Christ, such as the Anaphora of Thomas, the Anaphora of Gregory, and "Great Art Thou." The opposite is also possible: that such prayers were composed in reaction to the controversy. Unfortunately, these remain open possibilities since we have no evidence (at least as yet) that supports one or the other. What survives of Shenoute's defense of prayer addressed to Christ does not quote or refer to Gregory, Thomas, or the Epiphany prayer.[48] Of course, it is also possible that these three prayers had nothing to do with any controversy surrounding prayer to Christ.

B. Epicleses

In addition to the issue of prayer addressed to Christ and the polemics associated with it, "Great Art Thou" can also inform the issue of the history of epicleses. Some of the earliest epicleses invoked the Son as Logos or Dynamis. Spirit epicleses eventually became prevalent after the Council of Constantinople.[49] As Robert Taft has hypothesized, the earliest Spirit epicleses were probably interpreted as requesting the Spirit of the Son. Invoking the Spirit was thus tantamount to invoking the Son. This hypothesis based on the history

---

47. Aloys Grillmeier, "Das 'Gebet zu Jesus' und das 'Jesus-Gebet': Eine neue Quelle zum 'Jesus-Gebet' aus dem Weißen Kloster," in *After Chalcedon: Studies in Theology and Church History*, ed. C. Laga et al. (Leuven: Peeters, 1985), 187–202; and Grillmeier, *Christ in Christian Tradition*, trans. O. C. Dean (Louisville, KY: Westminster John Knox Press, 1996), 2:184–89.

48. Cristea, *Contra Origenistas*, 205–6, 213–15 (text), 274–45, 278–79 (translation).

49. See Robert Taft, "From Logos to Spirit: On the Early History of the Epiclesis," in *Gratias Agamus: Studien zum eucharistischen Hochgebet*, ed. Andreas Heinz and Heinrich Rennings (Freiburg: Herder, 1992), 489–502; and Mary K. Farag, "Δύναμις Epicleses: An Athanasian Perspective," *Studia Liturgica* 39 (2009): 63–79. Most studies on eucharistic epicleses focus on their form. See especially the following: Gabriele Winkler, "Weitere Beobachtungen zur frühen Epiklese (den Doxologien und dem Sanctus): Über die Bedeutung der Apokryphen für die Erforschung der Entwicklung der Riten," *Oriens Christianus* 80 (1996): 177–200; Sebastian P. Brock, "Towards a Typology of the Epicleses in the West Syrian Anaphoras," in *Crossroad of Cultures: Studies in Liturgy and Patristics in Honor of Gabriele Winkler*, ed. Hans-Jürgen Feulner, Elena Velkovska, and Robert F. Taft (Rome: Pontificio Istituto Orientale, 2000), 173–89; Sebastian P. Brock, *The Holy Spirit in the Syrian Baptismal Tradition* (Piscataway, NJ: Gorgias Press, 2008); and Anne McGowan, "In Search of the Spirit: The Epiclesis in Early Eucharistic Praying and Contemporary Liturgical Reforms" (PhD diss., University of Notre Dame, 2011).

of trinitarian theology finds clear substantiation in some of the epicleses in "Great Art Thou." The first epiclesis (passage 17) in the Greek version asks the Son to be present by the coming of his Holy Spirit. Similarly, the Coptic and Syriac versions request that the Son come by the descent of his Holy Spirit. According to these epicleses, the purpose of the Holy Spirit is to effectuate the presence of Christ. The Armenian version reflects this notion in the second epiclesis (passage 31) when the Son is asked to "draw nigh" through his Holy Spirit. The Son is thus asked to be "present" (Greek), to "come" (Coptic and Syriac), or to "draw nigh" (Armenian) by means of the Holy Spirit.

"Great Art Thou" thus furnishes us with christocentric Spirit epicleses that confirm a hypothesis surmised on the basis of theological history. The prayer supplies a missing intermediary step in the hypothesized transition "from Logos to Spirit" in epicleses.

VI. *Conclusion*

"Great Art Thou" is a late antique prayer that betrays its Hellenistic context in its terminology, bears a relationship to the *Apostolic Constitutions*, and has implications for the study of prayers addressed to Christ and of the history of epicleses. The prayer enjoyed as wide a circulation as, for instance, the Anaphora of Basil. It survives in the Armenian, Coptic, Ethiopic, Greek, and Syriac Epiphany rites and in the Greek baptismal rite. A comparison of as much of the manuscript tradition as has been edited and published reveals two independent traditions: one upon which the Armenian prayer is based and another upon which the Coptic, Syriac, and (presumably) Ethiopic are based. The Greek prayer draws upon both traditions. The prayer's particular author and provenance remain unknown, though it has been variously attributed to three different late antique theologians.

The theology of this prayer over water is christocentric. It ascribes to Christ three major acts: the act of creation ex nihilo, the act of sustaining the creation by providence, and the act of restoring the creation by the incarnation. The particular theme of providence has a long history in Hellenistic philosophy and Christian theology. In "Great Art Thou" the concept of providence is found in Christianized Stoic terms. All three themes and their particular formulation in Hellenistic and scriptural terms of four elements, four seasons, celestial luminaries, stretched heavens, an established earth, vital air poured out, seas bound by sand, and so forth, are found in *Apostolic Constitutions* 7.34, 7.35, and 8.12. This fact suggests a relationship between "Great Art Thou" and the *Apostolic Constitutions*.

A Shared Prayer over Water in the Eastern Christian Traditions 63

Not only does the prayer constitute a text important for the history of the *Apostolic Constitutions*, but it also enlarges our repertoire of prayers addressed entirely to Christ in the late antique period, a period in which such prayers were, at least in Egypt, a point of theological contention. The epicleses addressed to Christ in "Great Art Thou" support the hypothesis that Spirit epicleses were thought to invoke the presence of the Logos before the theology of the Holy Spirit as a distinct trinitarian person became firmly entrenched.

Appendix:
Comparative Chart of the Armenian, Greek, Coptic, Syriac, and Ethiopic Versions

The chart is based on the following editions:

1. Armenian: the translation is taken from Conybeare, *Rituale Armenorum*, 175–77. Used by permission of Oxford University Press. Note that the chart does not include any of the variants recorded in the edition's apparatus.

2. Greek: the translation is adapted from *The Great Book of Needs*, vol. 1 (South Canaan, PA: St. Tikhon's Seminary Press, 1998), 313–15, with reference to the Greek of the Barbarini euchologion in Conybeare, *Rituale Armenorum*, 399–400, 419. The text from *The Great Book of Needs* is used by permission of St. Tikhon's Seminary Press.

3. Coptic: the translation is adapted from Budge, *Blessing of the Waters*, 126–34.

4. Syriac: the translation is taken from Budge, *Blessing of the Waters*, 71–75. Note that Budge includes a translation of another Syriac manuscript on pages 91–96, the readings of which are not included here.

5. Ethiopic: the German translation is taken from Arnhard, *Liturgie zum Tauf-Fest*, 24–29.

Phraseological differences between the versions are in bold. Italicized phrases indicate diaconal or congregational responses. Scriptures alluded to in the prayers are included in the chart below according to passage number.

Passage No.	Scriptural Reference
1	Psalm 146:5, Judith 16:13
2	2 Maccabees 7:28
4-5	Psalm 148:3
6	Psalm 76:17, 103:2, Isaiah 40:22
7	Psalm 135:6
8	Jeremiah 5:22
9	Psalm 75:8
12	Philippians 2:7
16	Baruch 3:38, Psalm 73:13
24	Genesis 6-8
25	Exodus 13-14
26	Exodus 15
27	Exodus 17
28	3 Reigns 18
29	4 Reigns 2

A Shared Prayer over Water in the Eastern Christian Traditions 65

Armenian	Greek	Coptic	Syriac	Ethiopic
				Der Herr [sei] mit Euch Allen! [*und*] *mit Deinem Geiste!* Erhebet eure Herzen! *Wir haben sie [erhoben] zu Gott.* Danket ihm und preiset ihn! *Es ist billig und recht.*
		The love of God . . .		Im Namen Gottes, des Vaters, des Herrn der ganzen Welt und [im Namen] seines eingeborenen Sohnes, Jesus Christus, des Heilandes der ganzen Welt und [im Namen] des heiligen Geistes, welcher der ganzen Welt Leben gibt, Erster ohne Zeit (Zeitwechsel), Letzter ohne Ende;

Armenian (cont.)	Greek (cont.)	Coptic (cont.)	Syriac (cont.)	Ethiopic (cont.)
1. Great art thou, Lord, and wonderful are thy **works. And there is none** able to **tell the praise** of thy wonders.	1. Great art Thou, O Lord, and wondrous are Thy **works**; and **no word** shall be sufficient to **hymn** Thy wonders.	1. Great art Thou, O Lord, and marvellous are Thy **works**; there is **no word** which is sufficient for the **praise** of Thy wonders.	1. Great art Thou, O Lord, and marvellous are Thy **works, and no word** sufficeth [to declare] the **praise** of Thy wonders.	1. *Du* bist der grosse Gott, und wunderbar ist Deine **Herrlichkeit** und **Niemand** kann **verstehen** Deine Wunder.
2. For by thy **volition** thou broughtest all into being out of not-being; and by thy **authority** thou sustainest all creation, and **by thy providence thou orderest the world**. Thou out of four elements didst compact the world, and with four revolving seasons hast crowned **the ample measure of** the year's **fullness.**	2. For Thou, by Thy **will**, from nothingness hast brought all things into being, by Thy **might** Thou upholdest **creation**, and **by Thy providence Thou orderest the world**. From four elements Thou hast formed creation; Thou hast crowned the course of the year with four seasons.	2. For by Thy **power** out of the things which existed not Thou hast made to come into being everything which is, Thou sustainest all **creation** by Thy **power**, and **by Thy forethought dost direct the world**. Thou didst constitute creation from four elements, and Thou didst crown the circle of the year with the four seasons;	2. For having, by Thy **power**, brought everything [into being] from things which had no being, by Thy **might** Thou dost support **nature**, and **by Thy grace Thou dost fill the people with food**. Thou didst fashion creation out of four elements, and Thou hast crowned the course of the year with four seasons.	2. Mit Deiner **Macht** hast Du Alles, was existirt, geschaffen aus dem Nichts und Du hast die Welt und was sie erfüllt, befestigt; durch Deine **Erhabenheit, durch die Erkenntniss Deiner hast Du Deinen Geschöpfen Trost gespendet;** *Du* bist's, **der die Welt an den** vier Winkeln abgeschlossen **hat.** *Du* bist es, **der die Welt mit einem Kreise** von Tagen begrenzt hat;

3. Before thee the intelligible powers quail.	3. All the rational powers tremble before Thee.	3. **Thou art He through Whom, in the beginning,** the powers of the understanding were disturbed;	3. The hosts of rational beings tremble before Thee,
			3. *Du* bist *der Herr*, vor dem alle hohen Mächte zittern;
4. Thee the sun doth praise. Thee doth the moon glorify.	4. The sun hymns Thee. The moon glorifies Thee.	4. Thou art He Whom the sun blesseth; Thou art He unto Whom the moon ascribeth glory;	
			4. *Du* bist *der Herr*, den **Sonne und Mond** preisen;
5. Thee the companies of stars **magnify**.	5. The stars **meet together** before Thee.	5. Thou art He by Whom the stars **have been set in order**;	11. and the orders of the angels **praise** Thee, and the companies of the archangels **bow down** in homage [before Thee]; the six-winged Seraphim which fly [round about Thee] cry out unto Thee, and the **many-eyed** Cherubim shroud Thee in glory which cannot be approached.
			5. *Du* bist es, der **den Himmel mit** Sternen **gekrönt hat**;
6. Thee the light obeyeth. Before thee the abysses shudder. Thee the fountains serve. Thou	6. The light hearkens unto Thee. The deeps shudder before Thee. The springs of water serve	6. Thou art He Whom the light obeyeth; Thou art He Whom the depths hold in fear; and Thou art	
			6. *Du* bist es, dem allein die Lichter gehorchen; *Du* bist es, den diejenigen fürchten, welche unter

Armenian (cont.)	Greek (cont.)	Coptic (cont.)	Syriac (cont.)	Ethiopic (cont.)
didst spread out the heavens like a vault.	Thee. Thou hast stretched out the heaven as a curtain.	He unto Whom the seas minister. *O ye who are seated, stand.* Thou art He Who hast stretched out the heavens like a tent,		der Erde sind; *Du* bist es, dem die Quellen [der Wasser] dienen. *Die ihr sitzet, erhebet euch! Du* bist es, der den Himmel wie ein Gewölbe aufgehängt hat;
7. Thou hast **established** the earth in its foundation upon the waters.	7. Thou hast **established** the earth upon the waters.	7. Thou hast **made strong** the earth upon the waters,		
8. Thou hast ramparted the sea with sand. Thou hast poured out the winds **for the blast**.	8. Thou hast bounded the sea with sand. Thou hast spilled out the air **for breathing.**	8. Thou hast set the sand round about the sea **like a wall,** and Thou hast poured out the air for us **wherefrom we may draw our breath.** *Look ye towards the East.*		8. *Du* bist es, der das Meer eingehegt hat wie [mit] Sand; *Du* bist es, der dem **Luftkreis befohlen, es sollen diese Lüfte wehen**. *Blicket gegen Osten!*
9. Thou art terrible, and who can stand before thee?				

A Shared Prayer over Water in the Eastern Christian Traditions   69

11. The angelic hosts **praise** thee. The ranks of the archangels **worship** thee. The six-winged seraphim and the **multiform** cherubim mounting upwards are encircled and hidden in thy unapproachable light.	11. The Angelic Powers **serve** Thee. The choirs of Archangels **worship** Thee. The **many-eyed** Cherubim and the six-winged Seraphim, standing and flying round about, cover themselves with fear at Thine unapproachable glory.	11. The angelic powers **minister** unto Thee, and the company of the Archangels **bow down** unto Thee. **Thou art He Whose glory declare the Seraphim with six wings, who fly and stand in Thy presence, and the Cherubim with many eyes; they cover themselves with their**	4. The sun praiseth Thee; the moon glorifieth Thee; 5. the stars **praise** Thee; 6. the light is obedient unto Thee; the depths tremble before Thee; and the fountains of water serve Thee. Thou hast spread out the heavens like a curtain,	10. Wir bitten Dich, O Herr, ob Deines Erbarmens nicht ob unserem Werke, dass der heilige Geist über dieses Wasser wehe, damit es diene zur Heilung und Rettung der Seele Deiner Knechte. *Wir werden hinblicken.* 11. *Du* bist der, dem die erhabenen Mächte **dienen;** *Du* bist der, den die Erzengel **preisen;** Du bist derjenige, den **die Seraphim lobpreisen, welche Flügel haben, vor Dir stehend und Dich umgebend und welche voll sind von Augen und bedeckt mit** Lichtstrahlen, dass

Armenian (cont.)	Greek (cont.)	Coptic (cont.)	Syriac (cont.)	Ethiopic (cont.)
		wings because of Thy glory which cannot be approached, and they praise Thee saying, *Holy, Holy, Holy. . . .*	7. Thou hast **beaten out** the earth over the waters, 8. Thou hast shut in the sea with the sand, and Thou hast poured out the air **like a breath**.	Niemand Dir nahen kann. Sie preisen Dich, indem sie sagen: heilig. *Antwortet! Heilig, heilig, heilig ist der Herr!*
12. For thou art God **incircumscribable, ineffable, indescribable.** Thou camest upon earth, didst take the form of a servant, coming to be in the likeness of men, and wast found in form as it were man. For, **O Lord that lovest man**, thou couldst not bear, because of thy **manifold pity**, to look upon mankind **held in tyranny** by the	12. For Thou, who art God **inexpressible, unoriginate, and ineffable,** didst come down upon earth, taking the form of a servant, being made in the likeness of man. For Thou, **O Master**, for the sake of **Thy tender mercy**, couldest not endure to behold the race of man **tormented** by the **devil**; but Thou didst come and save us.	12. **Holy art Thou. Holy art Thou. Holy art Thou.** For Thou art the God Who art **incomprehensible, and without beginning, and Who canst not be described.** Thou didst come upon the earth and didst take the form of a servant, and didst dwell in the image of man, for, **O Lord**, by reason of the **compassion of Thy mercy**,	12. And Thou being God Who art **without end, and without beginning, and who canst not be comprehended**, didst come upon the earth, and didst take the form of a servant, and didst live in the form of **the children of** men. For by reason of Thy **saving mercy** Thou couldst not bear to see the race of the **children of** men **oppressed** by the	12. Du bist unser Gott, vollkommen in Deinem Wesen, keine Grenze hat Dein uranfängliches Sein und kein Aufhören Dein zukünftiges Sein, denn ewig ist es (Dein Sein), übersteigend menschliche **Erkenntniss**. Und Du bist herabgekommen auf die Erde, **hast hinweggenommen die Fesseln Deiner**

slanderer, but camest and savedst us.	Thou couldst not bear to see the race of men **oppressed** by the might of the **Devil**, and Thou didst come and deliver us.	**Calumniator**, but didst come and deliver [them].	**Knechte,** bist dem Menschen ähnlich geworden, **hast erduldet Versuchung, hast alle Werke der Menschen gethan, nur nicht Sünde, indem Du Alles auf Dich nahmst.** O Herr, gemäss Deiner **Erhabenheit ob der Menge Deines Erbarmens,** hast Du geblickt auf die Natur der Menschenkinder, wie der **Teufel** sie **unterjocht,** und hast ihrer in Deiner **Gnade** gedacht; Du bist gekommen, and Du hast sie gerettet. 13. So gedenke denn gleichermassen auch unser, o Herr! in Deinem

Armenian (cont.)	Greek (cont.)	Coptic (cont.)	Syriac (cont.)	Ethiopic (cont.)
				Erbarmen, und sende den heiligen Geist auf dieses Wasser, dass es diene zur Heilung unseres Leibes und zur Rettung unserer Seele und zur Abwaschung der Sünden Deiner Knechte.
14. We **laud** thy grace. We proclaim thy mercy. We hide not thy benevolence.	14. We **confess** Thy grace. We proclaim Thy mercy. We conceal not Thy benevolent acts.	14. We **confess** Thy graciousness, and we proclaim Thy mercy, and we do not hide Thy goodness **in that Thou didst come and deliver us**, *according to Thy mercy and not according to our sins.*	14. We **confess** Thy goodness, and we proclaim abroad Thy mercy, and we will not hide the fair beauty of that which Thou hast done.	14. **Wir wollen Dir Dank sagen und Dein** Erbarmen **suchen und Du** verbirg **nicht vor uns** Deine Güter. Du bist gekommen und hast sie gerettet
15. Thou hast **liberated** the offspring of our nature. Thou didst **sanctify** the	15. Thou hast **liberated** the offspring of our nature. Thou didst **sanctify** the	15. Thou hast **blessed** those who are brought forth by natural birth,	15. Thou didst **bless** the child of nature, and Thou didst by Thy birth	15. und Du hast die Menschenkinder dem **Tode vorgezogen**, und

A Shared Prayer over Water in the Eastern Christian Traditions 73

virgin's **womb** by thine **ineffable** birth. All creatures praise thee, revealed **Word God**.	the Virginal **womb** by Thy nativity. All creation hymns Thee who hast manifested Thyself.	and Thou hast **purified** the Virgin **Mother** by Thy birth; all creation praiseth Thee because Thou didst make Thyself manifest.	**sanctify** the virgin **womb**, and all creation praised Thee when Thou didst rise [on the world].	Du hast **stark gemacht den Leib** der Jungfrau, da Du in ihm getragen wurdest, und sie preisen Dich **in Ewigkeit**.
16. For thou art **our** God. On earth thou hast appeared and hast walked with men. Thou also didst hallow the Jordan's currents, **sending** from heaven thy holy Spirit. And thou didst bruise the head of the serpent that was lurking therein.	16. For Thou, **O our** God, wert seen upon the earth and hast dwelt among men. Thou didst sanctify the streams of Jordan, **sending** down from heaven Thy Holy Spirit, and didst crush the heads of the dragons that lurked therein.	16. For, **being God,** Thou didst make Thyself manifest upon the earth, and didst make Thyself a companion unto man in going about. Thou didst sanctify the floods of the Jordan having **drawn down** upon them from heaven Thy Holy Spirit, and Thou didst break in pieces the heads of the dragons that were hidden therein.	16. For Thou, **O our** God, didst appear upon the earth, and with the children of men Thou didst live and move. Thou didst sanctify the floods of Jordan when Thy Holy Spirit from heaven **smote** upon them, and Thou didst break the head of the dragon which writhed therein.	16. Und Du bist erschienen auf der Erde und Du bist gewandelt mit den Menschen. *Nach Deinem Erbarmen, o Herr, nicht nach unserer Sünde.* Du bist es, der mit Segnung geheiligt hat das Wasser des Jordan und vom Himmel herab den heiligen Geist über sie **gesendet** und zerschmettert die Häupter des Drachen in ihm (sc. in dem Wasser).

Armenian (cont.)	Greek (cont.)	Coptic (cont.)	Syriac (cont.)	Ethiopic (cont.)
17. And now we pray thee, **Lord** who lovest mankind, **send** thy holy Spirit from above into this water. **Bless and** hallow it, and endue it with the grace of the Jordan. And make it a fountain of blessing, and a gift of **incorruptibility**; a loosing of sin,	17. Do Thou Thyself, O **King**, the Lover of mankind, **be present** now through the **coming** of Thy Holy Spirit, and sanctify this water. And give it **the grace of redemption**, the blessing of the Jordan. Make it a fountain of incorruption, a gift of **sanctification**, a loosing of sins,	17. O our **Lord**, Thou man-loving God, **Jesus Christ, come now** again by the **descent** of Thy Holy Spirit. Sanctify this water, and give unto it the grace of the Jordan. Amen. Let it be a fountain of blessing. Amen. A gift of **purification**. Amen. A remission of sins. Amen.	17. Do Thou then, O **Lord**, Who lovest man, **come now** by the **descent** of Thy Holy Spirit, and sanctify these waters. Give [unto them] the grace of Jordan, and make them to be fountains of blessings, and gifts of **holiness**, and a loosing of sins,	17. Du bist der Liebhaber der Menschen, o **Gott; verlasse uns nicht wegen unserer Sünden, sondern nach der Fülle Deiner Barmherzigkeit schicke** den heiligen Geist, die Segnung des Jordan **durch Dein Erbarmen.** Amen. Mache ihn zur Quelle des Segens. Amen. Und zum Altar der **Reinigung.** Amen. Und zum Abwaschungsmittel der Sünde. Amen.
18. a healing of the sick,	18. a healing of sicknesses,	18. A driver away of sickness. Amen.	18. and a binding up of sicknesses,	
				19. Mache, o Herr, dieses Wasser zum Loslöser von den bösen Dämonen. Amen.

A Shared Prayer over Water in the Eastern Christian Traditions   75

19. dread ruin of demons, 20. health of the afflicted, 21. fearless of the power that confronts, filled full with **angelic** power.	19. a destruction of demons, 21. unapproachable by hostile powers, filled with **angelic might**, 22. that **all them that draw from and partake of it** may have it for the cleansing of souls and bodies, for the healing of sufferings, for the sanctification of homes, and for every useful purpose.	19. Let it be a terrifier of the demons. Amen. 21. And let not all the powers of the Foe draw nigh unto it. Amen. Let it be full of all **angelic** powers. Amen. 22. That unto **all those who draw therefrom, or who partake of it**, it may be a purification of soul, and **body, and spirit**. Amen. For a healing of pains. Amen. For a sanctification of houses. Amen. May it produce benefits of every kind. Amen.	19. And terrifiers [?] of devils, 21. and things unapproachable by opposing hosts, and things filled with **angelic** power, 22. so that they may become unto **all those who draw from and partake of them** for the cleansing of souls and bodies, and the healing of passions, and the sanctification of houses, and ready helpers to good things of every kind.	18. [Bereite es] zur Heilung der Leidenden, 21. auf dass kein unreiner Geist sich ihm nahe. Amen. Erfülle, o Herr, dieses Wasser mit Kraft. Amen. 22. **Wer damit sich gewaschen: mit der Kraft des heiligen Geistes werde es (sc. das Wasser) erfüllt zum Zwecke des Trinkens oder der Besprengung (zum Schutz gegen Zauber und Dämonen)** und diene zur Reinigung der Seele und des Körpers, und zur Heilung

Armenian (cont.)	Greek (cont.)	Coptic (cont.)	Syriac (cont.)	Ethiopic (cont.)
				der Kranken, und zur Weihe ihren Häusern. Amen. Mache, o Gott, [dasselbe] geeignet zu allem Thun. Amen.
	23. For Thou art our God, Who through water and the **Spirit** hast renewed our nature grown old through sin.	23. O Thou **Lord Jesus Christ,** Who didst renew again our nature, which had become old in sin, by water and by **Spirit**;	23. For Thou art He Who by **fire** and water didst renew our nature which had become old through sin.	23. *Du* bist es, o Gott, der die Natur der Menschenkinder erneuert hat, nachdem sie verfallen und herabgekommen war durch die Sünde **und Du hast sie himmlisch und geistig leuchtend, heilig und rein gemacht.**
	24. Thou art our God, Who through water didst drown sin in the days of Noah.	24. Who didst drown with water sin when it had become exalted in the time of Noah;	24. Thou art He Who by water didst drown sin in the days of Noah.	

A Shared Prayer over Water in the Eastern Christian Traditions 77

25. Thou art our God, Who through the sea, by Moses, didst free the Hebrew race from the slavery of Pharaoh.	25. Who didst set free the people of the Hebrews from the bondage of Pharaoh by Moses and the sea;	25. Thou art He Who by the sea didst set free the host of the Hebrews from the oppression of Pharaoh.	25. *Du* bist es, der die Kinder Israels frei machte von dem Dienste des Pharao, und sie wurden Freie durch **ihren Auszug aus Egypten und aus dem Meere** unter der Leitung des Moses.
26. For thou art our God, who didst in the desert in Moses' day sweeten with the tree the bitter waters and give to the thirsty people to drink.			
27. Thou art our God, Who didst cleave the rock in the Wilderness, and it gushed forth waters and poured out streams, and satisfied Thy thirsty people.			

Armenian (cont.)	Greek (cont.)	Coptic (cont.)	Syriac (cont.)	Ethiopic (cont.)
28. Thou art he that in Elisha's day with **fire and water** didst free Israel from Baal.	28. Thou art our God, Who through **water and fire**, by Elijah, didst convert Israel from **the delusion** of Ba'al.	28. Thou art He Who separated Israel from **the error** of Baal by water in the time of Elijah;	28. Thou art He Who by **water and fire** didst deliver Israel from **the error** of Baal by the hands of Elijah the Prophet.	28. *Du* bist es, der Israel befreit hat vom Götzendienst durch **Feuer vom Himmel** unter Elia.
29. Thou art he that in Elisha's day madest the bitter and barren waters wholesome with salt.	29. Thou art our God, Who treated the bitter and barren waters with salt in Elisha's day.			24. *Du* bist's, o Herr, der die Welt abgewaschen hat, die eingetaucht ward in das Wasser der Fluth, welche in den Tagen des Noah der Sünde wegen geschickt wurde.
	30. Thou art our God, Who revealed the inseparable harmony of the			

31. Do thou now thyself, **O Lord, draw nigh to us** through thy **holy Spirit**, and **bless** this water; 22. to the end that it may be for the **building** of houses, for the healing of the sick, for the **salvation** of soul and body, helpful for all uses and needs.	Triad in the Jordan and who manifested the consubstantiality belonging to Thy Father to us in Thyself. And now, 31. **O Master**, do Thyself **sanctify** this water with the **Holy Spirit**.	31. do Thou now also, **O our Lord, sanctify** this water by Thy **Holy Spirit**;	31. And now, **O our Lord**, whilst **sanctifying** these waters by Thy Holy Spirit,	31. Und nun, **o Herr!** bitten wir Dich, **dass Du mit dieser Deiner Kraft unser gedenkest nach Deinem Erbarmen,** und **gib** diesem Wasser die Segensweihe durch **Deinen heiligen Namen, damit nicht zu Schanden werde die Hoffnung** derer, die ihre **Hoffnung auf Dich setzen,**

Armenian (cont.)	Greek (cont.)	Coptic (cont.)	Syriac (cont.)	Ethiopic (cont.)
	32. Grant unto them that **touch it**, and partake of it, and **anoint themselves with it, sanctification**, blessing, cleansing, health.	32. and grant unto **those who shall make use of it in any form whatsoever,** whether one partaketh of it, **or drinketh therefrom**, that it may be unto them a **purification**, and a blessing, and a cleansing, and a healing;	32. grant unto those who **touch them**, or who partake of them, or who **make use of them in any way whatsoever in faith, holiness,** and blessing, and purification, and health,	32. mögen sie [darin] sich **baden** oder [damit] **besprengt** werden; bereite ihnen, o Herr! dieses Wasser **zur Rettung der Seele und des Leibes,** [mache, **dass es**] **abwasche die Sünde,** reinige von Befleckung, und heile die Krankheit und die Unreinheit, und löse den Zauber, den man am Menschen verübt, und löse die Fessel der Sünde, und sühne die Schuld Deiner Knechte.
33. **Because thou art God, merciful and loving mankind.** May all flee therefrom who	33. **And save, O Lord,** Thy servants, **our faithful kings,** and guard **them by Thy shelter in**			

devise evil against thy servants.	**peace**. Make **subject** to them every hateful and hostile thing. **Grant to them all the requests pertaining to salvation and everlasting life,**			
	35. so that through the elements and through human beings and through angels and through things visible and through things invisible,	35. that by the elements, and by the angels, and by men, and by things visible, and by things invisible,	35. so that by the material elements of this world, and by **the children of** men, and by angels, and by things visible, and by things invisible,	34. Und schreibe unsere Namen auf in dem Buche des Lebens und vereinige uns mit allen Deinen Heiligen nach der Fülle Deines Erbarmens;
				35. durch das Gebet Deiner Engel **und durch die Fürbitte Deiner Heiligen führe uns zu Dir**, denn von Dir sind alle sichtbaren und unsichtbaren Geschöpfe,

Armenian (cont.)	Greek (cont.)	Coptic (cont.)	Syriac (cont.)	Ethiopic (cont.)
36. **That we may call out, O Lord**, thy name, **great, glorious, and working wonders**; and offer unto thee **praise and glory**; to Father, **Son**, and holy Spirit, now and ever and for eternity.	36. Thy all-holy name may be **glorified**, with the Father and with Thy **Holy and good and life-giving** Spirit, now and always and unto the ages of all ages. Amen.	36. Thy Holy Name, **O Christ our God**, and Thy **good and spotless** Father, and Thy Holy Spirit, may be **glorified**, now and always.	36. Thy Name may be **praised**, together with Thy Father, and Thy Holy Spirit, now and always. *Amen.*	36. und **gepriesen** wird Dein heiliger Name **durch jede Handlung in unserem Herrn Jesus Christus, o Du Herr der ganzen Welt** und [auch] Dein heiliger Geist, **der lebenspendende**, jetzt und alle Zeit und von Ewigkeit zu Ewigkeit. Amen.

4

Migrating Nuns—Migrating Liturgy: The Context of Reform in Female Convents of the Late Middle Ages

Gisela Muschiol

I. Text and Context

Issues surrounding reform in female convents of the late Middle Ages, particularly in convents in the German-speaking world, have been looked into by linguists, historians, and theologians for quite a number of years.[1] Yet in most cases the term "reform" has been used (and continues to be used) in a very narrow sense, both by the reformers of the late Middle Ages and also by modern-day scholars: reform is understood as the introduction or reintroduction of enclosure—when this is done, a convent is considered a reformed convent. Once walls have been erected and doors locked, reform is achieved.

Reform, however, meant considerably more than just subjecting the nuns to a renewed, strict form of enclosure. Changes affecting convents were not restricted to their relationship to the outside world; reform always implied changes in the liturgy, too. These changes, as well as the forms in which they were implemented, have rarely been studied by scholars. The implementation of an altered liturgy, and of the reform as a whole, usually occurred in a specific way: sisters left their original convents and migrated into the convents that were

---

1. The present essay on the influence of nuns and sisters on liturgical change is the beginning of a larger research project on liturgy in female convents in the late Middle Ages.

to be reformed, taking with them a plan for liturgical celebrations that were—
or were supposed to be—truer to the monastic rules. In what follows, I will
inquire into the conditions and forms of these migrations of liturgy and into
their impact on the social and cultural identity of the convents to be reformed.

A. Female Convents in the Late Middle Ages

The following remarks concentrate primarily on monasteries in the German-speaking world. The general circumstances of late medieval female convents are broadly comparable, irrespective of the individual affiliation to a special order. By the twelfth century, a vast number of convents had been established, predominantly in towns and cities but also in rural areas. Whereas the communities founded in the early Middle Ages had chiefly been Benedictine—communities with restrictive admission rules—the advent of the Cistercians opened up enormous opportunities for women. By the late thirteenth century, more than 250 convents of Cistercian nuns had been established in the territory of the empire.[2] The period when the mendicant friars spread throughout Europe saw the establishment on a similar scale of female communities of Dominicans, Clarissans, Augustinians, and—not least—tertiaries of the Third Order of the Friars Minor. Initially, the male branches of the orders were troubled by concerns and discussions on how to provide, or ward off, pastoral care for these female communities,[3] yet by the end of the fourteenth century the nunneries were consolidated and had gained acceptance. At the same time, an intense reform movement developed, especially within the Dominican Order, known as the Observance. In connection with this Observance—along with reformist ideas within the church as a whole, articulated, for instance, at

---

2. Franz J. Felten, "Zisterzienserinnen in Deutschland: Beobachtungen und Überlegungen zu Ausbreitung und und Ordenszugehörigkeit," in *Unanimité et diversité cisterciennes: Filiations, réseaux, relectures de XIIe au XVIIe siècles*, Actes du quatrième Colloque international du CERCOR, Dijon, 23–25 Septembre 1998, ed. Nicole Bouter (Saint-Étienne: Publications de l'Université de Saint-Étienne, 2000), 345–400, here 348.

3. Brigitte Degler-Spengler, "'Zahlreich wie die Sterne des Himmels': Zisterzienser, Dominikaner und Franziskaner vor dem Problem der Inkorporation von Frauenklöstern," *Rottenburger Jahrbuch für Kirchengeschichte* 4 (1985): 37–50; idem, "The Incorporation of Cistercian Nuns into the Order in the Twelfth and Thirteenth Century," in *Hidden Springs: Cistercian Monastic Women*, ed. John A. Nichols and Lillian Thomas Shank, Medieval Religious Women, vol. 3, bk. 1 (Kalamazoo: Cistercian Publications, 1995), 85–134; Franz J. Felten, "Der Zisterzienserorden und die Frauen," in *Weltverachtung und Heilsgewißheit*, ed. Harald Schwillus and Andreas Hölscher, Studien zu Geschichte, Kunst und Kultur der Zisterzienser 10 (Berlin: Lukas Verlag, 2000), 34–135.

the councils of Constance and Basle—similar reform activities occurred in Benedictine and Cistercian communities. The reform communities of Kastl, Melk, and particularly Bursfeld reached not only male convents but nunneries as well.[4] In addition, this reform context includes Johannes Busch's reformist ideas for the Augustinians, as well as the birth of the *devotio moderna* in the Netherlands and in northern Germany, including the Windesheim Congregation.[5] At any rate, reform was on the agenda of men's and women's convents alike, whereas differences between the sexes characterized the content and the practice of reform.

B. The Context of Reform and Observance

The reformers aimed at "observance," understood as strict adherence to the monastic rules. Their activities centered on the notion of a return to the origins of monastic rules. This meant first and foremost adherence to the original rule in question, and furthermore a markedly stricter way of life in accordance with the threefold vows. At the same time, however, the motif of "return to the origin of the rule" often became a topos in and of itself. In the name of "the origin," individual reformers enforced what they themselves deemed appropriate and original.[6] Especially with respect to women's convents, return to the origin meant, above all, enclosure—regardless of whether or not this had been part

---

4. Johannes Linneborn, "Die Reformation der Benedictinerklöster im 15. Jahrhundert durch die Bursfelder Kongregation: Die Reformation der Frauenklöster," *Studien- und Mitteilungen aus dem Benediktiner- und Zisterzienserorden* 22 (1901): 48–71, 396–418; Inge Mager, "Bemühungen um die Reform der Klosterkonvente im 15. Jahrhundert: Grundzüge der Windesheimer und Bursfelder Reform," in *Trinitäts- und Christusdogma: Ihre Bedeutung für Beten und Handeln der Kirche*, FS Jouko Martikainen, ed. Jobst Reller (Münster: LIT, 2001), 223–43; Elke-Ursel Hammer, "Substrukturen, Zentren und Regionen in der Bursfelder Benediktinerkongregation," in *Religiöse Bewegungen im Mittelalter*, FS Matthias Werner, ed. Enno Bünz et al. (Cologne: Böhlau, 2007), 397–426; Anja Freckmann, *Die Bibliothek des Klosters Bursfelde im Spätmittelalter* (Göttingen: V&R Unipress, 2006).

5. Bertram Lesser, "Zwischen Windesheim und Bursfelde: Klosterreformen in Hildesheim im 15. Jahrhundert," in *Schätze im Himmel, Bücher auf Erden. Mittelalterliche Handschriften aus Hildesheim*, ed. Monika Müller, Ausstellung der Herzog-August-Bibliothek Wolfenbüttel (Wolfenbüttel: Herzog-August-Bibliothek, 2010), 31–40; Wybren Scheepsma, *Medieval Religious Women in the Low Countries: The "Modern Devotion," the Canonesses of Windesheim and Their Writings* (Rochester: Boydell Press, 2004); Mathilde van Dijk, "Disciples of the Deep Desert: Windesheim Biographers and the Imitation of the Desert Fathers," *Nederlands Archief voor Kerkgeschiedenis* 86 (2006): 257–90.

6. Gert Melville, "Aspekte zum Vergleich von Krisen und Reformen in mittelalterlichen Klöstern und Orden," in *Mittelalterliche Orden und Klöster im Vergleich: Methodische Ansätze*

of the original rule. Enclosure became the crucial hallmark and the essential ingredient of what constituted reform.[7]

In order to enforce their reformist ideas, the reformers—male in most cases—took a raft of measures. Ensuring enclosure by means of walls, gates, and grills constituted a principal measure. These changes to the monastic buildings were propped up by educational measures. Frequently, the introduction or reinforcement of enclosure carried with it instruction in reading, writing, and, above all, Latin, all deliberately introduced with regard to changes in the liturgy.[8] Simultaneously, women's convents rediscovered for themselves the value of the written word, with the number of chronicles and other texts written in convents rising significantly.[9] A quite common move—the consequences of which have yet to be explored—was the transfer of nuns from a reformed convent to a convent facing reform. This phenomenon will be dealt with in more detail below. Other reform measures included a reorganization of male supervision, conducted by secular or monastic clergy or, in economic matters, by male lay bailiffs.

C. The Written Evidence for Reform

Convent reforms of the late Middle Ages are exceptionally well documented. It is almost exclusively the reformers or the reformed convents who

---

und Perspektiven, ed. Gert Melville and Anne Müller, Vita Regularis 34 (Berlin: LIT, 2007), 139–60.

7. Sigrid Schmitt, "'Wilde, unzucht- und ungaistlich swestern': Straßburger Frauenkonvente im Spätmittelalter," in *Frauen und Kirche*, ed. Sigrid Schmitt (Stuttgart: Steiner, 2002), 71–94; Heike Uffmann, "Inside and Outside the Convent Walls: The Norm and Practice of Enclosure in the Reformed Nunneries of Late Medieval Germany," *The Medieval History Journal* 4 (2001): 83–108; Gisela Muschiol, "Versorgung, Unterdrückung, Selbstbestimmung? Religiöse Frauengemeinschaften als Forschungsfeld," *Rottenburger Jahrbuch für Kirchengeschichte* 27 (2008): 13–26, esp. 17.

8. Heike Uffmann, *Wie in einem Rosengarten: Monastische Reformen des späten Mittelalters in den Vorstellungen von Klosterfrauen* (Bielefeld: Verlag für Regionalgeschichte, 2008), 80–97; Marie-Luise Ehrenschwendtner, *Die Bildung der Dominikanerinnen in Süddeutschland vom 13. bis 15. Jahrhundert*, Contubernium Tübinger Beiträge zur Universitäts- und Wissenschaftsgeschichte 60 (Stuttgart: Steiner, 2004), 119–48; idem, "Puellae litteratae: The Use of the Vernacular in the Dominican Convents of Southern Germany," in *Medieval Women in Their Communities*, ed. Diane Watt (Cardiff: University of Wales Press, 1997), 49–71; Henrike Lähnemann, "Der Auferstandene im Dialog mit den Frauen: Die Erscheinungen Christi in den Andachtsbüchern des Klosters Medingen," in *Passion und Ostern in den Lüneburger Klöstern*, ed. Linda Maria Koldau (Ebstorf: Kloster Ebstorf, 2010), 105–34.

9. Uffmann, *Wie in einem Rosengarten*, 107–22; Ehrenschwendtner, *Die Bildung*, 277–86.

left records of the reform. Those convents that successfully resisted reform, and those individual monks and nuns opposed to reform who avoided it by leaving or changing their community, documented their unwillingness much less frequently. Reforms are recorded in various types of sources, prominent among them the historiographic texts written in the convents. Chronicles, displaying a visible interest in their subject matter, give a well-aimed account of the beginnings of the reform, of its progress, of its successes in all areas of monastic life, of its impact, and of its exemplariness.[10] A similar genre are the *Schwesternbücher*, "sister books," collections of short biographies of deceased sisters of a convent aiming to present role models for the living. Though most known sister books date back to the fourteenth century, that is, the period preceding the reform, a number of such books from the late fifteenth century, containing descriptions of sisterly lives led in an exemplary reformed fashion, have survived.[11]

A mostly personal view emerges from the few extant letters and collections of letters. When Katharina of Mühlheim, a nun from Schönensteinbach Abbey (where the Dominican Observance originated), wrote to her former prioress, she reported that, in seeking reform, she had to set off three times for new convents, thus revealing some of the troubles of the reform: "I would never have thought that I would have to spend my life alone with only one sister from Schönensteinbach. Know that it makes me very sad that I must live so far from Schönensteinbach, and also so far from all those sisters."[12]

Texts such as these provide information on everyday life and holidays, on the economy and the use of power, and also on the practice of the liturgy. Moreover, women's convents have also left a legacy of books explicitly intended for liturgical and paraliturgical use: antiphonals, breviaries, hymn books, psalteries, sequentiaries, and prayer books.[13] The Dominican women's convent

---

10. Anne Winston-Allen, *Convent Chronicles: Women Writing about Women and Reform in the Late Middle Ages* (University Park, PA: Pennsylvania State University Press, 2004); Antje Willing, *Literatur und Ordensreform im 15. Jahrhundert: Deutsche Abendmahlsschriften im Nürnberger Katharinenkloster* (Münster: Waxmann, 2004).

11. Anne Bollmann, "Frauenleben und Frauenliteratur in der Devotio moderna. Volkssprachliche Schwesternbücher in literarhistorischer Perspektive" (PhD diss., University of Groningen, 2004); Anne Bollmann and Nikolaus Staubach, eds., *Schwesternbuch und Statuten des St. Agnes-Konvents in Emmerich* (Emmerich: Emmericher Geschichtsverein, 1998).

12. *Seraphin Dietlers Chronik des Klosters Schönensteinbach*, ed. Johann von Schlumberger (Gebweiler: J. Boltz, 1897), 406; and Winston-Allen, *Convent Chronicles*, 105.

13. See the manuscripts and editions listed by Winston-Allen, *Convent Chronicles*, 293–301; Renate Giermann and Helmut Härtel, eds., *Handschriften des Klosters Ebstorf*, Mittelalterliche

in Nuremberg, for example, is the original home of a handbook for the nun sacristan, composed by the Katharina of Mühlheim, whose letter is quoted above.[14] The Benedictine nunnery of Preetz in Schleswig-Holstein preserves a so-called Buch im Chore (book in the choir) in which the prioress describes the proceedings of a late fifteenth-century church service—the realities as well as the ideals—where she renders visible the objectives of reform within a single convent.[15] Furthermore, various ceremonial books and *libri ordinarii* of the reform communities can be drawn upon in the quest for the migrations of the liturgy carried into the convents by migrating nuns and monks.[16]

II. Reform in Practice: The Migrating Nuns

Given the profusion of records just described, we have to confine ourselves to a selection here. The focus of the following remarks will be on two groups of female reformers: migrating nuns within the Dominican Observance and migrating nuns within the Bursfeld and Windesheim reform. With regard to the Dominican Observance, we will investigate the networks of nunneries in

---

Handschriften in Niedersachsen 10 (Wiesbaden: Harrassowitz, 1994); Karin Schneider, ed., *Die Handschriften der Stadtbibliothek Nürnberg*, vol. 1: *Die deutschen mittelalterlichen Handschriften* (Wiesbaden: Harrassowitz, 1965), xi–xxxvi; see http://www.manuscripta-mediaevalia.de for the manuscripts of the convent of St. Catherine in Nuremberg now housed in the Germanische Nationalmuseum and in the library of the city of Nuremberg; Christine Sauer, "Zwischen Kloster und Welt: Illuminierte Handschriften aus dem Dominikanerinnenkonvent St. Katharina in Nürnberg," in *Frauen—Kloster—Kunst: Neue Forschungen zur Kulturgeschichte des Mittelalters*, Beiträge zum Internationalen Kolloquium vom 13.–16. Mai 2005 anläßlich der Ausstellung "Krone und Schleier," ed. Jeffrey F. Hamburger and Carola Jäggi (Turnhout: Brepols, 2007), 113–30.

14. Gerhard Weilandt, "Alltag einer Küsterin: Die Ausstattung und liturgische Nutzung von Chor und Nonnenempore der Nürnberger Dominikanerinnenkirche nach dem unbekannten 'Notel der Küsterin' (1436)," in *Kunst und Liturgie: Choranlagen des Spätmittelalters: Ihre Architektur, Ausstattung und Nutzung*, ed. Anna Moraht-Fromm (Ostfildern: J. Thorbecke, 2003), 159–87.

15. Elfriede Kelm, "Das 'Buch im Chore' der Priörin Anna von Buchwald im Klosterarchiv zu Preetz," *Jahrbuch Plön* 4 (1974): 68–83; Johannes Rosenplänter, *Kloster Preetz und seine Grundherrschaft: Sozialgefüge, Wirtschaftsbeziehungen und religiöser Alltag eines holsteinischen Frauenklosters um 1210–1550*, Quellen und Forschungen zur Geschichte Schleswig-Holsteins 114 (Neumünster: Wachholtz, 2009).

16. Marcellus Albert, ed., *Caeremoniale Bursfeldenses*, Corpus Consuetudinum Monasticarum 13 (Siegburg: F. Schmitt, 2002); Albert Schmidt, *Zusätze als Problem des monastischen Stundengebets im Mittelalter* (Münster: Aschendorff, 1986).

southern and upper Germany.¹⁷ As to the Bursfeld and Windesheim reform, the so-called Heideklöster (heath cloisters) deserve special attention; they were a group of nunneries of Benedictine or Cistercian character situated in the heathland around Lüneburg, to the south of Hamburg. For a variety of reasons, the written records from these religious houses have been preserved much more fully than in other regions. The convents in question are Ebstorf (OSB), Isenhagen (OCist), Lüne (OSB), Medingen (OCist), Walsrode (OSB), and Wienhausen (OCist).[18]

A. Dominican Nuns on the Move

In his fifth *Buch der Reformacio Predigerordens* (book of the reform of the Dominican Order), Johannes Meyer, an observant Dominican living in the fifteenth century, describes in detail the events surrounding the reforms of the individual women's convents.[19] Introduction of the Observance in different women's convents shared one striking feature: reform was implemented not by handing over texts or books but by introducing a group of sisters from convents that had already been reformed. This phenomenon crisscrossed the southern parts of the empire: sisters from Colmar transferred to Basle, to Strasbourg, to Speyer, to Freiburg;[20] sisters from Schönensteinbach in Alsace transferred to Nuremberg, to Pforzheim, to Freiburg, to Medlingen near Augsburg;[21] sisters

---

17. Eva Schlotheuber, "Bücher und Bildung in den Frauengemeinschaften der Bettelorden," in *Nonnen, Kanonissen und Mystikerinnen: Religiöse Frauengemeinschaften in Süddeutschland*, ed. Eva Schlotheuber, Helmut Flachenecker, and Ingrid Gardill (Göttingen: Vandenhoeck & Ruprecht, 2008), 241–62; Hieronymus Wilms, *Das älteste Verzeichnis der deutschen Dominikanerinnenklöster*, Quellen und Forschungen zur Geschichte des Dominikanerordens in Deutschland 24 (Leipzig: O. Harrassowitz, 1928).

18. Ida-Christine Riggert, *Die Lüneburger Frauenklöster* (Hannover: Hahnsche Buchhandlung, 1996); Wolfgang Brandis, "Die Archive der Lüneburger Klöster," in *"In Treue und Hingabe": 800 Jahre Kloster Ebstorf*, ed. Marianne Elster and Horst Hoffmann (Ebstorf: Kloster Ebstorf, 1997), 275–82.

19. Johannes Meyer, *Buch der Reformacio Predigerordens*, ed. Benedictus Maria Reichert, Quellen und Forschungen zur Geschichte des Dominikanerordens in Deutschland 2/3 (Leipzig: O. Harrassowitz, 1908–9). The *Buch der Reformacio* is divided into five parts, called *Buch I* to *Buch V*. I quote from the edition of Reichert, naming the part of the *Buch* and the page of the detailed report of the migrations. The references that follow give the page numbers in *Buch V*.

20. Meyer, *Buch V*, from Colmar-Unterlinden to Basle, 52ff.; to Strasbourg-Nikolaus in undis, 80; to Strasbourg-St Agnes, 123; to Speyer, 198; to Freiburg-Adelhausen, 114f.

21. Ibid., from Schönensteinbach to Nuremberg, 64–66; to Pforzheim, 102f.; to Freiburg-Magdalen, 120; to Medlingen, 147f.

from Basle, for their part, transferred to Worms, to Strasbourg, to Bern;[22] and eventually those from Nuremberg, freshly reformed, transferred to Tulln (nowadays part of Austria), Pforzheim, Bamberg, Altenhohenau,[23] and so on. These migrating nuns took pivotal positions in their new convents, among them those of sexton[24] and singer,[25] positions directly linked to the liturgy. In addition, the migrating nuns regularly included sisters who were highly literate and especially able to write choir books.[26]

A vast amount of detail is provided by the accounts of the reform in the three Dominican women's convents in Freiburg im Breisgau, for the Dominican chronicler Johannes Meyer was obviously present there in person. The reform in Freiburg-Adelhausen began with a procession into the church. Having sung the antiphon *Sub tuum* at the altar of the Blessed Virgin Mary, the reform sisters proceeded to the nuns' choir, where they sang the hymn *Veni creator*, including the versicle. What followed was the appropriate *oratio*. Meyer refers to this sequence as "how one usually does it when a cloister is to be reformed." Similar things happened in the second convent, St. Agnes: three initial steps of reform were the procession into the church, a *Salve regina* sung in a kneeling position, and the hymn *Veni creator* sung in the choir. Likewise, in the last of the three convents in Freiburg, that of the Magdalen Sisters, the antiphon *Sub tuum* was sung, then the hymn *Veni creator*, and finally—in honor of the *matroness* (as the fifteenth-century account puts it)—the antiphon *Intercede*, followed by a concluding sermon.[27]

Johannes Meyer postulated an indissoluble link between the practice of reform and the practice of liturgy. This link was bolstered by all kinds of choir books written by the sisters. The Dominican women's convent in Nuremberg is the place of origin of a total of more than six hundred extant vernacular manuscripts, probably the largest library of a late medieval women's cloister in Germany, the major part written in the course of the reform.[28] The liturgical

---

22. Ibid., from the reformed convent of Basle to Worms-Hochheim, 78f.; to Strasbourg-Nikolaus in undis, 80f.; to Bern, 101f.

23. Ibid., from Nuremberg to Tulln, 95ff.; to Pforzheim, 102f.; to Bamberg, 107f.; to Altenhohenau, 122.

24. Ibid., in Strasbourg-St Agnes, 134; in Basle, 54.

25. In Nuremberg Sister Margareth Kartäuserin assumed the office of singer; ibid., 66.

26. In Comar-Unterlinden, ibid., 101.

27. Ibid., 118–20.

28. Willing, *Literatur und Ordensreform*, 22ff.; Barbara Steinke, *Paradiesgarten oder Gefängnis? Das Nürnberger Katharinenkloster zwischen Klosterreform und Reformation*, Spätmittelalter und Reformation Neue Reihe 30 (Tübingen: Mohr Siebeck, 2006), 56–61; Ehrenschwendtner, *Die Bildung*, 21–29, 334–37.

Migrating Nuns—Migrating Liturgy   91

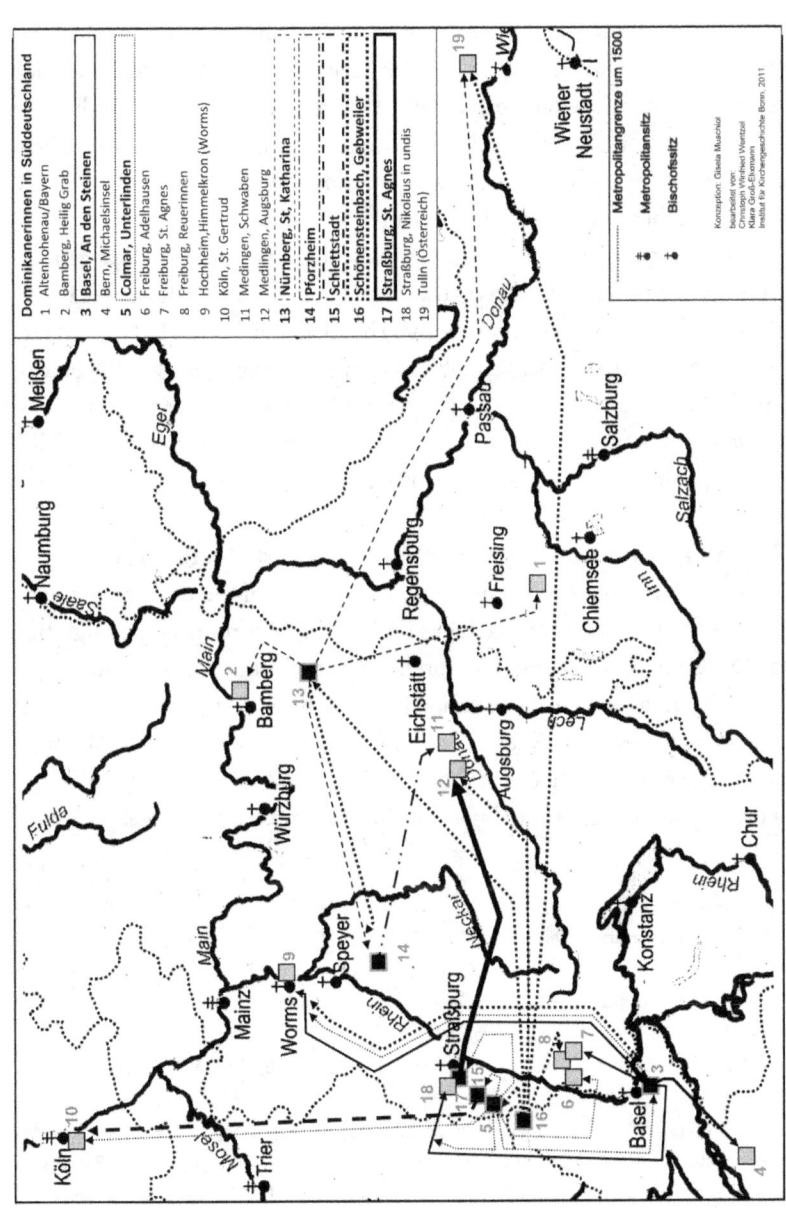

Routes of the migrating Dominican nuns in Southern Germany.

manuscripts from Nuremberg have not yet been analyzed in their entirety. According to Meyer, the reforming nuns on the move taught singing, reading, and writing.[29] Sister Margreth Kartäuserin may serve as a concrete example. She is reported to have held the position of *cantrix* for more than thirty years and, as one of the migrating reform sisters, to have written the hymn books afresh, all of them—according to the sources—of laudable artistic quality.[30]

The surviving records also document the exchange of books between observant women's convents: the Dominicans in St. Gall borrowed a gradual and an *evangeliar* from Nuremberg,[31] as well as a handbook for the sacristan, which described all the proceedings of worship in the course of the year, including the necessary preparatory work.[32] Likewise, the Dominican women in Nuremberg sent a *rituale* to Altenhohenau, thus supporting the reform endeavors of the sisters dispatched there from Nuremberg.[33]

These chronicles tell us that the migrating nuns brought with them a modified liturgy that they regarded as more accurate than the older rites and that they introduced in their new convents both by heart and by books. In Nuremberg, for instance, the reform changed the rules governing the Liturgy of the Hours. Henceforth, the so-called "seven times" (with Matins and Lauds fused into one) were to be sung in the sister's choir—and by all the sisters, the possibility of a leave of absence no longer being provided for.[34]

B. Migrating Nuns from the Bursfeld and Windesheim Reform

The women's convents in the Teutonia province of the Dominicans were not alone in considering the changes of the liturgy introduced by migrating nuns to be worth reporting. Comprehensive accounts of reform have also survived from the large zone of influence of the Bursfeld reform, whose exact size is no longer discoverable. As far as the "heath cloisters" in the Lüneburg area are concerned, pertinent accounts from Ebstorf, Lüne, and Wienhausen still exist;[35] in the case of Medingen we have a brief report, as well as a huge

---

29. Meyer, *Buch V*, 61.
30. Ehrenschwendtner, *Die Bildung*, 289.
31. Ibid., 291.
32. Weilandt, "Alltag einer Küsterin," 165.
33. Ehrenschwendtner, *Die Bildung*, 292.
34. Ibid., 152f.; that the rules could change is noted in the "Notel" of the sexton—cf. Weilandt, "Alltag einer Küsterin," 173.
35. Uffmann, *Wie in einem Rosengarten*, 123–33; Helmut Härtel, "Die Bibliothek des Klosters Ebstorf im späten Mittelalter," in *"In Treue und Hingabe": 800 Jahre Kloster Ebstorf*, ed. Marianne Elster and Horst Hoffmann (Ebstorf: Kloster Ebstorf, 1997), 109–22; Ernst Nolte,

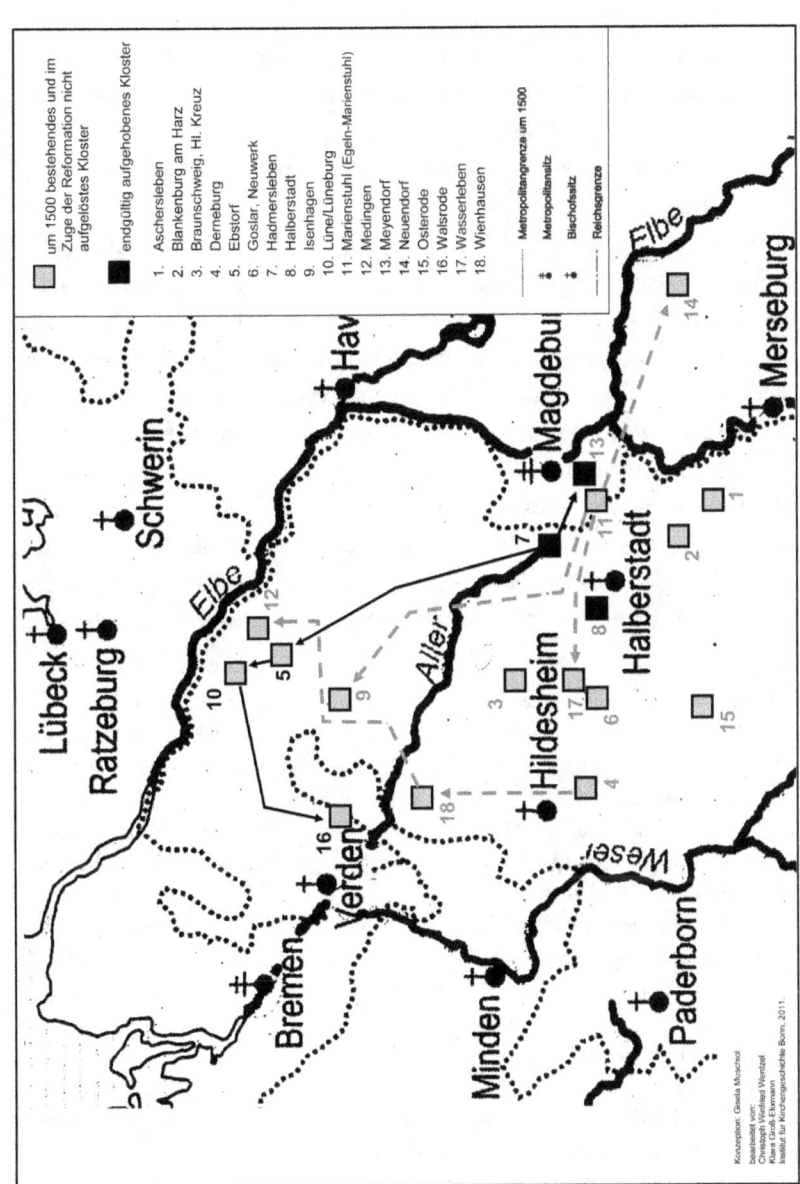

Routes of the migrating nuns from northern German convents.

number of manuscripts on liturgical matters that contain evidence of reforms.[36] None of these women's cloisters formally joined the Bursfeld Congregation or the Windesheim Congregation, yet all were affected indirectly by the reformist ideas emanating from Bursfeld and Windesheim.[37]

The reform in Ebstorf required two attempts: in 1469 the abbess of Hadmersleben Abbey in the Diocese of Halberstadt and some of her nuns came to Ebstorf, following the explicit request of the provost of Ebstorf, to introduce the new liturgy of the Bursfeld reform.[38] In December of 1469, they returned to Hadmersleben. Obviously, the roots put down by the new liturgy were not deep enough, and difficulties developed. Therefore, in January of 1470, two nuns from Hadmersleben were dispatched to Ebstorf once again: Mechthild of Niendorf, who became the new prioress, and another nun, whose name is not known.[39] The reform saw the production of numerous manuscripts in Ebstorf, mostly of a liturgical character. Even though the manuscripts for Mass and the Divine Office have been lost (due to the sixteenth-century Reformation), the extant manuscripts indicate that, apart from enclosure, the renewal of the liturgy constituted the main component of the reform. The surviving books from Ebstorf include four breviaries and an equal number of breviary fragments, as many as ten Latin and six Low German prayer books and an equal number of corresponding fragments, three collections of sermons, two psalteries, and several collections and fragments of hymnaries, antiphonals, and gradual books.[40] Looking at the library as a whole, we can see that the reform of the liturgy initiated by the nuns from Hadmersleben evolved in three stages.[41] During the first stage, which laid the foundation of the reform, the sisters in Ebstorf acquired writing skills as well

---

Quellen und Studien zur Geschichte des Nonnenklosters Lüne bei Lüneburg, vol. 1: *Die Quellen: Die Geschichte Lünes von den Anfängen bis zur Klostererneuerung im Jahre 1481* (Göttingen: Vandenhoeck & Ruprecht, 1932); Horst Appuhn, ed., *Chronik und Totenbuch des Klosters Wienhausen* (Wienhausen: Kloster Wienhausen, 1986).

36. See the research project of Henrike Lähnemann on the Medingen manuscripts: http://research.ncl.ac.uk/medingen/public_extern, accessed February 29, 2012. My thanks to Henrike Lähnemann for lively discussions.

37. Uffmann, *Wie in einem Rosengarten*, 126, 129, 132; cf. Philipp Hofmeister, "Liste der Nonnenklöster der Bursfelder Kongregation," *Studien und Mitteilungen zur Geschichte des Benediktinerordens und seiner Zweige* 53 (1935): 77–102; Albert, *Caeremoniale Bursfeldenses*, 19–25.

38. Uffmann, *Wie in einem Rosengarten*, 126.

39. Ibid., 127.

40. Härtel, "Die Bibliothek des Klosters Ebstorf," 118–21; cf. Giermann/Härtel, *Handschriften des Klosters Ebstorf*, with an overview of the all the manuscripts.

41. Härtel, "Die Bibliothek des Klosters Ebstorf," 109.

as a knowledge of Latin. The second stage consisted of catechetical instruction in the liturgy; in Ebstorf two explanations of the Mass, an exegetical text on the Lord's Prayer, and other catechetical texts have survived. The third stage of liturgical reform was a renewed and deeper grounding in prayer. The sixteen prayer books, though all unique and written by different sisters for their personal use, have one thing in common: they were in daily use, both for meditation during Mass and Divine Office and for the enrichment of the interim periods.[42]

Console with two nuns in the cloister of the convent of Ebstorf. Photo by author.

The reform of the liturgy, and of convent life as a whole, proved such a success that between 1477 and 1482 the Benedictine convent at Ebstorf reformed four other women's convents and dispatched nuns to these convents.[43] One of the religious houses reformed by the migrating nuns from the convent at Ebstorf was Lüne Abbey. In 1481 seven nuns were dispatched from Ebstorf to Lüne, headed by Mechthild of Niendorf, prioress at Ebstorf and former nun at Hadmersleben. Out of these seven migrating nuns, two spent the rest of their lives in Lüne, assuming leading positions there; two other nuns stayed for three years; and the three remaining nuns, among them the prioress, spent only a

---

42. Ibid., 113; cf. Johanna Thali, "*Qui vult cum Deo semper esse, frequenter debet orare, frequenter et legere*: Formen und Funktionen des Lesens in der klösterlichen Frömmigkeitskultur," in *Lesevorgänge. Prozesse des Erkennens in mittelalterlichen Texten, Bildern und Handschriften*, ed. Eckart C. Lutz, Martina Backes, and Stefan Matter, Medienwandel—Medienwechsel—Medienwissen 11 (Zürich: Chronos, 2010), 421–58.

43. Klaus Jaintner, "Das Benediktinerinnenkloster Ebstorf im Mittelalter (ca. 1165–1550)," in *Das Benediktinerinnenkloster Ebstorf im Mittelalter: Vorträge einer Tagung im Kloster Ebstorf vom 22.–24. Mai 1987*, ed. Klaus Jaintner (Hildesheim: August Lax, 1988), 1–25, esp. 20f.

brief spell in Lüne.[44] The reform itself began with the celebration of Mass.[45] The manuscripts written in Lüne preserve a remarkable piece of evidence illustrating the importance of the migrating nuns as vehicles of reform. The extremely strict enclosure regulations provided only one reason for which sisters were permitted to leave their cloister: *pro activa vel passiva reformatione*.[46]

About twenty years later, Lüne witnessed further liturgical changes enforced by a prioress who was influenced by the reform.[47] Excerpts from a manuscript of the *Caeremoniale Bursfeldensis*, written either still in Ebstorf or already in Lüne, have been handed down to us.[48] A comparison of this *Caeremoniale* with the manuscripts from men's convents of the Bursfeld Congregation reveals that most sections are the same, but female terms for the officers are used, and the chapter *De sacerdote* has been replaced in the manuscript from Lüne with a chapter *De collectoria*, dealing with the task of the female prayer leader in the Liturgy of the Hours.[49] One of the chronicles from Lüne provides in an initial section plentiful information on the organization of the liturgical year—for instance, the postponement of feasts of saints falling on a Sunday and the introduction of new feasts like that of St. Afra. In addition, special days of procession are mentioned, as well as special memorial Masses. A second section of the manuscript contains information on the burial rites that were presumably modified along the lines of the new liturgical regulations.[50]

Moreover, reform in Lüne found a very specific mode of expression that was regarded—rightly or wrongly—as typically female, namely, the resumption of the manufacture of embroidered tapestries, which had long been made by the nuns.[51] Thus, the first years of the sixteenth century, presided over by Abbess Mechthild Wilde, saw the manufacture of two embroideries for the nuns' choir, an Easter tapestry, and a resurrection tapestry.[52] The two tapestries not only

---

44. Nolte, *Quellen und Studien*, 127; cf. Uffmann, *Wie in einem Rosengarten*, 129.

45. Nolte, *Quellen und Studien*, 127: "Et post missam iuerunt processionaliter ad locum capitularum."

46. Linneborn, "Die Reformation der Benedictinerklöster," 65f.

47. Prioress Mechthild Wilde; see Uffmann, *Wie in einem Rosengarten*, 130.

48. The manuscript itself was burned in Hanover during World War II; Albert, *Caeremoniale Bursfeldenses*, 53.

49. Ibid., 22; Nolte, *Quellen und Studien*, 19f.

50. Cf. Nolte, *Quellen und Studien*, 31f.

51. Tanja Kohwagner-Nikolai, *"Per manus sororum . . .": Niedersächsische Bildstickereien im Klosterstick, 1300–1583* (Munich: Meidenbauer, 2006).

52. Tanja Kohwagner-Nikolai, "Zwischen Thomaszweifel und Nonnenglaube: Gestickte Bildteppiche für die Passions- und Osterzeit aus den Lüneburger Frauenklöstern," in *Passion*

illustrated the biblical stories but expressed a quite self-confident program: the resurrection tapestry shows three encounters of the women with the risen Christ. Christ's instruction that the women were to preach the resurrection is portrayed as an essential impulse of the reform and of the migration of the nuns. This instruction was intended to be right before the nuns' eyes during the celebration of the Divine Office.[53]

The Cistercian nuns at Wienhausen were another community whose reform was influenced by the ideas of the Windesheim Congregation. Johannes Busch, the most important reformer at Windesheim, personally initiated the changes at the Wienhausen convent. Once again migrating nuns set off. In 1469 five nuns left the Cistercian reform convent of Derneburg near Brunswick, among them the abbess and a nun by the name of Susanne Potstock, the future abbess at Wienhausen.[54] The prayer books and liturgical texts written in the wake of the reform have, as yet, been little studied. The late June Mecham has presented two remarkable essays on individual prayer books from Wienhausen.[55] A prayer book surviving in three different copies, the *Dornenkron* (crown of thorns) shows how the nuns at Wienhausen integrated a spiritual reform into their liturgical routine and testifies to the way in which the reforms brought about by the migrating nuns were adopted. Presumably, it was these reformed nuns who brought the meditation on the crown of thorns from Derneburg to Wienhausen, either directly or via another Cistercian community, the convent at Marienrode.[56] The prayer books united private and liturgical prayer, quoting from the liturgy as well as from meditative texts and from collections of prayers by reputable monastic writers.[57] According to the Wienhausen Chronicle, the new abbess brought plenty of liturgical books to Wienhausen with her (or, at later dates, made sure that such books were supplied) in order to have them copied for Wienhausen's own purposes. Many books are mentioned in the

---

und Ostern in den Lüneburger Klöstern, Kloster, ed. Linda Maria Koldau (Ebstorf: Kloster Ebstorf, 2010), 135–56, esp. 143, 153.

53. Ibid., 153f.

54. June L. Mecham, "Reading between the Lines: Compilation, Variation and the Recovery of an Authentic Female Voice in the *Dornenkron* Prayer Books from Wienhausen," *Journal of Medieval History* 29 (2003): 102–28, esp. 125, with an allusion to the reformer Johannes Busch.

55. Ibid., 113f., 116–18; June L. Mecham, "A Northern Jerusalem. Transforming the Spatial Geography of the Convent of Wienhausen," in *Defining the Holy: Sacred Space in Medieval and Early Modern Europe*, ed. Andrew Spicer and Sarah Hamilton (Burlington, VT: Ashgate, 2005), 139–60, esp. 151–53.

56. Mecham, "Reading between the Lines," 125.

57. Ibid., 121.

chronicle, among them antiphonals for the winter and the summer, as well as a breviary for sisters unable to attend the Divine Office in the church.[58] In addition, the nuns at Wienhausen adopted contemporary forms of piety. A pertinent example is provided by two manuscripts that present proposals for accommodating a Via Crucis within the monastic space. Stations of the Cross were established in many German towns and cities in the late fifteenth century.[59] Owing to enclosure, the sisters organized a meditative Way of the Cross in their own compound, thereby creating the possibility of a spiritual journey. June Mecham sums this up as follows: "Performance of the Stations thus dictated that a nun use the material space of the monastic complex, defined and regulated through architectural structures, to construct the imagined spaces of the earthly and heavenly Jerusalem, which were created through a combination of memory, movement and religious art."[60]

The reference to the presence of pious works of art touches on something else that influenced the liturgy in the reformed convents at Wienhausen and elsewhere. The special polychrome decoration of the nuns' choir at Wienhausen is overwhelming to the present day; it is unmistakably related to the liturgy, with particular emphasis on the liturgies of the passion and of Easter.[61] Within the confines of this essay, it is impossible to spell out the significance of the decoration for the history of art and of its relationship to the Divine Office or to the different liturgical celebrations within the year.[62] Suffice it to say here that during the course of the reform, in 1488 the new abbess, according to the chronicle, had the wall paintings in the nuns' choir repainted or restored by three members of her convent.[63] This artistic representation is not simply an illustration of Easter and the Easter liturgy; it is meant to place the liturgical actions of the nuns within the history of salvation as a whole. The program of decoration in the nuns' choir—supplemented by sculptures, stained-glass

---

58. Appuhn, *Chronik und Totenbuch*, 26, 27.

59. Susanne Wegmann, "Der Kreuzweg von Adam Kraft in Nürnberg: Ein Abbild Jerusalems in der Heimat," *Mitteilungen des Vereins für Geschichte der Stadt Nürnberg* 84 (1997): 93–118; cf. Mecham, "A Northern Jerusalem," 140.

60. Ibid., 147.

61. Susanne Wittekind, "Passion und Ostern im Bildprogramm des Wienhäuser Nonnenchores," in *Passion und Ostern in den Lüneburger Klöstern*, ed. Linda Maria Koldau (Ebstorf: Kloster Ebstorf, 2010), 157–86, esp. 160.

62. Ibid., 157, 160f., 174–76.

63. Appuhn, *Chronik und Totenbuch*, 28: "Ao. 1488 hat sie durch 3 Schwestern Gertrud genandt das Chor auffs neue bemahlen lassen. Da sie ao. 1495 einen Ohrt auff dem Chor mit Brettern übersetzen laßen."

windows, and wall paintings in the cloister and in the other monastic buildings, by textiles such as tapestries and antependia,[64] and by manuscripts for private and liturgical use—creates a quasi presence of the pivotal biblical events, which time and again immerses the sisters celebrating the liturgy in the visualization both of monastic history and of the history of salvation.[65] Precisely this reattachment to the roots of their monastic existence in the central act of salvation in Christ motivated the female reformers.

With Wienhausen successfully reformed, the tried and tested principle of migrating nuns was resorted to once again ten years later. In 1479, nuns left Wienhausen for the nearby Cistercian women's convent of Medingen and reformed it on the basis of the ideas developed at Windesheim and Bursfeld.[66] More than forty surviving illuminated manuscripts from Medingen give an impression of the remarkable writing and painting activities sparked off at Medingen by the reform. Moreover, the manuscripts reveal that, in addition to enclosure, the reformers regarded liturgical renewal as a second, equally important element of reform.[67] The manuscripts, most of them small in size, were not only used in the liturgy but could be taken elsewhere by the sisters. The rubrics, for instance, contain the instruction that certain prayers had to be said *dum exis de choro*, that is, on the way from the Liturgy of the Hours to everyday work.[68] These prayer or devotion books, along with the extant liturgical manuscripts, such as psalteries, antiphonals, and so forth, draw on the whole canon of monastic literature, both traditional works and contemporary reform literature. In Medingen also, what is remarkable is the depiction of the Easter events. According to Henrike Lähnemann, "The nuns at Medingen . . . enter Christ's communion with Mary of Magdala and the apostles and together with them encounter Christ and Mary."[69] The scenes convey a "new potential of imagery and significance" and prepare for the "inner vision of Christ during

---

64. Kohwagner-Nikolai, "Zwischen Thomaszweifel und Nonnenglaube," 153f.; Marianne Schmidt, "Der Osterteppich aus Kloster Lüne. Ein Bild der Liturgie und der Theologie der Osternacht," in *Jahrbuch des Museums für Kunst und Gewerbe Hamburg* 13 (1994/96): 55–86; Angela Karstensen, *Der Auferstehungsteppich zu Kloster Lüne. Bildtradition und Singularität* (Münster: LIT, 2009).

65. Wittekind, "Passion und Ostern," 185.

66. Lähnemann, "Der Auferstandene im Dialog," 105; cf. Uffmann, *Wie in einem Rosengarten*, 133.

67. See the website on the Medingen research project (http://research.ncl.ac.uk/medingen/public_extern) with a complete bibliography and a catalogue of the manuscripts.

68. Lähnemann, "Der Auferstandene im Dialog," 106.

69. Ibid., 129.

the performance of the liturgy."[70] Given the similarity of many manuscripts to text and images from Wienhausen and Lüne, Medingen too exemplifies the importance of the personal transfer of liturgical ideas, images, and books through the migrating nuns.

III. Migrating Nuns—Migrating Liturgy

Traditionally, investigations of the liturgical history of the Middle Ages focus above all on the written outcome of liturgical practice. Perceiving and interpreting liturgy as codified in books seems to be the best way of reconstructing historical forms of liturgical practice and their geographical migrations. Thus, wherever the surviving historical records are in short supply or lack useful information, scholars quickly reach the boundary of historical knowledge. Late medieval women's convents have handed down to posterity only a few codices explicitly and exclusively intended for use in the liturgy. Rendering visible channels of personal transmission widens the possibilities of detecting liturgical migrations. The Divine Office in the Dominican women's convents and in the convents of the Bursfeld and Windesheim congregations changed only when personal initiative came into play. The migrating nuns taught their new sisters first of all Latin, then singing, writing, painting, and embroidering—thus transplanting their own practice of liturgy into the convent to be reformed. The implementation of these new liturgical practices, however, is not restricted to the Divine Office but is reflected in renewed types of private prayer and devotion. Evidence of this liturgy in migration, far from being confined to the world of books, includes paintings, tapestries, prayer books, concepts of space, chronicles, sculptures, and the nuns themselves, whose spiritual and liturgical identity changed: human relics of a liturgy in migration.

---

70. Ibid., 129.

5

"From Many Different Sources": The Formation of the Polish and Lithuanian Reformed Liturgy

Kazimierz Bem

I. *The Early Years: 1550–95*

Tradition places the first public celebration of the Lord's Supper in the Reformed fashion in Pińczów, a private town in Lesser Poland (Małopolska), on 25 November 1550.[1] Only a month earlier its owner, Mikołaj Oleśnicki, had installed Francesco Stancaro as the town's pastor, expelled the Pauline friars and Catholic priests, and purged the town's churches of images and altars.[2] In November Oleśnicki convened the first national synod, attended by a handful of Protestant nobles and their clergy. The ministers, under the leadership of the savvy and learned Mantuan, adopted the 1543 Cologne Confession of Faith. It was then and there that the Protestant-inclined priest Jakub Sylvius[3] celebrated publicly, for the first time, the Lord's Supper in the Reformed fashion in Poland.

---

1. *Akta Synodów Różnowierczych w Polsce 1550–1559* (Warsaw: Państwowe Wydawnictwo Naukowe, 1966), 2 (hereafter ASR 1; all translations from Polish sources are done by the author). However, we know of individual nobles who established private Protestant congregations in their chapels and castles as early as 1547 (e.g., Jerzy Jazłowiecki in Jazłowiec in Podole).

2. Jacek Pielas, *Oleśniccy herbu Dębno w XVI I XVII wieku: Studium z dziejów zamożnej szlachty doby nowożytnej* (Kielce: Akademia Świętokrzyska, 2007), 151–56.

3. Agnieszka Biedrzycka and Jan Szturc, "Jakub Sylvius (zm. po 1583)," in *Polski Słownik Biograficzny* 46 (Kraków: Polskiej Akademii Umiejętności, 2009), 215–18 (hereafter PSB).

101

The acts of the first synod are surprisingly laconic about the form used, saying only, "Cena vere Dominica primo publice celebrata est per Iacobum Sylvium tunc ecclesiae Piniczoviensis pastorem."[4] Given Francesco Stancaro's presence, we can assume that he was instrumental not only in presenting a confession but also in suggesting a liturgy. We cannot say anything more with certainty about its form—in fact, we cannot even be certain that it was celebrated in Polish and not in Latin.[5] We should bear in mind that some of the nobles had been fostering a Lutheran-inspired reform on their estates, a legacy of their studies in Wittenberg or Leipzig or of their stay at the Lutheran court in Konigsberg, Prussia,[6] and Stancaro too was at this point sympathetic to Lutheranism. Whatever liturgy was used, it was probably not of a classical Reformed nature.[7] The Roman Catholic polemicist Orzechowski (clearly confusing the events of late 1550 and the summer of 1551) claims that Stancaro "began to establish the *error of Zwingli*. . . . According to these precepts he ordered that images be removed from the church, [and] an outlandish Lord's Supper be instituted in place of the usual one." Orzechowski insists that this was not done owing to fear of the king and that "for the present it was thought best to institute the Lord's Supper, but this should be only done privately in the castle, not publicly in the church. . . . In accordance with this view they permitted Stancaro to appoint the manner of the new Supper and to teach the use of it."[8] Orzechowski was probably correct in saying that a "foreign" liturgy was used, but he was wrong when he identified it as Zwingli's liturgy. Based on what we know of Stancaro and his theological views in the early 1550s, we can assume that some variant of Hermann von Wied's "Consultation" was employed. This

---

4. ASR 1:2.

5. The synod's minutes were kept in Latin until the 1580s. Only the Brethren in Greater Poland used Polish from the beginning.

6. Like Stancaro, the noble Stanisław Lasocki (d. 1563) had studied in Leipzig and Wittenberg, Stanisław Szafraniec (1530-98) was brought up and studied in Konigsberg at the Lutheran court of Prince Albrecht, and Krzystof Pilecki was accused of forcing Catholic clergy in his town of Łańcut to celebrate "Lutheran" ceremonies, which no doubt met with sympathy from the numerous German-speaking colonists there.

7. Darius Petkunas, *Holy Communion Rites in the Polish and Lithuanian Reformed Agendas of the 16th and Early 17th Centuries* (Klaipeda: Klaipedos Universitetas, 2007), 63–69.

8. Stanisław Lubieniecki, *History of the Polish Reformation: And Nine Related Documents*, trans. and ed. George Huntston Williams (Minneapolis, MN: Fortress Press, 1995), 105 (emphasis mine).

would explain the word "outlandish" (*peregrinam*) used to describe it.[9] We have no evidence for the claim that Stancaro and the others were using Zwingli's liturgy at this time, or at any other point for that matter.

Any development of this new church was thwarted in February of 1551 when Oleśnicki, under pressure from the king, allowed the monks to return to their monastery, reinstating Catholic Mass in the church and convent. The Protestant ministers were dispersed to Prussia (Stancaro), Silesia (Sylvius), and Lithuania (Zacjusz). Only Marcin Krowicki stayed, preaching and celebrating the sacraments in the castle chapel. When Oleśnicki once again expelled the monks in the summer of 1551 (this time permanently), Krowicki moved his services into the main church and then into the monastery church as well. However, for fear of persecution by the bishop of Kraków, he was forced in 1553 to flee to Wittenberg.[10] During the next few years the Reformation in Lesser Poland fell into chaos, becoming a highly decentralized, individualistic movement; this naturally did little to provide for a common liturgical practice. In fact, the years 1551–54 saw a growing radicalization on the part of both nobility and Reform-minded clergy. In the meantime Stancaro worked on his liturgy and had it published in 1552 in Frankfurt/Oder as *Canones Reformationis Ecclesiam Polonicarum*. This was translated, expanded, and published in Polish in 1553 as *Porządek naprawienia w kościelech naszych*.[11] As Petkunas rightly pointed out, it is more a directory than a set liturgy, with visible traces of Catholic ritual. Given that it was published in a Lutheran town, this is hardly surprising.[12] By the time the next Reformed synod met in November of 1554 in Słomniki, Stancaro's work seemed too conservative to many of the freshly converted nobles. It was criticized for intemperate language, and the nobleman Stadnicki suggested that it be burned. Nevertheless, the Reformed movement in Lesser Poland was in desperate need of uniformity of faith and worship, so those gathered accepted Stancaro's liturgy. This acceptance was probably understood to be for a limited time as the synod also resolved to begin talks with the Czech Brethren about a possible church union. It is doubtful whether Stancaro's *Porządek* was ever implemented in the Lesser Polish Reformed

---

9. The word might also suggest a version of the Basel liturgy, which Stancaro would have encountered during his 1540 stay in the town. Given the preference for the 1543 Cologne Confession and the still strong Lutheran sympathies of nobles and Stancaro, this does not seem probable.

10. Henryk Barycz, "Marcin Krowicki," PSB 15 (1970), 350–53.

11. It seems that all the copies of the Polish edition of 1553 printed in Kraków were burned.

12. Petkunas, *Holy Communion Rites*, 66–68.

Church to any wider extent; just one copy of it survives.[13] The talks with the Brethren in Greater Poland proceeded swiftly. The Brethren, first approached in March of 1555 in Krzęcice, were glad to hear of the Polish Protestants' zeal for unity but cautioned them to proceed slowly. The Lesser Poland Reformed would have none of it, and in April of 1555 they came to Koźminek, a center of the Brethren in Poland, where they forced themselves into an ecclesiastical and liturgical union with the Brethren.[14] When it came to liturgical questions, the Lesser Poles were remarkably candid, if not cavalier. They "desired" to adopt the Brethren's customs, but since there were not enough copies for them to take home and study, they suggested taking a closer look at them later. The Poles added a caveat: "And if these books are according to God's Word truly and rightly written, we will receive them gladly, and what we might not like about them, we will tell you so."[15] Naturally, the Brethren were not impressed and insisted that for a theological union to be effective it must entail liturgical unity as well. In the end, the more experienced Brethren acknowledged that this might take a while, and the Lesser Brethren agreed to work on implementing the Brethren liturgies: "Fourthly, that ceremonies in their [Lesser Poland Reformed] churches and congregations in all matters as are used by the Brethren are slowly to be led in. And for that end we have agreed to give them oversight so that they may in all these be strengthened and may all, with their congregations, unite with us. They also agreed that in all their counsels and needs to seek and use Brother Jerzy Izrael and our elders. To confirm that, they went with us to the eating of the Lord's Supper."[16]

During the Synod of Secemin in January of 1556, the Koźminek union was to be implemented by the Lesser Poland Reformed.[17] The synod did accept the Brethren liturgy and ordered ministers to follow it closely, but at the same time it also began to look west to Melanchthon, Calvin, and Jan Łaski for leadership. The synod was presided over by a lay delegate rather than by an ordained minister as in the Brethren fashion, a clear indication that the Lesser Polish Reformed were not all in agreement with the union, even if they elected three ministers to the position of seniors, following the Brethren fashion. Again, Lesser Polish uniqueness was reinforced when those assembled kept Feliks

---

13. ASR 1:2–3; Janusz T. Maciuszko, "Poglądy religijne Mikołaja Reja," in *Mikołaj Rej z Nagłowic: W pięćsetna rocznicę urodzin* (Kielce: n.p., 2005), 287–308.
14. ASR 1:5–45.
15. ASR 1:28.
16. ASR 1:41.
17. ASR 1:46–52.

Cruciger as their superintendent, a position not known in Brethren polity.[18] Regarding liturgical matters, no mention is made of the distribution of copies of the Brethren liturgy, which they intended to implement.

During the Synod of Pińczów in May of 1556, Brethren delegates and the supporters of the Union of Koźminek faced clear opposition. The clergy—notably the senior Sylvius and Linsmann—disliked both rites and theology. Sylvius described the liturgy bluntly as "way too long and not uplifting."[19] The Brethren realized, with some astonishment, that the Lesser Polish Reformed were "between Calvinists and Zwinglians" in their understanding of the Lord's Supper.[20] Objections were made not just to the understanding of the Lord's Supper, clerical celibacy, and the requirement that Brethren clergy work manually, but also to the public form of exercising church discipline. The synod ended in a stalemate. On the one hand, the Union of Koźminek was officially reaffirmed, and the Brethren were asked to teach the Lesser Polish clergy. At the same time, those assembled wrote to Calvin and Łaski, inviting them to come to Poland and to reform the Polish church. The bitter Brethren delegates wrote, "And thus we have seen that some of those lords and ministers hold this Koźminek union as if an eel by its tail and treat it lightly"[21] and then remarked sarcastically, "Calvin is for them as God, and whatever he says is accepted by them as true with no opposition or turning back."[22]

The differences between the Lesser Poles and the Brethren became clearer during a meeting of clergy from both sides in Krzęcice the following week.[23] Many issues were discussed, including the question of whether the Lord's Supper could be celebrated before the altars and images were removed from the churches. Marcin Krowicki stated, "When I was sent to Włodzisław by my elders, seeing that there were none from amongst the plebs who knew God's truth, I indulged them as little children; with the consent of my brothers I preached in a surplice, and bore the paintings, for more than half a year. Only when they began to accept the God's truth did I abandon the surplice, and the paintings [I] threw away without unnecessary scandal."[24] This commonsense

18. ASR 1:51–52.
19. ASR 1:70.
20. ASR 1:73.
21. ASR 1:73.
22. ASR 1:74.
23. ASR 1:114–71.
24. ASR 1:111. This is the first (and only) mention of vestment changes in the Lesser Polish church, indicating that Reform-minded ministers wanted to abandon the surplice.

attitude was met with approval from the Brethren, who remarked that in their churches "in Ostroróg and Koźminek images stayed for a long while, until the folk learned God's truth. Then we covered them with sheets, and when the folks cared less for them we took them down from the altars and railings and hid them in secret places, so they would not impede those more foggy in their faith."[25] In the following days the Brethren faced opposition to the union from certain ministers, headed by Stanisław Sarnicki.[26] When they accused him of being too lax and administering the Lord's Supper too generously, he retorted, "Who might know another's heart? I am not God to know it. And if I were not to serve [Communion] but only to those who made this agreement [the Koźminek Union], then only one [minister] would be needed in this region of Kraków; we would all not be needed."[27] These Lesser Polish ministers also acknowledged that "we do not keep all ceremonies . . . that you have, like the shaking of the hand with each other in Baptism, and then with the minister. Also with the Lord's Supper, some things are omitted and some are kept, because some of us did not have your agendas so that we could use them and be governed by them from the beginning. And thus the folk, and the ministers too, are used to some ceremonies that we shall keep."[28] Wisely, the Brethren were a bit more accommodating this time. However, with Jan Łaski on his way to Poland, their influence was waning among the nobility, and some clergy were becoming more hostile.[29] The arrival of Jan Łaski changed everything. Despite having repeatedly confirmed the Union of Koźminek, the Lesser Poland Reformed gave it to him for reconsideration and the amendments he thought necessary.[30] Not surprisingly, the 15–18 June 1557 Synod of Włodzisław was not a mellow one.[31] When the Brethren arrived in Włodzisław they remarked that "we saw the fashion of their service, simply different from ours in ceremonies, singing, exhortation, praying, and in preaching."[32] This did little to placate the Brethren, already annoyed with the duplicity of the Lesser Polish Reformed.

    25. ASR 1:113.
    26. Halina Kowalska and Janusz Sikorski, "Stanisław Sarnicki (1532–1597)," PSB 35 (1994), 217–23.
    27. ASR 1:148.
    28. ASR 1:153.
    29. Henryk Gmiterek, "Probelmy unifikacji liturgii braci czeskich i kalwinów w Rzeczpospolitej XVI–XVII w.," Annales universitatis Mariae Curie-Skłodowska 40 (1985): F 98–99.
    30. ASR 1:173 (in January 1557).
    31. ASR 1:179–207.
    32. ASR 1:195.

Łaski did manage to convince the Brethren of his good will, but from then on Łaski's *Forma ac Ratio* became the standard. Its use began to spread in Lesser Poland and, following his 1557 visit to Mikołaj Radziwiłł ("the Black"), in the Grand Duchy of Lithuania as well.[33] As the Lesser Polish admitted frankly a few years later to the Brethren, "When we learned of Stancaro's *Reformatio* we took it to be gold. Then your Brethren was far better to our liking. But the reverend Łaski even more. May you Brethren not hold it against us, that when we see something better thanks to the Grace of God, we accept it, and you Brethren should do so with us."[34]

The next few years pushed liturgical questions into the background. Łaski was trying to forge a theological union between the Brethren, the Calvinists, and the Lutherans, and so liturgical differences were secondary. Owing to Łaski's influence, use of his liturgy spread in the Lesser Polish church and beyond.[35] This was not to say that it was always well received: the September synod of 1558 in Włodzisław admitted that ministers and faithful alike were resisting some of its forms, and it twice admonished the ministers of the Reformed churches in Poland to conform and unify their liturgies based on Łaski's *Forma*.[36] This was especially important because this synod included the delegates of the Podlasie district of the Lithuanian Reformed Church, as well as delegates from the Chełm region in the east of Poland. Thus, copies of Łaski's *Forma* could have been sent home with those delegates for dissemination and implementation.[37] The issue of liturgical practice resurfaced briefly during the June 1559 synod in Pińczów. The Lesser Polish Calvinists met with a delegate from the Calvinist churches in the northern region of Kujawy and agreed in principle that the Lord's Supper "should be simple and humbly celebrated after the example of Christ, not pompous like the popish with their Masses and their superstitions—also not too difficult in ceremony, but adorned with the truth of God's word."[38] This is very interesting since we know from later

---

33. Petkunas, *Holy Communion Rites*, 156; Michael S. Springer, *Restoring Christ's Church: John a Lasco and the* Forma ac ratio (Burlington, VT: Ashgate 2007), 135–41.

34. *Akta Synodów Różnowierczych w Polsce (1560–1570)* (Warsaw: Państwowe Wydawnictwo Naukowe, 1972), 103 (hereafter ASR 2).

35. It was not fully translated into Polish until the twenty-first century—the first full Polish translation appeared in 2004: Jan Łaski, *Forma i całkowity porządek kościelnego posługiwania* (Warsaw: Wydawnictwo Naukowe Semper, 2004), 6. Petkunas does not mention this fact.

36. ASR 2:271, 279.

37. Petkunas, *Holy Communion Rites*, 157; Petkunas insists that this decision did not affect Lithuania, with which I strongly disagree.

38. ASR 1:302.

sources that the Reformed churches in Kujawy did not adopt Łaski's liturgy. Communion in the Kujawy churches was from the beginning received standing, as opposed to the Lutherans and the Brethren, who knelt.[39] No details were spelled out, but the Kujawy Calvinists were allowed to keep their own liturgy. Even after Łaski's death his liturgy was prescribed as the official form of the new church. When some ministers raised objections to it, those assembled resolved that "until such a time when by the grace of God all the churches in Poland are properly reformed," it was to be the liturgy used and followed.[40] The *Forma ac Ratio* was probably the one sent to the churches in Podole (in southern Poland by the Moldavian border), as well as to the heavily Reformed regions of Zator and Oświęcim, by the October 1560 Synod of Książ.[41] Łaski's liturgy for installing elders was explicitly reaffirmed during the January 1561 synod in Pińczów, when his son-in-law Stanisław Lutomirski (ca.1520–75)[42] was elected the new superintendent of Lesser Poland's Reformed Church.[43]

In the years from 1561 to 1595 we find very few references to liturgical matters in the Reformed camp.[44] We know that Łaski's liturgy continued to spread, probably by ministers making individual translations for their congregations' use. The practice of taking the Lord's Supper while seated took root, even in the congregations that went over to the Unitarian camp.[45] With theological differences apparently too subtle for most to detect, the Reformed in Lesser Poland and Lithuania needed a way of differentiating themselves from Unitarians. By the 1570s, perhaps under the influence of the Kujawy Calvinists, the Reformed began to promote the receiving of Communion standing. The Kraków synod of 1573, where tellingly the Kujawy Calvinist delegates were

---

39. ASR 2:195–56.

40. ASR 2:4.

41. ASR 2:38–39. The Latin minutes of the synod are very laconic. The Polish version written by the Brethren is more vivid but concentrates on the question of church discipline (or lack of it) in the Lesser Polish church and the heavy hand of the nobles in running it.

42. Halina Kowalska, "Stanisław Lutomirski (ca.1520–1575)," PSB 18 (1973), 144–46.

43. ASR 2:77, 91.

44. These years saw the Lesser Poland and Lithuanian Reformed churches engulfed in the Arian controversy. In December of 1561 Sylvius handed over the records to the Arian-inclined Lutomirski, and the taking of minutes ceased altogether. Thus, we have almost no materials to trace the development of liturgical practice in Lesser Poland's churches during this time. The minutes of the Lithuanian churches were burned during the anti-Protestant pogrom of 1611 in Wilno.

45. The Unitarians also accepted other parts of his liturgy, as Moskorzowski's 1646 Socinian Agenda testifies. See Petkunas, *Holy Communion Rites*, 157.

present, made it mandatory for the people to receive Communion standing and not seated.[46] This was reiterated during the 1583 synod in Włodzisław.[47] In 1566 the ministers agreed to administer the Lord's Supper quarterly, no doubt under Swiss influence.[48] Apart from frequency and the proper posture of the faithful while communicating, little else was agreed upon in those years. Both the Sandomir Agreement and the Confession of 1570 are strikingly silent regarding ceremonies and liturgical matters.[49] Given that they both tried to reconcile three different theologies of the Lord's Supper—Brethren, Lutheran, and Reformed—this is no surprise. In the chaotic and highly decentralized atmosphere of the Polish Reformed Church there were many variants in local church practice from the standard Łaski liturgy.

II. Kraiński's Forma of 1599 and 1601 in Lesser Poland

In his book Petkunas argues that it was during the July 1594 Lublin district synod[50] that the discussion regarding liturgies began. Those assembled desired uniformity in worship for their area, a request accepted in 1595, endorsed by the church of the whole province in 1599, and finally resulting in a new form in the 1601 version.[51] In his opinion, the Agenda was the product of Krzysztof Kraiński[52] (though the material was not), through whose erudition and influence it was accepted as the basis for liturgies in the whole Lesser Polish Brethren church.[53] There are a number of problems with this interpretation. First, the wording of the 1594 minutes does not necessarily mean that diverse practices existed in the Lublin district. In fact, it could be interpreted in the opposite way. The sentence reads as follows: "The form of serving the sacraments is to be agreed upon during the next synod, and there, if anything should require correction, we will agree on it."[54] Notice the "if"—in order to have corrections, something must need to be corrected. The future synod mentioned was the

---

46. *Akta Synodów Różnowierczych w Polsce: Małopolska 1571–1632* (Warsaw: Państwowe Wydawnictwo Naukowe, 1983), 12–13 (hereafter ASR 3).
47. ASR 3:79, 82.
48. ASR 2:203, 320.
49. ASR 2:251–304.
50. Petkunas mentions district synods, but he forgets to mention which ones—here it is that of the Lublin district of the Polish Reformed Church.
51. Petkunas, *Holy Communion Rites*, 115.
52. Janusz Tazbir, "Krzysztof Kraiński (1556–1618)," PSB 15 (1970), 92–93.
53. Petkunas, *Holy Communion Rites*, 115–25.
54. ASR 3:105.

Toruń synod of 1595, where the Reformed, Lutherans, and Czech Brethren were in attendance.[55] The district's delegation was headed by Kraiński himself and by the district's superintendent, Franciszek Jezierski.[56] It would be hard to imagine that they went to the synod with a plethora of rites from their region rather than one agreed-upon liturgy; we know of only one liturgical variant in the Lublin district, that centering on whether the Lord's Supper was to be received standing or kneeling.[57]

It would seem that by this time the Lublin Reformed had already achieved some measure of liturgical unity. This claim is, I think, reinforced by the fact that none of the Lublin district's minutes or church visitation records mention divergent liturgical practices.[58] If a wide range of liturgical practices had existed in the Lublin district before 1594, the absence of any complaints about this would be strange. All this taken together seems to suggest that some local liturgical uniformity had been achieved in the Lublin district before 1581, the date from which we have existing records. A peculiar note from a 1566 gathering of the seniors of the Lesser Polish and Lithuanian Reformed in Włodzisław reads as follows (my English translation mirrors closely the peculiarities of the Polish text):

> Concerning rites of the administrating of the sacraments. Moreover, as frequent alterations of the conformity of the sacred rites/ceremonies are unto a stumbling block for simpletons, for that reason the concealment of all of them is to be uniformly preserved by all of those in the sacred ministry. Verily, the rites are to be emplaced by the seniors in [the mode of] the utmost temperance, whose edification let it serve, on account of which reverence let be carried over to the administration of the mysteries of God, they have ordained as needing to be fashioned [as] in the wine press. Moreover for however long the private sheets of paper of the ceremony are written, for such a length of time the major changes will provide that which moreover will glorify itself, not likewise the contrary. But consequently there will be a future synod, which is assigned after the festival days of the Birth of the Lord, the extended volume [book] of the ecclesial ordinal the senior brothers will carry out.[59]

---

55. Wojciech Sławiński, *Toruński Synod Generalny 1595 roku* (Warsaw: Wydawnictwo Naukowe Semper, 2002), 147–56.
56. Lech Szczucki, "Franciszek Jezierski (zm. 1616/1617)," PSB 11 (1961), 200.
57. ASR 3:105.
58. ASR 3:44–74, 85–95, 103–5.
59. ASR 2:202–3.

Despite its clumsy Latin (which I tried to show in the translation), this is a very interesting passage. It suggests that despite promulgating Łaski's liturgy, some ministers continued to experiment with it—adding or subtracting as they saw fit—each having his own "sheet" or liturgy. The lack of any official translation of the *Forma* into Polish only encouraged such behavior. The ministers were ordered to hand over their sheets to the seniors, who were in charge of unifying the liturgies, at least in their own districts, in anticipation of a synod (which never took place). Such an endeavor could perhaps have been entrusted to Krzysztof Kraiński. We know little of his previous life, but by 1594, when he was appointed minister to the prestigious Lublin congregation, he must have had some influence. I would argue that it came from his work on the successful unification of the Lublin Reformed liturgies. We do not know how long this project took, but it must have involved careful inquiries into the liturgical fashions of the churches in Lublin, Bełz, and Chełm, as well as foreign ones.[60] The region boasted Dutch- and Swiss-educated nobles with extensive libraries containing theological books from the West, which he probably could consult.[61] We know that the Heidelberg Catechism began to exert strong influence on Polish Reformed catechisms at that time, and it would be odd if the Palatinate liturgy did not do so as well.[62] In fact, when Kraiński's liturgy was revised in 1601 its many sources were explicitly acknowledged: "Having looked zealously into the Form published in 1599, by our beloved brother Reverend Krzysztof Kraiński, which he has gathered *from many different forms* but agreeing in form and matter to God's Word. . . ."[63] Also, Kraiński himself mentions in the introduction to his liturgy that these new forms were in agreement with French, English, Scottish, Hungarian, Swiss, and Dutch forms and liturgies.[64] Finally, Kraiński took as his starting point not Łaski's *Forma* but rather some

---

60. The Bełz district was formed from the Lublin district in 1599, but the churches in the Chełm area stayed within the Lublin district; this means that all these areas had been using more or less the same liturgy (ASR 3:205).

61. Krzysztof Kraiński befriended the bibliophile members of the Słupecki family, educated in Basel, Heidelberg, and Leiden. When Feliks Słupecki (ca.1571–1616), later castellan of Żarnów, established a Reformed school in his town of Opole Lubelskie in 1598, he named Kraiński its head teacher. Their contact, however, must have dated to years before that, and Kraiński presumably used their extensive theological library in his endeavors. See Henryk Gmiterek, "Feliks Słupecki (ok. 1571–1616) kasztelan żarnowski," PSB 39 (1999): 102–5.

62. Dariusz Kuźmina, *Katechizmy w Rzeczypospolitej w XVI i początku XVII wieku* (Warsaw: n.p., 2002), 107–13.

63. *Porządek Nabożeństwa*, 1602 (emphasis mine).

64. *Porządek Nabożeństwa*, 1599, 83.

local liturgy, which he then creatively expanded on his own. To summarize: Kraiński's 1599 *Forma* was the fruit of an earlier harmonization of liturgy effected by the Lublin district of the Lesser Polish Reformed Church sometime between 1566 and 1581. While Kraiński was doubtless the author of most of the prayers and the editor of the final text, he used other liturgical sources, with Łaski's *Forma ac Ratio* neither the only nor the most important one. Kraiński was well aware of the liturgies in other Reformed churches in Europe.

No doubt it was Kraiński who pressed for liturgical uniformity in the Lesser Polish church. During the October 1598 synod in Ożarów he was elected superintendent of that church, and he convinced the others to pursue liturgical uniformity. During that same synod a surprising number of decisions were made in liturgical matters, unlike any previous Lesser Polish synod. Those gathered decided that each congregation should have its own Communion set (tray, chalice, baptismal basin, table cloth) and a Bible. They denounced the use of crucifixes and exorcisms and instructed that the Lord's Supper be celebrated at least four times a year, with permission to do so more often if "edifying." Krzysztof Kraiński's *Forma* was to be given to other seniors for review.[65] Owing to the lack of records, we cannot tell what each district thought of the *Forma*. We only know that the Chęciny (Kraków) district was not impressed and wanted it verified against Łaski's *Forma*.[66] During the next provincial synod, held in Ożarów in 1600, a special seven-person committee was appointed to study the *Forma*; this included a Brethren minister working in Baranów Sanodmierski.[67] The committee met in Czyżów in November that year and revised the 1599 *Forma* considerably.[68] It produced a unified liturgy so quickly that the Lublin delegates assembled at their district's synod in Kock in February of 1601 could already study it.[69] The Chęciny (Kraków) district synod approved the new liturgy and set aside a whole day so that ministers could make copies of it for their use.[70] The liturgy was finally approved during the 1601 provincial synod in Włodzisław, with the district seniors charged with making sure it was enforced.[71] The printed version came out in 1602 and was soon distributed to

---

65. ASR 3:197–98.
66. ASR 3:215.
67. ASR 3:217–18. Petkunas lists only four members, clearly a mistake (*Holy Communion Rites*, 117).
68. Petkunas, *Holy Communion Rites*, 116–20.
69. ASR 3:220.
70. ASR 3:221.
71. ASR 3:229.

the local synods—the Lublin district called it "sacrosanct," no doubt pleased with its input in this endeavor.[72] The provincial synod of 1602 once again affirmed it as the binding liturgical form for all districts.[73] Lesser Poland now had a unified liturgy—almost fifty years after its formation. Of course, its implementation took a while.

Now that they had their own unified liturgy, the Lesser Polish Reformed were confronted with two problems: rooting out any Catholic, or even Lutheran, vestiges in their own churches and reasserting themselves over and against the Brethren ministers who had started taking pulpits in Lesser Poland sponsored by their magnate patrons. In 1603 the Chęciny district synod ordered the sizeable congregation in Gorlice to cease using "ceremonies differing from our congregations' ceremonies, to which the folk have stubbornly attached themselves and which they are used to."[74] We have good reason to suspect these were Lutheran. The minister serving Gorlice from 1570 until at least 1595 was an ex-Catholic priest, and the bishop's visitation lists the congregation as Lutheran rather than Reformed. Given Gorlice's proximity to the border and the thriving Lutheran congregations in Slovakia, Lutheran influences and liturgy in that town would not be surprising.[75] In 1612 the Reformed in the Lublin district were very much annoyed when they found out that "in some congregations the bells are rung when the *Credo* is sung," and they asked that the provincial synod correct this error.[76] The provincial synod that met the same year in Ożarów complied and stated in its canon no. 6 that "in all congregations there should be order and sobriety, *citra superstitionem et idolatriam*, which *pastores loci* should attend to."[77] No exact details of places or customs were mentioned, unfortunately, and we do not know which congregations these minutes were discussing. For the next decade or so, no liturgical problems were mentioned in the minutes. Only during the provincial synod in Gliniany in 1624 did those assembled state again, "The order prescribed in the Agenda congregations are to follow in everything, especially before the service

---

72. ASR 3:236.
73. ASR 3:241.
74. ASR 3:244.
75. Mariusz Pawelec, *Bartłomiej Bythner starszy (ok. 1559–1629)* (Warsaw: Wydawnictwo Naukowe Semper, 2008), 82.
76. ASR 3:333.
77. ASR 3:336.

of the Lord's Supper."⁷⁸ Clearly, by that time Kraiński's *Forma* was followed more or less faithfully in all the congregations in the province.

A bigger challenge to Lesser Polish Reformed liturgical uniformity proved to be the trend of Greater Poland magnates and their chaplains moving to Lesser Poland.⁷⁹ When Andrzej Leszczyński moved to Baranów Sandomierski with his Brethren minister, Maciej Rybiński (1566–1612)⁸⁰ was quick to introduce Brethren liturgy and discipline in the town. Later, when Leszczyński inherited the Beresteczko estates in Volhynia (Wołyń) he installed there two ministers from the Brethren. Further, his sisters, after marrying into local families, brought their own Brethren chaplains with them and installed them on their estates. The Reformed resented this intrusion and demanded that the Brethren ministers present letters to the local Calvinist seniors for approval. Naturally, the Brethren would have none of that. Initially, the Brethren spoke from a superior position: their convocation in Gołuchów (1596) stated curtly that "he was sent properly by seniors of our confession and did not need or does not need a recommendation from anything or anyone else"⁸¹ and pressed on, "*Iurisdictiam* of seniors, as well as ceremonies used in congregations, not countries or lands, but confessions, to which the patron [adheres] the congregation and minister, *modum prescribere solent*."⁸²

The conflict was palpable throughout the early 1600s. In 1602 the noble Feliks Słupecki, married to Barbara Leszczyńska, asked his Reformed district for permission to call a Brethren pastor to his estate in Opole Lubelskie. This was granted, though with an important caveat: that the minister "be sent not with ceremonies [Brethren liturgy] but for ceremonies, not with government [Brethren church discipline] but to govern."⁸³ The latter's suspicion was not unfounded: at the same time, the Brethren agreed to send a minister to the lord Słupecki "to serve with *our* ceremonies."⁸⁴ The Brethren ministers in

78. ASR 3:462–63.
79. Henryk Gmiterek, "Duchowni Jednoty Braci Czeskich w zborach kalwińskich Małopolski i Litwy w pierwszej połowie XVII. wieku," *Historica: Acta Universitatis Palackianae Olomucensis Facultas philosophica (Historica Sborník prací historických)* 31 (2002): 157–64.
80. Henryk Gmieterk, "Maciej Rybiński (1566–1612)," PSB 33 (1992), 339–40.
81. *Akta Synodów Różnowierczych w Polsce: Wielkopolska (1569–1632)* (Warsaw: Wydawnictwo Uniwersytetu Warszawskiego, 1997), 118 (hereafter ASR 4).
82. ASR 4:118.
83. ASR 3:236.
84. ASR 4:169 (emphasis mine); Halina Kowalska, "Barbara z Leszczyńskich Słupecka (ok. 1582–1652)," PSB 39 (1999), 101–2; Henryk Gmiterek, "Feliks Słupecki h Rawa (ok. 1571–1616)," PSB 39 (1999), 102–5.

Baranów were notorious for ignoring the local Reformed synods, which did little to endear the local Calvinists to them. By 1610 the relations became quite tense—the Brethren synod of 1610 tersely stated that they were "full [fed up] of Rev. Kraiński's personal attacks."[85] In the end, Protestant solidarity and goodwill prevailed, no doubt rekindled after the civil war of 1606–9, which proved to be disastrous for Polish Protestants. A 1615 meeting of the leaders of the two churches finally worked out a resolution to these conflicts. Under this compromise the Brethren agreed to send no ministers to Lesser Poland without the local senior asking for him first. Once a Brethren minister was installed, he was to take part in the local synods and conform to the local liturgies.[86] Thus, by the 1620s the Reformed Church in Lesser Poland achieved liturgical conformity; moreover, it managed to enforce its liturgical customs on the Brethren ministers serving in the area.

III. Liturgical Developments in the Brethren Churches

Compared to the long, conflicted development of liturgy in Lesser Poland, worship in Brethren churches located in Greater Poland (Wielkopolska) was surprisingly uniform. The Brethren simply used their own liturgy. Minutes of the Brethren's synods mention few liturgical discrepancies. We do know that where the Brethren took over former Roman Catholic churches, side altars were removed, while the main altars were retained for a while to make the transition gradual and less shocking to "simpletons."[87] Only during the 1573 synod in Poznan were the ministers told to "cleanse idolatrous things from churches and sell them with the consent of patrons,"[88] a provision that was repeated at the synod two years later.[89] Underneath the surface of uniformity, however, were minor discrepancies.[90] We know that the laity wanted the Brethren to

---

85. ASR 4:225.
86. ASR 3:346–47.
87. ASR 1:113.
88. ASR 4:17.
89. ASR 4:41.
90. In 1608 a local patron, Adam Grodzicki (d. 1647), complained that the minister on his estate had introduced a new confessional liturgy. This, he claimed, "is actually good, but this custom seems to have been taken from the papacy and thus fosters the suspicion that we learn from papists." The minister in question was spoken to "in private," but it is not at all clear from the record that he was actually told to stop using it. Ironically, the patron so diligent in keeping watch for popish liturgical innovations himself converted to Roman Catholicism less than a decade later. Włodzimierz Dworzaczek, "Adam Grodzicki (zm. 1647)," PSB 8 (1960),

change the custom of praying quietly and demanded that prayers be said out loud. This demand was repeated in 1577, 1579, and 1600.[91] The seniors steadfastly refused, claiming this was not their church's custom, but they were out of touch with not only the faithful but also their parish clergy. That individual ministers simply introduced unison and set prayers without the bishop's approval is highly likely. The fact that after the death of the stern bishop Symeon Teofil Turnowski in 1608 the issue of set and unison prayers never came up again seems to point out that this practice took hold in the Brethren churches and that the earlier tradition of silent prayers was abandoned.

The most striking feature of the Brethren liturgical history is that from 1550, when they arrived in Poland, until 1637 the Brethren never actually produced a liturgy in Polish. A Reformation church, dedicated to services in the vernacular, operated for almost a hundred years without any official translation of its liturgy into the language of its people. What is equally interesting is that this seems to have been almost completely ignored by historians writing about the Brethren[92] or about the unification of Polish Reformed liturgy.[93] We do have a few surviving copies of private translations into Polish from the end of the sixteenth and the early seventeenth century done by individual ministers. These are ordination, marriage, and visitation liturgies, but we do not have any surviving copy of a personal translation of the liturgy for the Lord's Supper. Were they deliberately destroyed after 1637? Or, as hardly seems likely, were there no such translations at all? This lack of an official form in Polish must have led to some variations at the congregational level. In the early seventeenth century the Brethren expanded to include congregations in the Royal Prussia region with Polish, Dutch, German, and Scottish speakers, for whom liturgies in Czech would be of little use.[94] Additionally, by the end of the sixteenth cen-

---

620–22; Jolanta Dworzaczkowa, "Konwersje na katolicyzm szlachty ewangelickiej wyznania czeskiego w Wielkopolsce w XVI I XVII wieku," *Odrodzenie i Reformacja w Polsce* 50 (2006): 93.

91. ASR 4:59, 341, 345.

92. See Jolanta Dworzaczkowa, *Bracia czescy w Wielkopolsce w XVI I XVII wieku* (Warsaw: Wydawnictwo Naukowe Semper, 1997), 77, where the author devotes two sentences to this fact.

93. Stanisław Tworek, "Starania o ujednolicenie obrządku kalwińskiego w Polsce w XVII wieku," *Odrodzenie i Reformacja w Polsce* 16 (1971): 117–39, does not mention the fact at all! An exception is Henryk Gmiterek, *Bracia czescy a kalwini w Rzeczypospolitej: Połowa XVI-połowa XVII wieku* (Lublin: n.p., 1987), where this is discussed in a little more detail but with no conclusions drawn.

94. Aleksander Klemp, *Protestanci w dobrach prywatnych w Prusach Królewskich od drugiej połowy XVII do drugiej połowy XVIII wieku* (Wrocław: Zakład Narodowy im. Ossolińskich, 1994), 138–40.

tury a new generation of ministers grew up whose native language was Polish, English, or German, not Czech. These ministers were educated in Switzerland and the Netherlands, where set liturgies were the norm, and so the lack of a liturgy in Polish must have become increasingly problematic.[95] From the minutes of the Brethren synods we know that from at least the 1570s there were calls from clergy to translate the Brethren liturgy into Polish.[96] Synods in 1577 and 1578 pressed for a Polish hymnal (*Kancjonał*), which finally came out in 1587 in Toruń,[97] but no work had been done on the liturgy. In 1596 a translation of the liturgical form for parish visitation was finally approved, and it survives in manuscript.[98] The ministers grew frustrated, and in their petitions to the 1600 synod in Gołuchów they stated: "A request and a reminder for corrected agendas."[99] The time was also more opportune for this, as the Lesser Poland Brethren had in 1599 published their own liturgy.

The 1600 synod in Gołuchów thus had to deal with pressure both from within (ministers and laity) and from outside (the Lesser Polish Brethren and their liturgical work). It seems that Symeon Turnowski had been working on a liturgy for the Lord's Supper: "The prayer before serving with benediction bread and wine . . . by brother Symeon *ad imitationem* God's laws was written, read out loud, and evaluated; *item*, it is along the pattern of old Brethren agendas [and was] praised by a concordance *suffragio* of all elders; we are to give it to our Czech Brethren [for approval]."[100] The synod decided that "all our agendas are to be polished and made ready for the next, God willing, synod."[101] The 1600 synod also ordered that a separate liturgy be written for the visitation of the sick. Having done that, it felt it could now deal with the Lesser Polish Reformed and their desire to unify liturgy in the whole realm. With a condescending remark that the Rev. Kraiński published his liturgy "privately" and that it had "disturbed the church," the Brethren decided to raise the issue of liturgical conformity during a general synod of Polish Protestants. They added, "And that is why we should have ours, well polished and tried out, ready at hand."[102] But in the next years little happened.[103] In February of 1608,

95. Ibid., 138, 219–20.
96. ASR 4:343.
97. ASR 4:47, 50, 53, 99.
98. ASR 4:119.
99. ASR 4:365.
100. ASR 4:162.
101. ASR 4:162.
102. ASR 4:162–23.
103. ASR 4:174.

the seniors postponed a decision about the translation until the next synod.[104] The following year's synods reported modest progress, but the ministers put in charge of the translation grew increasingly old and soon died. In the end, the work came to nothing, except for a Polish translation of a liturgy for the ordination and installation of seniors, which the Brethren managed to finish by 1611.[105]

Since 1609, the Brethren had also been growing closer to the Calvinist churches in Kujawy and Royal Prussia.[106] The union was finalized in 1627 when the two pastors and the superintendent of the Kujawy Calvinists were received into the Brethren fold.[107] The Calvinist influence became stronger once Daniel Mikołajewski (1550–1633), the energetic and charismatic superintendent of the Kujawians, was chosen in 1627 to be the senior of the church.[108] We know that the 1627 fusion of the two churches, and Mikołajewski's election as senior, did not go over well with all the Brethren. Two years later Barbara Przyjemska removed the Brethren minister from her estate in Cienin and requested that the Brethren install a man of her choice, a renegade Roman Catholic priest. The Brethren refused, but she then replaced the ex-priest with a Lutheran minister. This has been traditionally interpreted as a result of her discomfort with the Calvinist doctrine of predestination.[109] However, this theory lacks one essential element: evidence that the senior Mikołajewski forced the Brethren minister in Cienin to preach on predestination. Another explanation is much simpler. Barbara Przyjemska disliked the Calvinist liturgy that she saw encroaching on her church. By the mid-1630s not only were former Kujawy Calvinist ministers in the Brethren churches, but talks with the Reformed churches of Lithuania and Lesser Poland were also occurring. Barbara, born into the Leszczyński family, was probably attached to the old liturgical worship style of the Brethren that was now eroding under Reformed influence. Moreover, the congregation in Cienin also had a tradition of ministers educated at Lutheran Wittenberg, which would make them especially resistant to Reformed liturgy.[110] Perhaps, then, her choice of a Lutheran minister in 1634 was not a theological dissent,

---

104. ASR 4:186.
105. ASR 4:198.
106. ASR 4:203–8.
107. ASR 4:310–12.
108. Maria Sipayłło, "Daniel Mikołajewski (1560–1633)," PSB 21 (1976), 154–56.
109. Jolanta Dworzaczkowa, Z dziejów braci czeskich w Polsce (Poznań: Instytut Historii UAM, 2003), 46–47.
110. Ibid., 42–44.

or not *only* a theological dissent, but rather a sign of her displeasure at the liturgical directions in which the Brethren were going and which was sealed by Włodawa.[111]

In summary, though much more liturgically unified than the early Calvinists of Lesser Poland, the Brethren too experienced some liturgical changes: the abandonment of silent prayer in worship by 1609, as well as the increasing influence of Reformed liturgies.

IV. Reformed Liturgy in the Grand Duchy of Lithuania 1550–1621

We know little about the liturgy used in the Lithuanian Reformed churches before 1611 because in that year a Catholic mob torched the Reformed church and its archives in Vilnius (Wilno). The cause of promoting the Reformation was espoused by Mikołaj "Czarny" ("the Black") Radziwiłł (1515–65), who in 1553 established a Protestant congregation at his court in Brześć Litewski. Initially a Lutheran sympathizer, by 1556 Radziwiłł the Black had moved to the Reformed camp.[112] In this move he was no doubt strengthened by his court preacher Szymon Zacjusz (ca. 1507–ca.1577). As we recall, Zacjusz, who was instrumental in establishing the first Reformed congregation in Pińczów in Lesser Poland, was forced to flee and found his way to the court of Radziwiłł the Black. It would be tempting to speculate that Zacjusz brought with him liturgical forms from Lesser Poland, but, as we have noted, the church there had none at that time. It would thus be safer to argue that Zacjusz and Radziwiłł began their own liturgical innovations and practices. In December of 1557 Radziwiłł moved Zacjusz to his residence in Vilnius, where Radziwiłł established the first official Reformed congregation and where, in January 1558, he was chosen as superintendent of the new church. The next years saw an explosion of Reformed congregations established on private estates as the nobility flocked to Calvinism from both Roman Catholicism and Eastern Orthodoxy.[113] Within two decades the elite of the Grand Duchy became thoroughly

---

111. Ibid., 46–47. In 1637 her eldest son Rafał Przyjemski recalled the Brethren minister who stayed there till his death in 1644, when the younger brothers converted to Catholicism, turned the church over to the Roman Catholics, and sold the property.

112. Henryk Lulewicz, "Mikołaj Radziwiłł zwany Czarnym (1515–1565)," PSB 30 (1987), 335–47.

113. Marzena Liedke, *Od prawosławia do katolicyzmu: Ruscy możni i szlachta Wielkiego Księstwa Litewskieh wobec wyznań reformacyjnych* (Białystok: Wydawnictwo Uniwersytetu w Bialymstoku, 2004).

Protestant, with at least 250 Reformed congregations established. In 1572, out of twenty-two lay senators from Lithuania, sixteen were Protestants (fifteen Calvinists and one Lutheran), three were Eastern Orthodox, and only three were Roman Catholic.[114]

Again, we have little information about the liturgical aspects of the new Reformed Church. We do know that in March of 1557 Jan Łaski visited Vilnius, where he met with Radziwiłł the Black and no doubt used this occasion to promote his *Forma ac Ratio*. As we recall, the Lesser Polish Reformed quickly embraced the *Forma*; given the ties between the two churches, there can be little doubt that this happened in Lithuania as well. Furthermore, during the 1558 synod in Włodzisław, the Lithuanian delegation headed by Zacjusz participated in discussions on both theology and liturgy. It is plausible that when those assembled there chose to designate Łaski's *Forma* as the liturgy for the new church, the decision was made with the Lithuanian delegates, and the consent included the Lithuanian churches as well. In the following years, most likely thanks to Radziwiłł, Łaski's liturgy translated into Polish became the liturgical standard of the Protestant churches in Lithuania.

All this happened while the Lithuanian church was becoming embroiled in the Arian controversy. Unlike in Lesser Poland, where the magnates opted for Calvinism, in the Grand Duchy the Arians found a staunch ally in Radziwiłł the Black and later in his nephew Jan Kiszka (d.1592), the palatine of Brześć.[115] When Zacjusz criticized the Unitarians, Radziwiłł simply fired him as his court preacher. During the 1565 synod in Mordy the majority of the Lithuanian clergy backed the antitrinitarian position. The years 1565–92 were thus extremely difficult for the Reformed: they struggled with the Unitarians and resurgent Roman Catholicism.

The cautious and gradual evolution of the Lithuanian church back to trinitarian Christianity is most evident in the publication of its catechisms. The 1563 Nieśwież Catechism was thoroughly antitrinitarian, and prayers were addressed to the "One God, the Father." It was revised in 1594 in Vilnius under the auspices of the Reformed. The new edition had an explicit polemic against Anabaptists and Judaizers attached, as well as an assortment of hymns where not just the Father but also the Son and the Holy Spirit were mentioned. However, prayers were still addressed to "three separate persons of one God-

---

114. Henryk Lulewicz, "Skład wyznaniowy senatorów świeckich Wielkiego Księstwa Litewskiego za panowania Wazów," *Przegląd Historyczny* 68 (1977): 425–32.

115. Janusz Tazbir, "Jan Kiszka (zm. 1592)," PSB 12 (1966–67), 507–8.

head" and lacked even one single reference to the term "Holy Trinity."[116] The 1594 *Katechizm* caused a scandal during the Protestant synod held in 1595 in Toruń.[117] Perhaps that embarrassment made the Lithuanian Reformed publish in 1598 another *Katechizm*, this time replete with references to the Holy Trinity in prayers and hymns—the material for which was taken mainly from Brethren hymnals![118] All of this should make us very cautious in accepting Petkunas's claim about "a unique and distinct Lithuanian liturgical theology."[119]

In their fight to distance themselves from the Unitarians, just as in Lesser Poland, the Lithuanian Reformed used liturgy, especially how to receive the Lord's Supper. We recall that the Unitarians adopted Łaski's instruction and received the sacrament seated. Now the Reformed insisted that the sacrament be received standing. These provisions were reiterated in the 1581 Lithuanian *Forma albo porządek*, which apart from that detail was basically Jan Łaski's *Forma ac Ratio* with minor corrections.[120] The same proscriptions were made in all subsequent printings of the liturgy (1594, 1598, 1600). All of them were printed in Polish, the liturgical language of the Lithuanian Reformed Church until the twentieth century.[121]

We have very little information for the period 1595–1612. We do know that the modified *Forma ac Ratio* became the prevalent liturgy in the duchy by the dawn of the seventeenth century, and we can safely assume that by that time the interiors of most Reformed churches had been purged of images, statues, and even organs. Exceptions were so few that they stand out: Jerzy Radziwiłł (1578–1613), castellan of Troki,[122] installed organs in his newly built Reformed church in Wiżuny. He also introduced liturgical vestments, fonts for holy water,

---

116. Wojciech Sławiński, *Toruński synod generalny 1595 roku: Z dziejów polskiego protestantyzmu w drugiej połowie xvi wieku* (Warsaw: Semper, 2002), 138–39.

117. ASR 3:134–35. For an excellent assessment of this conflict, see Sławiński, *Toruński synod*, 243–50.

118. Alina Kawecka-Gryczowa, *Kancjonały . . .*, 139.

119. Petkunas, *Holy Communion Rites*, 195.

120. Ibid., 165–66.

121. The first liturgy in the Lithuanian language was published in 1598, together with a Polish one on the facing pages. A separate Lithuanian liturgy was published in 1600, used only in some congregations in Samogitia as a supplement to the Polish. The church, however, did require until the twentieth century that those congregations be served by bilingual ministers. Petkunas, *Holy Communion Rites*, 166–68.

122. Henryk Lulewicz, "Jerzy Radziwiłł (1578–1613)," PSB 30 (1987), 234–36.

candlesticks, and other "popish" innovations.[123] The earliest information we do have for the Lithuanian Reformed liturgy comes from the acts of the July 1612 synod, which decided that liturgical matters would be dealt with the following year.[124] In 1613 three ministers were chosen to draft a new liturgy. Any changes or corrections were to be based on this modified liturgy.[125] This new liturgy did not satisfy everyone, and in 1617 another committee was appointed to work on a revision. What distinguished this initiative from any other in the commonwealth was that this committee included an equal number of laymen and ministers. The committee was specifically ordered not to leave Vilnius until they finished their work.[126] Unfortunately, the committee proved unable to fulfill its task. Either unhappy with the direction the committee was taking or perhaps hoping to be a catalyst for liturgical reform like Kraiński, the minister Jan Zygrowiusz (d. 1624) published his own private version of the liturgy in 1618 and promptly distributed it to a number of congregations. Though we do not have a copy of the 1618 liturgy, we have reason to believe that he drew on the liturgical reforms that were taking place in the church in Lesser Poland.[127]

The 1618 synod was furious and attacked the 1618 catechism for Unitarian inclinations—the fact that it was printed by the Unitarian printing press at Lubcza did little to help it. A new committee was appointed to investigate the matter and report to the following synod.[128] When it did so in 1619, a heated debate took place—some favored a completely new revision of the 1618 and earlier liturgies and catechisms, while others wanted to consult Lesser Poland's liturgies. In the end the synod called yet another committee, charged with revising the catechism and the liturgy. Any hymns with faint Roman Catholic or Anabaptist (still!) connotations were to be thrown out. The synod explicitly ordered that the catechism be based on the Heidelberg Catechism, but it

---

123. Perhaps his Lutheran wife, Zofia Zborowska, reinforced the duke's "high church" inclinations. What is fascinating is that even after his death these "innovations" were not removed but remained into the 1660s, when the Roman Catholics used them as a pretext to seize the church; Jadwiga Dyr, "Akcja ratowania zborów kalwińskich na Litwie," *Odrodzenie i Reformacja w Polsce* 17 (1972): 197.

124. *Akta synodów prowincjonalnych Jednoty Litewskiej 1611–1625*, Monumenta Reformationis Polonicae et Lithuanicae, Serya IV, Zeszyt II (Vilnius: n.p., 1915), 7 (hereafter AS 1915.)

125. AS 1915:16–17, 22.

126. AS 1915:42.

127. ASR 3:657.

128. AS 1915:46.

would seem from the wording that this referred to just the catechism part and not the liturgy.[129]

This was completed in 1620. It is interesting that, unlike in the Lesser Poland and Brethren churches, the liturgy was considered a part of the catechism, together with the hymnal. This says volumes about the Lithuanian clergy's awareness of the importance of liturgy. When it came to the Lord's Supper, however, it reached a fascinating decision, which, in my opinion, shows a deep division among the Lithuanian clergy on liturgical matters. Two liturgies were to be prepared, one based on Łaski's revised *Forma ac ratio* as used in Lithuania, and one by another group of ministers incorporating the forms of the Polish Reformed "presented to us by some of our brethren." No doubt not just Zygrowiusz but also other ministers were well aware of the liturgical developments in the other provinces of Poland-Lithuania. This conjecture is reinforced by the fact that the next canon was devoted to the increasing number of ministers coming from Poland and wanting to work in Lithuania.[130] The final decision as to which to use was left to Prince Krzysztof II Radziwiłł,[131] who chose the version "more pleasing to Lithuanian hearts." The 1621 *Katechizm* (and liturgy) was thus a small revision of Jan Łaski's *Forma ac ratio*. It was sent to all the congregations and declared the only permissible liturgy for the church.[132] It would seem that with relatively little strife and effort the Lithuanian Reformed achieved liturgical uniformity.

V. Toward a Unified Reformed Liturgy in Poland and Lithuania

The impetus for liturgical unification was a serious shortage of Bibles. As early as 1602 the Lesser Polish Calvinists suggested to the other churches that they work on a new translation of the Bible, as well as on a common liturgy. The Lesser Polish Calvinists returned to the idea a decade later (1613), calling on the Brethren to root these works in Scripture and therefore to give up the tradition of using a wafer for Communion. It was not the most tactful approach,

---

129. AS 1915:49–50.

130. AS 1915:55. The same synod also tried to prevent the noble Pakosz from calling a minister from Poland and ignoring the Lithuanian church authorities (AS 1915:59). A year later the synod officially acknowledged a shortage of ministers and allowed for calls from Poland (AS 1915:63).

131. Henryk Wisner, "Krzysztof Radziwiłł (1585–1640)," PSB 30 (1987), 276–83; AS 1915:55.

132. AS 1915:60.

and so it was tabled again.¹³³ The Lithuanian churches showed no interest in this venture, especially since in 1621 they printed a new catechism with a liturgy.¹³⁴ Things changed in 1622 when Prince Krzysztof II Radziwiłł ordered the Lithuanian churches to "consult without delay with the crown's lords *de uniformitate* of all prayers."¹³⁵ Those assembled in 1622 dared not say no to the duke directly. Pleading willingness to consult with the churches in Poland, they advised "another time, for this is too short notice," and expressed their reservation politely by adding, "if there be any need." Naturally, they thought there was none.¹³⁶ No doubt the idea of reworking a freshly printed liturgy was not to their liking, so they decided to stall and see if the duke's interest in the matter would fade. Having heard of the duke's intent, the Lesser Polish Brethren responded in 1625 during their synod in Oksza, where they called for a meeting close to Lithuania, at which the question of a new translation of the Bible and a correction of the agendas could be discussed.¹³⁷

Faced with all this, the Lithuanian church had little choice but to send in 1626 a high-ranking delegation to talk with the two churches in Poland. Their true feelings are expressed in the long instructions the delegates received, from which they were told not to depart under any circumstances. When it came to the Bible, the Lithuanians wanted only minor revisions of the 1563 Brześć Bible and were not at all interested in any new translation. When it came to hymns, these were to be unified with the Polish ones, provided the Lithuanian hymns from the recent editions be kept in toto.¹³⁸ The liturgical instructions were even more interesting: while desiring unification of the rites for the Lord's Supper, the Lithuanians were not to depart from their own form but were told to criticize the Lesser Polish one. Finally, they wished that the Lord's Supper liturgy be more restrained when it came to the number of hymns sung, unlike the Lesser Polish liturgy.¹³⁹ This sabotaged any talks on liturgical unification, since the only position the Lithuanians were willing to accept was that the

---

133. ASR 3:347.

134. Stanisław Tworek, "Starania o ujednolicenie," 117–23.

135. AS 1915:71.

136. AS 1915:73.

137. ASR 3:476–77. Sadly, the Brethren held no synods in the years 1623–27 but merely a convocation of seniors, and we have only short notes of what was discussed. ASR 4:306–9.

138. Marzena Liedke and Piotr Guzowski, eds., *Akta Synodów Prowincjonalnych Jednoty Litewskiej 1626-1637*, Semper (Warsaw: Wydawnictwo Naukowe Semper, 2011), 2 (hereafter ASR 5).

139. ASR 5:1–2.

other churches accept their liturgy.[140] In the end the meeting did not occur for political reasons, and the matter was dropped for a number of years.

The idea of liturgical unification was revived by the Brethren in 1632; they expressed a sentiment "that for the bigger advancement of God's glory there be *conformitas* in hymns, in catechisms, and in forms or agendas of church services," and they suggested that two ministers and one lay person be sent from each of the three churches to work out a suitable agreement.[141] As might have been expected, the church in Lesser Poland responded with enthusiasm. Anticipating Lithuanian opposition, they suggested that the three churches send delegations to Orla in Podlasie, the property of Janusz Radziwiłł[142] (son of Krzysztof II), in August 1633, putting the reluctant Lithuanians on the spot. Happy or not, the Lithuanians had little room to maneuver and agreed to play host. During their 1633 synod they expressed an "earnest desire" for conformity in rituals "in all congregations (in the Crown, the Grand Lithuanian Duchy, and adjacent principalities)" but then added their conditions: the Lithuanian hymnal of 1621 was to be retained, though new hymns could be added, together with new prayers for "opportune occasions." The Lithuanians agreed in principle to one liturgical Agenda but insisted that it be guided by "simplicity and purity." The fraction of the bread during Communion was to be retained, and the Lithuanians insisted on eliminating any attempts to allow kneeling when receiving Communion and using hosts instead of bread—something difficult for the Brethren to concede.[143]

The Orla convocation was a success. All three churches gave up something, and in the end those assembled agreed to print one Bible, one Agenda, and one Psalter, which were to be presented to the three churches for approval. The major part of the work fell on the shoulders of Tomasz Węgierski, who was probably the right person for this delicate job because of his Brethren background and his work in Lesser Poland's church. His work was to be presented to two Lithuanian superintendents, which ensured that all three churches would participate in the travails. Tellingly, he was in charge of the Communion liturgy that was presented, the most delicate part to handle. The Lithuanian superintendent was in charge of writing an introduction to the Agenda, the rite for

---

140. Stanisław Tworek, "Starania o ujednolicenie," 124.
141. ASR 5:330–31.
142. Tadeusz Wasilewski, "Janusz Radziwiłł (1612–1655)," PSB 30 (1987), 208–15.
143. ASR 5:114–15; Stanisław Tworek, "Starania o ujednolicenie," 117–23.

divorce, and the introduction to the hymnal.[144] As we recall, Tomasz Węgierski had to come up with a liturgy that would be simple and pure yet would honor the high church tendencies of the Brethren, as well as Jan Łaski's heritage of *Forma ac Ratio* and the Lesser Polish *Forma* of 1614, at the same time. The Brethren insisted on kneeling during Communion, while the Lesser Polish and Lithuanian Reformed found this unacceptable. The Reformed insisted on breaking the bread, while the Brethren wanted to use hosts, as was their tradition. His task seemed impossible.

The work produced by Tomasz Węgierski was rightly labelled by Petkunas "the most significant liturgical production of the Reformed churches in Poland and Lithuania."[145] In some ways it was completely new to all the provinces, but the biggest changes were in the Brethren liturgy, as well as in the Lithuanian form. The service of Holy Communion began with a call to worship in a fashion similar to the 1621 Lithuanian one. It then moved on to an exhortation to the Holy Spirit and the hymn *Veni Sancte Spiritus* in one musical setting, following the 1614 Lesser Polish *Porządek*. The excommunication of sinners followed, which was probably a nod to Lesser Polish and Lithuanian realities of competition with the Unitarians because this excommunication had an explicit mention of "any who blaspheme the holy, triune, one God or his word." An exhortation to make a confession, and a confession of sins, followed, based again on the 1614 Lesser Polish liturgy. As a nod to the Brethren, the prayers include the phrase "falling on our knees with our hearts," which, while it did not provide for kneeling as such during prayers, allowed the Brethren practice to continue. The liturgy also then provided for an optional singing of *Agnus Dei*—something the Lesser Polish and Lithuanian Reformed thought had "popish" undertones, but which was used by the Brethren. Again, Węgierski was wise enough to make this part of the liturgy optional. Then came the absolution, followed by a sung Apostles' Creed. At this point Węgierski departed from the Lithuanian and the Lesser Polish forms, and instead of having here the "prayer toward the words of Christ" he moved directly to the words of Christ's Testament with a lengthy explanation of the testament and a prayer of admonition. The Lord's Prayer followed, along with an invitation to God's table, and then the fraction. While Węgierski used the word *chleb* (bread), he never explicitly proscribed the use of hosts, which the Brethren continued to use until the mid-eighteenth century. The bread and the wine were to be distributed separately, as by the

---

144. For a more detailed assessment of the Orla convocation, see Henryk Gmiterek, *Bracia czescy a kalwini*, 130–35.

145. Petkunas, *Holy Communion Rites*, 177.

Lesser Poles—unlike the Lithuanians, who partook of the bread and wine at the same time. Then an admonition based on Łaski's "Credite et ne dubitate" was pronounced, something certainly to the liking of the Lithuanians as it was based on Łaski's *Forma*. Following the distribution, two prayers of thanksgiving were added: first a short one and then a lengthier one based on a Brethren liturgy. A final exhortation to do good works followed, and the service concluded with the Aaronic blessing and the singing of a hymn. All in all, the proposed liturgy was a careful and masterful work, combining three different traditions while retaining coherence and flow. The work of the committee was passed on to the three churches for approval.

During the 1634 Brethren synod in Ostroróg, the Orla agreements were approved even though the bishops were unhappy about them. This time it was the younger ministers and the lay delegates who showed up and influenced the outcome. The Lesser Polish Reformed synod in Bełżyce was very pleased with the results and suggested convening in September of 1634 in Włodawa. The Lithuanians, whose liturgy had been the one that was perhaps most altered, were naturally not ecstatic, but Petkunas exaggerates when he says they were "furious." The proceedings of the synod were visibly less enthusiastic than those of the Lesser Polish Calvinists, but nonetheless all the provisions of the Orla convocation were accepted.[146] Only minor reservations were made, mainly to the parts regarding the duties of junior clergy and the ordination of superintendents.[147] Whatever they must have thought about the changes, they were forced to keep their opinions to themselves and wait for the final convocation in Włodawa. Włodawa was chosen for the synod for a good reason: the city, though ecclesiastically part of the Lesser Polish church, politically lay in the Grand Duchy of Lithuania, and the majority of its inhabitants were Czech Brethren refugees from Bohemia.[148] Thus, Włodawa seemed like the place that already united all three provinces of the Polish and Lithuanian Reformed.[149] The Włodawa convocation turned out to be a unifying synod of Polish Calvinists, to a degree larger than the Toruń synod of 1595 or that of Sandomir in 1570. For the first time the three churches agreed to publish one common Bible—

---

146. ASR 5:128–29.
147. ASR 5:129–31; Stanisław Tworek, "Starania o ujednolicenie," 123–28.
148. Henryk Gmiterek, "Włodawa w dziejach reformacji i kultury staropolskiej," in *Dzieje Włodawy*, ed. Edward Olszewski and Ryszard Szczygieł (Lublin: Włodawa, 1991), 58–65.
149. Wacław Urban, "Rola Braci Węgierskich w podtrzymywaniu protestantyzmu polskiego," in *Religie, edukacja, kultura: Księga pamiątkowa dedykowana profesorowi Stanisławowi Litakowi*, ed. M. Surdacki (Lublin: n.p., 2002), 47–51.

the Gdańsk Bible. One hymnal was also planned for the three provinces, as well as, more importantly, one Agenda with a unified liturgy. Additionally, an effort was made to unify the structure of the three churches, making them more centralized and more Presbyterian in polity. The final pronouncements were signed by the seniors (or superintendents) of all three churches; the last changes were made in October of 1636, and the forms were sent to Gdańsk for publishing. It seemed as if after so many futile attempts, full liturgical unity was achieved. All three synods expressed their jubilation at the results, which were considerable. Even the reluctant Lithuanian synod proclaimed that it received the results of the Włodawa agreements "with due gratefulness, *unanimi et communi consensuet applausu* we approve, ratify, and promulgate."[150] The first copies of the Agenda arrived at all three churches in 1637.

At this point, at least in Lithuania, factions opposed to the new unification surfaced. Interestingly, they were led by Piotr Kochlewski, a former Brethren member and a Lithuanian delegate to the unification talks, someone who approved the proceedings of both Orla and Włodawa! We cannot know exactly why he did not like the results of the 1637 Agenda—perhaps having switched from one liturgical pattern to another, he did not want to repeat the experience, or perhaps he genuinely liked the liturgy used in the Grand Duchy. With the aging Duke Krzysztof II Radziwiłł absent from the 1637 synod, Kochlewski gathered around him a vocal group of ministers that began to obstruct the usage of the 1637 Agenda despite the efforts of the Lithuanian superintendent, Andrzej Dobrzański, to hold fast to the Włodawa agreements. By 1638 Kochlewski had managed to push the synod into a deadlock. The Lithuanians agreed to use some parts of the Agenda but requested that others be revised.[151] Naturally, the other two churches were not amused. Tomasz Węgierski wrote a personal letter and plea to the Lithuanian synod on their behalf, asking them what the problem was: Were they not present at the Orla and Włodawa meetings? Did they not agree there to all that was said and approved? Why did they now contradict themselves? "We now see that the zeal which you now display you did not use before, though present at the Orla and Włodawa convocations."[152] He also suggested that delegates from the three churches meet in Orla in 1639 to discuss what could be done, especially since the Agenda had already been paid for and printed. Perhaps the direct letter from Węgierski, and the pleas for unity, helped the Lithuanians come to their senses. In 1639 they agreed

---

150. ASR 5:144–45.
151. Stanisław Tworek, "Starania o ujednolicenie," 132.
152. Ibid., 133.

to meet with the other churches and discuss again the liturgical reservations they had about the Agenda. The Lesser Polish Calvinists and the Lithuanians prepared sizable delegations to meet, but two important things happened. First, a Roman Catholic mob sacked the Vilnius church building in 1640. Then, devastated by these events, Duke Krzysztof II Radziwiłł died. The next Lithuanian synod did not meet till 1641, and the delegates, shaken by recent events, were in a more conciliatory mood. The 1639 canon was reaffirmed, but the Lithuanians were preoccupied with the trial of the perpetrators of the tumult, which had, to their horror, morphed into a trial of the Vilnius congregation, which was forced to move outside the city walls in 1642.[153] In the meantime the Reformed from Lesser Poland pressed for talks, and finally in 1643 their superintendent, Tomasz Węgierski, went to the Vilnius synod himself to plead personally to get the matter settled. The synod acquiesced and once again the city of Orla was chosen as the place of meeting; all three churches were to send their delegations, and all three prepared well for it.

The Lesser Polish church sent an impressive delegation of lay leaders with their superintendent, Węgierski. They were told to listen to the Lithuanians patiently but to stick to the Włodawa agreements in all things. Any concessions were to be made only if the Brethren had agreed to them, too. The Brethren sent all their senior clerics to the meeting along with, in an interesting twist, Stanisław Kochlewski, a relative of Piotr Kochlewski, probably hoping to exert family influence if all else failed. The Lithuanians sent their own delegation of fifteen people, which was to express all the frustration of the Lithuanians and to press for a whole revision of the Agenda. They wanted to pit the Lesser Poles against the Brethren and to suggest that they unify the liturgy with the Lesser Poles. This was a political move to divide the delegations, but there was little chance the Lesser Polish church would accept a reversal to Łaski's *Forma ac Ratio*, which the Lithuanians were still using. But perhaps, despite what Petkunas or Tworek think, the Lithuanian delegation was not as unified as their instructions would have us believe. The senior from the Podlasie district was present, a place where Lesser Polish liturgical customs had considerable sway. Furthermore, one of the Lithuanian seniors, Andrzej Musonius, hailed from the Brethren and can hardly have been fiercely opposed to the 1637 Agenda.[154] We should also bear in mind that the 1640 Vilnius tumult showed the Lithuanian

---

153. Ibid., 137; Petkunas, *Holy Communion Rites*, 181–87.

154. He served in Lithuania from at least 1630. In 1652 he became superintendent of the Wilno district and died there in 1662/63. Information kindly supplied by Prof. Henryk Gmiterek from Lublin.

Reformed that they were not as safe and powerful as they considered themselves to be. With Duke Krzysztof II Radziwiłł dead and his son Janusz more involved with military than ecclesiastical affairs, they were in no position to alienate the other two churches and their political leaders, who still held sway in commonwealth parliamentary politics.

The outcome of the 1644 convocation in Orla was remarkable. The Lithuanians conceded on almost all points. While the other churches agreed to minor adjustments to the Lord's Supper liturgy, the substance of the 1637 Agenda service remained unchanged. Most of the Lithuanian concerns were worked into the pattern of the 1637 Agenda. The revised Lithuanian version was to be published as *Akta Usługi*, the term "Agenda" being reserved for the 1637 edition. The Lithuanians took what was offered, and its 1646 synod approved the *Akta Usługi*. The 1644 liturgy so quickly replaced the 1621 version that only one copy of the 1621 version remains!

VI. Conclusions

Much attention has been given to the fact that in the end the Lithuanian Reformed Church did not fully accept the Agenda and was very hesitant to accept the Gdańsk Bible. This is put forward as an alleged failure of the Włodawa agreements and even as a sign of Protestant "disintegration" in the Commonwealth of Two Nations.[155] I believe that is the exact opposite of what actually happened. In fact, during their 1635 synod the Lithuanian church fully accepted the Włodawa conclusions. While liturgical conformity was more convoluted by the mid-seventeenth century, the three churches achieved a remarkable sign of unity in liturgy with only minor differences in the order of some Communion prayers.[156] In fact, the 1637 Agenda remained the official liturgy in all three churches: in the Brethren until its dissolution in the Prussian Union Church in 1817, in the Lithuanian church until its extinction in 1945 (the revived Lithuanian branch of the church still uses the liturgy in Lithuanian), and in the Reformed Church in Poland to this very day.

155. Stanisław Tworek, "Starania o ujednolicenie," 138.
156. Petkunas, *Holy Communion Rites*, 63–69.

6

Methodism's "World Parish": Liturgical and Hymnological Migrations in Three Ecclesiastical Generations

Karen B. Westerfield Tucker

I. Characteristics of Early Methodist Worship

In the autobiography summing up his life, Silas Told remembers his first encounter with the Methodists and with the Anglican priest and Methodist founder John Wesley: a gathering in 1740 at the old royal cannon foundry (the "Foundery") in London that the Methodists had obtained for their use. Told writes:

> My friend, Mr. Greaves, stood close behind me, to prevent my going out, . . . to which I was strongly tempted, and had it not been for the multitude of people assembled together, so early in the morning as between four and five o'clock, and the striking consideration of such profound seriousness, which evidently appeared in the countenance of almost every person there, I must certainly have given way to the temptation, and thereby have lost the greatest blessing I ever experienced before. I tarried there a full half hour before the service began, during which my mind was sorely disturbed with many strange notions, as I had been so strongly attached to the church of England. Exactly at five o'clock a general whisper was conveyed through the congregation, and "Here he comes! Here he comes!" was repeated with the utmost pleasure. I was filled with curiosity to see his person, which, when I beheld, I much despised. The enemy of souls, who is never unprepared to hinder the salvation of individuals, suggested, that he was some farmer's son, who, not

able to support himself, was making a penny in this low and ignoble manner. He passed through the congregation into the temporary pulpit, and having his robes on, I expected he would have begun with the Church service; but, to my astonishment, the introduction to his preaching was the singing an hymn, with which I was almost enraptured; but his extemporary prayer was quite unpleasant, as I thought it savoured too much of the Dissenter's mode of worship, which at that time my prejudice could not abide. After which he took his text in the second chapter, of the first epistle general of St. John, twelve and thirteen verses. "I write unto you, little children, because your sins are forgiven you, &c." The enemy struck a deadly blow at me, and in that moment suggested, that he was a Papist, as he dwelt so much on forgiveness of sins; and although I had read this portion of Scripture many times before, yet I never understood that we were to know our sins forgiven on earth; supposing that it referred only to those to whom the apostle was then writing, especially as I had never heard this doctrine preached in the church. However, my prejudice quickly abated, through the excellent wisdom with which Mr. Wesley spoke: This clearly elucidated the subject, and proved the point. I then plainly saw I could never be saved without knowing my sins were forgiven me; and in the midst of his sermon the Spirit of God sealed the truth of every word upon my heart.[1]

This first meeting changed the course of his life, for Told, who had been forced to serve as a sailor on a slave ship, subsequently became a Methodist and a lay preacher, and in his final years was chaplain to condemned inmates at London's Newgate Prison. Although Told's principal purpose for recording this event was evangelical rather than liturgical, his eyewitness account exposes certain practices and expectations for worship that were typical of early Methodism. Since Methodists regarded themselves as a reform movement (a "Society") within the Church of England and not an emerging "Dissenter" church, Methodist worship was to occur outside of "church hours" so that Methodists, at least theoretically, could attend the church's Prayer Book liturgies and especially the celebration of the Lord's Supper. Gathering for Methodist worship between four and five in the morning thus was quite common during John Wesley's lifetime (d. 1791) and in fact, for a period, was formally advised in the Methodist rules.[2] This avoidance of "church hours," however,

---

1. Silas Told, *An Account of the Life and Dealings of God with Silas Told, Late Preacher of the Gospel* (n.p.: W. Cowdroy, 1805), 73–74.

2. "We are fully determined never to drop the morning preaching: and to continue preaching at five, wherever it is practicable, particularly in London and Bristol" (Q. 25, A., "Large Minutes," *Minutes of Several Conversations between the Rev. Mr. Wesley, and Others* [London: Printed at the Conference-Office; Thomas Cordeux, Agent, 1811], 15).

did not elevate the Methodist movement in the eyes of the majority of Anglican clergy, and indeed many of them refused Methodists access to the parish church for their distinctive worship. Thus Methodists, out of necessity as much as evangelistic zeal, held their worship in any space that could accommodate a crowd and were as comfortable with outdoor gatherings as with indoor. Told testifies to the report circulating in his day that Methodists were wont to convene in "subterraneous dens and caves" and undoubtedly in this light describes the Foundery as "a ruinous place" of "decayed timbers" containing a temporary pulpit constructed from "rough deal boards."[3] The presence of a pulpit, even in such a space, makes clear one intention of Methodist worship, which was further emphasized on the day of Told's visit by the subject of Mr. Wesley's sermon and his choice of Scripture text.

Told does not elaborate on his remark prior to Wesley's arrival that his "mind was sorely disturbed with many strange notions" because he was "so strongly attached to the Church of England." It may be that he witnessed during this time individuals engaging in hymn singing and extemporary prayer—both of which were not permitted during the Prayer Book liturgies; his evaluative comments on these practices are saved for when they are employed by a robed Reverend Mr. Wesley. The "strange notions" that disturbed him could possibly have come from observing the physical responses of tears, wailing, moaning, and jerking often freely expressed at Methodist gatherings when the mournful sinner was confronted with the mercy and forgiveness of a gracious God. Yet Told is quite intentional in recording that he was impressed by the "profound seriousness" displayed by many who were present.

Four characteristics and expectations of worship for Methodists in eighteenth-century England are thus addressed directly and indirectly by Silas Told's report. First, Methodists were to participate in the formal liturgies of the Church of England as well as in informal preaching services, prayer meetings, and personal prayer; the *Book of Common Prayer* was to continue to shape the habits of corporate prayer and private devotion even as Methodists engaged in more experiential practices. Second, any space could be used for worship that allowed for a clear hearing of the spoken word. Third, worship included the singing of newly composed hymns and songs (the majority by John Wesley's poet-priest brother Charles) as a vehicle for expressing both the *fides quae creditur* and the *fides qua creditur*. To engage the singer and the listener, tunes for these texts could be drawn from existing liturgical music, borrowed from

---

3. Told, *An Account of the Life*, 70, 73.

the broader culture (e.g., folk songs, music from the theater[4]), or freshly composed. Fourth, a variety of forms of prayer and styles of praying were as appropriate in large assemblies as in small groups and families, as well as in private. A fifth characteristic permeated the other four, as Told himself notes: while worship focused on offering love and gratitude to the triune God, the worshiper open to the movement of God's Spirit could experience a warmed heart, saving grace, and other blessings.

II. Three Ecclesiastical Generations

This scheme for worship was transplanted as the Methodists—Society members, lay preachers, and sympathetic Anglican and Dissenting clergy—happily disregarded parish boundaries[5] and national borders in their evangelistic enterprise to "reform the nation, particularly the Church, and to spread scriptural holiness over the land."[6] From bases in Bristol, Oxford, and London, Methodist work principally among the poor and lower-middle classes soon expanded to Ireland, Scotland, Wales, and parts of Europe and then across the Atlantic to "His Majesty's Dominions" in the West Indies, Bermuda, the Maritime provinces and parts of upper Canada, and the American colonies. During this initial missionizing period, the Methodists—at least officially—still regarded themselves as a movement and not as a church. Only after political, cultural, and ecclesiastical circumstances in the newly created United States demanded a separation from the Church of England did a Methodist group formally constitute itself as a church: the Methodist Episcopal Church was founded in 1784 and included Methodists in the United States and Canada.[7]

---

4. John Frederick Lampe, sometimes considered the first "Methodist" composer, drew inspiration from the English theater for his settings of hymn texts by Charles Wesley. George Frederick Handel also set at least three of Charles Wesley's texts. See Carlton R. Young, "John F. Lampe and *Hymns on the Great Festivals, and Other Occasions, 1746*," in *Hymns on the Great Festivals, and Other Occasions*, ed. Carlton R. Young et al., facsimile ed. (Madison, NJ: The Charles Wesley Society, 1996), 7–19.

5. Under the date of June 11, 1739, John Wesley wrote in his journal, "I look upon all the world as my parish; thus far I mean, that in whatever part of it I am, I judge it meet, right, and my bounden duty, to declare unto all that are willing to hear the glad tidings of salvation" (*The Works of John Wesley*, vol. 19, ed. W. Reginald Ward and Richard P. Heitzenrater [Nashville: Abingdon Press, 1990], 67).

6. Q. 3, A., "Large Minutes," *Minutes of Several Conversations*, 3.

7. The Methodist Episcopal Church encouraged the creation of an independent Methodist denomination in Canada in 1828.

Methodists in Britain continued to regard themselves as a "connection" and not as a "church," even though they steadily distanced themselves from the established church.

After Wesley's death in 1791, disputes soon erupted in the Methodist Episcopal Church and in the Methodist connection in Britain over such issues as Wesleyan identity, governance, leadership, race, and economics, and when amicable resolution was not possible new Methodist and Wesleyan denominations emerged.[8] These denominations created before or within thirty years of Wesley's death as the result of dissent and not intentional missionary activity may be considered—at least for our purposes—a first ecclesiastical generation.

Even during times of internal discord, the oldest Methodist bodies continued their spread of scriptural holiness to areas untouched by or indifferent to the Gospel. By 1816 first-generation Methodists from Britain and Ireland had visited Sierra Leone, South Africa, Australia, India, Ceylon (Sri Lanka), and Java (Indonesia). Methodists of the first generation in the United States set their sights early on the expanding west and on areas north and south of the border; by the mid-nineteenth century, they were sending missionaries to parts of Europe, Africa, and Asia. In some places, first-generation Methodists from both sides of the Atlantic worked together in missionary engagement; in other places, they established themselves in different regions within the same country. At first the missionized community was linked structurally to the first-generation group, but over time most came to be organized as a separate Wesleyan/Methodist denomination, thereby constituting a second generation. Among the second-generation autonomous denominations are the Methodist churches in Brazil, Hong Kong, Italy, New Zealand, Nigeria, and Sri Lanka.

The second-generation churches inherited the genetic impetus to spread scriptural holiness, so as the result of their work it is possible to identify a third ecclesiastical generation of Methodist/Wesleyan denominations or communities established, in some cases, in collaboration with churches of the first generation. For example, Methodism has been planted in Cambodia through the cooperative efforts of the United Methodist Church and the Wesleyan Church from the United States, both first-generation descendants, and several

---

8. In North America, for example, the Republican Methodist Church (1794), the African Methodist Episcopal Church (1816), and the African Methodist Episcopal Zion Church (1821). The predominant Methodist body in Britain was the Wesleyan Methodist Connexion, later named the Wesleyan Methodist Church in 1897. Other early British denominations included the Methodist New Connexion (1797), the Primitive Methodist Connexion (1811), and the Bible Christians (1815).

second-generation bodies: the United Methodist Church in Switzerland and France, the Methodist Church in Singapore, the Methodist Church in Malaysia, the Korean Methodist Church, and several Chinese churches through the World Federation of Chinese Methodist Churches. Although a distinct and autonomous Cambodian Methodist denomination is just emerging, Methodists in that country have already developed a unique identity with a Wesleyan imprint.

What is that Wesleyan imprint in the matter of worship? It appears that the four characteristics and expectations for worship exposed in Silas Told's eighteenth-century narrative generally have survived—migrated, if you will—though they have been adjusted according to their geographic, cultural, and generational locations. To explore this migration, the four characteristics—formal and informal worship, assembly space, hymns and songs, and prayer styles—will be examined by looking at the Sunday practices of a representative of each of the three generations. Cambodia, already mentioned, is a third-generation context.[9] The Methodist Church in Singapore, which was influenced by missionaries from Britain and from the Methodist Episcopal Church in the United States and hence by the liturgical practices of both those denominations, and which has established its own missionary work in Cambodia, will represent the second generation. The Methodist Episcopal Church will exemplify the first generation, although as a result of ecclesial mergers in 1939, a denomination under that name no longer exists.[10]

A. Formal and Informal, Texted and Untexted Worship

The establishment of the Methodist Episcopal Church in 1784 broke all ties with the Church of England except for one: a liturgical linkage that was kept by virtue of the new denomination's adoption of John Wesley's revision and reduction of the 1662 *Book of Common Prayer* under the title *The Sunday Service of the Methodists in North America with Other Occasional Services* (1784).[11] In

---

9. Information about Cambodian worship praxis is drawn from correspondence with Singaporean Methodists and United Methodists involved with the mission there and from the dissertation of a long-time Singaporean Methodist missionary to that country: Kevin Lowe Joo Oon, "A Cultural Analysis of Cambodian Methodist Church Worship Services and Their Implications for Evangelism" (DMin, Asbury Theological Seminary, 2007).

10. In 1939 the Methodist Episcopal Church reunited with two of the denominations that had separated from it—the Methodist Protestant Church and the Methodist Episcopal Church, South—to form the Methodist Church; that denomination in 1968 joined with the Evangelical United Brethren Church to create the United Methodist Church.

11. A partial reprint edition is available as James F. White, ed., *John Wesley's Prayer Book: The Sunday Service of the Methodists in North America* (Akron, OH: OSL Publications, 1991).

1792 the denomination, after its own revision of Wesley's liturgical revision, placed the "occasional" texts in a concluding section of its book of polity entitled *The Doctrines and Discipline of the Methodist Episcopal Church*.[12] What became known as the "Ritual" included rites for infant and adult baptism, the Lord's Supper, the solemnization of marriage, the burial of the dead, and the ordination of deacons, elders (presbyters), and bishops. Wesley's Sunday liturgies of Morning and Evening Prayer vanished, and in their place a series of rubrics related to worship were added to *Doctrines and Discipline* in a section outside the "Ritual." Lost too was Wesley's plan that the Methodist Episcopal elders (presbyters) administer the Lord's Supper every Lord's Day as a means of observing "constant" Communion.[13] Other peculiarly Methodist services continued after 1792, such as love feasts, covenant renewals, and watch night services,[14] but these were not scripted as published texts. While this shift eight years after its founding has been bemoaned as taking the denomination in a "nonliturgical" direction, a different reading is certainly possible. The liturgical diet of many Methodists was already informal preaching services and prayer meetings in combination with the formal eucharistic and occasional liturgies supplied by the Prayer Book, though admittedly the former were consumed more frequently than the latter. The 1792 revisions kept what many Methodists already knew and practiced; thus, they did not jettison entirely their liturgical inheritance from Wesley but moderated it to be in accord with their own context and experience of Methodist worship. Methodists had the freedom to engage in informal and unscripted worship open to community needs and the winds of the Spirit, but they also kept formal ritual texts for baptism, Eucharist, weddings, funerals, and ordination to preserve their Methodist theology and identity. Thus, a community might engage in informal prayers, singing, and preaching at the beginning of their Sunday worship together and conclude with a Lord's Supper liturgy that contained textual connections to the English Reformation and the medieval Sarum Use. Throughout the history of the Methodist Episcopal Church, the denomination's leadership affirmed

---

12. The earliest editions of the Methodist Episcopal Church's *Doctrines and Discipline* showed a strong dependence upon Wesley's "Large Minutes," and certain components from the "Large Minutes" persisted throughout the life of the denomination.

13. See John Wesley's letter of September 10, 1784, reprinted in *John Wesley's Prayer Book* (no pagination); cf. Wesley's sermon "The Duty of Constant Communion," in *The Works of John Wesley*, vol. 3, ed. Albert C. Outler (Nashville: Abingdon Press, 1986), 428–39.

14. See Karen B. Westerfield Tucker, *American Methodist Worship* (New York: Oxford University Press, 2001), 60–70.

that worship could be formal and informal, texted and untexted, solemn and revivalistic, though the extent to which that formality and freedom could be taken were constantly subjects for discussion and debate.

When examining the liturgical history of the Methodist Episcopal Church from its founding to its "end" as a distinct denomination in 1939, an unmistakable trend emerges. As the denomination settled into its identity as a church, its rapid growth made it for a time the largest Protestant denomination in the United States, and its constituency came to be drawn more from the middle and upper-middle classes. Church leaders made available printed prayers and other liturgical texts—both denominationally authorized and unofficial—for the "enrichment" of Sunday worship. By the middle of the nineteenth century there was renewed interest in Wesley's *Sunday Service*, and components from it (e.g., collects, psalmody) were introduced into the regular Sunday morning and evening preaching services in many congregations.[15] The last *Doctrines and Discipline* of the Methodist Episcopal Church in 1936 contained "An Order for Morning or Evening Prayer" adapted from the *Sunday Service* as well as two complete orders of worship that included printed prayers of confession and indicated a place for organ preludes and postludes, choral anthems, chanting of the *Venite* or *Te Deum*, responsive readings drawn from Scripture, and a sung *Gloria Patri*.[16] Thus, a greater confidence of being "church" was accompanied by a greater liturgical complexity for Sunday—with liturgical resources taken from its own origins as well as from the traditions of others. This liturgical complexity coexisted with the informal style of worship that was also part of the denominational roots. Both were integral to Methodist liturgical identity.

The trend, as an identity of "church" solidifies, toward a greater use of print resources for worship—while maintaining informal patterns—is also evident in churches of the second generation. Methodist Episcopal missionaries took with them the experiential and informal style of worship well suited to evangelism, along with the worship patterns printed in the book of *Doctrines and Discipline* and other liturgical practices (printed or not) that they personally preferred. The first Methodist worship service in Singapore, conducted by missionary James M. Thoburn in 1885, consisted of singing, prayer, Scripture reading, and preaching—what could be considered for Methodists the essential core of worship. In recalling the event, William F. Oldham noted that the service

---

15. See ibid., 8–20.

16. *Doctrines and Discipline of the Methodist Episcopal Church* (1936) (New York: Methodist Book Concern, 1936), nos. 1421–22.

Methodism's "World Parish" 139

was "exceedingly simple and the effect was so profound."[17] As the number of Methodists in Singapore increased—aided by the establishment of Methodist schools with mandatory chapel attendance—worship took on a more formal shape, patterned on what was predominantly in use in the American churches. The English-speaking Methodist communities easily drew on printed liturgical resources from the United States and Great Britain. Bahasa Melayu, Tamil, and Chinese-speaking (Mandarin, Cantonese, Foochow, Hakka, Hinghwa, Hokkien, and Teochew) communities resorted to translation or borrowing from materials imported from India and China. Liturgical borrowing, particularly with a westward orientation, continues today in the independent Methodist Church in Singapore, which is structurally organized along linguistic lines into three "annual conferences": Chinese speaking (Chinese Annual Conference), English speaking (Trinity AC), and Tamil speaking (Emmanuel Tamil AC).[18] As a result of the borrowing of liturgical texts and new worship trends, the worship of Methodists in Singapore reflects the influences of the charismatic and liturgical renewal movements; these in many ways have also brought it to consider its own liturgical heritage from the early Methodists. Work is currently underway to produce a denominationally authorized book[19] containing locally composed liturgical materials, a project made more complicated by the cultural diversity of the constituency, which in recent years has also included a strong presence of new Methodists from the Philippines, Indonesia, and Myanmar/Burma.

Worship in the emerging Cambodian Methodist congregations maintains the double tendency of formality/informality and texted/untexted. In 2001

---

17. W. F. Oldham, *Thoburn—Called of God* (New York: Methodist Book Concern, 1918), 133. Approximately 150 persons were reported to have attended the first meeting; on subsequent nights, the room was filled to capacity; see Bobby E. K. Sng, *In His Good Time: The Story of the Church in Singapore, 1819–1978* (Singapore: Graduates' Christian Fellowship, 1980), 107–8. Thoburn spent a significant part of his career in India; Oldham was born in Bangalore of British parents and after a period in the United States was sent to the mission field in Southeast Asia. Both men eventually became bishops in the Methodist Episcopal Church.

18. The "conference" in Methodism generally refers to a delegated body of clergy and laity with supervision of all or part of the legislative, judicial, and executive functions of the denomination. In Singapore the three annual conferences are each headed by an elected president and meet annually. The "general conference," which meets every four years, is made up of representatives from the three annual conferences. During the general conference, the delegates elect a bishop who has oversight of all three annual conferences.

19. Authorization would come from an affirmative vote by the denomination's general conference.

the missionizing denominations along with the Cambodian Methodists published a book in Khmer containing liturgies for Sunday and general worship, the sacraments, and selected occasional services under the title *Christian Hymn and Worship Book of the Cambodia Christian Methodist Association*.[20] Nevertheless, at this stage worship has more of an evangelistic flavor and is often done in the "praise and worship" style currently popular across global Methodism, which is also reminiscent of early Methodist "preaching service" praxis. In a nod to the cultural custom of showing respect at holy places, Cambodians remove their shoes for worship.[21] There is no shyness about conveying emotions during worship, so prayer and singing may be accompanied by such physical manifestations as jumping, fist pumping, wailing, and crying. Testimonies, once a staple of the Methodist love feast and Methodist revivals, are a regular occurrence on Sunday mornings and at other times. Preaching is intentionally interactive with the congregation and is done from behind a pulpit if one is available. Because of the commitment of the majority of the missionizing Methodist denominations to a frequent reception of the Eucharist, the Lord's Supper is often observed monthly and generally claims a higher attendance than the regular preaching services.[22] Communicants may approach the sacrament using a posture similar to that used by beggars in the street—"kneeling or squatting or crouching with outstretched hands clasped like a bowl [and] lifted way above their heads but never at any time daring to look up or open their eyes."[23] Cambodians have benefitted from the sensitivities to liturgical inculturation that emerged particularly in the mid-twentieth century, and thus worship takes place entirely in Khmer and integrates local custom in ways the people find appropriate. While liturgical resources from the missionizing groups are employed in translation, there has also been a concerted effort to produce indigenous liturgical materials.

B. Space for Worship

Methodists have been extremely pragmatic when it comes to places for worship since the mandate to spread scriptural holiness has never been contingent upon the availability of "consecrated" space. The itinerating Methodist Episcopal preacher Charles Giles captured the Methodist perspective when he

---

20. *Christian Hymn and Worship Book of the Cambodia Christian Methodist Association* (New York: General Board of Global Ministries, the United Methodist Church, 2001).
21. Lowe, "A Cultural Analysis," 88, 118.
22. Ibid., 90–95.
23. Ibid., 95.

recorded in his memoir published in 1844 that "pure spiritual worship, which emanates from the pious heart, can be offered acceptably in any place; and wherever Christ meets his worshipping saints, there is peace, paradise, and heaven."[24] Thus, Methodists have worshiped in every imaginable space and place until they have been able to build their own—and the construction of those spaces has been determined as much by demographics, geography, economics, and architectural preferences as by the style and practices of worship that the structure is to house. As was the case with the liturgy itself, greater longevity as a denomination led to greater complexities in the design of buildings and worship spaces and in the utilization of furniture and furnishings. For the Methodist Episcopal Church, the brush arbors, log cabins, and simple wooden structures used during its early years gave way to wood, stone, brick, and concrete buildings in Romanesque, Gothic revival, and auditorium designs by the beginning of the twentieth century.

The missionaries to Singapore took advantage of available spaces for their ministries: the town hall was the location for Thoburn's first service in 1885, and preaching services continued regularly there as well as at the already-constructed Christian Institute.[25] Methodists met in schools, homes, and "secular" spaces ornamented with the key furnishings of table and podium or temporary pulpit until their own houses for meeting and worship could be constructed. The image of church building in the mind's eye of the missionaries inevitably influenced the erection of places for worship; thus, the majority of Methodist buildings in Singapore could be mistaken for those in the United States or Britain. New or renovated constructions on the constricted land blocks available in Singapore rarely express the ethnic cultural backgrounds of the congregation; limited examples of inculturation can be found with the furnishings within and outside the worship space. Some redesign of the disposition of space and furnishings has been done to take into account the new concerns for the assembly itself and the centrality of the Eucharist as highlighted by the liturgical movement. For example, Trinity Methodist Church's outdoor immersion-style baptistery doubles as a cooling fountain when not needed for sacramental purposes.

---

24. Charles Giles, *Pioneer: A Narrative of the Nativity, Experience, Travels and Ministerial Labours of the Rev. Charles Giles* (New York: G. Lane and P. P. Sandford, 1844), 138.

25. Theodore R. Doraisamy, *The March of Methodism in Singapore and Malaysia* (Singapore: Methodist Book Room, 1982), 7–8.

The outdoor baptistery / cooling fountain at Trinity Methodist Church in Singapore. Photo by Alphonsus Loh and Philip Lim.

As did Methodists of the first and second generations early in their development as "church," so do the Cambodian Methodists of the third generation worship in whatever space can accommodate an assembly. Cambodians gather in public halls, under the platform of a house on stilts, in the open air, in private homes, and in Western-style church buildings when they are available. The furnishings are sparse: table, pulpit, an offering box, straw mats when there are no chairs or pews.[26] When possible, a red cross is erected on the exterior of the building, or chalked on the interior walls, or sewn onto a blue cloth typically draped behind the pulpit.[27] For the Cambodian Methodists, the color red that symbolizes commitment, steadfastness, and the laying down of one's life for a solemn purpose speaks about both the God they worship and who they are as a Christian people.[28] The inclusion of cultural forms at this early stage suggests a willingness to develop places for worship in the future that reflect an identity as both Christian and Cambodian.

C. Hymns and Songs

When the Methodist Episcopal Church was founded in 1784, not only did the new denomination take up John Wesley's *Sunday Service*; they also accepted the Wesley brothers' *A Collection of Psalms and Hymns for the Lord's Day* sent along with it, which was a slightly abridged version of an earlier collection.[29]

---

26. Lowe, "A Cultural Analysis," 85.
27. The color blue symbolizes peace, prosperity, and the presence of God (ibid., 115–16).
28. Ibid., 87, 136.
29. John and Charles Wesley, *A Collection of Psalms and Hymns for the Lord's Day* (London: Strahan, 1784); cf. John Wesley, *Collection of Psalms and Hymns* (London: Strahan, 1741).

Whereas a printed book of liturgical texts for Methodists was something new, a hymn book approved by John Wesley was not. Indeed, John Wesley appears to have been the first to publish a hymn collection in North America, having edited the book to assist his missionary work in the South Carolina and Georgia colonies.[30] After his return to England, he and his brother Charles together or singly brought out at least a collection a year for the next ten years, and they continued intermittently thereafter until 1787. Methodists immigrating to North America brought with them the various hymn books, hymn pamphlets, and tune books published in England by the Wesleys; Charles served as the principal poet for those books and is credited with writing over six thousand hymn texts on topics including the liturgical year, the Lord's Supper, and the Methodist way of salvation (*via salutis*).[31] The Wesley hymns were quite popular for corporate worship and for family or personal devotion: by 1773, printers in North America were reproducing the most widely used of the collections; and eighteenth-century manuscript diaries and journals contained favorite Wesley hymn texts copied by hand. Thus, it is not surprising that the first leaders of the Methodist Episcopal Church would legislate "keep[ing] close to Mr. Wesley's tunes and hymns" while at the same time restricting the use of unapproved hymns and hymn collections—a restriction put forward, the evidence shows, because certain Methodists were borrowing from other sources and composing their own material.[32] Methodist leaders were well aware of the hymn's capacity as a conveyor of the *lex credendi* and also as a tool for evangelism, and for this reason as well they encouraged all in the congregation to sing.[33]

While the Wesley hymn corpus continued in the first generation to be a source of Methodist identity even while the total number of Wesley hymns diminished in successive authorized hymnals (the decline more rapid in the United States than in Britain), the restrictions against the composition of new

---

30. John Wesley, ed., *Collection of Psalms and Hymns* (Charlestown, SC: Timothy, 1737); known as the "Charlestown collection."

31. In his preface to *A Collection of Hymns for the Use of the People Called Methodists* (1780), John Wesley noted that the collection was organized according to the "experience of real Christians," thus making it "in effect a little body of experimental [experiential] and practical divinity" (*The Works of John Wesley*, vol. 7, ed. Franz Hildebrandt and Oliver A. Beckerlegge [Nashville: Abingdon Press, 1983], 74).

32. Westerfield Tucker, *American Methodist Worship*, 156–61; cf. Q. 37, A. 9, "Large Minutes," *Minutes of Several Conversations*, 23; and Jesse Lee, *A Short History of the Methodists, in the United States of America; Beginning in 1766, and Continued till 1809* (Baltimore: Magill and Clime, 1810), 88.

33. Lee, *A Short History*, 190.

texts and tunes and the use of non-Methodist hymnological materials very quickly disappeared. The same musical spirit that animated Charles Wesley captured the hearts and pens of numbers of his spiritual descendants, though very few produced compositions of lasting quality. Examination of the style and content of the texts shows that many of them were intended for use at evangelistic meetings and that they were influenced by the theological and spiritual trends then current within the denomination and within wider American Protestantism. Among the more acclaimed hymn writers affiliated with the Methodist Episcopal Church should be named Fanny Crosby (who wrote hundreds of hymns under different pseudonyms), Mary Lathbury ("Day is Dying in the West"), and Frank Mason North ("Where Cross the Crowded Ways of Life"). Tunes that were adopted were influenced by folk melodies, music of different styles emanating from Europe, new homegrown compositions, and the latest popular style. Methodists continually debated which musical forms—and musical instruments—were the most appropriate for worship, though inevitably those at one time deemed highly inappropriate eventually came to be accepted. Congregational singing flourished throughout the life of the Methodist Episcopal Church.

The Wesleyan and other hymns commonly used in worship—whether from the authorized denominational hymnals or not—migrated with the Methodist Episcopal missionaries to Singapore. Those texts considered most beneficial to the work were quickly translated into the local languages, with texts in Bahasa Melayu being among the first, thanks to the translation talents of the English Methodist W. G. Shellabear, an officer stationed with the Royal Artillery.[34] But as was the case with the liturgical texts, few new hymns or songs were locally produced, even well into the twentieth century; most of the worship repertoire was translated Western imports—both text and tune. Even when many Singaporean Methodists embraced the so-called contemporary worship forms popular from the 1960s onward, the music they used and the instruments they played came from elsewhere. However, the last two decades of the twentieth century saw a gradual interest in locally produced music, a change that took place largely under the leadership of Mary Gan, founder of the Methodist School of Music established in 1997 (currently serving over five hundred students),[35] and Swee Hong Lim, a composer who had done his undergraduate training at the Asian Institute for Liturgy and Music in the Philippines. Singaporean Methodists had been hesitant to embrace Asian music styles and

---

34. Doraisamy, *The March of Methodism*, 15–16.
35. See http://www.msmusic.edu.sg.

Asian musical instruments for the reasons common to missionized peoples in regions dominated by other religions: out of concern that certain instruments and musical forms were associated with non-Christian worship and represented what was surrendered in order to become a Christian. Another factor was that many of the instructors and players of Asian instruments were non-Christians. The Methodist School of Music, with a Christian faculty, opened the door to the acceptance of inculturated musical forms and non-Western instruments, and Swee Hong Lim provided them with musical settings. Particularly striking are the melodies in Chinese style designed to accompany texts by Charles Wesley, such as the text "Still for Thy Loving Kindness."[36]

The emphasis on inculturated music in Singaporean Methodism and elsewhere in Methodism, coupled with the work on Cambodian indigenous music for the Christian community beginning in the 1970s that had been accomplished by the late British Overseas Missionary Fellowship missionary Alice Compain and by the Cambodian musician and Christian convert Sarin Sam (Som), meant that the *Christian Hymn and Worship Book of the Cambodia Christian Methodist Association* would contain original hymn and song texts in Khmer sung to Cambodian melodies. Compain had arrived in Cambodia in 1974 and discovered Christians writing their own texts to Western tunes. About the same time, the Cambodian musician Vinna Mao encouraged the composition of original tunes within the Christian community, but the ascendance of the Khmer Rouge resulted in the extermination of many of these Christian hymn writers, including Mao. Cambodian refugee camps in Thailand and elsewhere soon became the place for the creation of new Cambodian Christian songs and hymns, and it was there that Compain began painstakingly to notate these new indigenous songs. Compain met Sarin Sam in 1982, who started taking standard hymns (e.g., "O for a Thousand Tongues to Sing") and recasting them in Khmer idioms. The Christian Missionary Alliance (CMA) that had a long-time presence in Cambodia had translated Western hymns into Khmer and published them in a hymnal (*Tomnuk Domkerng*); with the collaboration and guidance of Compain and Sam, the CMA brought out in 1985 a second

---

36. See, for example, his published music in *Global Praise 2*, ed. S T Kimbrough Jr. and Carlton R. Young (New York: GBGMusik, General Board of Global Ministries, the United Methodist Church, 2000); and *Global Praise 3*, ed. S T Kimbrough Jr. and Carlton R. Young (New York: GBGMusik, General Board of Global Ministries, the United Methodist Church, 2004). See also his published dissertation *Giving Voice to Asian Christians: An Appraisal of the Pioneering Work of I-To Lo in the Area of Congregational Song* (Saarbrücken: Verlag Dr. Müller, 2008).

Text: Charles Wesley (from Hymns and Sacred Poems, 1740); music: Swee Hong Lim; music © 1988 General Board of Global Ministries, GBGMusik, 475 Riverside Dr., New York, NY 10115. All rights reserved. Used with permission.[37]

37. Found as no. 58 in Global Praise 1, ed. S T Kimbrough Jr. and Carlton R. Young (New York: GBGMusik, General Board of Global Ministries, the United Methodist Church, 1996).

edition (*Tomnuk Khmer Borisot; Holy Khmer Songs*) that contained indigenous texts with Cambodian tunes drawn from folk songs to opera. Later editions, produced with the assistance of Barnabas Mam (Mom), expanded the number of indigenously produced songs. An edition from 1993 contained over three hundred indigenous hymns.[38]

Because of Sarin Sam's knowledge of Cambodian musical sources, he was engaged as an editor for the Methodist *Christian Hymn and Worship Book* that was published in 2001. Material for the 194 hymns in the Methodist book came from texts and tunes composed by Sarin Sam and Barnabas Mam, in addition to Western tunes and Khmer translations of standard hymns (ten by Charles Wesley[39]) borrowed from the older CMA hymn books. Tunes associated with older Khmer melodies are specified for some of the hymns: five tunes are connected to "royal Khmer dance," four are "traditional Khmer," seven are "Khmer folk," nine are "Yee Keh drama songs," and one is a "Khmer harvest song." New "Methodist" lyrics and tunes were included in the book and were produced under the guidance of Swee Hong Lim at a Methodist Pastors' Training School held in Phnom Penh in February 1999.[40] Many of the Methodist churches in Cambodia have access to the 2001 book or one of the older books produced by the CMA. Yet new songs continue to be produced and sung in worship: texts and tunes in Khmer are still composed, but a new focus has developed on the cultivation of indigenous songs among minority communities that do not use Khmer musical idioms.

In performance practice, the lively singing of songs and hymns is occasionally accompanied by the Cambodian two-stringed *chepei* when native melodies are used; otherwise, the Western acoustic guitar is preferred, although some guitarists prefer to play only two of its strings.[41] Additional instruments found in worship, and particularly on Communion Sundays because of their

---

38. See Alice Compain, "Born across Borders, Raised in a Refugee Camp: The History of the Cambodian Hymnal," *EthnoDoxology* 1.1 (2002): 17–18. Cf. Lowe, "A Cultural Analysis," 86, 89.

39. The Charles Wesley hymns in Khmer translation are "O for a Thousand Tongues to Sing" (7), "Love Divine, All Loves Excelling" (22), "Hark! The Herald Angels Sing" (45), "Christ, the Lord, Is Risen Today" (67), "And Can It Be That I Should Gain" (80), "Jesus, Lover of My Soul" (83), "Arise, My Soul, Arise" (88), "O for a Heart to Praise My God" (113), "Still for Thy Loving Kindness" (161; the tune used is by Swee Hong Lim), and "Lo! He Comes with Clouds Descending" (191).

40. Swee Hong Lim, email message to author, February 18, 2011. Music in the *Christian Hymn and Worship Book* that was produced at the Pastors' School can be found as numbers 13, 20, 69, 77, 95, 112, 168, and 173.

41. Lowe, "A Cultural Analysis," 85.

148   Part One: Historical Moments of Liturgical Migration

[Musical score with Khmer, transliteration, and English text]

Khmer: ឱមនុស្សអើយ ព្រះបាន ឱ្យស្គាល់សេចក្ដីដែល
Translit.: O mnus oeuy Preah bahn bong-hagn neak heuy oy skorl sek-kdey del
English: For the Lord has shown to all of us and told us what is

loar teh Preah Am-Chas oy neak twer douch-mdeck nor keur
good; and what does God re-quire of us: to

oy pror-pret tair loar tahm plow soch-reth yutek-tor heuy
prac-tice jus-tice, and mer-cy al-ways love, to

sror-lagn kdey sobo-bros. Trov deur chear muy ning Preah ney
hum-bly walk with God, to prac-tice jus-tice, to love

kluon oy batin chorb snith morm moon doy kdey so-pheap reap teap.
mer-cy, and to walk hum-bly, hum-bly with our God.

Micah 6:8 paraphrase and music: Sarin Sam; English paraphrase: S T Kimbrough Jr.;
words and music © 1999 General Board of Global Ministries,
GBGMusik, 475 Riverside Dr., New York, NY 10115.
All rights reserved. Used with permission.[42]

42. Found as no. 101 in *Global Praise 2* and also as no. 116 in *Christian Hymn and Worship Book of the Cambodia Christian Methodist Association*.

Methodism's "World Parish" 149

Words and music: Sarin Sam; English: S T Kimbrough Jr.;
words and music © 2000 General Board of Global Ministries,
GBGMusik, 475 Riverside Dr., New York, NY 10115. All rights reserved. Used with permission.[43]

43. Found as no. 23 in *Global Praise 2* and also as no. 162 in *Christian Hymn and Worship Book of the Cambodia Christian Methodist Association*.

perceived ability to invoke the divine, are the *sko*, a handheld drum, and the *trow*, a two-string violin.[44] Passionate singing may encourage members of the congregation to dance, which is done Khmer style, with the initiator of the dance inviting others to join in a chain behind.[45] The sounds of worship are "Eastern, ethnic, and similar to songs and tunes used in Buddhist worship," a reality that may be uncomfortable to visitors from Singapore and elsewhere, especially those who were once Buddhists. But clearly the "discomfort is not extended to Khmer Christians," for whom "those sounds are great tools and bridges for the gospel."[46]

D. Prayer

Silas Told observed—and initially objected to—John Wesley's use of extemporary prayer, which, to his mind, "savoured too much of the Dissenter's mode of worship."[47] Indeed, the Methodists' employment of spontaneous and extemporary prayer that was often accompanied by physical and kinetic manifestations garnered similar disapproval from persons within the Church of England and without, and gave critics a "proof" of the Methodists' intention to separate from the established church, an accusation the Wesleys thoroughly denied.[48] The American Methodists thus inherited from John Wesley both the Prayer Book tradition of printed prayers and the custom of extemporary prayer, with the latter style received via the first Methodist immigrants in the 1760s. Since most Methodists were "fully satisfied that they could pray better, and with more devotion while their eyes were shut, than they could with their eyes open,"[49] extemporary prayer by a leader or by individuals in the assembly was a central component of Methodist worship in North America before and after the receipt (and rejection) of the Sunday parts of Wesley's *Sunday Service*. Those offering prayer were cautioned usually not to pray "*ex tempore* above eight or

---

44. Ibid., 116.
45. Ibid., 90.
46. Ibid., 86.
47. Told, *An Account of the Life*, 74.
48. "Although we call sinners to repentance in all places of God's dominion; and although we frequently use extemporary prayer, and unite together in a religious society; yet we are not Dissenters in the only sense which our law acknowledges, namely, those who renounce the service of the church. We do not: We dare not separate from it" (Q. 45, A., "Large Minutes," *Minutes of Several Conversations*, 28). Despite John Wesley's involvement in the creation of the Methodist Episcopal Church, he himself never formally separated from the Church of England.
49. Lee, *A Short History*, 107.

ten minutes (at most) without intermission,"[50] which suggests that spiritually inspired, as well as unfocused and long-winded, praying was quite common. Prayer was understood to be an instituted "means of grace"—instituted by Christ himself, who had supplied a model prayer—and was generally to include "deprecation, petition, intercession, and thanksgiving" whether offered on the knees[51] in private, in the family, or in public.[52]

From 1824, the *Doctrines and Discipline* specified that the Lord's Prayer was to be used as the conclusion for the first prayer in public worship, thereby acknowledging a place for "set" prayers in Methodist Episcopal congregations on Sunday. The acceptance of set and printed prayers continued throughout the century, as noted previously, so that by the turn into the twentieth century, authorized and unofficial prayer collections were in use for Sunday worship in many congregations.[53] Coinciding with this increase in the availability of printed prayers was a decline in the skills for offering prayer extemporaneously (according to commentators of the period)—even though spontaneous and extemporary prayer remained a hallmark of Methodist praxis and an unwritten expectation of the denomination's clergy and key lay leadership.

Although printed prayers were certainly available to Singapore's Methodist Episcopal and British Methodist missionaries, the option of extemporary prayer was generally taken because of the need for worship in simple English and in local languages and for prayers that spoke to the particular context and circumstances. As Methodism became more established and worship resources were imported and translated, extemporary prayer survived not only because it was considered a "Methodist" way of praying, but also on account

---

50. See Q. 37, A. 11, "Large Minutes," *Minutes of Several Conversations*, 23; and section 12, Q. 3, A. 9, *The Doctrines and Discipline of the Methodist Episcopal Church in America* (Philadelphia: Parry Hall, 1792), 28.

51. Although the "Large Minutes" specify that prayer is to be offered kneeling (Q. 37, A. 16, "Large Minutes," *Minutes of Several Conversations*, 24), by 1792 the Methodist Episcopal *Doctrines and Discipline* no longer carried the instruction, though the practice of kneeling for prayer even in public worship continued well into the nineteenth century in some congregations.

52. See Q. 48, A. I.1, "Large Minutes," *Minutes of Several Conversations*, 30; and section 13, Q. 2, A. I.1, *The Doctrines and Discipline of the Methodist Episcopal Church in America* (1792), 29. The specification of the content of prayer survived through to the (final) *Doctrines and Discipline of the Methodist Episcopal Church (1936)*, par. 428, no. 1.

53. For example, Charles LeVerne Roberts, ed., *Divine Service: A Compilation of Collects and Psalms for Use in the Public Worship of God in the Methodist Episcopal Church* (Cincinnati: Jennings and Pye, 1903); and Wilbur P. Thirkield, *Service and Prayers for Church and Home* (New York: Methodist Book Concern, 1918, 1928).

of conservative and charismatic trends that developed first in the Chinese-speaking churches and then in the English- and Tamil-speaking congregations—approaches that inclined toward a less "scripted" approach to worship. The preference for spontaneous and extemporary prayer can particularly be found today in Singaporean Methodist congregations of all language groups that have embraced the so-called contemporary worship style, given the demand and desire for liturgical flexibility.[54]

Initially lacking print resources, Cambodian Methodist Christians learned to pray "from the heart" and "with the spirit and the mind" (1 Cor 14:15). Such an approach to prayer remains strong even with the availability of Methodist texts from other places translated into Khmer. The most prominent style is for the entire congregation to pray their personal prayers aloud simultaneously, a practice similar to the Korean exercise of *tongsung kido* and to what is found in some charismatic communities. Thus, on Sunday morning among Cambodian Methodists,

> the worship leader begins verbalizing his or her prayers and soon the entire congregation is caught up in the frenzy of praying. A holy buzz or a droning sound arises when the prayers first begin and subsequently pick up in volume like chants.
>
> It is distinctly audible, and soon many are lost in the spirit of praying. Sometimes they are beside themselves in a good way, in that they are oblivious to those around them. They pray uninhibitedly. They pray earnestly. Often times they shout with fists pumped up into the air as a sign of intensity or a declaration of victory that their prayers have been heard by God or in a celebration that God will answer and act from their prayers. Sometimes they wail and cry. They all stand to pray, heads bowed or lifted and eyes closed. Some clasp their hands in the same manner as in their traditional greeting, while others raise their hands. Just as naturally as the prayers had begun, the congregation similarly soon tapers to a hush and complete silence without prompting after all have prayed. The worship leader again prays on behalf of the congregation and finally asks the congregation to pray aloud together the Lord's prayer.[55]

---

54. Swee Hong Lim, "Chinese, Tamil, and English Congregations: Sunday Worship of the Methodist Church in Singapore," in *The Sunday Service of the Methodists: Twentieth-Century Worship in Worldwide Methodism*, ed. Karen B. Westerfield Tucker (Nashville: Kingswood Press, 1996), 210–14.

55. Lowe, "A Cultural Analysis," 92.

Such a description also has strong resonances with the prayer practices of the early Methodists in Britain and in America, a people who understood their hearts to be "strangely warmed."

III. Conclusion

What preliminary observations can be made regarding Methodist liturgical and hymnological migrations crossing generations and geography?

Because of its origin as a movement—an evangelistic movement charged to spread scriptural holiness—Methodism assumed migration to be part of its self-identity. The effective transmission of the Gospel required attention to the contexts of the hearers, and the pragmatic Methodists quickly discovered that informal worship consisting of the core components of prayer, singing, Scripture reading, and preaching could easily be adapted to most situations. As we have seen, this "core" migrated across each of the three ecclesiastical generations. Although texted liturgical forms were also transplanted in each generation, those forms, at least as pertaining to Sunday or general worship, were not as quickly and readily accepted as were the forms for occasional practices—perhaps precisely because they were occasional forms. Over time, however, the use of texted liturgical resources in a given community became more widespread. Perhaps it can be said, drawing on the Methodist example, that the simpler the liturgy, the more easily it migrates across borders of time and place.

The examples of the Methodist Church in Singapore as a second ecclesiastical generation, and Cambodian Methodism as a third generation, raise questions about the transmission, adaptation, and creation of liturgical texts. Up until the last twenty-five years or so, the Methodist Church in Singapore looked to its originating denominations for liturgical materials, with little interest in adapting those liturgies or in creating their own. The same is true for the liturgical texts used by the Korean Methodist Church and African Methodist denominations with their roots in British Methodism. The impetus for creativity in these churches appears to have resulted in part from the attention to inculturation given in the years after the Second Vatican Council. But what other factors may have caused continued reliance on the "liturgies of origin" long after these churches had become independent denominations? Focus on other ecclesiastical issues? Residual compliance with the missionaries' idealization of Western forms and practices? Satisfaction that the inherited texts were genuinely and appropriately "Methodist"? The delay of the second generation is striking when measured against the liturgical creativity of the third generation. This certainly is an area for more research.

Each generation has borne witness to the evangelical and "catholic" aspects of its Wesleyan heritage, with the latter best represented by the attention given to the importance of the Lord's Supper. The renewed interest in the Wesleyan heritage that began in the final decades of the nineteenth century along with the influences of the liturgical movement in the first half of the twentieth century have enabled the third Methodist generation, like their spiritual ancestors, to own the sacrament as a place of encounter with their risen Lord.

It is often said that Methodism was born in song. Yet it is also clear that Methodism is sustained by song. The translation of an old repertoire and the creation of a new repertoire have been important within each generation and across the generations. But what in the end binds these generations and locations together is the hymns of the Wesleys:

> Partakers of the Saviour's grace
> The same in mind and heart,
> Nor joy, nor grief, nor time, nor place,
> Nor life, nor death can part.[56]

---

56. Stanza 5, "Blest Be the Dear, Uniting Love" (no. 520), in *A Collection of Hymns for the Use of the People Called Methodists* (1780), The Works of John Wesley, 7:713.

7

An Immigrant Liturgy: Greek Orthodox Worship and Architecture in America

Kostis Kourelis and Vasileios Marinis

Greek Orthodox Migrations to America

The Greek Orthodox Archdiocese of America comprises its main district, New York, and eight metropolises, which spread from New Jersey to California. According to official records, the archdiocese includes about 540 parishes, 800 priests, and 1.5 million faithful, although this number is certainly an exaggeration.[1] Nowadays worship is conducted mostly in English, with only parts in Greek, except in parishes in such areas as Astoria, New York, where there is still a large concentration of first-generation immigrants. The setting of Greek American worship is a hybrid, combining strong elements derived from Byzantine and post-Byzantine architectural and artistic traditions with "Western" influences stemming from the practices of other mainstream denominations, Catholic and Protestant, and from major twentieth-century trends, such as modernism. The current situation is the end result of a lengthy and at times painful process of liturgical migration that began in the late nineteenth century.

---

1. For a more realistic estimate, see Charles Moskos, "The Greeks in the United States," in *The Greek Diaspora in the Twentieth Century*, ed. Richard Clogg (New York: St. Martin's Press, 1999), 107.

Leaving a home country where Greek Orthodoxy was the denominational mainstream, as well as the national church, Greeks found themselves in the position of a religious minority with rites and customs that appeared unconventional to the host population. On a fundamental level, the migration of the Greek Orthodox liturgy should be examined in the general context of Greek immigration and settlement in the United States.[2] Liturgical practice, as well as its apparatuses, accoutrements, and architectural accommodations, were and still are part of the discourse of identity (ethnic, national, and transnational) of Greek communities in America. The mission, stated or implied, of the Greek Orthodox Church in America and, by extension, its liturgical practice has always been strongly tied to the life, aspirations, and hopes of the parishes that compose it.

The mission of the church has changed dramatically over time.[3] Immigration to the United States started in the late nineteenth century and peaked after the end of World War I. It is calculated that about half a million Greeks immigrated to the United States, close to one-quarter of Greece's working-age male population.[4] One of the first acts of these communities was to organize and consecrate a church. In the absence of a central authority, clergy were brought from the Patriarchate of Constantinople, or from Greece, at the initiative of

---

2. On the history of the Greek American community, see, inter alia, Thomas Burgess, *Greeks in America* (Boston: Sherman, French, 1913; repr., 1970); J. P. Xenides, *The Greeks in America* (New York: G. H. Doran Co., 1922; repr., San Francisco: R. and E. Research Associates, 1972); Theodore Saloutos, *The Greeks in the United States* (Cambridge, MA: Harvard University Press, 1967); Alice Scourby, *The Greek Americans* (Boston: Twayne Publishers, 1984); Charles C. Moskos, *Greek Americans: Struggle and Success*, 2nd ed. (New Brunswick, NJ: Transaction Publishers, 1989); Babis I. Marketos, *Hoi Hellenoamerikanoi* (Athens: Papazeses, 2006).

3. See Theodore Saloutos, "The Greek Orthodox Church in the United States and Assimilation," *International Migration Review* 7/4 (1973): 395–407; Vasileios Th. Zoustes, *Ho en Amerike Hellenismos kai he drasis autou: He historia tes Hellenikes Archiepiskopes Amerikes Voreiou kai Notiou* (New York: n.p., 1954); Miltiades B. Efthimiou and George A. Christopoulos, eds., *History of the Greek Orthodox Church in America* (New York: Greek Orthodox Archdiocese of North and South America, 1984); Nicon D. Patrinacos, "The Role of the Church in the Evolving Greek American Community," in *The Greek American Community in Transition*, ed. Harry J. Psomiades and Alice Scourby (New York: Pella, 1982), 123–36; Demetrios J. Constantelos, ed., *Encyclicals and Documents of the Greek Orthodox Archdiocese of North and South America: Relating to Its Thought and Activity the First Fifty Years (1922–1972)* (Thessalonike: Patriarchal Institute for Patristic Studies, 1976); Paul Manolis, ed., *The History of the Greek Church in America: In Acts and Documents* (Berkeley, CA: Ambelos Press, 2003); Nicolas Prévélakis, "Église orthodoxe et diaspora grecque," in *Arméniens et Grecs en diaspora: Approches comparatives*, ed. Michel Bruneau et al. (Athens: École française d'Athènes, 2007), esp. 511–16.

4. Moskos, *Greek Americans*, 8.

each parish.⁵ Some order was imposed with the incorporation of the Greek Orthodox Archdiocese of North and South America in 1921, some thirty years after the arrival of the first wave of immigrants.⁶

These circumstances had two unforeseen but interconnected consequences for the organizational structure of the Greek Orthodox archdiocese. First, the communities were impervious to interference from a central authority because each one paid for the construction of its church building, financed its activities, and was responsible for the priest's salary.⁷ Thus, even today Greek churches in the United States follow the presbyterian system, something unheard of in Greece, where the church is sponsored by the state and clergy are civil servants. Second, these communities experienced an unprecedented autonomy, which also affected liturgical and architectural practice.

The usual self-narrative of Greek immigrants to the United States focused on the temporariness of their status: their proclaimed goal was to amass wealth and return home. Because of this, immigrants were anxious to preserve their identity, especially their language, their customs and traditions, and certainly their faith. The church, especially in the early decades, played the role of defender and guarantor of Greek identity. This is not surprising, given that the mainstays of Greek life are organized around the religious calendar, with festivals culminating such major holidays as Easter, Christmas, and the feast of the Dormition of the Virgin on August 15. Furthermore, the church in Greece has had a real or imagined role as a leader in education, a role carried to the United States.

The preservation of ethnic identity proved to be challenging for the church, at least at the beginning. There were very few Greek-language schools, and these were located far from people's homes. The Immigration Acts of 1921 and 1924 introduced quotas that brought mass immigration to a stop.⁸ The shortage of newcomers from Greece was coupled with high rates of intermarriage and defection from the church.⁹ Finally, the Great Depression took a heavy toll on Greek parishes, both demographically and financially.¹⁰

---

5. For some examples, see Saloutos, *The Greeks*, 123–26.
6. On the organization of the Greek Orthodox archdiocese, see James S. Counelis, *Inheritance and Change in Orthodox Christianity* (Scranton, PA: University of Scranton Press, 1995), 74–78.
7. Saloutos, *The Greeks*, 129; Counelis, *Inheritance and Change*, 76–78.
8. Saloutos, "The Greek Orthodox Church," 399.
9. See the concerns of Athenagoras, archbishop of North and South America (1931–1948), in Constantelos, *Encyclicals*, 122.
10. Saloutos, "The Greek Orthodox Church," 401.

In the decades after World War II, there was a shift in the mission of the church. Rather than preserving Greek national identity, the church turned its attention, first, to sustaining the Orthodox faith and, second, to preserving the Greek language in the context of a multicultural America.[11] Thus the church stressed its role as a religious rather than an ethnic institution. However, the Immigration Act of 1965 brought a fresh flow of immigrants whose ideology, customs, and religious practices often clashed with those of the established Greek Americans who wanted greater use of English during church services and favored integration rather than ghettoization. The tension between old and new immigrants continued well into the 1990s, although further quotas in the 1980s stopped immigration again. This resulted in a majority of second- and third-generation Greek Americans whose primary language was English and whose primary cultural identity, either confessed or pragmatic, was American.[12] The creation of the Holy Cross School of Theology in 1937 (originally in Pomfret, Connecticut, and now in Brookline, Massachusetts), dedicated to the training of clergy, further reduced the need for imports from Greece.[13] Indeed, the vast majority of clergy serving today in the Greek Orthodox Church grew up in the United States and graduated from Holy Cross.

The migration of Greek American Orthodox worship to the United States and its subsequent evolution occurred within such complex social, cultural, and historical contexts. The mechanics of these processes are especially evident in three areas: language, liturgical practice, and architecture.

Language in Worship

The language of worship in the Greek American Orthodox Church largely reflects the fluctuations of the church's position toward national Greek identity. Athenagoras, one of the most influential archbishops of North and South America (1931–48) and subsequently ecumenical patriarch (1948–72), considered the preservation of the Greek language of the utmost importance. During his tenure the use of English for worship and preaching was discouraged,

---

11. See, for example, Constantelos, *Encyclicals*, 1106–9, 1114–15, 1119–26.

12. See Alexander Kitroeff, "Greek American Identity in the 1980s," in *Arméniens et grecs en diaspora: Approches comparatives*, ed. Michel Bruneau et al. (Athens: École française d'Athènes, 2007), 299–306.

13. For a history of this seminary, see Nomikos M. Vaporis, *A Chronicle of Hellenic College / Holy Cross Greek Orthodox School of Theology* (Brookline, MA: Holy Cross Orthodox Press, 1988).

even for American-born priests.[14] Archbishop Michael (1948–58) allowed English in Sunday schools and permitted clergy to preach in both languages, but English was not sanctioned for use in worship, despite claims, even by scholars and church leaders from Greece, that clinging to a language understood by only a fraction of the people would lead to isolation and would jeopardize the future of the church.[15] The situation began to change during the long tenure of Archbishop Iakovos (1959–96), a controversial but visionary leader. The Clergy-Laity Congress of 1964 suggested that the epistle and gospel lections, as well as the Creed and the Lord's Prayer, be repeated in English.[16] In an encyclical issued on October 3, 1968, Iakovos himself wrote:

> Our Church is not homogeneous, comprised of one generation. Our flock includes two, not to say three and four generations. . . . Furthermore, the Archdiocese has not one, two, or ten parishes but over four hundred. . . . Therefore the Archdiocese recommends measured use of one or the other language. . . . What will contribute to the understanding and experience of Orthodoxy is not so much language but rather participation in the ceremonies.[17]

The Clergy-Laity Congress of 1970 in New York City recommended the use of English in the Divine Liturgy and the translation of the texts of other sacraments.[18] The negative reaction against this initiative in both the United States and Greece was substantial and dramatic, although it was based on gross and largely intentional misinterpretation of what the congress had suggested.[19] The problem eventually solved itself, as Greek competency among Greek Americans declined. Unfortunately, we have no reliable statistics about this issue. In a study published in 1999, Charles Moskos estimated that about one-third of those attending church regularly had Greek as a mother tongue, but this figure would vary by practice.[20] As early as 1980 a study of the New York metropolitan area (where most Greek immigrants are located) indicated that 96.7 percent of second-generation Greek Americans claimed to speak

---

14. See George Papaioannou, *From Mars Hill to Manhattan: The Greek Orthodox in America under Athenagoras I* (Minneapolis, MN: Light and Life, 1976), 232–34.

15. Ibid., 234–37.

16. See Iakovos's comments in Constantelos, *Encyclicals*, 757.

17. Ibid., 745.

18. Saloutos, "The Greek Orthodox Church," 404–6.

19. See, for example, the comments in Marketos, *Hellenoamerikanoi*, 191–92.

20. Charles Moskos, "The Greeks in the United States," in *The Greek Diaspora in the Twentieth Century*, ed. Richard Clogg (New York: St. Martin's Press, 1999), 111.

Greek. The percentage fell to 57.8 percent when it came to third-generation Greek Americans.[21] Nowadays, the Greek Orthodox Archdiocese of America wisely allows each parish to decide the proportions of Greek and English used in worship, depending on the demographics of the congregation.

The dramatic debate over the use of English in worship overshadowed the important issue of the mechanics of translation of the Divine Liturgy. During the tenure of Archbishop Michael (1948–58), the archdiocese offered an English translation of the Divine Liturgy for the use of those who could not follow the Greek. In the 1960s there were about a dozen such translations.[22] However, it quickly became evident that simply "translating the words" was not enough. As Alexander Schmemann noted in 1964,

> Most of our translators seem to forget that the basic "key" to the liturgy is primarily of *aesthetical* and not of rational, nature. Liturgical texts are not mere statements. . . . The aesthetical element in the liturgy: in liturgical poetry, music and rite—is not accidental but essential.[23]

Despite several false starts, there exist today adequate and sensible translations of the Divine Liturgy, most notably the Holy Cross edition and the one currently used in the Archdiocese of Thyateira and in Great Britain.[24] Yet the intense focus on the Liturgy had the result that the translation of the texts of other services, such as *Orthros* (Matins) and *Hesperinos* (Vespers), was largely neglected. In contrast to the Divine Liturgy, which has few "proper" (variable) elements and is mostly read or intoned, the hymns in both Vespers and Matins comprise most of the service, change daily, and are sung. Their translation has been plagued by seemingly insurmountable difficulties because these hymns are essentially poems, composed in the Middle Ages and set to music. The need for the text to fit the traditional melody must be balanced by a translation that makes logical and theological sense. Here is one characteristically unsuccessful

---

21. Alice Scourby, "Three Generations of Greek Americans: A Study in Ethnicity," in *The Greek American Community in Transition*, ed. Harry J. Psomiades and Alice Scourby (New York: Pella, 1982), 116. See also Alice Scourby, *Third Generation Greek Americans: A Study of Religious Attitudes* (New York: Arno Press, 1980).

22. Saloutos, "The Greek Orthodox Church," 406.

23. Alexander Schmemann, "Problems of Orthodoxy in America: The Liturgical Problem," *St. Vladimir's Seminary Quarterly* 8 (1964): 166.

24. *The Divine Liturgy of Saint John Chrysostom* (Brookline, MA: Holy Cross Orthodox Press, 1985); *The Divine Liturgy of Our Father among the Saints, John Chrysostom* (New York: Oxford University Press, 1998).

example from the web site of the Greek Orthodox Archdiocese of America, the *kontakion* of St. James, the brother of the Lord:

> O wondrous Iakovos, God the Logos, only-begotten of the Father, who dwelt among us in latter days, declared you, the first shepherd and teacher of Jerusalem, and faithful steward of the spiritual mysteries. Wherefore, we all honor you, O Apostle.

Setting aside the awkwardness of syntax and grammar, one has to reach almost the middle of the hymn to realize that Iakovos is not God the Logos, nor is he the only-begotten Son of the Father! What constitutes a successful translation of these hymns remains a subject of debate among musicians, scholars, and leaders of worship.[25] Despite some recent efforts, the lack of reliable and comprehensible translations, in combination with the shortage of appropriate musical settings that underscore rather than obscure the meaning of the liturgical texts, contributed to the disappearance of many hymns from the communal consciousness of Greek American worshipers. This and the deficiency of educational programs for laity that pertain to the meaning, symbolism, and structures of Orthodox worship have greatly affected liturgical practices.

Liturgical Practices

A host of canons, rubric books, and liturgical calendars regulate virtually every aspect of the liturgical practice of the Greek Orthodox Church.[26] Such uniformity is a relatively recent phenomenon.[27] Until the advent of the printing

---

25. See Alexander Lingas, "Tradition and Renewal in Greek Orthodox Psalmody," in *The Psalms in Community: Jewish and Christian Textual, Liturgical, and Artistic Traditions*, ed. Harold W. Attridge and Margot E. Fassler (Atlanta: Society of Biblical Literature, 2003), 341–56; idem, "Performance Practice and the Politics of Transcribing Byzantine Chant," *Acta Musicae Byzantinae* 6 (2003): 56–76.

26. For a succinct history of this practice, see Robert F. Taft, *The Byzantine Rite: A Short History* (Collegeville, MN: Liturgical Press, 1992). See also Hans-Joachim Schulz, *The Byzantine Liturgy: Symbolic Structure and Faith Expression* (New York: Pueblo, 1986); Hugh Wybrew, *The Orthodox Liturgy: The Development of the Eucharistic Liturgy in the Byzantine Rite* (London: SPCK, 1989).

27. On questions of evolution, change, and local variations of the Byzantine Rite, see Robert F. Taft, "How Liturgies Grow: The Evolution of the Byzantine Divine Liturgy," *Orientalia Christiana Periodica* 43 (1977): 355–78, repr. in Robert F. Taft, *Beyond East and West: Problems in Liturgical Understanding*, 2nd ed. (Rome: Edizioni Orientalia Christiana, 1997), chap. 11; Thomas Pott, *Byzantine Liturgical Reform: A Study of Liturgical Change in the Byzantine Tradition* (Crestwood, NY: St. Vladimir's Seminary Press, 2010).

press and the ensuing ossification of the Byzantine Rite, of which the Greek Orthodox Church is an inheritor, liturgical variations, primarily regional, were not unusual. In this context innovation in liturgical practice in Greek American Orthodoxy can be considered a positive result of its presbyterian structure and its distance from the spiritual center. However, such phenomena are not always a response to theological, liturgical, or even internal practical developments. For example, already in the 1950s the problem of unauthorized shortening of services and the introduction of "foreign" practices was significant enough to require an encyclical by Archbishop Michael:

> Several priests continue to curtail parts of the Divine Liturgies and the most holy sacraments; others still introduce innovations foreign to the holy tradition of the Church. . . . All priests should follow the rubrics in the liturgical calendar, otherwise they would face spiritual court. They should stop reading the prayer of absolution [συγχωρητική] to people who are about to receive communion, who had not participated in the sacrament of confession.[28]

The encyclical is vague in the particulars, yet with minor adjustments it could be circulated today. In some parishes Sunday Matins has been curtailed to its essentials and is just long enough for the celebrant to prepare the eucharistic gifts for the liturgy. Very few, if any, laity participate. Attendance in Saturday Vespers is equally low. The question of why these services have become effectively irrelevant for some communities merits a separate study, but it is not coincidental that we lack adequate translations and musical settings for the hymns sung in these services.[29] Whether the people can understand the meaning of a church ritual and comprehend what is said in it is of paramount importance.

The encyclical's last sentence is of particular significance as it pinpoints another area of friction, namely, the acceptance of "Western" practices. In the Orthodox tradition confession is a sacrament that takes place between the confessing person and the priest or bishop in a private space. The encyclical's text implies that under Protestant influence some priests had started reading the prayer of absolution on behalf of the whole congregation right before Communion, something that Archbishop Michael rightly considered a noncanonical practice.

The angst over "foreign" (Protestant or Catholic) influences affecting worship was expressed in another encyclical from the 1970s. Priests were instructed to

---

28. Constantelos, *Encyclicals*, 527–28.
29. The translations published by Narthex Press, although useful, are of variable quality.

preach for no more than fifteen minutes and to avoid using Catholic and Protestant sermons or quotations from foreign sources.[30] From another contemporary document we learn that in some parishes a wedding march was played before the beginning of the sacrament of marriage, obviously at the request of the participants. Interestingly, priests were instructed not to repeal this practice. "Rather," the source says, "if it is necessary to play it, this should happen in a hushed and quiet way [ἐλαφρῶς καὶ ὑποκώφως] and separately from the sacrament."[31]

The sacrament of marriage has been amenable to such additions because of the large number of inter-Christian marriages. According to official statistics, nearly two-thirds (63 percent) of all marriages conducted in the Greek Orthodox Archdiocese of America are designated as inter-Christian.[32] A noteworthy recent inclusion in some parishes is the recitation of the wedding vows in the narthex of the church before the sacrament proper. The Orthodox service does not include vows; indeed, the couple does not utter a single word during the service.

The most unmistakable change attributed to Western influence is the use of the organ—actually an electronic variation thereof—and polyphonic choirs. Both are foreign to the Greek Orthodox Church, and many organists and choir members are volunteers or, at most, part-time employees, so the results have been mixed (and, on occasion, distressing). Such choirs cannot hope to reach the uncanny musical perfection of a high church Anglo-Catholic parish, and as a matter of fact, they should not. Amateur choirs are heralds of a renewed emphasis on congregational participation. In Greece even today the liturgy is a segregated affair, with the clergy celebrating and a professional cantor chanting the appropriate parts. In the United States there is a deliberate effort, at least in some parishes, to involve the faithful in the act of worshiping God. Examples range from the recital of the Creed and the Lord's Prayer by the people to congregational singing of responses and hymns during the liturgy.

Architecture

In the Orthodox tradition architecture has developed into a codified container of ritual, iconography, and symbolic meaning.[33] Like liturgical practice,

---

30. Ibid., 847.
31. Ibid., 845–46.
32. Greek Orthodox Archdiocese of America, Department of Marriage and Family, http://www.goarch.org/archdiocese/departments/marriage, accessed 16 September 2010.
33. See Vasileios Marinis, "Defining Liturgical Space," in *The Byzantine World*, ed. Paul Stephenson (New York: Routledge, 2010), 284–302.

architectural design is tightly controlled by ecclesiastical authority, which, to many Western viewers, explains the conservative, seemingly unchanging character of Byzantine visual culture. Basilicas became the first architectural model for Christian churches beginning with Emperor Constantine I in the fourth century. Although basilican forms continued to dominate the architecture of the Catholic West, the centralized domed building has been the canonical type for churches in the Orthodox East from the seventh century to the present.[34] This singular model contrasts greatly with the variety in Christian architecture that developed in the West, especially after the Italian Renaissance and the Protestant Reformation. Orthodox churches in Greece continue to be built on the medieval model even when modern materials like reinforced concrete are used. Shared by all Orthodox Christians, the liturgical commitment to a prescribed architectural space is a force that has kept religious experience consistent across the Orthodox Ecumene through the centuries. Central ecclesiastical control, moreover, has guaranteed that every new church is approved by a test of tradition.

Between 1900 and 1920 over four hundred thousand Greeks immigrated to North America, making it the largest population movement of Greeks until the Greek-Turkish War of 1922. In spite of the demographic magnitude of this phenomenon, no statistical figures exist for ecclesiastical establishments, including the phases of development from impermanent to permanent real estate holdings. In 1930 there were about two hundred Greek Orthodox churches in the United States.[35] Although not all Greek migrants were faithful Christians, they sought communal solidarity through the establishment of churches.[36] No systematic history of Greek American buildings has been written, but a survey of churches reveals a diversity of religious architecture unmatched in any other Orthodox context.[37] Strategies of appropriation and reuse, coupled

---

34. For a history of Byzantine architecture, see Richard Krautheimer, *Early Christian and Byzantine Architecture*, 4th ed. (New York: Penguin, 1986).

35. Moskos, *Greek Americans*, 12, 36.

36. For an introduction to the cultural experiences of Greek immigration, see Alexander Kitroeff, "He hyperatlantike metanasteuse," in *Historia tes Hellados tou 20ou aiona*, 1/1, *Hoi aparches 1900–1922* (Athens: Vivliorama, 1999), 122–71; and Ioanna Laliotou, *Transatlantic Subjects: Acts of Migration and Cultures of Transnationalism between Greece and America* (Chicago: University of Chicago Press, 2004).

37. See John J. Yiannias, "Coping with the Imported Past: A Theme in Greek and Greek American Church Architecture," in *Anathemata Eortika: Studies in Honor of Thomas F. Mathews*, ed. Joseph D. Alchermes (Mainz: Von Zabern, 2009), 318–26; Panos Fiorentinos, *Ecclesia: Greek Orthodox Churches of the Chicago Metropolis* (Chicago: Kantyli, 2004); and Kostas Baroutas, *Hoi naoi to Hellenon metanaston* (Athens: Karakotsoglou, 2006).

with creative license, have created a unique set of architectural expressions. Even if the basic liturgical narrative remains fundamentally medieval, the liturgical experience of Greek communities in the Unites States has been spatially different from the experiences of the home country. Such variation from prototypes is significant and, given the central role that architecture plays in the Orthodox liturgy, it has transformed liturgical experience. In our overview of Greek American churches, which follows below, we identify three phases of distinct architectural change. Phase I covers the formative first century, circa 1850 to 1950, and exhibits a strategy of adaptation and architectural variety. Phase II, from the 1950s to the 1980s, is a period of modernist liberties. Phase III, from the 1980s to the present, consists of a centralized return to historicist correctness.

During phase I, many congregations began their liturgical practices in preexisting buildings, whether rented or bought from Protestant congregations. The volatile ebb and flow of American capitalism created an unstable real estate market. Working-class immigrants populated industrial neighborhoods, forming ethnic ghettos. In many cases the older inhabitants of those neighborhoods moved out of the new slums. Upwardly mobile Protestant and Catholic buildings were suddenly separated from their congregations, which moved to suburban neighborhoods. This "white flight" generated a surplus of abandoned buildings, which the new immigrants exploited.

Greek communities with enough funds to build new ecclesiastical structures opted for a variety of models. Most prominent was the twin-tower façade imported directly from Greece. During the Ottoman period (1453–1821), churches in Greece were heavily regulated. Restrictions on size, bell towers, and domes curtailed any visual competition that Christian churches might exert on mosques with their prominent minarets. After the War of Greek Independence, ecclesiastical architecture sought to celebrate a newly acquired liberty by physical magnitude, exaggerated bell towers, and prominent domes. The Orthodox Church in Greece otherwise retained the liturgical model of narthex, domed *naos*, centralized plan, and screened sanctuary. Moreover, the modern Greek nation-state sought to distinguish itself from its Ottoman medieval past by aligning its cultural expression with the West. The Bavarian crown's religious preferences, moreover, assisted in the theological incorporation of Western ideas. In architecture, this translated into the adaptation of Renaissance decorations.[38] Renaissance forms replaced Byzantine architectural details. In the

---

38. See Demetris Philippides, *Neoellenike architektonike* (Athens: Melissa, 1984), 93–98.

United States many of the new churches, such as the neo-Romanesque Greek Orthodox Cathedral of the Holy Trinity in New York City (1929–31) and the Church of Constantine and Helen in Chicago (1927–28), were non-Byzantine in style. The first newly constructed Greek Orthodox Church in America, Holy Trinity in New Orleans, illustrates adherence to American vernacular models such as the Louisiana shotgun house.

Phase II, from the 1950s to 1980s, corresponds with the Greek community's entrance into the middle class and with assimilation. This generation of American-born Greeks wished to prove their progressive achievements and to highlight the social distance from their lower-class parents and the miseries of their experiences. Competing successfully in the economics of urban capitalism, they could abandon the ethnic ghetto and establish new congregations in the suburbs. The new suburban architecture was new not only in its geography but also in its architectural expression. High modernism, disfavored by the Church of Greece, became the style of choice for new suburban Greek Americans. Churches dedicated to the Annunciation in Milwaukee, Wisconsin (1956–61), designed by Frank Lloyd Wright, in Oakland, California (1960), and in Atlanta, Georgia (1964–70), resembled futuristic spaceships, reflected the ecclesiastical autonomy of the Archdiocese of North and South America from the Church of Greece, and also suggested awareness of architectural trends in other American denominations. For instance, Greek Americans were keenly aware of the Second Vatican Council (1962–65) that liberated Catholic churches from historical prototypes and precipitated an explosion of wild designs among the Irish, Italian, and Hispanic populations with whom Greeks socialized and intermarried. For the Greeks back in Greece, Vatican II was totally irrelevant. The mid-century modern phase of Orthodox architecture is the only period that has attracted extensive scholarly attention, particularly by American Byzantinists who have identified a typological inheritance from Hagia Sophia.[39] During the second phase of architectural expression, we also note the establishment of Greek architectural offices.[40]

---

39. Anthony Cutler, "The Tyranny of Hagia Sophia: Notes on Greek Orthodox Church Design in the United States," *The Journal of the Society of Architectural Historians* 31 (1972), 38–50; Robert S. Nelson, *Hagia Sophia, 1850–1950: Holy Wisdom Modern Monument* (Chicago: University of Chicago Press, 2004), 195–214.

40. Steven Papadatos and Chris Kamages were the most prominent Greek American architects; see Steven Peter Papadatos, "Development of Orthodox Architecture," in Efthimiou and Christopoulos, eds., *History of the Greek Orthodox Church in America*, 293–302.

Finally, phase III reflects a self-conscious reaction against the liberties of modernism, a move toward historicism, and a return to canonical Byzantine prototypes. This last architectural phase has resulted from a newfound search for cultural authenticity that all American minorities articulated in debates on multiculturalism during the 1980s. But more importantly, the historicist idiom reflects the postmodernist trends dominating architectural practice and education. Certainly, the historicism of the 1980s reflects a self-conscious rejection of modernism, but it also marks a political effort by the ecclesiastical authorities to exert control over church aesthetics. Rejecting the chaotic variety of phase I and the creative license of phase II, the Greek Orthodox Church in North America sought a system of authentication. In 2005 a new requirement was issued in the Uniform Parish Regulations of the archdiocese requiring the approval of all architectural and iconographic projects by the parish's metropolitan bishop.[41] The presbyterian model of architectural choice that had been exercised during the first hundred years of Greek American Orthodoxy was terminated.

As we have already suggested, immigration to the United States introduced a new set of variables, both global and transient, that ecclesiastical tradition had not anticipated. As a result, Greek American architecture developed great divergences from the canon of the homeland. Unlike the situation in Greece, where the church is nationalized, Greek Orthodox churches in the United States were private organizations and had to compete in America's "religious marketplace." Beyond symbolic connections to the homeland, the new immigrants needed to compete in the symbolic arena of the American city and the availability of preexisting real estate.[42] Greek American parishes took unprecedented creative license, compounded by the presbyterian model of their organization. In spite of their architectural richness, Orthodox churches in North America have not received systematic attention. Professional architectural historians have dismissed them as accidental vernacular expressions. The haphazard processes of their design and construction, moreover, have relegated them into the category of kitsch.

A First Case Study

In order to illustrate the liturgical significance of Greek American church architecture, we will use a case study from Pennsylvania, focusing on the cities of

---

41. Art. 16, sect. 4, in Yiannias, "Coping with the Imported Past," 322.

42. See Jeanne Halgren Kilde, *Sacred Power, Sacred Space: An Introduction to Christian Architecture* (New York: Oxford University Press, 2008), 161–96.

the metropolitan church of Philadelphia and a provincial church in Lancaster.[43] Philadelphia witnessed the arrival of Greek immigrants as early as the 1870s. Like many immigrant communities, the first Greeks in Philadelphia were poor working-class folk, struggling to make a living and sending their savings back home. When permanent communities developed with a need for congregational spaces, they typically bought abandoned churches cheaply available on the market. Thus, the earliest liturgical experience of the Greek community took place in abandoned Protestant spaces with radically strange internal organization. In Philadelphia this took place in 1908 and in 1921.

The first Greek Orthodox congregation was formalized in 1875. By 1908 the Greek community was able to buy a building that had just lost its congregation, the nineteenth-century building of All Saints Episcopal Church.[44] In 1921 the architectural landmark Church of St. Andrew was on the market, and the Greeks had saved enough to make a down payment for a mortgage. The original structure had been Philadelphia's premiere Episcopalian church, built in the fashionable Greek Revival style of 1822 (see fig. 1). John Haviland, the building's original designer, was one of America's first architects, a member of the congregation who chose to be buried in the building's crypt.[45] Ironically, St. Andrew was one of the first American congregations to do missionary work in Greece after the Greek War of Independence. Although Haviland utilized ancient Greek prototypes, he could have never imagined that living Greeks would eventually inhabit his showpiece and mausoleum.

A century after the construction of St. Andrew, its neighborhood had turned into a working-class slum. Blaming the influx of African Americans and immigrants (such as the Greeks), the Episcopalians fled to the prosperous suburb of West Philadelphia and took Haviland's body with them. They hired the premiere Philadelphia firm of Zantzinger, Borie and Medary to design a towering Gothic Revival chapel that formed the core of the Philadelphia Divinity School. Stalled by the Great Depression, the Divinity School campus was never completed. In 1974 it merged with the Episcopal Theological School in Cambridge, and

43. See Kostis Kourelis, "From Greek Revival to Greek America: Archaeology and Transformation in Saint George Orthodox Cathedral of Philadelphia," in *The Archaeology of Xenitia: Greek Immigration and Material Culture*, ed. Kostis Kourelis, New Griffon 10 (2008): 28–36.

44. Dedicated to the Annunciation, this first Greek Orthodox church no longer exists; it was sold in 1963 and torn down. The congregation then moved to the prosperous suburb of Elkins Park, not far from Frank Lloyd Wright's Beth Sholom Synagogue.

45. See Agnes Addison Gilchrist, "John Haviland before 1816," *The Journal of the Society of Architectural Historians* 20 (1961): 136–37.

the grounds were sold to the University of Pennsylvania.[46] St. Andrew of 1822 and St. Andrew of 1925 are radically different architecturally and illustrate the evolutionary variety of Episcopalian tastes from Greek Revival in the nineteenth century to Gothic Revival in the twentieth. Unlike architectural changes in Orthodox church architecture, the Episcopalian shifts of taste occurred via a fundamental liturgical reorientation during the Ecclesiological Movement.[47]

When the Greeks bought St. Andrew in 1924, they dedicated the building to St. George (see Fig. 1, p. 174). In order to understand how an old Episcopalian building affected Orthodox liturgy, we must reconstruct the original space. This task is harder than one might think. Historical photos of Orthodox interiors are rare, owing to an unspoken taboo against photographing liturgical space. The great majority of historical photographs of the church are staged on the secular exterior, along the building's steps. The only visual record of the interior comes from the 1873 pamphlet celebrating St. Andrew's semicentennial.[48] We note the presence of the pews and the lack of an altar screen. For comparison we can turn to another Haviland church whose original interior survives, the Miller Chapel at Princeton Theological Seminary.[49] The chapel today still shows the prominent organ and the pristinely white classical interior, a far cry from Orthodox mysticism. But in effect, this became the liturgical framework in which the Orthodox liturgy was performed during the first decade of St. George's Greek American parish.

Not until the congregation had paid off its mortgage and a fire destroyed the roof in 1930 did the Greeks seek a Byzantinizing facelift to their Episcopalian space. A one-to-one comparison between 1873 and the interior today illustrates the changes. The coffered ceiling was not replaced, leaving the beams exposed, a wooden screen divided the altar from the nave, and the semidome above the apse was decorated with a canonical image of the Mother of God completed in 1942 in time for the state visit of Greece's King George II. Taking its cue from a darkly

---

46. George E. Thomas, "Zantzinger, Borie and Medary (1911–1931)," in *Drawing toward Building: Philadelphia Architectural Graphics 1732–1986*, ed. James F. O'Gorman et al. (Philadelphia: University of Pennsylvania Press, 1986), 193–95.

47. Developing in England out of the Oxford Tractarian Movement and the Cambridge Camden Society, the Ecclesiological Movement traveled to the United States via Philadelphia. The Episcopal Church of St. James the Less at Laurel Hill Cemetery (1846–48) was built on drawings sent to Philadelphia by the Cambridge Camden Society. See Michael J. Lewis, *The Gothic Revival* (New York: Thames and Hudson, 2002).

48. Wilbur F. Paddock, ed., *Half-Century of Church-Life: Semi-Centennial Commemoration of St. Andrew's Church, Philadelphia* (Philadelphia: M'Calla & Stavely, 1873).

49. Raymond Rhinehart, *Princeton University: The Campus Guide* (New York: Princeton Architectural Press, 2000), 150.

enameled screen, the rest of the church's previously white wood was stained dark and accentuated with gold. Small details, like the double-headed eagle light fixtures puncturing the old gallery, effectively Byzantinized the Protestant interior. Despite the Byzantinification of the church, tensions still exist between the church's Protestant skin and its Orthodox furniture, between the un-iconic Episcopalian stained-glass windows, for instance, and the gilded Greek icons.[50]

A Second Case Study

Elsewhere in Pennsylvania we see similar, and perhaps more extreme, examples of early integration. When a small Greek American community formed in Lancaster, in the heart of Pennsylvania German country, its liturgical practices were entirely dependent on the visitation of a priest from St. George in Philadelphia, eighty miles away. Being without a building, Lancaster's Greeks were invited to worship at St. John's Episcopal Church. Surprisingly, the Greek Orthodox bishop Alexandros officially permitted the Episcopal clergy of St. John's to minister to the Greeks of Lancaster.[51] The arrangement between the Episcopal clergy and the Greek community was an ecumenical gesture sanctioned by Patriarch Meletios IV of Constantinople and Bishop Alexandros, who were trying to establish a Greek Orthodox archdiocese in America. The Episcopal ministry to Lancaster Greeks in the Church of St. John illustrates a fascinating moment in church history when in the early twentieth century Anglican and Orthodox churches discussed union.

While borrowing space, the Greek community raised funds to buy its own building. In 1914 St. Paul's Methodist Church upgraded from its modest brick building of 1861 into a grand stone cathedral across the street. The Greeks bought the old building in 1922 and dedicated it to the Annunciation (see fig. 2, p. 175). The Methodist shell served the Greek community for a generation, until 1959, when the Greeks built their own church of the Annunciation at the outer limits of the city. Just as their Methodist predecessors had done in 1914, the Greeks sold the old building to the next needy population, an African American congregation.[52]

---

50. On the gilding of the icons and a votive ethnography of the church, see Robert T. Teske, *Votive Offerings among Greek-Philadelphians* (New York: Arno Press, 1980).

51. See Nikitas J. Zervanos, "The Early Greek Settlers of Lancaster County, 1896–1922, and the Annunciation Greek Orthodox Church," *The Journal of the Lancaster County Historical Society* 110/3–4 (Fall/Winter 2008–9): 94–200.

52. It has served as Glad Tidings Temple, Assembly of God (1960–72), Water Street Mission's Grace Chapel (1972–81), and Brightside Baptist Church (1981–present). From its

An Immigrant Liturgy: Greek Orthodox Worship and Architecture in America   171

Unlike Greeks back home, Greeks in the United States found themselves subject to real estate volatility. Rapid changes in the labor markets and property values had, after all, transformed an elite Anglo-Saxon neighborhood into a Greek ghetto. Just as the Greek proletariat had caused the Episcopalians to flee to more prosperous suburbs, so were upwardly mobile Greeks pushed away by a new ghetto. Once the Greek working class had risen to middle-class status, they could not tolerate the growing levels of African American poverty. As beautifully dramatized in Jeffrey Eugenides's 2002 novel *Middlesex*, the race riots of the 1960s turned the old Greek towns into crime-ridden ghettos, and Greeks orchestrated their own white flight from the inner cities. Eugenides describes the motivation of Detroit's new Orthodox church clearly: "To show the world the financial wherewithal of the prospering Greek American community."[53] As Yiorgos Anagnostou has so eloquently argued, during the 1920s Americans did not consider Greeks to be of the same Caucasian race.[54] By aggressively embracing forms of whiteness, including the appropriation of Western architecture spaces, the Greeks transformed their social status. By the 1960s they could in turn practice forms of racism against African Americans and engender their own white flight to the suburbs.

The suburban exodus and ethnic assimilation had an interesting architectural character. One way to prove financial coming of age was to employ the vocabulary of success, which in the 1960s was modernism. Averse to the spatial subcompartmentalization of historical architecture, modernism sought expansive unitary spaces celebrating aesthetic freedom and expression. The Greeks hired architects like Frank Lloyd Wright to design ultramodern Orthodox spaces.[55] The now-standard pews were arranged in centralized theatrical fashion. Although the separation between chancel and *naos* was maintained by loose sanctuary barriers, the aesthetic effect was one of universal space. It

---

construction in 1861 until today, the Methodist Church of St. Paul's has served no fewer than six different ecclesial communities; see A. Hunter Rineer Jr., *Churches and Cemeteries of Lancaster County, Pennsylvania: A Complete Guide* (Lancaster, PA: Lancaster County Historical Society, 1993), 212–13, 222.

53. Jeffrey Eugenides, *Middlesex* (New York: Picador, 2002), 220.

54. Yiorgos Anagnostou, "Forget the Past, Remember the Ancestors! Modernity, 'Whiteness,' American Hellenism, and the Politics of Modernity in Early Greek America," *Journal of Modern Greek Studies* 22 (2004): 25–71; *Contours of White Ethnicity: Popular Ethnography and the Making of Usable Pasts in Greek America* (Athens, OH: Ohio State University Press, 2009).

55. See Neil Levine, *The Architecture of Frank Lloyd Wright* (Princeton: Princeton University Press, 1996), 301–8; and Dimitri Tselos, "Frank Lloyd Wright and World Architecture," *Journal of the Society of Architectural Historians* 28 (1969): 58–72.

is interesting to note that Wright had encountered immigrant populations in Hull House, a settlement house in Chicago founded in 1889 by Jane Addams.[56] Wright encountered Orthodox liturgies through his wife, who was raised in the Serbian Orthodox Church.[57] Milwaukee's Annunciation Church may have some vague associations with Hagia Sophia in Constantinople, but it is ultimately a Unitarian space. Wright, who was born into one of America's most important Unitarian families, developed his ideals of sacred space at Unity Temple in 1905.[58] Those ideas were translated interdenominationally in his Beth Sholom synagogue in Elkins Park and in his Greek Orthodox church in Milwaukee, both executed in 1954. Wright conceived of the *naos* as an auditorium in the round. The central axis through the narthex twists at the center of the circle, redirected left toward the altar. Although the altar is marked by a sanctuary barrier, this screen is a translucent, decorative surface, in contrast to the traditional Byzantine opaque sanctuary. Such a dissolution of the barriers between altar and *naos* is evident in many Midwestern churches, like SS. Constantine and Helen in Merrillville, Indiana, and, in the Northeast, at the Koimesis Church in Poughkeepsie, New York.[59]

The desire to break away from any Orthodox liturgical norms, and to embrace modernist abstraction, is evident throughout the United States. Many of the architects of these churches were Greek Americans and were trained as modernists. As American designers, they were engaged in the debates on church architecture that Vatican II unleashed. The modernists' Orthodox buildings are an interesting anomaly, unparalleled by any contemporary works in traditionally Orthodox countries. No traveler from the Patriarchate of Constantinople, from Greece, the Soviet Union, or the Balkans, would have recognized these buildings as churches at all, just as they would not have understood the presence of an organ, the pews, or the use of English. Start-

---

56. In 1901 Frank Lloyd Wright delivered one of his most important lectures at Hull House, "The Art and Craft of the Machine," reprinted in *Frank Lloyd Wright Collected Writings*, vol. 1, *1894–1930*, ed. Bruce Brooks Pfeiffer (New York: Rizzoli, 1982), 58–69.

57. Joseph M. Siry, *Beth Sholom Synagogue: Frank Lloyd Wright and Modern Religious Architecture* (Chicago: University of Chicago Press, 2012), 505–18.

58. Wright's mother, Anna Lloyd-Jones, belonged to a prominent Unitarian family. Her brother, Jenkin Lloyd Jones, was an important figure in the Unitarian Church of the Midwest. Joseph M. Siry, *Unity Temple: Frank Lloyd Wright and Architecture for Liberal Religion* (Cambridge: Cambridge University Press, 1996), 244.

59. The Merrillville church inspired Angela Volan, a young Greek American, to study Byzantine art. On this church, see Robert M. Taylor, *Indiana: A New Historical Guide* (South Bend, IN: Indiana Historical Society), 573–82, 589–90.

ing with the clean slate of modernism, Greek American congregations were able to dissolve the liturgical tensions that would be evident in a traditional building. In effect, they created a unique American liturgical space, more recognizable by Americans of other denominations than by other Orthodox practitioners. This American modern aesthetic can surely be explained by cultural assimilation and by intermarriage, most evident in the brave new world of the suburbs. We would like to suggest, however, that this sudden aesthetic freedom did not emerge simply as a vehicle for expressing status and prosperity. We believe that the experience of appropriating non-Orthodox buildings in the earlier phase taught the Greek Americans a spatial flexibility that the home country did not offer.

We should note that the Orthodox churches of the 1950s and 1960s show great variety. Not all of them were radically new modern monuments, but most incorporated some elements of modernism. An empirical study of all the churches would reveal interesting regional expressions and statistical trends. The cathedral in Los Angeles, for instance, shows allegiance to a Hispanic tradition in its baroque interiors. This church was financed by the Greek movie mogul Spyros Skouras, founder of Twentieth-Century Fox Studios in Hollywood. The Los Angeles cathedral is assimilated into a fantasy of Pan-Mediterraneanism linking Greeks and Mexicans. In the 1980s Los Angeles's Greek Town had been so thoroughly incorporated into the Latino environment that it is now called the Byzantine-Latino Quarter.

The exuberance and variety of the mid-twentieth century was terminated with the third phase of architectural taste in the 1980s. Almost overnight modernism was demonized. The new generations wanted not assimilation but multicultural difference. A new search for roots, coupled with postmodernism's critique of all things modern, brought about strict adherence to a new stylistic historicism, an almost direct copy of Byzantine prototypes. The Church of SS. Nicholas, Constantine, and Helen in Roseland, New Jersey, for example, is conceived as a sixth-century building. A new liturgical conservatism and tighter aesthetic control by the metropolitan hierarchy introduced another dimension of liturgical complexity, whose consequences have not yet been studied. What has been happening to Greek American churches in the last ten years is the introduction of non-Greek congregations from newer immigrant groups not populous enough to house their own communities. Newer Orthodox immigrants from Ethiopia, the Middle East, and eastern Europe are adding new elements to the melting pot. The newcomers have more conservative liturgical forms than the Greek Americans, who have already experimented for over a century. The liturgical and aesthetic shifts of the future will be as interesting as those of the past.

Figure 1: Saint George Greek Orthodox Cathedral of Philadelphia, Pennsylvania, previously Saint Andrew Episcopal Church. John Haviland, architect, 1822. Photo taken by Kostis Kourelis.

An Immigrant Liturgy: Greek Orthodox Worship and Architecture in America 175

Figure 2: Annunciation Greek Orthodox Church, Lancaster, Pennsylvania, previously Saint Paul Methodist Church, 1861.
Photo taken by Kostis Kourelis.

PART 2

Contemporary Liturgical Migrations

8

Eastern Christian Insights and Western Liturgical Reforms: Travelers, Texts, and Liturgical Luggage

Anne McGowan

A contemporary Anglican visitor to an Orthodox Vespers service in Canada remarked that "worship in parishes of the Orthodox Church in America is the best liturgy this side of heaven. Beautiful, dignified, comfortable with itself and with very few concessions to the countervailing culture, always oriented toward the Trinity."[1] The overall impression of splendor and transcendence communicated to many outside observers by Eastern Christian worship has a long history. This anonymous visitor's impressions, for instance, resemble the legendary reaction of ambassadors sent by Prince Vladimir of Kiev more than one thousand years earlier to explore the worship of other peoples in order to determine the religion of their realm. After attending Divine Liturgy at the Church of Hagia Sophia in Constantinople, the prince's servants recalled that

> the Greeks led us to the edifices where they worship their God, and we knew not whether we were in heaven or on earth. For on earth there is no such splendor or such beauty, and we are at a loss how to describe it. We only know that

---

The author wishes to thank the community of the Yale Institute of Sacred Music for a generous fellowship during the 2011–12 academic year and for helpful comments on an earlier version of this essay.

1. Mystery Worshipper report, "362: The Sign of the Theotokos, Montreal, Canada" (2001), accessed 9 February, 2012, http://ship-of-fools.com/mystery/2001/362Mystery.html.

179

God dwells there among men, and their service is fairer than the ceremonies of other nations. For we cannot forget that beauty.²

The comments of the twenty-first century "Mystery Worshipper," however, also allude to another element of Eastern Christian worship that may help to explain its intermittent appeal to Western Christians in the modern era: its slow development over time can give the impression that it is countercultural and ritually conservative. Although both Eastern and Western liturgies have been deeply formed by the cultures that produced and celebrated them, and both exhibit some degree of evolution over time, there is the perception that the Eastern rites have preserved intact (or at least relatively unchanged) many very ancient ritual practices that might otherwise have been lost to the vicissitudes of history. Reflecting both deep admiration and critique of the development (or lack thereof) of the Eastern Orthodox Church, for example, the Roman Catholic liturgical scholar Adrian Fortescue wrote in the early twentieth century that "the way in which she clings to one stage of development is altogether unjustifiable theologically, but it results in a number of very curious and picturesque remnants of a past age, which exist only in her services."³ In a similar vein, Olivier Rousseau, an early historian of the Roman Catholic liturgical movement, commented, "Among Catholics it is a truism that the Orthodox Church has preserved the liturgical spirit of the Early Church, and that it continues to live this spirit, to drink from it as from its purest source. . . . This Church *has never departed in its piety and its offices from the liturgical spirit of the Early Church*, to which it has always remained faithful."⁴

Although some Western liturgiologists and other interested travelers have had the opportunity to experience Eastern liturgies celebrated in the geographical regions where these Eastern incarnations of Christianity originated,⁵

---

2. Samuel Hazzard Cross and Olgerd P. Sherbowitz-Wetzor, eds. and trans., *The Russian Primary Chronicle: Laurentian Text* (Cambridge, MA: The Mediaeval Academy of America, 1953), 111. This event is placed in the year 987.

3. Adrian Fortescue, *The Orthodox Eastern Church* (London: Catholic Truth Society, 1907), 404–5, n. 2, as quoted in Anthony Dragani, *Adrian Fortescue and the Eastern Christian Churches* (Piscataway, NJ: Gorgias Press, 2007), 71.

4. Olivier Rousseau, *Histoire du mouvement liturgique*, Lex Orandi 3 (Paris: Éditions du Cerf, 1945), 188, as translated by Robert F. Taft, "Eastern Presuppositions and Western Liturgical Renewal," *Antiphon: A Journal for Liturgical Renewal* 5 (2000), 13; emphasis added.

5. For a visual portrayal of the geographical distribution of Eastern Christian churches, see the maps in John Binns, *An Introduction to the Christian Orthodox Churches* (New York: Cambridge University Press, 2002), xii–xiv.

many more Westerners have been exposed to the ritual practices and theological ethos of Eastern Christian worship as a result of the westward migration of Eastern liturgies. These liturgies took up residence in the West when they accompanied groups of Eastern Christians who settled in the West temporarily or permanently; in various times and places, such communities might have comprised scholars, entrepreneurs, wealthy tourists and expatriates, and political refugees (among others). Eastern liturgical texts also traveled west, and the dissemination of printed editions and translations in western Europe from the sixteenth century onward made these texts available to a much wider audience of interested parties than was possible before, given the more limited circulation of manuscript copies. Finally, the Western fascination with certain aspects of Eastern liturgy and spirituality has contributed to their adaptation and use in Western liturgical contexts. It appears that increased exposure to Eastern Christian practitioners, texts, and liturgical units motivated some Westerners to view Eastern liturgies as a potential complement or corrective to their own and to consider incorporating selected insights from Eastern liturgies into Western worship. Theological and/or ecumenical concerns provided the immediate impetus for some of the modern Western interest in Eastern liturgies, and, for this reason, it is worth considering briefly the general attraction of Eastern liturgies in the modern West before exploring particular instances of Eastern migration and Western "borrowing" in more detail.

I. The Appeal of the (Ancient) Christian East in the Modern West

The quotations above from Fortescue and Rousseau on the relatively "unchanging" character of Eastern liturgical practice (and thus the implied outward continuity between twentieth-century Eastern worship and that of the early church) exaggerate the evidence and reflect an overly romantic notion of Eastern liturgies. Nevertheless, from the sixteenth century onward, the natural growth of Western liturgies, both Protestant and Catholic, was clearly interrupted. Protestant reformers molded liturgical rites consistent with their own theologies of worship, and the Roman Catholic Church engaged in a process of reform and standardization of its own.[6] The supposed testimony, therefore, that Eastern rites and Eastern authors provided for the worship

---

6. Therefore, the perception advocated by scholars such as Anton Baumstark who promoted a view that "only the liturgies of the East continued to develop organically according to the laws which sprang from their common being" is understandable. See Fritz West, "Baumstark's Tree and Thoughts after Harvest," in *Comparative Liturgy Fifty Years after Anton Baumstark* (1872–1948),

practices of the primitive church proved useful in the early modern period regarding claims that the rituals of various churches in the West either were or were not consistent with those of the postapostolic age that provided the earliest written witness besides Scripture to the tradition of the one, undivided church.[7] In later centuries, the use of Eastern liturgies turned from polemical to pastoral purposes as representatives of various Western churches considered incorporating elements from Eastern liturgies to meet the perceived needs of later ages—sometimes without sufficient concern for the native context or theology of these "enrichments" to Western liturgies.[8]

On one level, many of those involved in Western reforms that appropriated components of Eastern liturgies clearly expressed admiration for Eastern Christian traditions, frequently accompanied by a sincere desire that theological obstacles to fuller unity between Western and Eastern churches might soon be overcome. Given the widespread impression that what was Eastern was also more likely to reflect the practice of the *early* church, however, looking East was also a way to put Westerners in touch with the liturgical roots of their own tradition. Thus, whatever the superficial rationale for appealing to the East, the underlying motives could be significantly more complex. Robert Taft has written, "It has long been a theological device to turn eastwards in search of supporting liturgical evidence for what one has already decided to do anyway. . . . The underlying presupposition seems to be that the Eastern practice will reflect a more ancient—indeed *the* ancient—tradition of the undivided Church."[9]

Taft observes elsewhere that the West "has tended to define eastern liturgy in terms of what it perceives itself as lacking," interpreting these rites in light of its *own* pressing pastoral concerns and desires rather than modeling its patterns of worship after current Eastern usages.[10] Many of the perceived Western needs that prompted—at least indirectly—liturgical borrowings from the East have to do with aspects that the Christian East has seemingly maintained whereas the West has apparently neglected or "lost" them, particularly qualities that appear to

---

ed. Robert F. Taft and Gabriele Winkler, Orientalia Christiana Analecta 265 (Rome: Pontificio Istituto Orientale, 2001), 172. The quote is West's paraphrase of Baumstark's view.

7. See, for example, Bryan D. Spinks, *Western Use and Abuse of Eastern Liturgical Traditions: Some Cross-Sections in Its History*, Placid Lecture Series 14 (Rome/Bangalore: Centre for Indian and Inter-Religious Studies / Dharmaram Publications, 1992), 47–62.

8. Several examples are discussed at length in Spinks, *Western Use and Abuse*, 47–62.

9. Robert F. Taft, "Ex Oriente Lux? Some Reflections on Eucharistic Concelebration," in *Beyond East and West: Problems in Liturgical Understanding*, 2nd rev. and enlarged ed. (Rome: Pontifical Oriental Institute, 2001), 111; emphasis his.

10. Taft, "Eastern Presuppositions," 13.

have been common to both East and West in the idealized "golden age" of liturgical creativity and synthesis (circa the fourth and fifth centuries). Among these qualities, Taft identifies in Eastern liturgies a balance between high Christology and an accessible human Christ, a deep trinitarian consciousness, an awareness of a transcendent, unknowable God who merits human worship simply by virtue of existing, a holistic synthesis of symbol and ritual, a theological alternative to Western scholasticism, and a sense of tradition as "integral and indivisible."[11]

The remainder of this essay seeks to provide an overview of how Eastern Christian insights have impacted Western liturgical reforms in the past several centuries, especially through unofficial or official changes to ritual structures. Some of these changes were proposed by marginal groups and had a relatively limited impact in their own time and in later ages. Other reforms were implemented on a much broader scale and impacted large swaths of Western Christianity. This overview will proceed with an examination of the "migration" of people, texts, and traditions that illustrate Eastern influence on Western reforms. The limited scope of this essay will permit little more than select consideration of a few "postcards" or "snapshots" of moments in this process of migration rather than a full vision of all the complicated motives and interactions that were involved in various times and places.

The focus will be the selective use of aspects of Eastern liturgies to "enrich" Western theology and practice at points where it was perceived to be lacking. There have been other Western involvements with Eastern liturgies that will not be discussed here. For example, at certain points representatives of Western churches have imposed Western concerns on Eastern liturgies, such as proposing the use of a clear institution narrative in Eastern eucharistic prayers that, according to the judgment of much more recent scholarship, lacked this element, not because of a defective eucharistic theology, but because eucharistic prayers like the East Syrian Anaphora of Addai and Mari predated the regular inclusion of the narrative as a standard feature of the eucharistic prayer.[12] Other aspects important to the wider issue of East-West liturgical exchange from the

---

11. See ibid., 14–17.

12. Thus, the focus will be on the second of the three areas of Western "use and abuse" of Eastern liturgical traditions identified by Spinks: "There is adding or changing parts of the liturgy on the grounds that the Western is better or more Christian—for example the concern over the words of institution or confirmation; there is the use of selective parts of the Eastern liturgies to assist Western theological disputes, as at the Reformation; and finally the use of early Eastern material where doctrines are still undeveloped to support Western rationalism and heterodoxy, as with [William] Whiston and [John] Henley. What all these approaches have in common is a failure to treat Eastern rites on their own grounds with their own integrity" (Spinks, *Western Use and Abuse*, 145).

Eastern side will not be addressed, such as Eastern reactions to the Western use of Eastern liturgies, or Eastern rites as celebrated by Eastern Christians in full communion with Western churches (such as the twenty-two distinct Eastern ecclesiastical entities in full communion with the Roman Catholic Church,[13] or the Mar Thoma Syrian Church of Malabar, which is in full communion with the Anglican Church[14]). Parallel influences in the other direction (i.e., the voluntary adoption of Western elements in Eastern liturgies) will likewise be passed over in silence, such as the phenomenon known as "Western Rite Orthodoxy" in which largely Western liturgies are adapted and celebrated in Eastern churches.[15] Since liturgical reforms are carried out by people (who, by virtue of being human, are susceptible to biases, idiosyncrasies, and mixed motives), the human element of this phenomenon of liturgical migration from East to West will be examined first.

II. Patrons and Travelers, Emigrants and Scholars: Points of Personal Contact between East and West

Some interest in Eastern texts and traditions was made possible because of the prior movement of people. From at least the fourth century, pilgrims to the

---

13. For a concise overview of the complex history of these churches, see the section on "The Catholic Eastern Churches" in Ronald G. Roberson, *The Eastern Christian Churches: A Brief Survey*, 7th ed. (Rome: Edizioni Orientalia Christiana, 2008). The entire text is available online at http://www.cnewa.org/default.aspx?ID=123&pagetypeID=9&pageno=1 (last modified 7 December, 2010).

14. This church originated as a reform movement within the Malankara Orthodox Syrian Church in India. On its history, see Alexander Mar Thoma, *The Marthoma Church: Heritage and Mission* (Tiruvalla: Christava Sahitya Samithy, 2010); and Zac Varghese Kanisseril and Mathew A. Kallumpram, *Glimpses of Mar Thoma Church History* (London: Society of St. Thomas and St. Augustine, 2003).

15. For more on Western Rite Orthodoxy, see Jack Turner, "The Journey Thus Far: A Review of the Literature of Western-Rite Orthodoxy," *St. Vladimir's Theological Quarterly* 53:4 (2009): 477–505; and idem, "Orthodoxy and the Western Rite: The Question of Necessity," *The Canadian Journal of Orthodox Christianity* 5:3 (Fall 2010): 107–25, available at http://www.cjoc.ca/pdf/Vol5_F-3WesternRite.pdf. Western liturgies celebrated in Orthodox churches include the Liturgy of St. Gregory (an adapted form of the Roman Missal of 1570 with an Anglo-Catholic flavor), the Liturgy of St. Tikhon, which has its origins in the 1892 and 1928 editions of the *Book of Common Prayer* of the Episcopal Church, and the Liturgy of St. Germanus, which incorporates aspects of Gallican liturgies from an age preceding the Great Schism of 1054. These rites are discussed briefly in John Madey, "Orthodox Churches and Western Liturgies," *Christian Orient: An Indian Journal of Eastern Churches for Creative Theological Thinking* 19:4 (1998): 193–96, and much more extensively in Gregory Woolfenden, "Western-Rite Orthodoxy: Some Reflections on a Liturgical Question," *St. Vladimir's Theological Quarterly* 45:2 (2001): 163–92.

Holy Land returned with stories of the ritual practices of Jerusalem and piqued the interest of those elsewhere in imitating aspects of the celebrations of the place where Jesus Christ died and rose from the dead. The travel narrative of the Spanish pilgrim Egeria from the late fourth century, for instance, provides many ritual details about practices in and around Jerusalem for a presumably interested audience back home.[16]

On the eve of the Reformation, several events in western Europe served to arouse interest in the Greek fathers and, by extension, in Eastern liturgies. While the people involved may not have contributed directly to Western liturgical reforms, their efforts and encounters raised awareness of the Eastern churches and their rites in the West and laid some of the scholarly foundations that made subsequent reforms possible. An informal network of Byzantine scholars was active in the Italian city-states in the fifteenth century, following the Council of Ferrara-Florence (1438–39), which discussed several important issues related to the sacraments and the reunion of the separated Eastern and Western churches, and the fall of Constantinople to the Ottoman Empire in 1453.[17] Charles Stinger judges that, in addition to the patronage of popes and cardinals committed to the humanist agenda, the presence of Byzantine *émigré* scholars in Rome "provided the major inspiration for Greek studies there, including patristics."[18] Some of these scholars, along with Italian humanists, were engaged in studies and translations of Greek patristic texts—including texts of liturgical importance.[19] The motivations for this scholarship were mixed. While "there was a tendency to see work on major Greek patristic texts as an end in itself, as recovering 'monuments' of ancient Christian eloquence and wisdom," there were also concerns among some to

---

16. There are many editions of this text, including John Wilkinson, trans. and ed., *Egeria's Travels*, 3rd ed. (Warminster: Aris & Phillips, 1999).

17. See Charles L. Stinger, "Italian Renaissance Learning and the Church Fathers," in *The Reception of the Church Fathers in the West: From the Carolingians to the Maurists*, vol. 2, ed. Irena Backus (New York: E. J. Brill, 1997), 488–91. For more on the role of Byzantine scholars in Italy, see John Monfasani, *Byzantine Scholars in Renaissance Italy: Cardinal Bessarion and other Émigrés* (Aldershot, UK: Variorum, 1995); and Nigel Guy Wilson, *From Byzantium to Italy: Greek Studies in the Italian Renaissance* (London: Duckworth, 1992).

18. Stinger, "Italian Renaissance Learning," 493.

19. Cardinal Bessarion (1403–72) was a leading figure in this movement. He had arrived at the Council of Ferrara in 1438 as a member of the Greek Orthodox delegation but soon joined the Roman Catholic Church. He became the head of an informal group of Byzantine *émigré* scholars and was committed to preserving the cultural and intellectual legacy of Greece and Byzantium in the West. Stinger, "Italian Renaissance Learning," 491.

elevate the status of Rome as a hub of learning and culture and to mine the fathers for moral and spiritual advice pertinent to contemporary concerns, both practical and theological.[20] In terms of liturgy and sacraments, the debates at the Council of Florence had sparked interest in certain Greek texts pertinent to disputed points of sacramental doctrine as well as in a form of theology grounded in Scripture and the writings of the church fathers rather than the scholastic method of argumentation.

Once movements for reform got underway in western Europe, several churches reached out to the churches of the Christian East, especially their nearest geographical neighbors, the Byzantine Orthodox churches. These churches provided a model for worship and church governance that had equal authority and claim to the tradition of the early church, yet without being subject to the authority of Rome. Steven Runciman remarked, "It was inevitable that, sooner or later, the Protestant Churches, protesting against Roman autocracy, should seek to find out about a Church which had made such a protest from the earliest times."[21] Early on, the Hussites made contact with Orthodox leaders in Constantinople in 1451, but circumstances in Constantinople at that time, and then the fall of the city in 1453, ended these initiatives.[22] A more extended conversation unfolded between German Lutherans and the Greek Orthodox patriarch of Constantinople, Jeremias II, between 1574 and 1581. While the two sides could not reach doctrinal agreement—a situation complicated by political circumstances on both sides—lines of communication remained open on other fronts.[23]

---

20. Promoting papal authority and opposing conciliarist ecclesiology were particularly important in this regard. See Stinger, "Italian Renaissance Learning," 495ff.; the quote above is from 496.

21. Steven Runciman, *The Great Church in Captivity: A Study of the Patriarchate of Constantinople from the Eve of the Turkish Conquest to the Greek War of Independence* (New York: Cambridge University Press, 1968), 238.

22. Ibid. See also M. Pavlova, "L'Empire Byzantine et les Tchèques avant la Chute de Constantinople, " *Byzantinoslavica* 14 (1953): 203–24. The incident is also discussed more extensively in Günther Thomann, *The Western Rite in Orthodoxy: Union and Reunion Schemes of Western and Eastern Churches with Eastern Orthodoxy: A Brief Historical Outline*, 3rd ed., rev. and corr. (Nürnberg: G. H. Thomann, 1995).

23. See Runciman, *Great Church in Captivity*, 247–56, and Paschalis M. Kitromilides, "Orthodoxy and the West: Reformation to Enlightenment," in *The Cambridge History of Christianity*, vol. 5, *Eastern Christianity*, ed. Michael Angold (New York: Cambridge University Press, 2006), 189–91. One incident that demonstrated an ongoing connection was the subsequent invitation extended to some Greek theological students to continue their studies in Lutheran Germany. For a short time (1728–29), there was an endowed theological seminary

Anglican Christians have shown what Nicolas and Militza Zernov described as a "sporadic interest" in Eastern Christians for several centuries.[24] During the seventeenth century, with Puritan groups in the ascendancy in the Church of England, several high church Anglicans developed an extremely positive regard for Eastern churches. This regard extended to the publication in England of several serious studies on the topic, as well as the production of experimental liturgies that incorporated Eastern elements. In the early eighteenth century, the group known as the Nonjurors[25] initiated discussion with Eastern patriarchs about the union of their churches, seeking spiritual and political benefits from the potential ecclesiastical merger. Correspondence flowed between the West and the East on this matter between 1716 and 1725, but the theological differences between the two sides were too great to make rapprochement realistic.[26] The climate in the remainder of the eighteenth century was not amenable to reopening such negotiations, but the Catholic revival connected to the Oxford Movement in the nineteenth century reawakened interest in closer ties with Eastern Christian churches. Various societies were formed to work toward communion, raise awareness of, and cultivate relationships between Anglicans and Orthodox Christians, including the Eastern Church Association (established in 1863–64) and the Anglican and Eastern Orthodox Churches Union (in 1906); the latter developed a Russian offshoot devoted to exploring Anglicanism. After the First World War, the two societies merged as the Anglican and Eastern Churches Association and continued their work, at

---

for such students at Halle in Saxony. Runciman, *Great Church in Captivity*, 257, mentions this development briefly, noting that "the inspiration for the seminary came from the orientalists J. H. and C. B. Michaelis, and from the former's son J. D. Michaelis."

24. Nicolas and Militza Zernov, "The History of the Fellowship of St. Alban and St. Sergius: A Historical Memoir by Nicolas and Militza Zernov" (Oxford: Fellowship of St. Alban & St. Sergius, 1979). The text is also available online: http://www.sobornost.org/Zernov_History-of-the-Fellowship.pdf; the quoted material is found on page 2 of the PDF. Subsequent references will cite the pagination of the electronic version.

25. The Nonjurors refused to swear an oath of allegiance to William III and Mary II after the Revolution of 1688 (or, later, to the House of Hanover). For a recent reassessment of the significance of the Nonjurors' liturgical positions, see James David Smith, *The Eucharistic Doctrine of the Later Nonjurors: A Revisionist View of the Eighteenth-Century Usages Controversy*, Alcuin/GROW Liturgical Study 46 (Cambridge: Grove Books, 2000).

26. Runciman, *Great Church in Captivity*, 319, writes, "Looking back from the vantage-point of later centuries, we can see that attempts to bring the Orthodox and Protestant Churches into communion with each other were premature. The only strong common basis was a mutual fear and dislike of Rome." This incident is discussed in greater detail on 310–19 as part of a chapter entitled "The Church and the Churches: The Anglican Experiment."

this time mainly centered on efforts to promote recognition of Anglican orders from the Orthodox side.[27]

Eastern insights were also circulating in the West through scholarly centers founded for the general and/or theological education of Eastern Christian students. Western Christians served as patrons for many of these institutions, and the students and teachers at these schools helped increase contact between the West and the East. As mentioned earlier, Greek students came to study in Italy in the fifteenth century, and Greek students continued to study at Venice in the sixteenth century and circulated among Catholics elsewhere in Italy.[28] Pope Gregory XIII founded the College of St. Athanasius at Rome in 1577 for the education of Greek boys; though the majority of its students were from Greek Catholic families, some Orthodox students attended as well, owing to the efforts of Jesuit missionaries in the area around Constantinople. The Jesuits went on to found several schools within the Ottoman Empire itself.[29] Some of the Jesuit missionaries who worked in these areas collected Eastern manuscripts and translated texts, some of them liturgical, and shared their knowledge of the East and its liturgies through their writing and teaching in the East and the West.[30]

The renewal in Orthodox theology in the twentieth century led to the founding of new institutions of higher learning where Orthodox theology could be studied as a scholarly discipline. These schools also provided points of contact between Western and Eastern Christians. The Theological Institute of St. Sergius was established in Paris in 1925 by emigrants from Russia. American schools also played an important role; especially notable among them are Holy Cross Greek Orthodox School of Theology (which originated in Pomfret, Connecticut, in 1937 and moved to Brookline, Massachusetts, in 1946) and St. Vladimir's Orthodox Theological Seminary (which held its first classes in 1938 in New York City and relocated to Crestwood, New York, in 1962).[31] By the mid-twentieth

---

27. Zernov and Zernov, "History of the Fellowship," 2–3.

28. Runciman, *Great Church in Captivity*, 228–29.

29. Ibid., 231. For more on the College of St. Athanasius, see Ludwig Freiherr von Pastor, *The History of the Popes from the Close of the Middle Ages*, ed. and trans. F. I. Antrobus, R. F. Kerr, Ernest Graf, and E. F. Peeler (London: Kegan Paul, Trench, Trübner & Co., 1881–1928), vols. XIX (247–49) and XX (584–85); and Placide de Meester, *Le Collège Pontifical Grec de Rome* (Rome: Collège Grec, 1910).

30. For examples, see Dominique Bertrand, "The Society of Jesus and the Church Fathers in the Sixteenth and Seventeenth Century," trans. Antoinina Bevan, in *The Reception of the Church Fathers in the West*, ed. Backus, 2:889–950.

31. See Dragani, *Adrian Fortescue and the Eastern Christian Churches*, 137–38. See also Timothy Ware, *The Orthodox Church*, new ed. (New York: Penguin Books, 1993), 178–79, 183. For more

century, Eastern Catholic theology was experiencing a renaissance, partly thanks to the creation of the Pontifical Oriental Institute in Rome by Pope Benedict XV in 1917. Benedict founded the institute "in the hope that one day Catholic and Orthodox students would there work side by side."[32] This hope has come to pass, and the institute has become "an important point of intellectual contact between Eastern Catholics and Orthodox Christians."[33]

Some segments of the Orthodox diaspora in the West were open to increased contact and dialogue with Western Christians.[34] Nicolas Zernov notes that after the founding of St. Sergius, "contacts were established with different branches of the ecumenical movement and Russian professors and students were invited to participate as observers at its conferences."[35] One example of the liturgical impact of such contacts is the Fellowship of St. Alban and St. Sergius. It was established in England in 1928, growing out of the Anglo-Russian student conferences in 1927–28. The fellowship now has numerous branches and a wider ecumenical scope, promoting contact among Orthodox, Anglican, Reformed, and Catholic Christians. Its activities have introduced important Orthodox theologians to Anglophone Christians, its conferences and symposia explore Eastern and Western theological perspectives, and its journal, *Sobornost*, promotes dialogue between Eastern and Western Christians. Its events have included Orthodox liturgies celebrated in English, and members of the Fellowship have developed experimental forms of worship for their gatherings derived from both Eastern and Western liturgical sources.[36]

---

on the history of these institutions, see http://www.hchc.edu/holycross/about/history_of _holy_cross.html (for Holy Cross) and http://www.svots.edu/about/history (for St. Vladimir's).

32. As quoted in Michael O'Carroll, *Light from the East: The Ecumenical Patriarch Bartholomew I* (Santa Barbara, CA: Queenship Publishing, 1998), 27–28. Patriarch Bartholomew is among the notable Orthodox scholars and ecclesiastical leaders who completed their studies at the Institute. For more on the significance of the school, see Gabriele Winkler, "The Achievements of the Pontifical Oriental Institute in the Study of Oriental Liturgiology," in *Il 75° Anniversario del Pontificio Istituto Orientale: Atti delle celebrazioni giubilari, 15–17 ottobre 1992*, ed. Robert F. Taft and James Lee Dugan, Orientalia Christiana Analecta 244 (Rome: Pontificio Istituto Orientale, 1994), 115–41.

33. Dragani, *Adrian Fortescue and the Eastern Christian Churches*, 139.

34. Nicolas Zernov, "The Significance of the Russian Orthodox Diaspora and Its Effect on the Christian West," in *The Orthodox Churches and the West*, ed. Derek Baker (Oxford: Basil Blackwell, 1976), 319.

35. Ibid., 316.

36. "Our History, Fellowship of St. Alban and St. Sergius," accessed 9 February, 2012, http://www.sobornost.org/about-4.html. See also Zernov and Zernov, "History of the Fellowship," 5ff. Nicolas Zernov recalls that "its conferences had a distinctive liturgical character. Each day

In the mid-twentieth century, the liturgical movement in French Catholicism was influenced by connections with Russian Orthodox refugees who had fled to France after the Bolshevik Revolution of 1917. Over two million Russians had left Russia by 1926, and most resettled in western Europe.[37] There had been a few Russian churches under the diocese of St. Petersburg, located in the capital cities of Europe and in locales popular with Russian tourists, but these proved insufficient to meet the needs of a much larger diaspora population cultivating renewed attachment to the religion of their ancestral homeland. Consequently, new Russian Orthodox parishes were established in places where they had not been before.[38] Through personal friendships with such figures as Abbé Paul Couturier (1881–1953) and Dom Lambert Beauduin (1873–1960)—one of the "founders" of the liturgical movement and a friend of Pope John XXIII (who convened the Second Vatican Council)—Russian exiles may have indirectly influenced some of the liturgical reforms undertaken in the Roman Catholic Church in the late twentieth century.[39] Whatever the impact of these personal connections, it is clear that the involvement of Eastern Catholics at the Second Vatican Council directly helped to shape their own liturgical vision as well as that of Western Catholics in their postconciliar reforms. Taft notes that the elements of postconciliar reform first proposed by the Melkites, for example, at Vatican II is "simply astonishing"; the breadth of their vision belied their small numbers in terms of overall representation at the council. The list of reforms first suggested by the Melkite delegation included "liturgy in the vernacular, eucharistic concelebration and communion under both species in the Latin liturgy . . . [and] the permanent diaconate."[40]

---

started with the celebration of the eucharist, which followed alternatively the eastern and western rite. The members prayed at each others' service, but refrained from taking communion, for intercommunion was not authorized at that time. This method proved to be most efficient and many barriers melted away and genuine unity of belief and common purpose was established." (See his "The Significance of the Russian Orthodox Diaspora," 318.)

37. Zernov, "The Significance of the Russian Orthodox Diaspora," 307, 312. For an overview of the Russian church at the turn of the twentieth century, see 308–12.

38. Ibid., 312.

39. Ibid., 324. Anglicans such as the bishop and liturgical scholar Walter Frere, CR (1863–1938) and the Reverend Fynes Clinton (1875–1959) also lent "financial and moral support to the Russian theological academy in Paris, the Russian student Christian movement in exile and the fellowship of St Alban and St Sergius" (ibid.).

40. See Taft, "Eastern Presuppositions," 10–11, quote at 10. For more information on the Melkite contribution at Vatican II, see Saba Shofany, *The Melkites at the Vatican Council II: Contribution of the Melkite Prelates to Vatican Council II on the Renewal of Moral Theology* (Bloomington, IN: AuthorHouse, 2005) which, despite its title, includes significant treatment

While much of this section has focused on "travelers" from the East influencing the West, people were moving in the other direction as well. John Cosin (1594–1672), a follower of the Anglican bishop Lancelot Andrewes (who had promoted meditation on Eastern liturgies as a private devotion),[41] did more than study the texts of various Eastern liturgies. While exiled in Paris, Cosin struck up a friendship with Cyril, archbishop of Trebizond, and attended Divine Liturgy. Geoffrey Cuming observes that "Cosin's approach is much more that of the modern liturgical scholar, anxious both to be familiar with the rite in its contemporary practice, and to get back as far as possible to its original form."[42] George Percy Badger (1815–88), an Anglican missionary in the Middle East, not only studied the rites of the Assyrian Church of the East but also experienced them firsthand, from which he collected material for a book on East Syrian liturgies.[43] William Palmer (1811–79), a member of the Anglican clergy associated with the Oxford Movement, devoted much of his career to establishing closer relations between the Anglican Church and Eastern churches. In the process, he undertook several visits to Russia and the Near East and wrote a number of works on Eastern Christianity, including a six-volume study of the Russian patriarch Nikon (1605–81).[44] Individuals such as these, however, are somewhat exceptional. Most of those who had contact with Eastern liturgies in the modern period knew about them primarily through *texts* rather than through direct contact with Eastern Christians in the European diaspora or in the eastern lands where these churches and their rites originated.

III. Western Rites and Eastern Liturgies: Traveling Texts, Armchair Scholars, and Liturgical Collections

The distinction between the movement of people and the movement of texts is somewhat artificial, since in many cases texts moved from East to West

---

of issues of liturgical interest. For more on the revival of Eastern Catholic theology in general, see Robert F. Taft, "Eastern Catholic Theology: Slow Rebirth after a Long and Difficult Gestation," *Eastern Churches Journal* 8:2 (2001): 51–80.

41. See *The Preces Privatae of Lancelot Andrewes, Bishop of Winchester*, trans. with an introduction and notes by F. E. Brightman (London: Methuen & Co., 1903).

42. Geoffrey J. Cuming, "Eastern Liturgies and Anglican Divines 1510–1662," in *The Orthodox Churches and the West*, ed. Derek Baker (Oxford: Basil Blackwell, 1976), 236.

43. George Percy Badger, *The Nestorians and Their Rituals: With the Narrative of a Mission to Mesopotamia and Coordistan in 1842–1844, and of a Late Visit to Those Countries in 1850* (London: Joseph Masters, 1852).

44. Zernov and Zernov, "History of the Fellowship," 2.

because people did. For example, what is now the earliest-known manuscript of the Byzantine liturgy, *Barberini gr. 336*, was likely produced not in Constantinople but rather in southern Italy in the second half of the eighth century.[45] Some of the Greek scholars discussed in the previous section brought Greek manuscripts with them when they migrated west after the fall of Constantinople.[46] Among the first texts of Eastern liturgies to be printed in the West were, perhaps surprisingly, Ethiopic texts, and the reason for this has to do with Jesuit missionaries sent from Portugal to Ethiopia. Relationships developed, some Ethiopians visited Rome, and as a result Ethiopian liturgical texts were printed there in 1548.[47]

For those who did not have personal relationships with Eastern Christians or firsthand experience of their liturgical rites, however, it is hard to determine how extensive knowledge of Eastern liturgies would have been in the West before printed editions became more widely available in the mid-sixteenth century.[48] Even in cases where researchers now have some indication of what editions of printed texts *might* have been available to particular humanist scholars and reformers, this does not provide an exhaustive catalogue of the full range of texts that *could* have been available, nor does this determine for certain whether a particular scholar or theologian had actually read and used a specific work.[49] However, many of the reformers of the sixteenth and subsequent centuries were apparently well versed in at least the better-known patristic and liturgical

---

45. For recent theories about the origin of this codex and a review of its subsequent history, see Stefano Parenti and Elena Velkovska, eds., *L'Eucologio Barberini gr. 336 (ff. 1–263)* (Rome: C.L.V.-Edizioni Liturgiche, 1995), xxiii–xxv; cf. F. E. Brightman, ed., *Liturgies Eastern and Western*, vol. 1, *Eastern Liturgies* (Oxford: Clarendon Press, 1896; reprint, Piscataway, NJ: Gorgias Press, 2004), lxxxix.

46. Cuming, "Eastern Liturgies and Anglican Divines," 231.

47. See Aidan Nichols, *Rome and the Eastern Churches: A Study in Schism*, rev. ed. (San Francisco: Ignatius Press, 2010), 110–11. For more details on these relationships, see also Girma Beshah and Merid Wolde Aregay, *The Question of the Union of the Churches in Luso-Ethiopian Relations, 1500–1632* (Lisbon: Junta de Investigações do Ultramar, 1964); and Philip Caraman, *The Lost Empire: The Story of the Jesuits in Ethiopia, 1555–1634* (Notre Dame, IN: University of Notre Dame Press, 1985).

48. Cuming, "Eastern Liturgies and Anglican Divines," 231.

49. First of all, scholars of the sixteenth century may still have been reading manuscripts in addition to print editions. Also, in many cases, "the fact that the work had been available does not prove that it had been read, but only the possibility that it could have been read." In some instances, much more is known about works that a reformer had a hand in editing or translating or had owned and notated. See Hughes Oliphant Old, *The Patristic Roots of Reformed Worship* (Zürich: Theologischer Verlag, 1975), 156–58, quote at 156–57.

sources available at the time, even if they did not draw on them specifically in framing their own forms of worship.[50]

The supposed echoes of Christian antiquity found in the Eastern rites may have contributed to a desire to learn more about these liturgies, especially their earliest extant representatives. According to Hughes Oliphant Old, "The Reformers believed that the worship of the Church must be 're-formed' according to the Word of God. They wanted nothing less than to find again the traditions established by Christ, handed down by the Apostles, and practiced by the ancient Church."[51] This was a hope shared by many engaged in the process of reforming worship in the sixteenth century—to pare down the interpolations and accretions of later ages and return to a "purer" form of Christian worship.[52] In many cases this involved crafting rites whose prayers and rubrics were felt to be consistent with the practices of the early church—incorporating, for example, such features as liturgy in the vernacular, the regular use of preaching, and Communion for all under the forms of both bread and wine rather than bread alone. In other cases, reformers explicitly incorporated elements from early liturgies into their own forms of worship; sometimes there is clear evidence that Eastern sources were the basis for these additions.

Thomas Cranmer, for example, had included a section entitled "A Prayer of Chrysostome" in his English Litany of 1544—the predecessor of the 1549 *Book of Common Prayer*. This Litany translates (and to some extent adapts) a prayer used at the beginning of the Liturgy of the Catechumens in the Divine Liturgy of St. John Chrysostom.[53] In this way, sources of Christian authority outside of

---

50. See, for example, Old, *Patristic Roots*, 180. On Thomas Cranmer's awareness of and approach to patristic texts, see George B. Soroka, "An Eastern Heritage in a Western Rite: A Study of Source and Method for Archbishop Cranmer's Inclusion of 'A Prayer of Chrysostome' in the English Litany of 1544," *Reformation and Renaissance Review* 7:2–3 (2005): 249–67.

51. Old, *Patristic Roots*, 38. While Old is speaking particularly of the Reformed tradition, the impetus to return to a form of worship that more closely resembled that of the apostolic and postapostolic age was present to a greater or lesser degree in many of the "reformations" that occurred in this era, including that of the Roman Catholic Church. The Council of Trent, for instance, had advocated that the Roman Missal be restored "to the pristine norm of the Holy Fathers" (Pius V, *Quo Primum*, 14 July 1570), as quoted in Frederick R. McManus, "Back to the Future: The Early Christian Roots of Liturgical Renewal," *Worship* 72 (1998): 390.

52. This did not mean, however, simply imitating supposedly "primitive" forms merely because of their antiquity. Soroka notes that, for example, "regaining an authentic Christianity for Cranmer . . . entailed a synthesis of what he judged as scripturally sound material, both ancient and more recent, into a context wherein it became meaningful in a contemporary sense" ("An Eastern Heritage in a Western Rite," 252).

53. See ibid.

the purview of Rome were tacitly deemed acceptable resources for the reform of the English church.[54] While the inclusion of an epiclesis of the "holy spirite and worde" in the 1549 *Book of Common Prayer* and other possible allusions to Eastern texts, such as the Liturgy of St. Basil, could have been inspired by Western sources as well,[55] the mere fact that the 1549 Prayer Book *had* an epiclesis provided a link to ancient Eastern Christian eucharistic practice and may have helped to spark interest in texts such as *Apostolic Constitutions* 8 and the Anaphora of St. James, especially among Anglican scholars and theologians.

This interest was facilitated by the wider availability in the West of printed editions and translations of Eastern liturgical texts—both those currently used in Eastern rites and those that were no longer used, if they had ever been used at all. The Greek text of the liturgies attributed to St. John Chrysostom and St. Basil was first printed at Rome in 1526. The major Byzantine service books had come off the presses by 1545, and other Eastern liturgies continued to appear regularly throughout that century, giving interested Westerners access to all the major Eastern liturgical texts known at that time except those from the East Syrian tradition. The Greek text of the Liturgy of St. James, for example, was published in 1560; a Latin translation of the Syriac version of this liturgy followed in 1572. *Apostolic Constitutions* was first printed in 1563. The liturgies of St. Mark (1583) and St. Peter (1589) soon followed, and Latin translations of Coptic liturgies (St. Cyril, St. Basil, and St. Gregory) were published in 1604.[56]

Once such texts were recovered and put into wider circulation through the use of printing, they were available as weapons for those engaged in disputes over how to celebrate and interpret liturgical rites. The voices of Christian antiquity enshrined in liturgical texts, and theological reflection upon them, were made to speak for or against the practices of the various churches emerging in western Europe and to criticize those of the Catholic Church.[57] Texts associated with, for example, Basil of Caesarea and John Chrysostom had authority by virtue of their authors and their standing in the larger church. Thus, one strategy available to

---

54. Ibid., 252. Another reason why Eastern Orthodox liturgies in particular might have appealed to English reformers was the long practice of conducting liturgical services in the vernacular (or "protovernacular").

55. See Cuming, "Eastern Liturgies and Anglican Divines," 232–33.

56. Ibid., 231, 233–34. For a list of Byzantine texts available in the West, see Brightman, *Liturgies Eastern and Western*, 1:lxxxiii ff., and Charles Anthony Swainson, *The Greek Liturgies, Chiefly from Original Authorities*, ed. and trans. C. Bezold (New York: Cambridge University Press, 1884; reprint, New York: Georg Olms Verlag, 1971), v–xiv.

57. Ralph Keen, "The Fathers in Counter-Reformation Theology in the Pre-Tridentine Period," in *The Reception of the Church Fathers in the West*, ed. Backus, 2:703.

reformers, Protestant or Catholic, to mitigate the authority of such texts was to question their attribution to famous authors and defenders of the faith. Another way to dismiss ancient Eastern (or Western) evidence was to question the antiquity of a particular source. There was no absolute standard for what time period defined the boundaries of the "early church." Many would admit evidence from the first four to six centuries of the Christian era as a relatively reliable witness to the apostolic interpretation of Scripture, but others defined the temporal span of "primitive" Christian tradition much more narrowly, limiting it, for example, to the first three centuries—which would conveniently eliminate "any liturgy then known, other than those attributed to one or all of the apostles; and the authenticity of the latter was by no means universally accepted" even then.[58]

Thus, concerned to safeguard the prestige and theological orthodoxy of their own traditions, early liturgiologists, as George Every notes, "had a practical interest in the antiquity of fixed liturgies, but also in making distinctions, where they were required by controversial needs, between present uses and the original forms."[59] If current attacks on, for example, the Roman Canon or the English *Book of Common Prayer* could be deflected by an appeal to ancient tradition, all the better. Consequently, much of the early use of Eastern liturgical texts was apologetic or polemical in intent rather than oriented toward developing "new" liturgical initiatives. The polemic was undertaken from the Catholic side by those concerned to defend the traditions of their church with selected evidence from the East. Those who had parted ways with the Roman Catholic Church, however, wielded evidence from the East that highlighted just how far the practice of the contemporary Catholic Church had departed from that of the first few centuries of the church, which was perceived to be more faithful to the will of Christ and the earliest apostles. However, almost every generalization has exceptions, and there were also a few Catholic irenicists among the apologists, people who, according to Ralph Keen, "ventured into Reformation colloquies with sincere proposals for reunion, theologians willing to concede that the protestants' distaste for contemporary practices in the church was not unjustified. Like the reformers, they contrasted the ancient church with that of their

---

58. Cuming, "Eastern Liturgies and Anglican Divines," 237. Cf. Spinks, *Western Use and Abuse*, 51.

59. George Every, "Edmund Bishop and the Epiclesis," in *Rediscovering Eastern Christendom*, ed. A. H. Armstrong and E. J. Barbara Fry (London: Darton, Longman & Todd, 1963), 77.

own time; they did not, like their [Roman Catholic] polemicist counterparts, seek to compare them."[60]

As the study of texts proceeded, however, scholars became more acutely aware that liturgical texts were part of the genre of "living literature" and thus subject to changes and adaptations as the texts were used over time.[61] With this rise in critical awareness, for example, liturgical scholars "became more conscious of the variety in Byzantine liturgical manuscripts, and of the unreliability, by such standards as those provided, of modern editions intended for use."[62] The seventeenth century also saw the rise of the scientific method, which was applied to patristic texts and liturgies as in other fields.[63] In terms of liturgical studies, massive projects of collection and translation were undertaken in the seventeenth and eighteenth centuries by the Maurists such as Jean Mabillon and the Jesuit Bollandists, among others.[64] Eastern liturgies had fallen out of favor in Roman Catholic circles by the mid-eighteenth century in the quest to promote Roman usages. In the nineteenth century, however, sustained interest in Eastern liturgies resurfaced, thanks in part to the Oxford Movement within the Church of England, whose goals included the restoration of this church's "catholic" identity. Scholars of this era who made important contributions

---

60. Keen, "Fathers in Counter-Reformation Theology," 724–25. These irenicists, particularly Georg Witzel and Johann Gropper, are discussed in more detail on 724–28. For further information on these figures, see Pontien Polman, *L'Element historique dans la controverse religieuse du XVIe siècle* (Gembloux: J. Duculot, 1932), 388–90; Michael B. Lukens, "Witzel and Erasmian Irenicism in the 1530s," *Journal of Theological Studies* 39:1 (1988): 134–36; and Walter Lipgens, *Kardinal Johannes Gropper 1503–1559 und die Anfänge der katholischen Reform in Deutschland*, Reformationsgeschichtliche Studien und Texte 75 (Münster: Aschendorff, 1951).

61. Living literature "is material which circulates within a community and forms a part of its heritage and tradition but which is constantly subject to revision and rewriting to reflect changing historical and cultural circumstances." See Paul F. Bradshaw, *The Search for the Origins of Christian Worship: Sources and Methods for the Study of Early Liturgy*, 2nd ed. (New York: Oxford University Press, 2002), 5.

62. Every, "Edmund Bishop and the Epiclesis," 77. *Apostolic Constitutions* 8 had been misattributed to Clement of Rome (hence the designation "Clementine" liturgy); both it and the Liturgy of St. James were once thought to belong to an authentic "apostolic tradition" dating back to the primitive church. See Cuming, "Eastern Liturgies and Anglican Divines," 237.

63. Bertrand, "The Society of Jesus and the Church Fathers," 936.

64. Taft, "Eastern Presuppositions," 11. Among those who focused on Eastern liturgies in particular, Taft mentions Jacques Goar (d. 1653), Jean Morin (d. 1659), Isaac Habert (d. 1668), Eusèbe Renaudot (d. 1720), Leo Allatios (d. 1669), Joseph Simon Assemani (d. 1768), and Joseph Louis Assemani (d. 1782).

included Charles Hammond, Charles Swainson, Frank Brightman, and Frederick Conybeare.[65]

In addition to studying early Eastern liturgies, some Anglican scholars and theologians were also *using* them to some extent. For example, Edward Stephens (1633–1706), Johannes Grabe (1666–1711), and Thomas Rattray (1684–1743) drafted eucharistic liturgies for private, experimental use that developed out of their study of early liturgies. Stephens compiled several liturgies intended for private congregations of worshipers based on ancient liturgies, especially book 8 of the *Apostolic Constitutions*, as well as the 1549 *Book of Common Prayer*.[66] Grabe used Eastern eucharistic prayers (including the anaphoras of St. James, St. Gregory of Nazianzus, St. Mark, St. Basil, St. John Chrysostom, and St. Cyril of Alexandria) to build his case that eucharistic consecration is accomplished by both the words of institution *and* the priest's prayer for the coming of the Spirit. Based on these convictions, Grabe penned two eucharistic liturgies of his own, both representing modifications of the 1662 *Book of Common Prayer* and modeled closely after the liturgies of Edward Stephens—but containing additions, adaptations, and expansions reflecting Grabe's own theological commitments.[67] The last section of Rattray's book, *The Ancient Liturgy of the Church of Jerusalem*,[68] consists of a practical application of his historical liturgical scholarship (including efforts to

---

65. See ibid., 20, n. 10.

66. See W. Jardine Grisbrooke, *Anglican Liturgies of the Seventeenth and Eighteenth Centuries*, Alcuin Club Collections XL (London: SPCK, 1958), 37–55 (and 201ff. for the texts of the liturgies); and Bryan D. Spinks, *Liturgy in the Age of Reason: Worship and Sacraments in England and Scotland, 1662–c.1800* (Burlington, VT: Ashgate, 2008), 111–12.

67. See J. E. Grabe, *De Forma Consecrationis Eucharistiae etc., Or a Defence of the Greek Church, against the Roman, in the Articles of the Consecration of the Eucharistical Elements . . . Written in Latin . . . together with a Translation . . . to Which Are Added Some Papers concerning the Oblation of the Body and Blood of Christ* (London: Richard King, 1721); and Spinks, *Liturgy in the Age of Reason*, 113–16.

68. *The Ancient Liturgy of the Church of Jerusalem, Being the Liturgy of St. James, Freed from All Latter Additions and Interpolations of Whatever Kind, and So Restored to It's* [sic] *Original Purity* . . . (London: James Bettenham, 1744). This text was published anonymously the year after Rattray died. Stuart G. Hall summarizes the principles that undergirded Rattray's rendition of the "primitive" Jerusalem liturgy: "He believed in an original apostolic liturgy, and sought it behind the evidence. What he was really handling was the evidence for liturgical reform in the fourth and fifth centuries. . . . But in fairness it should be said that in terms of the times in which Rattray worked his error was understandable." Stuart G. Hall, "Patristics and Reform: Thomas Rattray and *The Ancient Liturgy of the Church of Jerusalem*," in *Continuity and Change in Christian Worship: Papers Read at the 1997 Summer Meeting and the 1998 Winter*

reconstruct the earliest form of the anaphora used at Jerusalem from various Eastern sources) in the form of *An Office for the Sacrifice of the Holy Eucharist, Being the Ancient Liturgy of the Church of Jerusalem*.[69] This portion, which could be a stand-alone booklet of its own,[70] features an adapted version of Rattray's "original" Jerusalem liturgy in English translation, incorporating elements from other ancient liturgies in addition to offertory sentences from the Prayer Book tradition (especially the Scottish Prayer Book of 1637), resulting in a hybrid text that is neither purely ancient nor modern.[71] The rubrics and other directions imply that the text was intended at least as a model for liturgical celebration.[72]

On the one hand, efforts such as these reflect a move from purely polemical use of Eastern liturgical texts to practical pastoral application. Eastern anaphoras thought to reflect the usage of an earlier age were translated and adapted for the spiritual benefit of modern Western worshipers. On the other hand, these hybrid liturgical compositions—as enacted liturgical rites—affected very few. The transfer of substantial sections of Eastern text into Western liturgy was largely the project of marginal groups within a more mainstream tradition, resulting in liturgical texts that had limited use and impact. This situation changes quite dramatically in the twentieth century, however, as a number of liturgical units that seem to have originated in the East settle into Western rites and take up more permanent residence there.

Meeting of the Ecclesiastical History Society, ed. R. N. Swanson (Rochester, NY: Boydell Press, 1999), 254.

69. The full title of this section is *An Office for the Sacrifice of the Holy Eucharist, Being the Ancient Liturgy of the Church of Jerusalem, to Which Proper Rubrics Are Added for Direction, and Some Few Notes at the Foot of the Page, &c.* The text is reproduced in Grisbrooke, *Anglican Liturgies of the Seventeenth and Eighteenth Centuries*, 319ff.

70. While the pagination continues from earlier parts of the book, the fact that the *Office* has a title page of its own, lacks cross-references to other parts of *The Ancient Liturgy*, and duplicates information already discussed elsewhere in the book in its footnotes suggests that it was designed to be circulated independently, and there is some evidence that it did. See Hall, "Patristics and Reform," 249, 256.

71. "We are therefore offered a pedantic intention to restore the ancient text whole and perfect, which strays into creative liturgy-writing nevertheless." See Hall, "Patristics and Reform," 254–55, here 255.

72. While it is unclear whether Rattray's *Office* was used liturgically in the years following his death, there has been at least one celebration of it—in Edinburgh on 22 May 1994. See A. M. Allchin, "Thomas Rattray: After 250 Years," *Scottish Episcopal Church Review* 4 (1995): 50–63.

IV. The Migration of Liturgical Units from East to West in Twentieth-Century Liturgical Reforms

During the latter half of the twentieth century in particular, many Western churches sought to reform their liturgical rites. Interest in historical liturgical scholarship, increasing ecumenical awareness, and pastoral problems affecting Christian communities in an increasingly secular world contributed directly or indirectly to changes in worship practices that aligned them more closely to the perceived rites of the early church. Members of many Western churches, now better informed about the origins of Christian worship than would have been possible in previous centuries and looking to reforms currently underway or recently completed in other churches as examples of what might be possible in their own, developed rites whose individual components sometimes resembled those of Eastern Christian churches. Robert Taft has suggested that "what was being done was not so much an imitation of *existing* eastern usage, as deciding what should be done on the basis of several factors, above all perceived pastoral need, and then finding justification and support in patristic and eastern precedents as interpreted—even reinterpreted—in the light of those perceived present needs."[73] Nonetheless, the end result is that Western rites have picked up a number of elements in recent years that have either rough parallels or direct correspondence with Eastern worship practices and/or texts.

Like people and texts, liturgical units have likewise been on the move for a long time. More so than entire liturgies, or even texts of liturgies, liturgical units are highly portable.[74] The Latin West has borrowed much from the East through the centuries, including the *Kyrie eleison*, the *Gloria in excelsis*, the recitation of the Creed in Sunday worship, the *Sanctus*, and the *Agnus Dei*, and further loaning of Eastern elements is likely found in non-Roman Western rites, particularly the Gallican and Mozarabic expressions of Western Christianity.[75] However, like travelers bringing souvenirs home and integrating them into their collection of possessions, the process of transferring liturgical units from one rite to another is somewhat selective. Key components are taken out of their native context and sometimes set alongside parts that had never before resided nearby. Sometimes the contrast is quite obvious, as when "borrowed" liturgical units turn up in a different location and perhaps with a different function than they had in their

---

73. Taft, "Eastern Presuppositions," 13; emphasis added.

74. On the concept of liturgical units, see Robert F. Taft, "The Structural Analysis of Liturgical Units: An Essay in Methodology," in *Beyond East and West: Problems in Liturgical Understanding*, 2nd rev. and enlarged ed. (Rome: Pontifical Oriental Institute, 2001), 187–202.

75. For a more extensive discussion of these and other elements, see Bryan D. Spinks, "Some Early Liturgical Borrowing from the East," in *Western Use and Abuse*, 16–30.

rite of origin. In the process of liturgical evolution, then, the structure of a liturgical unit may be preserved even when its original intent and meaning are not.[76]

Tracing the movements of liturgical units (in terms of locating their likely origin(s) and subsequent path(s) of diffusion) is the work of comparative liturgical scholarship and can be a complex undertaking. Identifying overt borrowings of Eastern liturgical units in twentieth-century Western liturgical revisions, however, is often much easier. Some of the minor details about theological and practical motivations can be hard to trace—since many revised Western liturgies are the product of committee work rather than of individuals. As Spinks notes, "Since much of this revision has been undertaken in an ecumenical atmosphere, with cross-fertilization of scholarship and theology, it would be an endless task to trace which committee member in a particular denomination had taken a good idea from some Eastern rite, or had advocated some particular insight from a particular scholarly study on the Eastern liturgies."[77] Yet the fact that Western churches have imported Eastern liturgical units is obvious in many cases. The migration of two liturgical units from East to West will be considered here as examples. The first unit is very small, consisting of a single phrase. In an effort to connect a postbaptismal handlaying and/or anointing to the gift of the Spirit given in baptism, several Western churches have picked up the chrismation formula from the Byzantine Rite. The second unit is larger, drawing upon a complete Eastern prayer. As an ecumenical gesture, a number of Western churches have adopted a translation or adaptation of the Egyptian version of the Anaphora of Basil.

Example 1: The Byzantinization of Western Postbaptismal Anointings

In their overall shape and in certain ritual details, Western initiation rites have experienced a degree of "Easternization" or "Byzantinization" in recent decades.[78] A blatant Eastern borrowing occurred in the revised Roman rite of confirmation, in which the traditional Roman formula (i.e., "I sign you with the sign of the cross and confirm you with the chrism of salvation. In the name of the Father and of the Son and of the Holy Spirit") has been replaced since 1971 by an adaptation of the Syro-Byzantine formula, "N., be sealed with the gift of the Holy Spirit." Pope Paul VI, in the apostolic constitution on the sacrament of confirmation that introduced the new rite, gave a hint of the rationale behind the preference for the Eastern formula:

---

76. Taft, "Structural Analysis," 189.

77. Spinks, *Western Use and Abuse*, 126.

78. See Aidan Kavanagh, *Confirmation: Origins and Reform* (New York: Pueblo Publishing Company, 1988), 93.

As regards the words pronounced in confirmation, we have examined with the consideration it deserves the dignity of the respected formulary used in the Latin Church, but we judge preferable the very ancient formulary belonging to the Byzantine Rite. This expresses the Gift of the Holy Spirit himself and calls to mind the outpouring of the Spirit on the day of Pentecost (see Acts 2:1-4, 38). We therefore adopt this formulary, rendering it almost word for word.[79]

Several aspects of this description suggest that the motives for opting for the Eastern formula were that it is "very ancient" and that it effectively carries the biblical allusion to the Pentecost event constitutive of the Christian community in Acts. Given the comment elsewhere in this document that "it has been our wish also to include in this revision what concerns the very essence of the rite of confirmation, through which the faithful receive the Holy Spirit as Gift,"[80] the clear pneumatology of the Byzantine formula was probably a crucial reason for its adoption. Here the Eastern chrismation formula definitively conveyed a theological truth that the Roman West may have "lost" or neglected. Furthermore, the Eastern phrase was also amenable to the development of a theology of confirmation as a strengthening or completion of baptismal grace (rather than as something quite distinct from the rest of the process of Christian initiation).[81]

In the Byzantine baptismal ritual, this formula occurs in the context of the postbaptismal chrismation usually administered by a presbyter (or by whoever happens to baptize). It is clearly not a rite of prayer, handlaying, and anointing reserved to a bishop—and thus often separated temporally from the baptismal event. In the Roman rites of initiation developed since Vatican II, priests who baptize older children or adults or receive baptized persons into full communion are expected to confirm them on the same occasion. Thus, in practice, it is *only* in the case of those baptized as infants in the Catholic Church that Roman confirmation retains its "traditional" role as a postbaptismal anointing *reserved to the bishop*. The renegotiation of the practice and theology of confirmation along the lines of Eastern models has effectively resulted in two different ritual structures depending on a person's age and circumstances at baptism. Considering the evidence, Aidan Kavanagh concludes, "It might be argued that confirmation structurally has been given up in all but name in the case of adults and children

---

79. Paul VI, "Apostolic Constitution on the Sacrament of Confirmation," in *The Rites of the Catholic Church as Revised by the Second Vatican Ecumenical Council*, vol. 1 (Collegeville, MN: Liturgical Press, 1990), 477.

80. Ibid., 473.

81. Making a clearer connection between this sacrament and the rest of the process of Christian initiation was one of the goals stated in *Sacrosanctum Concilium* 71.

of catechetical age, but is retained as a separate structure for those baptized as infants. This anomalous situation is the weakest aspect of the reform since it does not restore anything peculiarly Roman but creates something new on grounds that are liturgically syncretistic and may well turn out to be pastorally problematical."[82] Regardless of the details, the East has a postbaptismal anointing associated with the gift of the Holy Spirit, and it consists of a *single* postbaptismal anointing conferred by the baptizing minister. The Roman Rite, in the case of infants, has not one but *two* postbaptismal anointings—a messianic and christic postbaptismal anointing (which is omitted if confirmation follows immediately) and an episcopal pneumatic anointing accompanied by handlaying and prayer.

This liturgical unit has been similarly transferred in some form to many other Western churches that celebrate some form of the postbaptismal gift of the Holy Spirit. However, its theological situation is less complicated because in those churches it typically occurs as a postbaptismal anointing performed by the minister of baptism. The postbaptismal rites in the *Lutheran Book of Worship* (1978) and in the *Book of Common Prayer* (1979) of the Episcopal Church, USA, for example, seem to have adopted a variation of both the handlaying prayer for the sevenfold gift of the Holy Spirit *and* the chrismation formula from the 1971 Roman rite of confirmation.[83]

Byzantine Rite[84]	Roman Rite of Confirmation (1971) (reproduced in 1973 in the Rite of Christian Initiation of Adults)[85]	Lutheran Book of Worship (1978) (postbaptismal anointing)	Episcopal Book of Common Prayer (1979) (postbaptismal anointing)

---

82. Kavanagh, *Confirmation*, 93.

83. See Maxwell E. Johnson, "Baptism as 'New Birth *ex Aqua et Spiritu*': A Preliminary Investigation of Western Liturgical Sources," in *Comparative Liturgy Fifty Years after Anton Baumstark (1872–1948)*, ed. Robert F. Taft and Gabriele Winkler, Orientalia Christiana Analecta 265 (Rome: Pontificio Istituto Orientale, 2001), 801. For the ritual texts, see the *Book of Common Prayer* of the Episcopal Church, USA (New York: Church Hymnal Corp., 1979), 308; and *Lutheran Book of Worship* (Minneapolis/Philadelphia: Augsburg Pub. House, 1978), 124 (= 311 of the ministers desk edition). The rubrics have been italicized in this table.

84. See E. C. Whitaker, *Documents of the Baptismal Liturgy*, rev. and expanded by Maxwell E. Johnson (Collegeville, MN: Liturgical Press, 2003), 123.

85. Rite of Confirmation, no. 27, in *The Rites*, 490–91.

And the priest anoints those that have been baptized with the holy oil, making the sign of the cross on the forehead and eyes and nostrils and mouth and both ears, saying: The seal of the gift of the Holy Spirit.	The bishop [celebrant] dips his right thumb in the chrism and makes the sign of the cross on the forehead of the one to be confirmed, as he says: N., be sealed with the Gift of the Holy Spirit.	The minister marks the sign of the cross on the forehead of each of the baptized. Oil prepared for this purpose may be used. As the sign of the cross is made, the minister says: name, child of God, you have been sealed by the Holy Spirit and marked with the cross of Christ forever.	Then the Bishop or Priest places a hand on the person's head, marking on the forehead the sign of the cross [using Chrism if desired] and saying to each one N., you are sealed by the Holy Spirit in Baptism and marked as Christ's own for ever.

Example 2: Western Versions of the Egyptian Anaphora of Basil

The eucharistic prayer is another aspect of recent Western reforms that has seen significant potential "Eastern" influence. Before the reforms of the last several decades, it was customary in Western traditions to have only one eucharistic prayer in use at any one time, perhaps with some changeable components, such as prefaces, to add variety suitable to liturgical seasons and feasts. Following the example of the East, it is now the norm for Western churches to have several eucharistic prayers in their repertoire, and many of these prayers follow the West Syrian or Antiochene form.[86] One anaphora of this type, the Alexandrian or Egyptian form of the Anaphora of Basil, has been used extensively in recent Western reforms. Prayers inspired by or adapted from this anaphora can be found as Eucharistic Prayer IV in the Roman Missal of Paul VI, as Prayer

---

86. A West Syrian anaphora traditionally contains the following elements: *Sursum corda*, preface, pre-*Sanctus*, *Sanctus*, post-*Sanctus*, institution narrative, anamnesis, offering, epiclesis, intercessions, and doxology. Its structure is outlined in R. C. D. Jasper and G. J. Cuming, *Prayers of the Eucharist, Early and Reformed*, 3rd ed., revised and enlarged (Collegeville, MN: Liturgical Press, 1990), 6. Ancient anaphoras that fit this pattern, thought to have emerged by the late fourth century, include the anaphoras of St. Basil, St. James, and St. John Chrysostom, as well as the *Apostolic Constitutions*.

D in the Episcopal Church's *Book of Common Prayer*, as Great Thanksgiving F in the Presbyterian Church's *Book of Common Worship*, and as Prayer F in the Church of England's *Common Worship*. The Egyptian form was chosen as the base text because scholarly consensus identified it as the most primitive of the several related forms of this anaphora. As a eucharistic prayer text, the Anaphora of Basil had broad ecumenical appeal, for it has been and still is used by many Eastern churches. The Egyptian form is used in the Coptic Church, and a longer version is prayed in the Greek and Russian Orthodox churches. A number of Eastern Catholic churches still use it as well, and it has also been celebrated by the Armenian, Georgian, and Syrian churches.[87]

Unlike the prior example of the migration of a single phrase from East to West, the length and complexity of an anaphora—a large liturgical unit comprising many subunits of its own—likely contributed to a more involved process of reception in the West. Western churches did not simply translate the Anaphora of Basil into contemporary vernacular languages but also adapted some of its components to better suit the theological milieu of the churches in which the prayer would find a new home. The epiclesis, which in the Eastern version of the anaphora requests both consecration of the bread and wine and other benefits for those about to share in Communion after the anamnesis section, is one component of the prayer that was frequently adjusted by Western churches. The inclusion of an explicit pneumatic epiclesis in Western eucharistic prayers is still relatively new in most traditions, and this element often migrated into Western prayers as one component of prayers imported from the East. For this reason, it is worthwhile to examine the epiclesis in more detail. The epiclesis of the Egyptian Anaphora of Basil reads:

> And we, sinners and unworthy and wretched, pray you, our God, in adoration that in the good pleasure of your goodness your Holy Spirit may descend upon us and upon these gifts that have been set before you, and may sanctify them and make them holy of holies. Make us all worthy to partake of your holy things for sanctification of soul and body, that we may become one body and one spirit, and may have a portion with all the saints who have been pleasing to you from eternity.[88]

---

87. Spinks, *Western Use and Abuse*, 128.
88. English text from Jasper and Cuming, *Prayers of the Eucharist*, 71.

In several contemporary renditions of the Anaphora of Basil, the epiclesis is as follows:

Roman Missal (1970) Eucharistic Prayer IV (Translation: International Commission on the Liturgy [ICEL], 2010)[89]	"A Common Eucharistic Prayer" (1975)[90] = Book of Common Prayer (Episcopal Church in the United States of America, 1979), Eucharistic Prayer D =Book of Common Worship (Presbyterian Church, USA, 1992), Great Thanksgiving F	Common Worship (Church of England, 2000) Eucharistic Prayer F[91]
[I.] Therefore, O Lord, we pray: may this same Holy Spirit graciously sanctify these offerings, that they may become the Body and Blood of our Lord Jesus Christ for the celebration of this great mystery, which he himself left us as an eternal covenant. . . .	Lord, we pray that in your goodness and mercy your Holy Spirit may descend upon us, and upon these gifts, sanctifying them and showing them to be holy gifts for your holy people, the bread of life and the cup of salvation, the body and blood of your Son Jesus Christ.	As we recall the one, perfect sacrifice of our redemption, Father, by your Holy Spirit let these gifts of your creation be to us the body and blood of our Lord Jesus Christ; form us into the likeness of Christ and make us a perfect offering in your sight.

---

89. *The Roman Missal*, third typical edition (Collegeville, MN: Liturgical Press, 2011), nos. 118 and 122 (pp. 658 and 660). The Roman Catholic prayer splits the epiclesis into two sections, indicated by Roman numerals in this chart: (I) a petition before the institution narrative for the sanctification of the offerings and (II) a prayer after the anamnesis for the fruits of Communion.

90. Episcopal Church, USA, *Book of Common Prayer*, 375; The Theology and Worship Ministry Unit for the Presbyterian Church (USA) and the Cumberland Presbyterian Church, *Book of Common Worship* (Louisville, KY: Westminster/John Knox Press, 1993), 148. The only difference between the two texts is the capitalization of the words "body," "blood," and "name" in the former but not in the latter.

91. The Church of England, "Eucharistic Prayers for Use in Order One," http://www.churchofengland.org/prayer-worship/worship/texts/principal-services/holy-communion/epsforonefront/prayerf.aspx.

Roman Missal (cont.)	"A Common Eucharistic Prayer" (cont.)	Common Worship (cont.)
[II.] Look, O Lord, upon the Sacrifice which you yourself have provided for your Church, and grant in your loving kindness to all who partake of this one Bread and one Chalice that, gathered into one body by the Holy Spirit, they may truly become a living sacrifice in Christ to the praise of your glory.	Grant that all who share this bread and cup may become one body and one spirit, a living sacrifice in Christ, to the praise of your name.	*All:* Amen. Come, Holy Spirit.

Although there were initial discussions in committee following the Second Vatican Council to use this prayer of St. Basil as it was, it proved an insurmountable difficulty for theologians of the Roman Rite to include an invocation of the Spirit for the consecration of the elements *after* the words of Christ had already been spoken in the institution narrative. The Roman Catholic version opted, as with all eucharistic prayers composed since the council, to split the epiclesis of this ancient prayer, reworking it into a consecratory petition before the institution narrative and a Communion petition after the anamnesis. In English translation, much of the original prayer is unrecognizable owing to extensive reworking of the text. The texts of the epiclesis in the Episcopal Church's Prayer D and in the Presbyterian Church's Great Thanksgiving F are identical, as both of these texts are based on "A Common Eucharistic Prayer," which was the result of an ecumenical project.[92] Most of the text represents a

---

92. "A Common Eucharistic Prayer," copyright 1975 by Marion J. Hatchett for the Committee for a Common Eucharistic Prayer. For more details on this prayer, see Leonel L. Mitchell, "The Alexandrian Anaphora of St. Basil of Caesarea: Ancient Source of 'A Common Eucharistic Prayer,'" *Anglican Theological Review* 58:2 (1976): 194–206; and Marion J. Hatchett, *Commentary on the American Prayer Book* (New York: Seabury Press, 1980), 377–78. In hopes that the prayer might be prayed by members of a variety of Christian traditions with different

different English translation of the Latin text of the Roman Catholic Church's Eucharistic Prayer IV, with the most significant changes in the anamnesis and epiclesis section. The group deleted the preliminary epiclesis found in the Catholic prayer and reintroduced a shortened form of the epiclesis of the Egyptian Anaphora of Basil in its traditional location after the anamnesis, also restoring the accompanying offering of the bread and wine at this point in the prayer.[93] This translation follows the pattern of the ancient prayer quite closely. The Church of England's rendering of the Egyptian Anaphora of Basil also follows the general themes of the original, with the addition of a concluding acclamation, "Amen. Come, Holy Spirit." However, the sense of unity through sharing in Communion, as well as the eschatological orientation of the original text, seems to have been "lost" (or at least diminished) in translation.

What all these variations suggest is that Western churches are open to using eucharistic prayers inspired by Eastern anaphoras, but they are not always content with the theology these prayers convey. In the case of the Anaphora of Basil and its epiclesis, a liturgical unit was imported from the East, but some of its features, particularly the location of the epiclesis within the prayer and some of its language, were changed to make the prayer resonate better with the expectations of Western eucharistic theology.

V. Conclusion

The above survey of the movement of people, texts, and liturgical units between East and West suggests that the motives for the fascination with Eastern

---

expectations about the standard contents of a eucharistic prayer, options in the text included conforming the text of the institution narrative to match that of the church in which it was prayed and omitting the intercessions. Hatchett comments: "The text of the prayer up to the institution narrative is a translation of the Latin original of the Roman sacramentary. The institution narrative [in the Episcopal *Book of Common Prayer*] is that of Prayers A and B. The anamnesis, oblation, and epiclesis are basically those of the earliest known manuscript of the prayer, with the addition of the phrase, 'the bread of life and the cup of salvation, the Body and Blood of your Son Jesus Christ,' from later manuscripts. The petition for the communicants is based on the Roman sacramentary Latin version; the petition for the church is from the earliest manuscript, and the bracketed intercessions are based on those of the Roman sacramentary. The final petition, that we may find our inheritance with the saints, contains phrases from the early manuscripts and from the old Roman prayer. The concluding expression of praise and the doxology are from the Latin version of the Roman sacramentary" (377).

93. H. Boone Porter, "Episcopal Anaphoral Prayers," in *New Eucharistic Prayers: An Ecumenical Study of Their Development and Structure*, ed. Frank C. Senn (Mahwah, NJ: Paulist Press, 1987), 70.

liturgies since the reformations of the West have varied with time and place and the theological inclinations of those who studied, used, and borrowed the texts. Yet several elements seem to recur—especially a fascination with the East as both deeply traditional and exotic and as retaining in near-constant use elements that Western liturgical theology and practice had forgotten or long neglected. Much of the migration of Eastern liturgies into Western reforms described in this essay was not the fruit of scholarly work in comparative oriental liturgiology. Rather, this migration was the result of Western admiration and selective adaptation often based on a limited exposure to the world of the Eastern Christian churches. Increased exposure to people, texts, and liturgical units led to a desire to incorporate aspects of Eastern liturgies into Western rites—in order to reflect a share in the common heritage, East and West, of the undivided ancient church or to express solidarity with contemporary Eastern practice. Thus, some contemporary Western worshipers need not venture outside churches of their own ecclesial tradition to see images of Western saints done in the style of Byzantine icons or hear Eastern phrases in their baptismal, eucharistic, or other prayer texts.

What seems to be happening is that Western liturgists, historians, and scholars have created—either intentionally or unintentionally—a vision of early Christian worship and of Eastern Christian worship that could inform *current* issues in their own churches just as much as they were retrieving Eastern traditions that had been neglected or "lost" in the West. This is a trend that is likely to continue in an age when members of both traditional churches and emerging churches in the West are searching for identity. Thomas Pott draws attention to the interplay of identity and tradition in liturgical reform that encompasses past, present, and future. Although he is addressing reform in the Byzantine tradition, his words convey something of what was happening and continues to happen in the process of overlaying Eastern elements on a Western liturgical identity. "Every liturgical reform, whether consciously or subconsciously, seeks to connect a certain vision of the future in relation to a certain vision of the present reality. It is particularly in this vision of present reality that the question of identity plays itself out. . . . The greater the ideological weight of identity, the more the vision of tradition is exploited, the less the properly liturgical aim of the reform is transparent."[94]

---

94. Thomas Pott, *Byzantine Liturgical Reform: A Study of Liturgical Change in the Byzantine Tradition*, trans. Paul Meyendorff (Crestwood, NY: St. Vladimir's Seminary Press, 2010), 259–60.

9

Hispanic Migrations: Connections between Mozarabic and Hispanic Devotions to the Cross

Raúl Gómez-Ruiz, SDS

Among Roman Catholic Hispanics, processions in the popular realm have precedents and parallels in the liturgical realm. This suggests a migration of processions—possibly back and forth—between the liturgical and popular realms. For processions in the liturgical realm, processions come to mind that are part of Corpus Christi celebrations, Palm Sunday services, the Holy Thursday reposition of the Blessed Sacrament at the end of Mass, and the exposition of the cross during the Good Friday liturgy. In addition, every Roman Catholic sacrament is celebrated in a liturgical context and involves a procession of some sort or other. At the same time, the liturgical processions have parallels that take place beyond the liturgical realm yet are linked to the liturgies of those days. This becomes particularly visible on Good Friday among the Mozarabs[1] or "Old Christians" of Toledo, Spain, and among Hispanics in San Antonio, Texas.

---

1. Present-day Mozarabs are a Spanish ethnic group comprised of the descendants of those Hispano-Roman and Visigothic Christians who held onto their faith despite the vicissitudes of the Islamic invasion and the need to adapt to the dominant culture. Through the centuries these Christians mingled and intermarried with subsequent conquerors and inhabitants of Toledo, including Arabs, Berbers, Syrians, Castilians, Galicians, and French, who made their home among them. During the more than 370 years of Islamic domination, they spoke Arabic and acquired the cultural characteristics of the dominant Arabic culture. See among other works

In this essay, I address the theme of "liturgy in migration" by examining these two sites and their particular forms of devotion to the cross, which are expressed in processions in both the liturgical and popular realms. My first example is the processions of the Hispano-Mozarabic liturgy that take place on Good Friday in Toledo, Spain, together with the popular piety practiced by the Mozarabs on that day. My second example is the Good Friday procession conducted by Hispanic Catholics in San Antonio, Texas, a procession that incorporates both liturgical and popular elements. Parallels will become visible between these processions. I then offer some reflections on the particular devotion to the cross expressed here and on how the processions themselves might have migrated, by way of what Jan Assmann has called "cultural memory," between the liturgical and popular realms.

I. Good Friday Processions among Mozarabs in Toledo, Spain

The cross appears central to the spirituality of Mozarabs and to their identity. This is most evident on Good Friday when they gather for two liturgies and then take part in processions that wend their way through the city.[2] Toledo, the city that inspired the painter El Greco in the sixteenth century, sits atop a rugged promontory hedged in on three sides by a loop of the Río Tajo. The city's core, the *casco antiguo*, whose crooked streets tend to be narrow and often impassable by car, has remained relatively unchanged. The parish church of Santa Eulalia y San Marcos, where Mozarabs usually celebrate their liturgy, is hidden on a steep, narrow, cobblestoned street in an out-of-the-way barrio of the *casco antiguo*. The church was first built in 559 during the Visigothic era, under the reign of King Athanagild (554–67),[3] and has undergone reforms, rebuilding, abandonment, and reconstruction over the ensuing centuries. The building was abandoned in 1842, repaired in the late 1960s when electricity

---

Richard Hitchcock, *Mozarabs in Medieval and Early Modern Spain: Identities and Influences* (Burlington, VT: Ashgate, 2008).

2. For more on the Mozarabic rituals described here, see my *Mozarabs, Hispanics, and the Cross* (Maryknoll, NY: Orbis Books, 2007), and "Ritual and the Construction of Cultural Identity: An Example from Hispanic Liturgy," *Perspectivas* 12 (Fall 2008): 9–32.

3. For more, see A. Arellano, "La Parroquia Mozárabe de Santa Eulalia," *Crónica Mozárabe* (=CM) 6 (1982): 12; Francisco de Sales Córdoba, "Las iglesias mozárabes de Toledo," CM 11 (1984): 9–10; Ignacio Gallego Peñalver, "La iglesia mozárabe de Santa Eulalia de Toledo," CM 17 (1986): 7–9; and Sixto Ramón Parro, *Toledo en la Mano*, 2 vols., Serie IV Clásicos Toledanos 6 (Toledo: Instituto Provincial de Investigaciones y Estudios Toledanos, 1978; repr. of *Toledo en la Mano* [Toledo: Severiano López Fando, 1857]), 2:189–91.

was installed, and reconsecrated for worship in 1973.[4] It has recently undergone further repairs owing to the deterioration of its western wall, and it was reconsecrated on 20 February 2011. The building is a modified Visigothic- and Mozarabic-style basilican construction with Mudéjar elements.[5]

The Mozarabs' devotion to the cross is focused on a relic of "the wood of the true cross," the *Lignum Crucis*. This relic is housed in a reliquary in the shape of a Latin cross that sits atop the tabernacle in the Blessed Sacrament chapel of the church. The relic of the true cross was found in a small coffer when repairs were made to the church in the mid-fifteenth century; the reliquary was made in 1636.[6] A box at the foot of the Latin cross contains the relics of Santa Eulalia, the patron saint of the parish. The Hermandad Mozárabe takes the reliquary out in procession on Good Friday. The main reason Don Enrique Carrillo Morales, the pastor, gives for the placement of the reliquary atop the tabernacle is liturgical. The Lignum Crucis is placed over the tabernacle, he says, "so that because of the singular veneration given to [the tabernacle] by the Catholic liturgy, the reliquary is assimilated to and united to that which the Church gives to the presence of Jesus in the Blessed Sacrament."[7] Thus, Don Enrique deliberately wants to link the Lignum Crucis to the Blessed Sacrament. Indeed, the reliquary is treated as if it were a monstrance containing a particle of the sacramental presence of Christ when it is taken out in procession under the *palio*, a canopy that goes over the Blessed Sacrament in liturgical processions.

The ***ad tertiam*** **service** is the first liturgical service of Good Friday. Celebrated anew at Santa Eulalia only since 1996, it is a recovery of a service found in the *Liber ordinum* (ca. 1039)[8] that was altered and combined with the *ad nonam* service under Cardinal Ximénez de Cisneros, archbishop of Toledo, in 1500. *Ad tertiam* refers to Terce, the third hour of liturgical prayer, which usually takes place at 9:00 in the morning. The liturgy nowadays includes a procession of the assembly with the Lignum Crucis, and two venerations of the relic. Don Enrique begins the liturgy with a brief greeting and prayer. Then he instructs the assembly to leave the church in procession and starts a

---

4. See Córdoba, "Las iglesias mozárabes de Toledo," 9.

5. For Visigothic, Mozarabic, and Mudéjar architecture, see Xavier Barral i Altet, *The Early Middle Ages: From Late Antiquity to A.D. 1000*, Taschen's World Architecture series (Cologne: Benedikt Taschen Verlag, 1997), 99–117.

6. Enrique Carrillo Morales, "Las Reliquias de Santa Eulalia," CM 20 (1987): 2.

7. Ibid., 3 (translation mine).

8. Marius Férotin, *Le Liber ordinum en usage dans l'église wisigothique et mozarabe d'Espagne du cinquième au onzième siècle*, Monumenta Ecclesiae Liturgica 5 (Paris: Firmin-Didot, 1904).

hymn to the cross, ¡*Victoria! Tú reinarás*.⁹ The people sing as they go out of the building into the plaza, descend the hill, circle back, and return inside. At the rear of the procession a minister swings the thurible filled with incense; Don Enrique follows carrying aloft the Lignum Crucis. Back inside, the people go to their pews while the ministers return to the front of the altar, with Don Enrique continuing to hold high the Lignum Crucis. He then calls on all to venerate the wood on which hung Christ the Savior. The ritual unfolds as the Lignum Crucis is venerated twice. During the second veneration, people come forward in procession and make various forms of reverence. All do so from a slight distance before then nearing the reliquary to kiss or touch it. During the veneration rite, which lasts about twenty minutes, Don Enrique intones the ancient Latin hymn *Vexilla regis*¹⁰ followed by the contemporary hymn ¡*Victoria! Tú reinarás*. After the veneration Don Enrique carries the reliquary to the altar. He invites the people to stand and acclaim the cross in a litany of praise, which opens by extolling the holy cross on which Christ hung, whose blood washed our wounds. After the litany, all kneel for a closing prayer. Thus ends the morning service.

The **ad nonam pro indulgentia** service, the second liturgy of the day at Santa Eulalia, takes place in the afternoon. The title in English means "at the ninth hour, for mercy." This service is longer than the morning one, lasting about ninety minutes; in a sense it is a continuation of the morning service. A special feature is the Litany for Mercy (*Indulgentia*)¹¹ decreed by the Fourth Council of Toledo (633).¹² Because penance and the reconciliation of peni-

---

9. This is an idiosyncratic introduction by Don Enrique. The *Missale Hispano-Mozarabicum* (Archdiocese of Toledo, 1991) and the *Liber ordinum* offer the text of a Latin hymn, but owing to the lack of notation, Don Enrique has substituted a hymn of recent vintage. Its title in English is "Victory! You will reign." It was composed by F. X. Moreau; another version is available in the hymnal *Flor y Canto* (Portland, OR: OCP Pub., 1989), no. 194, where the title is simply *Tú reinarás*.

10. This sixth-century hymn is directly related to an earlier procession with another relic of the true cross, this one sent to Queen Radegunde for her convent near Poitiers. Radegunde asked Venantius Fortunatus to compose a hymn for the procession of this relic to her church. For more, see Anne-Madeleine Plum, *Adoratio Crucis in Ritus und Gesang: Die Verehrung des Kreuzes in liturgischer Feier und in zehn exemplarischen Passionsliedern*, Pietas Liturgica Studia 17 (Tübingen: A. Francke Verlag, 2006), 194–215.

11. *Indulgentia* can be translated as "indulgence," "pardon," "tenderness," or "mercy"; the latter word best conveys the request for mercy in the plea for forgiveness.

12. José Vives, Tomás Marín Martínez, and Gonzalo Martínez Díez, eds., *Concilios Visigóticos e Hispano-Romanos* (Barcelona: Consejo Superior de Investigaciones Científicas, Instituto Enrique Flórez, 1963), 210 (canon 55).

tents were public in the Visigothic church, this service was to be the sacramental reconciliation liturgy. The Litany for Mercy played a major role in the completion of penance and incorporated the rest of those present into a communal penance service.[13]

The service begins with a procession in which the ministers file in from the sacristy in silence. As in the morning service, Don Enrique carries the Lignum Crucis with a humeral veil covering his hands and the base of the reliquary. He places the Lignum Crucis on the altar between votive lamps or tapers, where it remains throughout the liturgy (although direct references to it never occur). In this way, the reliquary remains a ritual focal point. After the service it is taken to the other Mozarabic Rite parish, Santas Justa y Rufina, near the city center, where it will be prepared for the evening processions through Toledo. Those carrying the reliquary to Santas Justa y Rufina form what can be called an informal procession since they follow the person carrying the reliquary but in no set order and with no particular displays of reverence.

For the **Good Friday Evening Procession**, the Mozarab processants begin to arrive at Santas Justa y Rufina around 7:30. People from other parts of Spain come to take part, joining those who live in Toledo. The processants include men and women, boys and girls. The men come dressed in the distinctive royal blue mantle of the Hermandad; a large cross emblem adorns its left arm. Each wears a *venera* (Mozarab emblem) around his neck on a blue and gold ribbon. The women arrive dressed in black, each with a Spanish *peineta* (comb) and a *mantilla* (lace veil) on her head. Their emblem, the cross of Alfonso VI attached to a blue and gold ribbon in the form of a *lazo* (bow), is pinned over their hearts. Don Enrique arrives wearing the Mozarab cross emblem on a blue and gold band around his neck. Only processants may be in the church at this time. The archdiocese assigns a chaplain to each group; in this way the popular religious practice of Holy Week processions is legitimized and integrated into the ecclesial life of Toledo. Three other groups are in the building, assembling and putting the final touches on their *pasos* (the biers for carrying the statues in procession), which will go out that evening.[14] The first group to leave at

---

13. Jorge Perales, "The Reconciliation of Public Penitents in Spain during the First Millennium" (Collegeville, MN: Saint John's University, unpublished paper written for a seminar in liturgical studies [LTS 470], 1986), 39 pp., here 4–5.

14. On the development of Spanish *cofradías*, see Ricardo García-Villoslada, *Edad media (800-1303): La cristiandad en el mundo europeo y feudal*, 5th ed., vol. 2 of *Historia de la Iglesia Católica en sus cinco grandes edades: Antigua, media, nueva, moderna y contemporánea* (Madrid: BAC, 1988), 852–55.

the onset of the procession is the one that accompanies the *descendimiento paso*. The Hermandad y Cofradía del Santísimo Cristo del Descendimiento (Brotherhood and Confraternity of the Most Holy Christ of the Descent from the Cross) takes in procession a seventeenth-century tableau of Christ being taken down from the cross.[15] Then follows the group accompanying the *paso* of the Virgen de las Angustias. This is the Venerable, Real e Ilustre Hermandad de Nuestra Madre María Inmaculada en su Mayor Angustia, Piedad y Desamparo (Venerable, Royal and Illustrious Brotherhood of Our Mother Mary Immaculate in her Great Anguish, Pity and Helplessness—popularly known as *Angustias*, "Agonies"); the group takes a Pietà in procession. The image of the Virgin was made in 1999, while the image of Christ laid over her lap is from the seventeenth century. Each penitent member wears a navy velvet cape, stiff pointed hood with face mask (*capirote*), and cincture over a white habit. The *capirote* and habit, or *Sambenito* (literally "St. Benedict"), of the penitents was instituted by the Inquisition in the fifteenth century. In the eighteenth century this costume was taken over by the *cofradías* (confraternities) and *gremios* (guilds) for Holy Week processions.

Processants dressed in seventeenth-century armor are next. Most of these are young people since the armor is for those of smaller physical stature. The group includes girls as well as boys, young women as well as young men. Still, the armor is fairly heavy and requires much stamina to wear in procession. Some accompany the members of the Knights of the Holy Sepulcher who escort a *carroza* (cart) carrying an eighteenth-century sculpted image of Christ in a glass coffin called either the *Santo Sepulcro* (the Holy Sepulcher) or the *Santo Entierro* (Holy Burial). Each member wears a heavy white mantle with a large red Jerusalem cross on his left arm, white gloves, and a biretta topped by a red pom-pom. A young man in armor drags a black pennant attached to a spear behind him as he goes ahead of the dead Christ in the glass coffin. After this comes the Hermandad Mozárabe with the Lignum Crucis.[16] The Hermandad is followed by more soldiers. The last *paso* is that of Nuestra Señora

---

15. For the link between *cofradías* and their images, see Antonio Mestre Sanchis, "Religión y cultura en el siglo XVIII español," in *Edad moderna: La época del absolutismo monárquico (1648-1814)*, vol. 4 of *Historia de la Iglesia Católica en sus cinco grandes edades: Antigua, media, nueva, moderna y contemporánea* (Madrid: BAC, 1991), 596–97.

16. Cardinal González Martín in 1976 decreed the participation of the Hermandad in the Good Friday processions and indicated its placement behind the *Santo Sepulcro paso*. See Marcelo González Martín, "Decreto sobre el 'Lignum Crucis' de la Parroquia Mozárabe de Santa Eulalia y San Marcos," *Boletín Eclesiástico del Arzobispado de Toledo* 132 (1976): 208–9.

de la Soledad carrying a nineteenth-century image of the Sorrowful Mother, *la Soledad*. It is taken out by the Real e Ilustre Cofradía de Nuestra Señora de la Soledad (Royal and Illustrious Confraternity of Our Lady of Sorrows). The female penitents wear black dresses and *mantillas* along with the group's emblem. The male penitents wear ivory capes and habits with black hoods and girdles; they also wear the group's emblem around their necks.

By maintaining this processional, moving tableau—in which Jesus is taken down from the cross, placed on the lap of his weeping mother, escorted by soldiers, and laid out in a coffin, leaving the cross empty (the Lignum Crucis reliquary) and his mother weeping—the gospel narrative describing Jesus' passion is reenacted for all to see and own.

About 10:00 p.m., the Lignum Crucis reliquary emerges from the church. The *paso* is carried by four Mozarab young men who are led by two boys dressed as altar boys, one swinging a thurible. The *paso* is flimsier than the earlier ones; any movement is easily seen in its canopy. Its simplicity and starkness are striking. Spotlights on the *paso* are focused on the reliquary, making it shine underneath the canopy. It is carried in silence over the entire route.

Civic and military officials are the last to line up; they approach the church from the lower part of Santa Justa Street as the Hermandad Mozárabe emerges at 8:30. These officials include members of the city council and the provincial government, military officers, and officers of the Guardia Civil. They are led by the mayor, who wears the Mozarab cross emblem on a gold chain as a symbol of the city government's role of civil protector of the Hermandad Mozárabe.[17] Archdiocesan officials also participate in the procession, walking before the civic and military officials. At the center is the archbishop, who may also wear the Mozarab cross emblem on a gold chain, a sign of his role as the ecclesiastical superior of the Hispano-Mozarabic Rite and titular head of the Hermandad Mozárabe.[18] The group leaving Santas Justa y Rufina will join with two other

---

17. *Constituciones de la Ilustre y Antiquísima Hermandad de Caballeros Mozárabes de Nuestra Señora de la Esperanza, de la Imperial Ciudad de Toledo, Capítulo de Toledo* (Toledo: Arzobispado de Toledo, parroquias Mozárabes de San Marcos y de Santas Justa y Rufina, 1966), as revised in 1984, art. 5; as revised in 1999, arts. 14 and 25.

18. *Constituciones* (1984), arts. 1 and 5; *Constituciones* (1999), art. 13. Archbishop Francisco Álvarez Martínez, designated a cardinal by Pope John Paul II in 2001, retired in 2005 and was replaced by Cardinal Antonio Cañizares Llovera, who served as the archbishop of Toledo until 2009 when he was named prefect for the Congregation for Divine Worship and the Discipline of the Sacraments. Cardinal Cañizares made some significant changes in the processions by taking a more active quasi-liturgical role in them. His successor, the current archbishop of Toledo, Don Braulio Rodríguez Plaza, has not continued most of the practices introduced by

groups leaving from other churches, resulting in a huge, blocks-long procession made up of hundreds of men, women, and children dressed as penitents or in formal attire. They wend their way through the *casco antiguo* and at one point pass through Zocodover, the main square, where seats have been set up for paying viewers. Three drum and bugle corps and ten *pasos* are interspersed among them. The *pasos* for the most part are very elaborate and bedecked with colorful, fresh flowers. All are sizeable except for one, the small Lignum Crucis under its canopy. It elicits attention and quiet respect, surpassed only by the reverence paid to the image of Christ in the glass coffin. All together, the *pasos* form a tableau of the passion of Jesus Christ. The thousands of observers are temporarily suspended in time as they return to the moments of Jesus' suffering and death. They are moved to pity for the Virgin as she weeps her beloved son's death. The ritual enables the passion narratives to come to life before all who have eyes to see. The drama allows the ugliness of Christ's ignominious death to be transformed into a beautiful and majestic pageant of victory.

Once the processants return to the church, they sing the *Salve* and then disperse to go their separate ways. The Lignum Crucis is taken from its *anda* (platform) and will be returned quietly to Santa Eulalia, where it will be affixed to the top of the tabernacle again to remain there until next year's Holy Week.[19]

II. The Good Friday Procession in San Antonio, Texas

A large crowd gathers in front of a long platform that has been set up as a stage at one side of a plaza in the Mercado or old Market Square, a tourist-oriented, open-air shopping mall near the heart of San Antonio, Texas.[20] There

---

his predecessor. Nonetheless, as did Don Antonio, Don Braulio joins the processants at Santas Justa y Rufina as they prepare to leave on procession rather than meeting them at the cathedral and then joining them.

19. For such processions as "bearing the sacred," see Ronald L. Grimes, *Beginnings in Ritual Studies*, rev. ed. (Columbia, SC: University of South Carolina Press, 1995; first pub. in 1982 by University Press of America), 51–53. For Grimes, liturgy declares "this is the way things are," and it does this by "re-presenting" events and "event-ualizing" structures. These traits appear in the case of the Lignum Crucis as the Mozarabs take their *paso* out in procession.

20. In 1998 I was a consultant as part of a study group that observed, analyzed, and reflected upon the events organized by the staff at San Fernando Cathedral, San Antonio, TX. The study, funded by the Lilly Foundation and the Mexican American Cultural Center, was later published in various sources. For a particular description and interpretation of these events, see Virgilio P. Elizondo and Timothy M. Matovina, eds., *San Fernando Cathedral, Soul of the City* (Maryknoll, NY: Orbis Books, 1998), 90–96. Also see the video "Soul of the City / Alma del Pueblo," a

is excitement in the air as men and women, boys and girls dressed in costumes reminiscent of first-century Palestine make their way through the crowd to the stage. These participants had gathered earlier at San Fernando Cathedral, their parish, to pray, get costumed, and prepare for the drama that will unfold later in the day. They also had roles the evening before at the Holy Thursday liturgy and reenactment of Christ's agony in the garden of Gethsemane.

At the onset of the Good Friday event, ministers of various Christian denominations mount the stage. Most of them are dressed in alb and stole according to their liturgical practice. Among them is the Roman Catholic archbishop of San Antonio, who will preside at a short service to begin the passion of Christ reenactment. As part of the service a brief sermon and prayers are offered. Immediately following, a commotion occurs as a trumpet sounds: men dressed in Roman armor arrive, bringing with them a man costumed as Christ in chains. The representatives of the churches descend, while actors taking on the roles of Pontius Pilate, Herod, and their courts take over sections of the stage. A centurion announces that Pilate will hear the case against this so-called Jesus. The trial of Jesus before Pilate, then Herod, and back to Pilate is then enacted, following the gospel accounts of the passion. As part of this reenactment the actors in Middle Eastern costumes call for Jesus' crucifixion in place of Barabbas's. Pilate accedes, washing his hands. After Jesus' condemnation, he and two other men are laden with large wooden crosses and led to the street. The crowd presses to get out of the way and to the street.

Wearing a crown of thorns, Jesus begins to carry the cross through the streets of San Antonio. On the sidewalks along either side of Dolorosa Street, leading from the Mercado to the plaza in front of the cathedral, are thousands of spectators. They watch somberly as the Roman soldiers push Jesus and the two thieves forward. Occasionally, the soldiers yell at them and crack their whips. As they move down the street, the stations of the Via Crucis (the Way of the Cross) are enacted, including Jesus' three falls and his encounters with the weeping women of Jerusalem and with Veronica, who wipes his face. I take note of a child who covers his ears and weeps at the terrible scene of violence against Jesus. At one point the archbishop takes the cross from Jesus, as if he were Simon of Cyrene. People are watching in respectful silence. Some are very moved, while others are not sure what to make of this scene. Along the way, the procession will pass the justice center with its courthouse and jail; the banking

---

project of the Mexican-American Cultural Center, prod. Adán M. Medrano (San Antonio: JM Communications/MACC, 1996).

district of San Antonio is located nearby, as is the famous Alamo, from which the commotion on the street draws people away to see what is happening.

Finally, about midday, the actors arrive at the plaza in front of San Fernando Cathedral. The street here is named Soledad, the title of the Blessed Virgin Mary in her great sorrow as she mourns the death of her son. The crosses carried by the three men are laid across the steps leading into the cathedral, and the soldiers proceed to strip and nail Jesus to the cross. The eerie pounding of nails into the wood and the cries of anguish are so realistic that many people begin to weep. As the crosses, with the men attached to them, are elevated, the rest of the passion narrative is enacted until Jesus expires on the cross about 3:00 p.m. Throughout the reenactment Jesus' "seven last words" are pronounced by the one acting as Christ. After Jesus expires the cross ensemble is lowered and then carried in procession into the cathedral, where it is laid in front of the altar. Afterward, another cross with an articulated image of Christ replaces the one carried in procession, and people stream in to touch or kiss this cross or make some other sign of reverence. The crowd that had gathered for the procession disperses slowly. Soon there will be a liturgical Good Friday service that lasts about forty-five minutes, with a more formal reading of the passion and a veneration of the cross. In the evening at 7:00, a large crowd will fill the cathedral to capacity for a service called the Pésame a la Virgen (an expression of condolences to the Virgin). During this service the articulated image of the dead Jesus on the cross will be laid on a bier, and people will come forward to pay their respects and place flowers on the body until it is completely covered. Some kiss the feet; others touch the face or feel the hands before returning to their pews for the ending of the service.

III. Reflections on the Mozarabic and Hispanic Good Friday Processions

Scholars have noted the growing practice of Good Friday processions conducted by Hispanic Catholics through city streets in the United States.[21] These processions are usually called the Via Crucis, the Way of the Cross, and involve large numbers of people who normally leave from a local Hispanic parish to move through the streets, making periodic stops where Jesus' route

---

21. I use the term "Hispanic" broadly to describe peoples in the world, especially in the United States, who share history and familial connections derived from Spain, a key element held in common by those identified as Hispanic. See Jorge J. E. Gracia, *Hispanic/Latino Identity: A Philosophical Perspective* (Malden, MA: Blackwell, 2000).

to his crucifixion and death are reenacted before returning to their starting point. In most cases in the United States this involves actors who take on the roles of the various personages described in the gospel narratives of Christ's passion, including an actor who takes on the role of Jesus carrying his cross. The structure of the Via Crucis follows the pattern established by the Lenten practice of weekly Friday Stations of the Cross services and the processions that take place inside Roman Catholic parish churches, usually led by a liturgical minister such as a priest or deacon. Though both the Stations of the Cross and the Via Crucis processions are considered expressions of popular piety that focus on devotion to the cross, they represent the migration of liturgical processions into the popular realm. Such Via Crucis processions in the United States, however, themselves represent a migration of devotional practices that originated in Spain and during the colonial period were taken to various Latin American countries and to the Philippines prior to taking root in the United States. These Good Friday processions continue to take place in Latin America and the Philippines as well as in Spain. Over the centuries the processions have developed some characteristics found only in one place and not another, but many traits continue to be shared across geographic distances. Certainly, devotion to the cross plays a central role in all these processions. At the same time, some of the innovations introduced in one place have migrated back to Spain, particularly the practice of choosing actors to create living tableaux of Christ's Good Friday passion.[22]

The San Antonio Good Friday service is unique because of its setting and the well-developed dramatic elements that take place from mid-morning until late in the evening. However, the use of actors who reenact the Way of the Cross on Good Friday also occurs in many cities in the United States, including Chicago, Milwaukee, and Washington, DC. Virgilio Elizondo notes that in terms of the Good Friday services and processions, "public rituals are a collective way of experiencing God in which all the people act and appear as one body, the body of Christ."[23] That is, rituals are important because they engage the participants bodily and lead them to internalize meanings. Or, as the adage says, "Where the body goes, the mind follows." Elizondo goes on to say that "through these religious rituals, each person experiences the truth of the past here and now in a very active way by actually reliving the events."[24] Jan Assmann's concept of

22. As is the case, for example, in the Via Crucis in Riogordo (Málaga).
23. Virgilio P. Elizondo, "The Sacred in the City," chap. 7 in Elizondo and Matovina, *San Fernando Cathedral, Soul of the City* 81.
24. Ibid., 82.

"cultural memory" is helpful here to understand how this works in the Good Friday processions in Toledo and in San Antonio.

Cultural Memory

Hispanics have taken liturgical elements and applied them to their everyday lives by means of popular religious practices, which continue to be linked to what happens at worship. These popular religious practices bear what Jan Assmann has called "cultural memory." For Assmann cultural memory is a "collective concept for all knowledge that directs behavior and experience in the interactive framework of a society and one that obtains through generations in repeated societal practice and initiation."[25] One way Hispanic popular religious practices, such as Good Friday processions, can be understood to represent a migration of the liturgy is through the cultural memory they carry and hand on. Cultural memory, for Assmann, is contained in objectivized cultural elements such as rites, texts, images, buildings, monuments, cities, and even landscapes, as well as in everyday exchanges such as jokes and ad hoc comments. All these elements hold the identity of a particular group and make this identity accessible to its members to own.[26] An important element in Assmann's theory is the notion of "communicative memory," which involves everyday communications that form part of the collective memory of a group.[27] He says that train rides, waiting rooms, or the common table, among other things, foster—and to a certain extent predetermine—such communications. Thus, "through this manner of communication, each individual composes a memory which . . . is (a) socially mediated and (b) relates to a group."[28] In Assmann's view, memory and objectivized culture are coupled. Rites, texts, and images, for example, are cues that hold memory and link the everyday to the past. Such memory is maintained "through cultural formation (texts, rites, monuments) and institutional communication (recitation, observance, practice). We call these 'figures of memory.'"[29] Assmann attributes the power of cultural memory to "mnemonic energy," claiming that "in cultural formation, a collective experience crystal-

---

25. Jan Assmann, "Collective Memory and Cultural Identity," trans. John Czaplicka, *New German Critique* 95 (Spring/Summer 1995): 125–33 (originally published in *Kultur und Gedächtnis*, ed. Jan Assmann and Tonio Hölscher [Frankfurt/Main: Suhrkamp, 1988], 9–19).

26. Assmann attributes his work to the foundation set in the 1930s by the sociologist Maurice Halbwachs and the art historian Aby Warburg, who independently developed two theories of a "collective" or "social" memory; see ibid., 125.

27. Ibid., 126, building on Halbwachs.

28. Ibid., 127.

29. Ibid., 128–29.

lizes, whose meaning, when touched upon, may suddenly become accessible again across millennia."[30] Following Assmann, Hispanic religious practices can be understood to hold a cultural memory and a mnemonic energy that help Hispanics develop their identity as a unique part of God's people. This identity is shaped both by the official liturgy and by popular devotions such as processions. One of the characteristics of cultural memory is that it preserves accumulated knowledge from which a group derives an awareness of its unity and uniqueness. Another characteristic is its "capacity to reconstruct" or relate knowledge to an actual contemporary situation. Assmann claims that "cultural memory exists in two modes: first in the mode of potentiality of the archive whose accumulated texts, images, and rules of conduct act as a total horizon, and second, in the mode of actuality, whereby each contemporary context puts the objectivized meaning into its own perspective, giving it its own relevance."[31] In sum, cultural memory contains the values and self-knowledge of a group and holds its memory of these by means of figures of memory, that is, rites, texts, customs, and so forth, that help the group access the values and identity contained therein (communicative memory).

How may we apply Assmann's thinking to the Good Friday processions described above? The participants in these processions may be said to access, embody, and express the mnemonic energy that gives dynamism to the cultural memory from whence these processions come. Processants provide to themselves and to observers access to cultural memory by means of figures of memory such as the Lignum Crucis, the Via Crucis, and penitential practices, investing them with more mnemonic energy that can be communicated to others. Processants also invest these processions with meanings that are expressed ritually and interpreted individually as well as collectively. Theologically put, it seems, then, that as a bearer of cultural memory processions in both liturgical and popular realms have the mnemonic energy to provide people with an encounter with Christ and his cross in their lives. The cross is a symbol that elicits devotions and is embraced through self-sacrifice and joining one's own suffering to Christ's. This helps Mozarabs and Hispanics generate certain figures of memory that give them access to this encounter in worship and in popular religious practices. It also helps them see their lives as related to Christ's, particularly his passion; Mozarabs and Hispanics thus find the liturgy in their lives and their lives in the liturgy. Good Friday processions as figures of memory are a way to make this link. Moreover, through the cultural memory they contain,

30. Ibid., 129.
31. Ibid., 130.

they reveal a migration of liturgy into the popular realm and facilitate a possible return to the liturgy. If this were not the case, I believe that Hispanics would abandon the practice. For this reason Mozarabs can say that to go in procession on Good Friday is to engage in "an act of recollection. It means to accompany the Lignum Crucis. It is to do penance."[32] Don Mario Arellano García asserts that taking the Lignum Crucis in procession is very important: "It is the most important element in the procession of Good Friday since it is the authentic relic of the cross. The rest are just statues."[33]

Historic Roots and Routes

Processions entered the cultural memory of Hispanics through centuries-old practices of processions that form part of their identity. Even before Christianity took root in Iberia, pagans used processions as acts of worship, and we can expect the language and practices of pre-Christian religions to have had some impact on Christian worship in Iberia. For instance, Simon Keay describes various pre-Christian festivals that took place in the second to the fourth centuries CE in Iberia.[34] These included processions with devotees carrying sacred images. An example is the great spring festival in honor of Cybele and Attis that took place between 15 and 27 March.[35] One of its processions involved carrying a sacred pine tree representing the death of Attis, a youth personifying death and resurrection. Clearly, there appear to be links between contemporary Hispanic practices of Holy Week and earlier practices, which may have included ways of commemorating death and resurrection that appealed to early Iberian Christians. These practices were adapted and transmitted to later generations and made their way into Holy Week celebrations. But pagan practices alone were not the only influence on the religious practices of Christians in Spain. Christian practices in other ecclesial centers also played a role in the development of Holy Week in Spain. This is especially true of liturgical practices in Jerusalem, Rome, and Constantinople,[36] all of which knew religious processions.

32. Jurado Lozano family, interviewed by author in Toledo, 2 June 1999: "Es un acto de recogimiento. Significa acompañar al *Lignum Crucis*. Es completar la penitencia."
33. Mario Arellano García, interviewed by author in Toledo, 20 May 1999: "Es el elemento más importante de la procesión de Viernes Santo puesto que es la reliquia autentica de la cruz. Lo demás es solamente imágenes."
34. See S. J. Keay, *Roman Spain*, Exploring the Roman World 2 (Berkeley, CA: University of California Press, 1988).
35. More in Ibid., 164–65.
36. John F. Baldovin, SJ, *The Urban Character of Christian Worship: The Origins, Development, and Meaning of Stational Liturgy*, Orientalia Christiana Analecta 228 (Rome: Pont. Institutum

As John Baldovin has noted, "the late antique world of the Mediterranean was a world of processions."[37] Processions were an especially important feature of the liturgies of Holy Week in Jerusalem. A major source of knowledge about the Christian practice in Jerusalem comes from the fourth-century Spanish pilgrim Egeria, who describes these in her diary,[38] noting the uniqueness and similarities between practices in Jerusalem and at home.

Penitential practices as part of processions also have a long history in Spain. There is explicit evidence of processions in Spain during the sixth century that tended to be penitential in character,[39] a trait that continues to mark Holy Week processions both in Toledo and in San Antonio to this day. As noted above, the Good Friday *ad nonam pro indulgentia* liturgy in Toledo was the yearly public penance service when penitents were reconciled. More dramatic elements entered the celebration of Holy Week in the ninth century in Spain.[40] Indeed, liturgical drama such as mystery plays as part of Holy Week celebrations began with the Carolingians in their region in the same era and spread elsewhere in Europe.[41] Processions were an element that at times formed part of the liturgical dramatization of the events of the Lord's passion. The current Holy Week processions in Spain have their firmest foundation in the sixteenth century when many confraternities were established, and sculpted processional images were introduced for this purpose.[42] The baroque era saw the development of elaborate biers borne aloft by carriers and accompanied by *nazarenos* (literally "Nazarenes") dressed in the penitential garb of pointed hood and face

---

Studiorum Orientalium, 1987), 39: "Jerusalem, Rome, and Constantinople all had a major symbolic significance for the late antique and early medieval world, and were the centers of liturgical influence that left their imprint most clearly on subsequent rites."

37. Ibid., 165.

38. *Egeria: Diary of a Pilgrimage*, trans. George E. Gingras, Ancient Christian Writers 38 (New York: Newman Press, 1970).

39. See Baldovin, *Urban Character of Christian Worship*, 160.

40. Jaime Lara, "The Liturgical Roots of Hispanic Popular Religiosity," in *Misa, Mesa y Musa: Liturgy in the U.S. Hispanic Church*, comp. and ed. Kenneth G. Davis, OFM, Conv. (Schiller Park IL: World Library Publications, 1997), 31.

41. See Jaime Lara, "Stages for Rituals of Conversion," chap. 6 of *City, Temple, Stage: Eschatological Architecture and Liturgical Theatrics in New Spain* (Notre Dame, IN: University of Notre Dame Press, 2004), esp. 178, 190, 193.

42. See *Semana Santa Toledo '99: Programa de actos y cultos* (Toledo: Junta de Cofradías y Hermandades de Semana Santa de Toledo, 1999, booklet); *Semana Santa '99 Toledo: Programa de actos y cultos* (Toledo: Junta de Comunidades de Castilla-La Mancha, Asociación Provincial de Empresarios de Hostelería de Toledo, pamphlet). These are the official programs for Holy Week of 1999.

mask introduced by the Inquisition for those doing "public" penance for their transgressions. (This garb is still used today and disturbs those from the United States because it has been appropriated by the Klu Klux Klan.)

Processions were a means of proclaiming faith publicly and of taking the liturgy hidden in churches into the street. In this way, the city became liturgical space. John Baldovin in fact asserts that the processions themselves are liturgical in nature. He highlights certain characteristics that are mirrored in current Hispanic practice in general and in the processions in Toledo and San Antonio in particular: "Processions of all sorts are, of course, public in nature, but popular liturgical processions differ in that they are much larger in scale and succeed in bringing together people of diverse backgrounds and status. Thus, as a kind of democratic form in a very undemocratic world, they succeeded in bringing liturgy onto the streets."[43] It is important to note in addition that the Directory on Popular Piety and the Liturgy issued by the Holy See in 2001 affirms processions among Roman Catholics as worthy liturgical and devotional practices meriting renewal and participation by all the faithful.[44]

Today in the United States the public aspect of religion and its practices is being limited due to the insistence on the separation of church and state. Though this has led to attempts to delimit religious practices to the private and personal realms, Hispanics have taken to the streets on Good Friday anyway. Without the means to mount large processions and carry expensive images illustrating the events of Christ's passion, they have substituted actors, with the end result being a living tableau of Christ's passion that is linked to the cultural and social context in which Hispanics find themselves. Reflections on the different stations of Christ's carrying the cross to Calvary often incorporate prayers and comments on the social events having an impact on Hispanics today. The Via Crucis processions frequently take place in poor barrios, and sometimes the route takes them by jails and other institutions that evoke social justice themes.[45] In structure and in certain other details, the Good Friday Via Crucis processions taking place in the United States contain vestiges of

---

43. Baldovin, *Urban Character of Christian Worship*, 160.

44. Cf. Congregation for Divine Worship, Directory on Popular Piety and the Liturgy: Principles and Guidelines, official English trans. (Vatican City: Libreria Editrice Vaticana, 2002), nos. 245–47.

45. See Karen Mary Davalos, "'The Real Way of Praying': The Via Crucis, Mexicano Sacred Space, and the Architecture of Domination," in *Horizons of the Sacred: Mexican Traditions in U.S. Catholicism*, ed. Timothy Matovina and Gary Riebe-Estrella, SVD (Ithaca, NY: Cornell University Press, 2002), 41–68.

practices found elsewhere in contemporary Latin America and Spain, as well as throughout the history of these processions. The reverse is also true, in that the practice of using actors for living Via Crucis processions has occurred in various parts of Spain.

IV. Conclusion

Though no direct cause and effect of migration can be established between processions in the liturgical and popular realms, history shows that Christians took pre-Christian practices and incorporated them into their own liturgies. This included processions and the bearing of sacred images or artifacts as part of them.[46] That today in the United States Good Friday processions are beginning to occur wherever sufficient numbers of Hispanic Catholics gather is possible because of the first migration of processions from pre-Christian into Christian worship. The practice appears to have migrated later from the liturgical realm to the popular realm, especially during the medieval era when other phenomena such as liturgical mystery plays also developed. Along the way, Good Friday processions took on traits that reflected the cultural context in which they took root, whether in Jerusalem, Constantinople, Rome, or Toledo. As noted, during the baroque era these processions took on many characteristics still found today in Spain, Latin America, the Philippines, and the United States.

A key element of Good Friday events such as the Mozarab processions in Toledo and the Via Crucis in San Antonio is the focus on the cross. That the cross is a central element in the spirituality and identity of the Mozarabs is most evident on Good Friday. The ritual use of the Lignum Crucis, in the two liturgies and in the procession in the evening, helps us gain a deeper understanding of its significance as a symbol of the cross for Mozarabs in particular and for Hispanic spirituality in general. Because Mozarabs and their rite reflect the liturgy and spirituality of the earliest Hispanics, they and their liturgy are an apt source for examining the roots of much contemporary Hispanic spirituality, especially as expressed in popular religious practices such as the Via Crucis. Roberto Goizueta, reflecting on the processions in San Antonio, notes that in the Via Crucis of Good Friday, Hispanics engage in a practice that, as an act of "accompaniment," constitutes and empowers them as persons and as a

---

46. For more, see Sabine Felbecker, *Die Prozession: Historische und systematische Untersuchungen zu einer liturgischen Ausdruckshandlung*, Münsteraner Theologische Abhandlungen 39 (Altenberge: Oros Verlag, 1995).

community of faith.⁴⁷ For Hispanics the cross and resurrection are intimately related. The Good Friday events thus provide a way for Hispanics to stress the passion as an active, communal undertaking over against the suffering passively endured by a solitary individual: "Suffering shared is suffering already in retreat."⁴⁸ Goizueta avers that the source of hope is not the resurrection of a solitary individual but "the ultimate indestructibility of the community that accompanies Jesus on the Via Crucis and is reconciled with him in the Resurrection."⁴⁹

The Mozarabs' sense that one must embrace the cross, as seen in the Hispano-Mozarabic Rite, has its parallel in the Good Friday processions found among Hispanics all over the world where individuals perform penitential acts of self-sacrifice. *Mandas* and *promesas*—penitential vows and promises made by individuals to God, Mary, and the saints—are a way of doing this. Carrying the cross in everyday life is expressed by such concepts as "Hay que sacrificarse por sus hijos" (One must sacrifice oneself for one's children), or "No hay mal que por bien no venga" (There is no evil that does not come for some good), or "No hay gloria sin la cruz" (There is no glory without the cross). These are common ways of speaking among Hispanics as they face problems and try to make sense of them in light of their faith in Christ and his sacrifice on the cross.

Good Friday popular processions linked to the liturgy of Good Friday migrated with the peoples who left Spain to colonize the Americas. Those migrating to what has become the United States have brought their religious expressions with them, including taking those expressions to places not previously under Spanish control. And as before, Good Friday processions take on particular cultural traits that reflect the context in which they have taken root. As many others have done, Hispanic Catholics could have abandoned the practices of their forebears, but they instead have sought to put them to use in the new cultural context. Part of what has facilitated this is the cultural memory transmitted through figures of memory associated with the liturgy and popular piety, as well as through the symbiotic relationships among liturgy, popular piety, and figures of memory.

Today, facilitated still by migrations of peoples, as well as by newer social means of communication such as television, newspapers, magazines, DVDs,

---

47. For his development of this concept, see Roberto S. Goizueta, *Caminemos con Jesús: Toward a Hispanic/Latino Theology of Accompaniment* (Maryknoll, NY: Orbis Books, 1995).

48. Roberto S. Goizueta, "A Matter of Life and Death: Theological Anthropology between Calvary and Galilee," *Catholic Theological Society of America Proceedings* 53 (1993): 4.

49. Ibid., 5; Goizueta draws on Hans Urs von Baltasar here.

films, and the internet, people's knowledge of these processions has expanded. Consequently, people pick and choose aspects that appeal to them and continue to adapt and develop these events into dynamic and meaningful practices. In this way participants are both reconstructing and composing cultural memory as they generate new forms that combine the old with the new via the context, place, and time, adding to the store of mnemonic energy. Perhaps this is why using actors to fill the roles of Jesus, Mary, the Roman soldiers, and so forth, in the United States has led to the reintroduction of this in parts of Spain, thereby facilitating a migration back to where Good Friday processions entered into the religious sensibility and its expression among Hispanics. Even so, they have been able to have recourse to figures of memory, such as Good Friday processions, that facilitated the reappropriation of certain aspects of practices from the past (e.g., mystery plays) in order to be able to do this.

As noted earlier, the specific pattern of the migration of liturgy and related practices back and forth is difficult to establish definitively because it is hard to say which came first. Nonetheless, here and there appear practices that we find in one place and then encounter elsewhere. A sign of this is the participation of liturgical officials such as the archbishops of Toledo and San Antonio in the Good Friday processions. It is not clear to what extent, if any, these have occurred spontaneously, or to what extent people have reached into their cultural memories to extract practices of earlier times and imbued them with new aspects and meanings while still forming part of what processions are in the liturgical and popular realms. Clearly, Good Friday processions among Mozarabs and Hispanics point to their identities as well as to the interrelationship of liturgy and popular piety and the migration of cultural meaning between the two, especially in terms of devotion to the cross.

10
Sounding the Challenges of Forced Migration: Musical Lessons from the Ethiopian Orthodox Christian Diaspora

Kay Kaufman Shelemay

In the lives of many immigrants, liturgy holds a place of privilege. Liturgical practices, materials, and the experience of performance can help bridge distances of time and space, rendering a new homeland familiar. Yet an expectation that liturgy should inevitably function as a site of stability during periods of stress surrounding migration may in fact be unrealistic. Periods of forced migration can provide signal challenges to long-standing patterns of liturgical continuity. Transitional moments demand a good measure of creativity from those experiencing spatial and cultural displacement.

In this essay I will present a case study from the Ethiopian Orthodox Church tradition that suggests that the more complex the historical liturgical tradition, the more difficult may be its transplantation and maintenance abroad. The complexity of the Ethiopian Orthodox Church—complexity in several domains, ranging from esoteric musical content to the unusual clerical structure for transmitting the musical liturgy—has presented special hurdles for perpetuating the tradition abroad. I will suggest that the perpetuation of liturgy can present a daunting, perhaps even insurmountable, challenge for those establishing new lives in exile. At the same time, the process of establishing a postmigration liturgy can provide very interesting insights into the nature of creative responses that may reshape liturgy in the wake of crisis and forced mobility.

My reflections will be divided into four sections: (1) a brief introduction to the history and musical practice of Ethiopian Orthodox Christianity; (2) a look at the experience of recent forced migration from Ethiopia and the ways in which this experience disrupts liturgical practice and performance; (3) an analysis of musical domains where transitions under conditions of forced migration appear to be particularly marked: liturgical performance, liturgical transmission, and the musical dynamics between clergy and congregation; and (4) a concluding summary of "musical lessons" that this case study offers, spanning insights into the challenges to, and emerging changes in, liturgical transmission and performance.

I. The History and Musical Practice of Ethiopian Christianity

In contrast to most of African Christianity, which arose through European missionary efforts of the seventeenth through twentieth centuries, the establishment of Ethiopia's church dates to the conversion of the Ethiopian court by shipwrecked Christians from Tyre in the early fourth century.[1] It appears that from a very early date Ethiopian Christianity was a literate tradition, with its indigenous liturgy codified according to church traditions in the sixth century in the ancient Semitic language Ge'ez. The Ethiopian Synaxary (*Mashafa Sənkəssar*) records in some detail the musical inspiration of St. Yared, a church musician said in oral traditions to have lived during the sixth-century reign of Emperor Gabra Masqal and to have received the corpus of chants through inspiration from the Holy Spirit.[2]

The conversion of the Ethiopian court served to unite the political and religious domains in Ethiopia from a very early date. By the thirteenth century additional layers of mythology from a source titled *Kəbra Nagast* (Glory of the Kings) linked the history of Ethiopian Christianity and the royal dynasty that assumed power in that era with Judaic traditions. These included the myth that

---

1. See Gianfranco Fiaccadori, "Salama," in *Encyclopaedia Aethiopicae* 4 (Wiesbaden: Harrassowitz Verlag, 2010), 484–88.
2. The first complete edition of the Synaxarium was edited by E. A. Wallis Budge in 1928: *Mashafa Sənkəssar: The Book of the Saints of the Ethiopian Church; A Translation of the Ethiopic Synaxarium; Made from the Manuscripts Oriental 660 and 661 in the British Museum* (Cambridge: Cambridge University Press, 1928). See Gérard Colin and Allessandro Bausi, "*Sənkəssar*," in *Encyclopaedia Aethiopicae* 4 (Wiesbaden: Harrassowitz Verlag, 2010), 621–22, for the history of the Ethiopian Synaxarium, based initially on fourteenth-century Coptic sources, and for a summary of recent critical editions.

Menelik, the fabled son of King Solomon and the queen of Sheba, brought the ark of the covenant to Ethiopia from Jerusalem.³

As we consider the challenges to the Ethiopian liturgical tradition through forced migration in the later twentieth and early twenty-first centuries, we should note that about five hundred years ago the Ethiopian liturgical tradition encountered the only other major challenge to its survival. Between 1529 and 1541 virtually all of highland Ethiopia was overrun by Muslim forces led by Ahmad b. Ibrahim al-Gazi (known as Grañ or Gragn).⁴ The invaders destroyed the majority of Ethiopian monasteries and churches and ravaged their extraordinary manuscript and artistic holdings. By the time Ethiopia managed to repel the invaders, many of the clergy had been exterminated and most of the monasteries and churches were in ruins. We know that performance of the liturgy was disrupted because within a decade or two after the invasion, two surviving clerics innovated a system of musical notation to help reinforce oral transmission. This extraordinary act of musical and liturgical creativity provided a mnemonic system, based on the Geʻez syllabary, in which melodies from the liturgy were represented by abbreviations of the liturgical texts with which they were associated. Continued performance of the liturgy and knowledge of the oral tradition were necessary, however, to use the notation.⁵ Here, then, we see a creative response to exigencies of time and place and a concerted effort to rescue the tradition. We will shortly see how creative impulses in the musical domain also characterize the current era of forced migration, but through very different initiatives with very different outcomes.

The period from the seventeenth to the twentieth centuries witnessed a series of Ethiopian emperors who once again centralized church authority, first in the north of the country and then, by 1900, in the central highlands in the present capital, Addis Ababa. They revived and rebuilt the network of monasteries and expanded the boundaries of their Christian empire. The Mass remained a musical domain of straightforward plainchant, but over the years

---

3. See Paolo Marrassini, "Kəbrä Nägäśt," in *Encyclopaedia Aethiopicae* 3 (Wiesbaden: Harrassowitz Verlag, 2007), 364–68, for an account of the disputed history of the *Kəbra Nagast* as well as for details of its critical editions.

4. Franz-Christoph Muth, "Ahmad b. Ibrahim al-Gazi," in *Encyclopaedia Aethiopicae* 1 (Wiesbaden: Harrassowitz Verlag, 2003), 155–58.

5. For a history of the church musical tradition and its notational system, see Kay Kaufman Shelemay and Peter Jeffery, *Ethiopian Christian Liturgical Chant: An Anthology*, 3 vols, with CD (Madison, WI: A-R Editions, Inc., 1993, 1994, 1997). For a concise discussion of the notational system, see my "Mələkkət," in *Encyclopaedia Aethiopica* 3 (Wiesbaden: Otto Harrassowitz, 2007), 916–17.

the music performed for the Cathedral Office, termed the *Mahlet*, became ever more highly elaborate, being performed in vigils that lasted throughout the night. The historic system of three musical modes credited to St. Yared was elaborated when sung in distinctive regional vocal styles associated with different monasteries and was enhanced by new styles of dance accompanied by drums and sistra. While priests and deacons alone performed the Mass, a large group of nonordained liturgical musicians (*dabtara*) was responsible for performing and transmitting the Cathedral Office. A single priest with an assisting deacon could perform the Mass (*Qeddase*), but to fully realize the Cathedral Office and all aspects of Hymnary (*Dəggwa*) performance practice, a full cohort of twenty-four knowledgeable musicians, led by one or more even more highly trained head musicians, the *marigeta*, was needed.

II. *The Dimensions of Forced Migration*

Beginning in the spring of 1974, the long-standing hierarchies of Ethiopian religious and political life were turned upside down. With the overthrow of Emperor Haile Selassie I, the church lost its symbolic head and, with the nationalization of rural and urban lands, its economic base as well. The assumption of power by a Marxist military committee known as the Derg—officers who overthrew and eventually murdered the emperor—resulted in all manner of trauma and dislocation. One outcome was the marginalization of the church, so long associated with the ruling, Christian elite, who were among the first targets of the revolution.

Beginning in late 1974, Ethiopian daily life became increasingly chaotic: Ethiopian students who had at the beginning helped to spark the rebellion were sent to the countryside as part of a supposed educational initiative in which many died; members of the former government and aristocracy were thrown into prison or executed. Beyond the loss of the church's power and economic base, strictly enforced urban curfews stretching from 6:00 p.m. to 6:00 a.m. severely disrupted ecclesial life, especially the performance of the Hymnary and Mass. To add to the church's woes, the convening of large groups of people was formally forbidden. Thus, Ethiopian Christians came under direct threat for the first time since the sixteenth-century Grañ invasion, and most of the small number of Ethiopians then living abroad simply did not return home. As an example we can take Moges Seyoum, today the leader of the musicians at one of the largest Ethiopian churches in Washington, DC, who was studying in Greece in 1974 and has not returned to Ethiopia since that time. He has received asylum in the United States. In 1982 he helped to found a church in Garland, Texas, and in 1989 he accepted an invitation from Debre Selam Kidist Mariam Ethiopian Orthodox Tewahedo Church in Washington, DC, to lead its liturgy.

Many Ethiopians fled their country, taking whatever routes they could to escape, especially during the trauma of the Red Terror of 1977–78, a particularly violent chapter of the Ethiopian revolution. Bodies of individuals, picked up and murdered by the regime of Mengistu Haile Mariam, were left in the roads as a warning to others. The impact of the revolution was devastating. Clergy who had received land through the church lost it; high church officials were humiliated, being instructed to wear khaki uniforms instead of clerical garb, and they were put to work sweeping the streets of the capital. I quote Father Tsehai Birhanu, an Ethiopian priest and *marigeta* who today leads St. Michael's Church in Mattapan, Massachusetts. He discussed with me the revolution's long-term impact, as many priests and liturgical musicians left church employment in order to survive:

> [The church] is affected very, very badly. . . . In Ethiopia nowadays . . . everybody . . . is struggling even to get daily food. Even in the countryside . . . you cannot find any scholars. They left the church, and now they live in different cities and they are working daily to survive. . . . The scholars are not enough to serve the church. It is very sad for the church nowadays. (Tsehai Birhanu, 17 September 2010)

The Ethiopian revolution ended in 1991 with the overthrow of the Derg's revolutionary government. This transition, however, sparked another round of marginalization for the church and especially for the Christian Amhara ethnic group long at its center. With a new policy favoring a multiethnic state, and with Christianity no longer the official state religion, many thousands, especially Christian Amharas, left the country. The years since 1975 have thus seen the establishment of a worldwide Ethiopian diaspora, with its largest concentration in North America. Approximately 250,000 Ethiopians and Eritreans live in the Washington, DC, metropolitan area alone; this is the largest Ethiopian community outside of the homeland and the second largest new African community in the United States.[6]

---

6. For an introduction to the history and culture of the Ethiopian diaspora, see Kay Kaufman Shelemay and Steven Kaplan, "Creating the Ethiopian Diaspora," special double issue of *Diaspora: A Journal of Transnational Studies*, 15/2–3 (2006, published in 2011). This essay introduces a collection of articles prepared by an interdisciplinary group of scholars who participated in a conference I organized at Harvard University's Radcliffe Institute for Advanced Studies during the spring of 2008.

Before moving on to part 3 of this essay, I must briefly note one musical development that took place just before the advent of the Ethiopian revolution and that has had a global musical impact subsequently. In 1968 Father Tsehai Birhanu, the Ethiopian priest and *marigeta* quoted above, was a rising church musician in Addis Ababa. Father Tsehai tried to arouse the interest of urban Christian youth in Addis Ababa by composing hymns in Amharic, the national language. Father Tsehai recalls:

> Yes, the new style. . . . I composed this hymn book while I was studying [at] Holy Trinity College in Addis Ababa. I was assigned by the bishop to teach Bible and song at every church in Addis Ababa. At that time, [I was] creating every new hymn. So I decided to make a book of compositions. I sent it to the bishop. He just put his sign on [it] to be sent to the Department of Evangelization. They said, "If it is published, it will be helpful for the younger generation of the church." . . . And it was published. Soon everybody, even the bishops, the archbishops, the scholars—they had that book. (Tsehai Birhanu, 12 April 2008)

Thus, Father Tsehai was the creator of the most important musical innovation in the Ethiopian church in the later twentieth century. His hymns quickly became popular among young people, and little more than five years later, during the revolution, the songs were used by youth as a cover for Sunday meetings in the church. The hymns, known as the "Sunday school songs," are today circulated and widely performed both in Ethiopia and worldwide and are known through cassettes, CDs, and oral tradition. The Sunday school songs have provided a channel through which young people, and especially women of all ages, become active in liturgical performance. The Sunday school songs have revolutionized Ethiopian Christian liturgical performance in the diaspora. In the words of a young deacon who assists Father Tsehai at St. Michael's Church in Boston,

> It's been popular . . . thanks to Father Tsehai; he started these Sunday school *mazmurs* [songs] that are in Amharic. . . . Now if you go through the streets of Addis Ababa, you hear [them] through the streets, through the stores, . . . [in] taxis—whatever you take, you hear these kind of *mazmurs*. . . . And you have, like, more than twenty artists publishing five, six CDs of this type, and he [Father Tsehai] was the first to start it. (Gabriel Alemayehu, 26 October 2010)

I will return to the signal importance of the Sunday school songs in the context of the migrating Ethiopian Christian liturgy.

III. Sounding Three Musical Domains

To "sound" a domain is to probe it, to seek information about its depth, breadth, and other qualities. In what follows, I sound three domains integral to musical activity, taking account of their impact on Ethiopian liturgy in migration: liturgical performance, liturgical transmission, and the musical dynamics between clergy and congregation.

Liturgical Performance

In diaspora, reestablishment of what was an accustomed aspect of life presents overwhelming hurdles. For Ethiopians in diaspora (especially outside of Washington, DC) to have a priest present on a regular basis is unusual, let alone a musician (*dabtara*) or an accomplished *marigeta*. Thus, liturgical performances by the full cohort of musicians at St. Mary's Church in Washington, DC, are the great exception to the diaspora rule.

To give a contrasting example, four Ethiopian Orthodox congregations in the Boston metropolitan area serve an Ethiopian population of about fifteen thousand.[7] All four Orthodox churches are small, and each is led by a single priest assisted by one or, in one case, two young male deacons recruited from the congregation. Father Tsehai officiates with a single deacon at St. Michael's Church in Mattapan, the congregation of several hundred families that in 2001 succeeded in attracting him to Boston. In the case of St. Michael's, the deacon is also exceptional: Gabriel Alemayehu is a theology student at a local divinity school, familiar with the liturgy from his formative years in Ethiopia and interested in its study.

Moreover, St. Michael's Church in Mattapan is doubly fortunate in that Father Tsehai is both a priest and a highly trained *marigeta*, as well as the first composer of the Sunday school song repertory. That other churches in Boston have one priest each, and no accomplished musicians, provides an incentive for all the area churches to come together to observe major holidays. Therefore, choirs play an increasingly prominent role in most Ethiopian diaspora churches. The choirs range from those constituted entirely of women of various ages to the large coed ensembles seen at major churches such as St. Mary's in Washington, DC.

Liturgical Transmission

Even more daunting than the weekly challenge of performing liturgy is the prospect of transmitting it to the younger generation. In Ethiopia various

---

7. There are also Ethiopian evangelical churches, a number of local Ethiopian Muslims who attend different Boston mosques, and religiously unaffiliated Ethiopians.

aspects of church literature, poetry, and music were historically transmitted in special schools located at monasteries scattered across the country. Truly learned church musicians traditionally spent more than twenty years at a series of church schools, where they acquired the chants of the different service books, studied instrumental musical practices and dance, and learned improvised poetic traditions. Father Tsehai emphasizes that these special bodies of knowledge are required for church musicians and that an enormous amount of time is needed to achieve expertise:

> Anybody can be a priest in Ethiopia. [One is not required] to know *zema* [chant]. Just if you want to be a priest, you can be; you can be ordained, and you can lead the Mass—that's it. It is very easy to be priest. But to be a qualified *marigeta*, you have to study hard. (Tsehai Birhanu, 5 October 2010)

In my interview with him, Father Tsehai also provided a summary of what a knowledgeable musician should know:

> So you want to be a *marigeta*. You have to learn Ge'ez, you have to learn *senasel* [sistrum], you have to learn *zema* (chant), you have to learn *aqwaqqwam* [instrumental practice and dance]. If you have only *marigeta* of *Deggwa* [Hymnary] and do not know *aqwaqqwam*, it is nothing. . . . You have to learn [these] not at one time but one by one, yeah. [You] have to go to another place, [to study with] another *marigeta*, [so that] you can find some different knowledge from the other. [By] not only staying [with] one *marigeta*, you can have huge knowledge. Because of that, you have to go [from] one place to another place. When I finished in . . . my [native] country, I went . . . to another province to get more education and to get that certificate that I am a *marigeta* of *Deggwa* [Hymnary]. . . . It is very difficult. You [need] to sleep, . . . [but] at midnight you have to stand. And your *marigeta* is waiting for you. And you have to go there and you have to [do] oral study. It is a collection of books, hymns. . . . In daytime, you have to study some *Deggwa*, *Dawit* [Psalms], *Som* [chants for fast days], and portions of the hymns. So to be a teacher, or to be a *marigeta*, you have to accomplish all these things and you have to learn, you have to study . . . day and night. (Tsehai Birhanu, 17 September 2010)

The fragility of the transmission process poses a threat to the future of this liturgy in diaspora, and some efforts have been made recently in the United States to ensure transmission. The accomplished *marigeta* Moges Seyoum has since 2000 offered a class each week on Saturday mornings to teach a group of men from his church portions of the rituals in Ge'ez as performed on various holy days. Currently, plans are underway to build an Ethiopian monastery in Houston, Texas, where Ethiopian liturgical education in the United States can be centralized.

Other factors also constitute barriers to transmission for a community of recent immigrants. Given the enormous economic constraints of a struggling refugee community, life in diaspora locales requires regular work with people often holding two or even three jobs, which does not permit long periods to be devoted to study. Even mounting the nocturnal Ethiopian rituals so integral to the Ethiopian liturgical cycle presents a signal challenge, with most rituals scheduled on the weekend nearest to their calendrical date in order not to disrupt secular work demands. Thus the liturgical calendar is attenuated in immigrant communities, and rituals are much shorter, reducing the time the congregation (and prospective priests and musicians) have to acquire the liturgy through regular exposure. A further challenge in diaspora is the lack of knowledge, beyond the clergy trained in Ethiopia, of the liturgical language, Ge'ez. Indeed, even knowledge of the Amharic vernacular has declined greatly among second-generation Ethiopians born and raised in the United States.

For a tradition of such historical depth and liturgical complexity, as well as of extraordinary musical demands, the realities of migration require a good measure of creativity. As Moges Seyoum pointed out in an interview,

> I have to teach. I have an idea, to approach the younger generation. . . . When I was in Ethiopia, it was OK; I didn't have any problem, because a lot of students needed to follow the *zema* [chant], the *aqqwaqwam* [dance]. Now we don't have time in this country. You know, everybody works, and just the younger generation follows a class in English language. (Moges Seyoum, 2 August 2007)

To close this gap, Moges Seyoum has published a set of CDs containing the complete chants for the annual cycle of holidays. He also aspires to record a DVD that will transmit his singing along with its accompanying movements. "Maybe a lot of people can't come to see [the liturgy] in church. But you know, the DVD is very important to everybody. So at home you can follow it" (Moges Seyoum, 2 August 2007).

Dynamics between Congregation and Clergy

The changing dynamics between clergy and congregation include some the most dramatic postmigration changes and are where the future of the musical liturgy is most clearly in ferment. In Ethiopia the church is administered by the Ethiopian patriarch and professional administrators drawn from the ranks of the priests and *dabtara*. In diaspora, Ethiopian congregations themselves have become heavily engaged in church administration. The political structure of the diaspora churches is quite complex, and American Ethiopian churches are formally split between those affiliated with the Ethiopian patriarch and those who follow an American patriarch. In their organization and construction, however, all of the churches increasingly reflect American congregational models.

When I first visited St. Michael's Church in Boston's Mattapan neighborhood, I was introduced with great formality to a female congregant named Mary Alemu Walker. One of the early Ethiopian immigrants to the Boston area in the 1970s, married to an African American, and owner of her own beauty salon in a distant suburb, Mrs. Walker was introduced as the founder of the church. She told me that she had mortgaged her house to help the congregation buy its building. When I commented to Mrs. Walker how impressed I was that a woman had built this Ethiopian church, she responded that she models herself after the queen of Sheba and the Virgin Mary!

Ethiopian church architecture has changed to an American congregational model. In the homeland, Ethiopian churches were constructed in the round: three concentric circles, with a Holy of Holies at its center where only the priests (or king) could enter, a second ring for the offering of Communion, and an outer circle where the musicians performed the Hymnary. The congregation could enter this outer circle, with women restricted to the south side. Today virtually all diaspora churches have dispensed with the threefold division of interior space. Most have a single large space with the Holy of Holies delineated by a screen or wall with three portals and the rest of the space open for the congregation, with the women on the left side and the men on the right (from the perspective of the officiating clergy).[8]

In the diaspora, the relationship of the clergy and the congregation has also become more collaborative, with the congregations exercising authority in hiring priests and recruiting liturgical musicians. As women have become more active in the choirs that perform Sunday school songs and have learned to manage the sistrum, prayer staff, and drum, they have begun to participate in the core musical liturgy. In St. Michael's Church in Mattapan, the majority of the performers, other than Father Tsehai and the deacon, are in fact the women of the choir. More women than men are present at most church services I have attended in Ethiopian communities across the United States.

---

8. Marilyn Heldman, "Creating Sacred Space: Orthodox Churches of the Ethiopian American Diaspora," in "Creating the Ethiopian Diaspora," 285–302.

Sounding the Challenges of Forced Migration 239

The Sunday school choir from St. Michael's Ethiopian Orthodox Church in Mattapan, MA. Photo by author.

When Father Tsehai Birhanu brought a choir to sing Sunday school songs at a conference I hosted at Harvard in 2008, he also had the choir perform a standard portion from the *Deggwa* in Ge'ez. Yet he and most other priests still conceive of the role of women as restricted to the Sunday school songs, as Father Tsehai indicated in an interview:

> Oh, you see, traditionally in [the] Ethiopian Orthodox Church tradition, women do not sing. . . . Even to attend the Mass, they stand formally [and] they don't respond. . . . But nowadays, since Emperor Haile Selassie [was] crowned, little by little they start to respond while the Mass is going. . . . They stand firm and they listen, even [when] they don't understand . . . the Ge'ez. When it is finished they go home—that's it. . . . Since 1950 [or] something like that, [they have] started . . . to follow the gospel. But before, not so. (Tsehai Birhanu, 26 October 2010)

The impact of the Sunday school songs in shaping a new liturgical role for women has helped catalyze major changes in the clergy-congregation relationship. One innovation can give rise to others, and several churches have recently mounted major performances of Sunday school songs featuring choirs, secular instruments, and well-known popular singers. These events are used for fundraising, with elaborate DVDs widely marketed throughout diaspora Ethiopian communities internationally.

Conclusion

The Ethiopian diaspora is a new reality, with millions of Ethiopians dispersed worldwide. That Ethiopians celebrated their millennium in 2007[9] in part with a huge gathering beneath the Washington monument in Washington, DC, is not at all coincidental. With their future in the United States now assured, many Ethiopian immigrants live transnational lives, taking trips back and forth to Addis Ababa. Most remit funds to support relatives, and some either have reclaimed houses nationalized in Ethiopia or have bought new second homes there.

Yet a shadow looms over the Ethiopian Christian future. As we have seen, the complexity of the Ethiopian liturgy, its esoteric musical performance practice, and a complicated clerical structure all constrain processes of liturgical transmission and performance abroad. Thus, Ethiopian Christians in America (and other diaspora locales) have had to be enormously inventive and to work creatively to maintain aspects of their historical religious tradition. These initiatives range from Moges Seyoum's classes for congregants to ensure that he has a critical mass of *dabtara* for major holidays, to the proliferation of the Sunday school songs, a new genre that at once opens the liturgical experience to vernacular (Amharic) expression and democratizes the liturgy for participation by women and young people. Clearly, late twentieth-century forced migration has presented a structural threat to Ethiopian liturgical practice comparable to that of the sixteenth-century Islamic invasion.

Here, then, we arrive at the creative initiatives called forth by migrating liturgies. I will invoke categories of creativity recently proposed by the sociologist Donald Levine.[10] In his earlier books on Ethiopian culture,[11] Levine suggested that Ethiopians had long practiced "creative incorporation," a process through which external inspirations in areas ranging from art to literature are incorporated and immediately transformed and indigenized. But Levine and

---

9. The Ethiopian calendar is based on the Julian calendar and is approximately seven and a half years behind the Western calendar.

10. See Donald N. Levine, "On Cultural Creativity in the Ethiopian Diaspora," in "Creating the Ethiopian Diaspora," 215–20.

11. Donald N. Levine, *Wax and Gold: Tradition and Innovation in Ethiopian Culture* (Chicago: University of Chicago Press, 1965), and *Greater Ethiopia: The Evolution of a Multiethnic Society* (Chicago: University of Chicago Press, 1974).

others studying the creation of the Ethiopian diaspora now view creativity as extending beyond "creative incorporation" and including a much greater array of factors that interact and overlap. A brief summary of these factors (based on Levine's work[12]) will anchor my final comments.

A provisional semantic matrix for different types of creativity might identify the following four: creativity associated with problem solving, with finding new ways of combining existing elements, with spontaneous expression of energies, and with the invention of novel forms. I suggest that processes to sustain the migrating Ethiopian Christian liturgy draw on all four categories of creativity, and I offer a final example for your consideration.

The celebration of *Masqal* (festival of the true cross) 2009 in Cambridge, MA. The congregation is circulating around the *demera* (bonfire) that does not burn. Photo by David Kaminsky.

On the holiday of *Masqal* (festival of the true cross), the ritual culminates in a bonfire (*demera*) lit at sunset. In Ethiopia huge bonfires are constructed in major urban spaces and are surrounded by clergy and congregants processing, dancing, and singing. In the diaspora the bonfire is a much more modest affair, if indeed a bonfire can be burned at all. In some places, such as Cambridge, Massachusetts,

---

12. Levine, "On Cultural Creativity," 218.

local fire ordinances prohibit burning open fires within the city limits. Given this prohibition, in 2007 the inventive Ethiopian Americans of Cambridge constructed a bonfire that does not burn: a bonfire-like wooden frame is covered in gold cloth that reflects the light of the setting sun to provide a facsimile of flames.

I would argue that the Cambridge *Masqal* bonfire provides (1) a lively example of problem solving that constitutes the first and most basic form of creativity and (2) is a great example of combining existing elements in new ways in order to achieve an outcome that would otherwise be impossible. To address points 3 and 4 of Levine's creativity matrix, I refer to a subsequent Cambridge *Masqal* observance, in 2009, that demonstrates a spontaneous expression of energies. Two years after the innovation of the bonfire that does not burn, we find additional levels of creativity (point 3). The congregation circles the cloth bonfire, holding sparklers and lit candles. Thus the congregation itself spontaneously "becomes the fire," reinventing the bonfire yet again in a new mode.

The invention of novel forms (point 4) is also present in Ethiopian diaspora *Masqal* musical practice. Here I offer the participation of women at *Masqal* as the congregation circles the bonfire, with female drummers playing the large *kebaro* drums. No longer relegated to accompanying only the Sunday school songs, female drummers become part of the culminating event of the *Masqal* ritual, at once a striking and novel innovation but one deeply integrated into the fabric of the ritual.

In sum, I would suggest that music lessons from the Ethiopian Christian diaspora teach us about the multifaceted challenges to migrating liturgies, most especially in cases of forced migration. To understand the lessons they offer, we have to sound not just the liturgy but the lives and institutions of those who carry the liturgy from place to place. They bear witness to the extraordinarily creative responses of the people whose mobile lives demand more than a full measure of resilience.

11

Asian American Catholics and Contemporary Liturgical Migrations: From Tradition-Maintenance to Traditioning

Jonathan Y. Tan

In this essay I examine the implications of hybridities, multiple belongings, and multiple migrations for the liturgical practices of Asian American Catholics in the contemporary United States. First, I will argue that the ahistorical essentialism of early theologies of liturgical inculturation emphasized the ideals of cohesive group identity, overarching harmony, and unity, thereby subsuming differences to the exclusion of the particularities and conflicts that are generated by generational shifts, multiple belongings, and manifold border crossings. The uncritical attempt to create inculturated Asian American liturgies by transplanting romanticized and essentialized cultural forms from the Asian motherlands raises more questions in the face of the complicated experiences of the 1.5 generation,[1] US-born children of first-generation Asian immigrants,

---

1. The term "1.5 generation" was first coined by the Cuban American sociologist Rubén G. Rumbaut to refer to those who immigrate to a new country between the ages of six and twelve. For in-depth discussion of the significance and implications of the 1.5 generation, see Rubén G. Rumbaut, "The Agony of Exile: A Study of the Migration and Adaptation of Indochinese Refugee Adults and Children," in *Refugee Children: Theory, Research, and Services,* ed. Frederick L. Ahearn Jr. and Jean L. Athey (Baltimore: John Hopkins University Press, 1991), 53–91; Rubén G. Rumbaut, "Ages, Life Stages, and Generational Cohorts: Decomposing the Immigrant First and Second Generations in the United States," *International Migration Review* 38 (2004): 1160–1205; and Kyeyoung Park, " 'I Really Do Feel I'm 1.5': The Construction of Self and Community by Young Korean Americans," *Amerasia Journal* 25 (1999): 139–63.

Asian American adoptees of white parents, and bi/multiracial Asian Americans. Second, I will make the case that the essentialized categories of racial-ethnic, cultural, and faith identities have to be deconstructed, challenged, contested, and, finally, remixed in new keys and forms to address the implications of hybridities, multiple belongings, and multiple border crossings within contemporary Asian American Catholic communities. Third, I will propose that Asian American Catholic liturgies move away from classical *tradition-maintenance* to the creative remix of *traditioning*, from liturgies that uncritically reinscribe the past to liturgies as creative and dynamic endeavors that seek to encompass the multiplicity of pluralistic, hybridized, and conflicting constructions of faith and identity.

For the purposes of this essay, I am using the term "Asian American" as a generic and convenient shorthand to categorize all Americans of Asian ancestry and heritage—whether they are US-born second or later generations, the 1.5 generation, or first-generation immigrants—with their diverse languages, cultures, and traditions. At the same time, I also acknowledge that the term "Asian American" masks distinct racial-ethnic communities under the façade of a homogenous and monolithic pan–Asian American identity that exists more in theory than in reality. In reality, the category of "Asian Americans" encompasses groups of peoples of diverse languages, cultures, spiritual traditions, worldviews, socioeconomic classes, and generational levels, such that all attempts at generalizations run a significant risk of error. Instead of viewing the Asian American identity in rigid and normative terms, perhaps this identity is better understood as diverse and multiple, constantly in flux and shaped by, as well as shaping, historical, social, cultural, and political contexts.[2]

More significantly, labels such as "Asian American," "Vietnamese American," "Chinese American," "Filipino American," "Korean American," and so forth, are double-edged swords. On the one hand, they are useful generic shorthand to identify and categorize distinct ethnic Asian American communities, giving them a united and collective voice vis-à-vis the dominant white mainstream. On the

---

2. The Asian American scholar Lisa Lowe explains the implications of Asian American heterogeneity as follows: "What is referred to as 'Asian American' is clearly a heterogeneous entity. From the perspective of the majority culture, Asian Americans may very well be constructed as different from, and other than, Euro-Americans. But, from the perspectives of Asian Americans, we are perhaps even more different, more diverse among ourselves. . . . As with other diasporas in the United States, the Asian immigrant collectivity is unstable and changeable, with its cohesion complicated by intergenerationality, by various degrees of identification and relation to a 'homeland,' and by different extents of assimilation to and distinction from 'majority culture' in the United States." Lisa Lowe, "Heterogeneity, Hybridity, Multiplicity: Marking Asian American Differences," *Diaspora* 1 (1991): 22–44, here 27.

other hand, they are also problematic insofar as the categories break down when confronted with the 1.5 generation, the American born, and adoptees, as well as bi/multiracial Asian Americans who are the products of interracial marriages. Indeed, the presence of adoptees and bi/multiracial Asian Americans challenges the uncritical presumption of a normative, monolithic, and static notion of "Asianness," "Chineseness," "Vietnameseness," and so on. The incongruity arising from their presence serves as a reminder that identity is negotiated and constructed, neither given nor born, and neither static nor fixed. Are the 1.5-generation, US-born, adoptee, and bi/multiracial Asian Americans authentically Asians and Americans? How would Asian American liturgies address their needs, concerns, and hopes?

I. The Limits of Liturgical Inculturation as Tradition-Maintenance

In 2007 a friend of mine participated in the annual Lunar New Year Eucharist at St. Mary's Cathedral in San Francisco and shared with me the photos he took of the ancestor veneration ceremony that was incorporated into the Lunar New Year liturgy. Bishop Ignatius Wang, then auxiliary bishop of San Francisco and the first Chinese American bishop in the US Catholic Church, led the concelebrants in offering prayers and incense at the ancestral altar that was specially set up for this ritual. The concelebrants were followed by members of the assembly in a well-choreographed and picture-perfect ritual. As my friend showed me the photographs, he turned to me and acknowledged that while the ritual meant a great deal to the older generation, it did not speak to him and his peers. He was plainly uncomfortable with the ritual; he thought that it was oriented toward the migrant or first-generation Asians in the United States, who long for the sociocultural world in which they grew up but which is no longer present in the United States for both 1.5-generation and US-born Chinese. As far as my friend was concerned, the ancestor veneration ritual emphasizes filial piety, patriarchy, and patrilineal transmission, all of which are incongruous with his values, aspirations, and hopes, as well as those of his peers. He pointed out that his generation and the next value and celebrate individuality, independence, and the freedom to define their own lives.

This conversation reminded me of a conversation that I had with a Vietnamese elder several years back. We were admiring the new parish hall, and an extension to the existing church building, of a Vietnamese American national parish. This elder turned to me and said that he despaired of the younger generation of US-born Vietnamese Catholics who were turning away from the Vietnamese language and culture that his generation is fighting so hard to preserve in the Vietnamese diaspora in the United States. He expressed his disappointment at the teens and young adults in the parish who leave for English-language services elsewhere because the Vietnamese parishes no longer hold any meaning or significance for them. What was more troubling for him is that the US-born Vietnamese no longer see the strict preservation and uninterrupted transmission of Vietnamese language and culture as essential and normative of "Vietnameseness," the essence of Vietnamese identity.

Remembering these two conversations, I cannot help thinking about the implications of hybridities, multiple belongings, and multiple migrations on the liturgical practices of Asian American Catholics in the contemporary United States in general and the question of Asian American Catholic liturgical inculturation in particular. Liturgical inculturation is commonly understood as integrating liturgical worship with a community's sociocultural tradition. This task may appear to be deceptively simple, but in reality determining the ambit and limits of tradition, as well as identifying who gets to define what a community's tradition is and is not, is fraught with difficulty. While the two examples cited above are textbook accounts of liturgical inculturation in the Chinese and Vietnamese American Catholic communities in the United States, both examples reveal the limits of liturgical inculturation in Asian American communities. Specifically, both highlight the complexity, ambiguity, and plurality of the question of whether it is possible, let alone desirable, to identify specific normative elements as defining the sociocultural tradition that lies at the heart of liturgical inculturation.

To complicate matters, when one attempts to define the "tradition" that underlies liturgical inculturation, one realizes that the term "tradition" raises further questions that defy easy and simplistic answers. Even scholars and experts have differing opinions on what constitutes tradition. For example, according to the Protestant theologian Paul Tillich, tradition is more than simply "a set of memories which are delivered from one generation to the other"; it is rather "the recollection of those events which have gained significance for the bearers and receivers of the tradition."[3] By contrast, Catherine Bell, a scholar of religion and ritual, asserts that tradition "is not created once and then left to its own momentum," but rather "exists because it is constantly produced and reproduced, pruned for a clear profile, and softened to absorb revitalizing elements."[4] Going one step further, the Marxist historian Eric Hobsbawm, who sees tradition as "a set of practices, normally governed by overtly or tacitly accepted rules and of a ritual or symbolic nature, which seek to inculcate certain values and norms of behavior by repetition, which auto-

---

3. Paul Tillich, *Systematic Theology* (Chicago: University of Chicago Press, 1963), 3:300.
4. Catherine Bell, *Ritual Theory, Ritual Practice* (New York: Oxford University Press, 1992), 123.

matically implies continuity with the past,"⁵ has strenuously argued the case for tradition to be viewed as invented fictions, explaining that "insofar as there is such a reverence to a historic past, the peculiarity of 'invented' traditions is that the continuity with it is largely fictitious" because they are, in reality, "responses to novel situations which take the form of reference to old situations, or which establish their own past by quasi-obligatory repetition."⁶ He points to the period between 1870 and 1914 in Europe as the period that witnessed the deliberate invention of new traditions as a means of defining and propping political power and social identity.⁷

In response to Hobsbawm, the Catholic theologian Terrence Tilley counters that "traditions can be made and remade without being deliberately invented" because "they adapt with integrity to changing circumstances."⁸ He points out that traditions mutate as they are transmitted, explaining that the "environments in which traditional beliefs, practices, and attitudes are transmitted and the items from other traditions that their holders encounter change their significance."⁹ He explains that if traditions are "perfectly rigid, they either die as contexts change because that elite can no longer maintain the identity of the tradition" or the tradition becomes the possession of an esoteric elite who "keep the old traditions alive" as a compartmentalized practice or set of practices and beliefs."¹⁰

Moving from theorizing to practical realities, it should come as no surprise that many first-generation Asian Americans insist that tradition is stable and fixed, timeless and unchanging, invariant and immutable, anchoring their identity in a turbulent new world of contemporary US society. For them, tradition represents an authoritative and prescriptive precedent, a treasured family heirloom that they brought with them from their homelands in Asia to their adopted land of the United States, which they hope to transmit lock, stock, and barrel from their generation to the next. Woe betide anyone who dares to tinker with tradition or challenge its ontological certitude! The first wave of Asian American Catholic liturgical inculturation took for granted such idealized and essentialized

---

5. Eric Hobsbawm, "Introduction: Inventing Traditions," in *The Invention of Tradition*, ed. Eric Hobsbawm and Terence Ranger (Cambridge: Cambridge University Press, 1983), 1.
6. Ibid., 2.
7. Hobsbawm, "Mass-Producing Traditions: Europe, 1879–1914," in Hobsbawm and Ranger, *The Invention of Tradition*, 263–307.
8. Terrence W. Tilley, *Inventing Catholic Tradition* (Maryknoll, NY: Orbis Books, 2000), 41.
9. Ibid., 30.
10. Ibid., 36.

biological and cultural notions of what constituted identities of "Asian," "Vietnamese," "Chinese," "Korean," "Filipino," and so on. Their underlying theology of liturgical inculturation assumed a romanticized and essentialized understanding of tradition that defines culture and identity—that is, identity definitions and cultural norms that are stable, normative, homogeneous, and unchanging. The problem with this approach is its nostalgic tendency to essentialize and reify, as well as romanticize and idealize, tradition, failing to recognize its oppressive elements (e.g., patriarchy, misogyny, etc.). Going back to my first example above, we see that first-generation Chinese Americans perceive ancestor veneration as an important and definitive element of being Chinese and incorporate this ritual into an inculturated Lunar New Year liturgical celebration. Yet my friend rightly asks whether an uncritical use of ancestor veneration ignores underlying problems with this ritual. For example, ancestor veneration emphasizes maleness and male succession, marginalizing the position and roles of women, traditionally excluded in the patrilineal and patriarchal orientation of ancestor veneration. It is also a ritual reminder of submission and obedience to elders in a world where younger Asian Americans, especially women, bi/multiracial people, adoptees, and LGBTs, are seeking the freedom to define and construct new identities that are meaningful for themselves.

No tradition is truly pure and innocent, devoid of shortcomings. The failure to engage in critical reflections on its challenges and shortcomings is often justified by the need to ensure the uninterrupted intergenerational transmission of cultural traditions and values in the face of the difficult challenges of dislocation, discrimination, and assimilation in the United States. This means that inculturated Asian American liturgies often ignore differences and particularities, focusing instead on harmony and unity as overarching Asian values. What is being overlooked here is the reality that culture and identity constructs are dynamic and affected by the ambiguities that emerge as a result of the blurring and confusion of boundaries caused by generational differences, adoptees, and bi/multiracial family frameworks.

For example, the Japanese American biblical scholar Frank Yamada questions the uncritical privileging of essentialized notions of what constitutes "Asian American," arguing that culture and identity constructions are shaped by forces of hybridity and heterogeneity. Specifically, he asserts that cultural identity for third and later generations of US-born Asian Americans is messy, complicated, and conflicting. He contends that one "must move beyond idealized and essentialist notions of culture" and a tendency to utilize the immigrant experience of marginality and liminality as normative of all Asian Americans to "emphasize particularity, contradiction, and complexity in order to counter oversimplified personifications of what constitutes Asian American."[11] In particular, Yamada insists that themes of marginality and liminality are based upon stable, essentialized notions of what it means to be Asian and American.[12] As a result, he stresses hybridity and heterogeneity over essentialism, with the later generations breaking down fixed boundaries and "pure" notions of culture that earlier generations have uncritically assumed.[13]

Similarly, Henry Morisada Rietz and Mary Foskett have criticized the essentialism of the category "Asian American" in their theological reflections, especially with regard to the life experiences of Asian Americans who fall outside conventionally defined categories, challenging the uncritical privileging of certain essentialist traits that purport to define the Asian American identity. Rietz focuses on himself as a biracial *hapa-haole* who claims both German and Japanese ancestries, acknowledging that his mixed heritage prevents him from claiming one identity completely so that he is the "other" to both Asian Americans and white Americans. He asserts that his *hapa* identity reveals the limitations of essentialism and homogeneity in Asian American identity constructions that are usually based on boundaries defined by the commonalities of the members while at the same time accentuating their differences from biracial and multiracial Asian Americans, who do not fit neatly into traditional constructions of Asian American identities. In doing so, Rietz unmasks the painful tension between *inherited* (i.e., biological or "blood") reproduction and *constructed* reproduction. He challenges the privileged position of the former by articulating the controversial view that the Asian American identities could be constructed without reference to inherited biological ("blood") reproduction. As a solution, he proposes a new model of identity construction that is modeled on *differences* or *particularity* as the basis for community and communication, emphasizing that Asian American identities are not transmitted by inheritance but shaped by the dynamic process of identity-construction politics.[14]

---

11. See Frank M. Yamada, "Constructing Hybridity and Heterogeneity: Asian American Biblical Interpretation from a Third-Generation Perspective," in *Ways of Being, Ways of Reading: Asian American Biblical Interpretation*, ed. Mary F. Foskett and Jeffrey Kah-Jin Kuan (St. Louis, MO: Chalice Press, 2006), 166.

12. Ibid., 169

13. Ibid., 172–73.

14. Henry Morisada Rietz, "My Father Has No Children: Reflections on a *Hapa* Identity toward a Hermeneutic of Particularity," *Semeia* 90/91 (2002): 145–57; see also "Living Past: A Hapa Identifying with the Exodus, the Exile, and the Internment," in Foskett and Kuan, *Ways of Being*, 192–203.

As an ethnic Chinese who was adopted by a white American family, Mary Foskett explores the plight of Asian American adoptees of white American families, an in-between group that has historically been ignored in many Asian American communities. According to Foskett, Asian American adoptees have to contend not only with the ambiguity and confusion of defining their identity but also with their invisibility and double marginalization within the wider Asian American communities. She rejects the essentialism of Asian American cultural traditions and norms within many Asian American communities and in doing so confronts the tension between biological reproductions vis-à-vis cultural reproductions in the construction of Asian American communities. In her rereading of Exodus 2:1-22 she offers a new vision of Moses' lost identity as replaced by a newly gained one through his adoption by the Egyptian princess, as well as through the ensuing bicultural socialization that resulted in his having to confront painful choices. By interpreting Moses' story as an adoptee's struggle to come to terms with his own identity and purpose in life, Foskett challenges Asian Americans to overcome their indifference toward the plight of Asian American adoptees in the United States and to discover ways of defining Asian American identity without essentializing cultural and bloodline identities.[15]

In other words, increasing hybridity and heterogeneity in Asian America is exemplified not only by the 1.5-generation and US-born children of first-generation Asian immigrants (see Frank Yamada), but also by Asian Americans who marry outside their group and end up with bi/multiracial identities (as discussed by Henry Morisada Rietz) and by Asian adoptees of white American families (see Mary Foskett). Indeed, neither Rietz nor Foskett fits neatly into essentialized and clearly demarcated, biologically defined racial and ethnic categories of Asian Americans. Rietz's writings reveal that he considers himself both Asian and white American. Does that make him any less Asian or white American?

II. From Tradition-Maintenance to Traditioning

How do Asian American liturgies go beyond essentialist and normative views of Asian cultural traditions and heritage to include the concerns, hopes, and dreams of the 1.5-generation and US-born children of first-generation

---

15. Mary Foskett, "The Accidents of Being and the Politics of Identity: Biblical Images of Adoption and Asian Adoptees in America," *Semeia* 90/91 (2002): 135–44; see also her "Obscured Beginnings: Lessons from the Study of Christian Origins," in Foskett and Kuan, *Ways of Being*, 178–91.

Asian immigrants, bi/multiracial Asian Americans, and Asian adoptees? This question points to the difficult task of identifying content, as well as the processes of transmission and reception. In response, I would like to propose that contemporary Asian American liturgies move away from *tradition-maintenance*, that is, clinging to ethnic-bound traditions, customs, and theological positions from the "Old World" at all costs, in favor of what I would call *traditioning*, which I define as the largely unconscious and ongoing process of shaping, constructing, and negotiating new traditions, practices, and theological positions that seek to address the issues and questions confronting all Asian Americans, be they immigrant, US-born, bi/multiracial, or adopted. In some sense, tradition-maintenance is akin to a classical symphony in that both emphasize the ideals of overarching group harmony and unity, subsuming differences. By contrast, I see traditioning as comparable to the remix culture that is transforming the contemporary music scene: both traditioning and remixing challenge, contest, deconstruct, and reenvision essentialized categories, theological or musical, in new keys and forms. As the contemporary musical scene shifts away from the classical symphony to remixing, so too Asian American liturgies are shifting away from tradition-maintenance of age-old cultural ideals to creative traditioning, giving birth to new insights into worship and celebration that address contemporary challenges and concerns.

From a theological perspective the process of traditioning is not something altogether new. Although the Catholic theologian Yves Congar did not use the term, he nevertheless argued against an essentialist understanding of tradition in favor of a dynamic perspective of tradition as something that is passed on, stating that "tradition is not primarily to be defined by a particular material object, but by the act of transmission, and its content is simply *id quod traditum est, id quod traditur* [that which is handed on or handed over]."[16] Similarly, although the late Jaroslav Pelikan did not use the terms *tradition-maintenance* and *traditioning*, he captures succinctly the sense of these two terms when he writes, "Tradition is the living faith of the dead, traditionalism is the dead faith of the living."[17] In a subsequent interview with Joseph Carey that appeared in *U.S. News & World Report*, Pelikan articulated a profound understanding of traditioning:

---

16. Yves Congar, *Tradition and Traditions: An Historical and a Theological Essay*, trans. Michael Naseby and Thomas Rainborough (New York: Macmillan, 1967), 296.

17. Jaroslav Pelikan, *The Vindication of Tradition* (New Haven, CT: Yale University Press, 1984), 65.

Tradition is not fixed for all time. . . . It is the perpetuation of *a changing, developing identity*. Tradition is the living faith of the dead; traditionalism is the dead faith of the living. Tradition lives *in conversation with the past*, while *remembering where we are* and *when we are* and that *it is we who have to decide*. Traditionalism supposes that nothing should ever be done for the first time, so all that is needed to solve any problem is to arrive at the supposedly unanimous testimony of this homogenized tradition.[18]

Pelikan's insights have far-reaching consequences for Asian American Catholics who are endeavoring to make sense of their cultural and ethnic traditions in the contemporary United States. Although he did not use the specific phrase, it is clear from the extended quotation that the verb "traditioning" best describes what Pelikan had in mind when he spoke about a tradition that "lives *in conversation with the past,* while *remembering where we are* and *when we are* and that *it is we who have to decide.*" In other words, Pelikan unequivocally eschewed the static traditionalism that clings tenaciously to past precedents without any regard for the contemporary context and its specific needs, in favor of an active and dynamic traditioning that pays attention to contemporary social locations and challenges.

More recently, theologians such as Dale Irvin,[19] Simon Chan,[20] Carmen Nanko-Fernández,[21] Orlando Espín,[22] and Gary Riebe-Estrella[23] have reflected on the implications of traditioning in their theological writings. Within contemporary Asian theology, the Singaporean Chinese theologian Simon

---

18. Joseph Carey, "Christianity as an Enfolding Circle," *U.S. News & World Report* 106/25 (26 June 1989): 57, emphasis added.

19. Dale Irvin, *Christian Histories, Christian Traditioning: Rendering Accounts* (Maryknoll, NY: Orbis Books, 1998).

20. Simon Chan, *Pentecostal Theology and the Christian Spiritual Tradition* (London: Sheffield Academic Press, 2000).

21. Carmen Nanko-Fernández, "Traditioning latinamente: A Theological Reflection on la lengue cotidiana" (unpublished); "Language, Community and Identity," in *Handbook of Latino/a Theologies*, ed. Edwin Aponte and Miguel de la Torre (St Louis, MO: Chalice Press, 2006), 265–75; and "Handing on Faith en su propia lengua," in *Theologizing en Espanglish: Context, Community, and Ministry* (Maryknoll, NY: Orbis Books, 2010), 61–76.

22. Orlando O. Espín, "Traditioning: Culture, Daily Life and Popular Religion, and Their Impact on Christian Tradition," in *Futuring Our Past: Explorations in the Theology of Tradition*, ed. Orlando O. Espín and Gary Macy (Maryknoll, NY: Orbis Books, 2006), 1–22. Espín is currently working on a full-length monograph exploring this issue.

23. Gary Riebe-Estrella, "Tradition as Conversation," in *Futuring Our Past*, ed. Espín and Macy, 141–56.

Chan observes that traditioning ensures that the Pentecostal faith tradition is handed down to a new generation "in a way that *takes account of the new context of a new generation of faithful.*"[24] For Chan, tradition, "far from confining a community to a static existence," is "the bearer of real change."[25]

Dale Irvin has articulated his understanding of traditioning as an antithesis to tradition as conformism with its "illusion of timeless and unchanging identity,"[26] citing Walter Benjamin's essay "Theses on the Philosophy of History" (1940) with approval: "In every era the attempt must be made anew to wrest tradition away from a conformism that is about to overpower it."[27] In particular, Irvin speaks of traditioning as an "ongoing, constructive activity" that is "found wherever people in community remember a past and claim it as their own," as well as "a practice that makes present the historical past as memory and identity."[28] He views traditioning not in terms of seeking "to render an account of the past that is bound to its evidence," but rather as seeking "to render a meaningful account of the relationship of the past to the present."[29] For him, traditioning is "a renewing practice of faith"[30] that is not merely the repetition of the past, for mere repetition often indicates a loss of vitality and a failure of transmission.[31] In support of the foregoing, he cites Eugen Rosenstock-Huessy, who insisted that "*each generation has to act differently precisely in order to represent the same thing.*"[32] More importantly, Irvin insists that traditioning goes beyond simply "an act of passing on the authentic memory and identity of the past in a new historical situation" to encompass "an act of betrayal and treason":

> In every act of authentic traditioning there remains something of an act of treason, otherwise it would not be an authentic act of handing over, of change. Without a bit of treason performed in the act of handing over, the tradition remains inseparably bound to the world in which it was formed, hence not

---

24. Chan, *Pentecostal Theology*, 20, emphasis added.
25. Ibid., 17.
26. Irvin, *Christian Histories*, 42.
27. Walter Benjamin, *Illuminations*, ed. Hannah Arendt (New York: Schocken Books, 1969), 255, cited in Irvin, *Christian Histories*, 42.
28. Irvin, *Christian Histories*, 29.
29. Ibid., 35.
30. Ibid., 124.
31. Ibid., 28.
32. Eugen Rosenstock-Huessy, *The Christian Future; or, The Modern Mind Outrun* (New York: Harper and Row, 1966), 130 (emphasis in the original), cited in Irvin, *Christian Histories*, 28.

only irrelevant but also incomprehensible. Acts of treason and betrayal, on the other hand, are not unambiguous signs of the rejection of a tradition, but moments of contending for its authenticity. Acts of treason presuppose a traitor's decision to contend for the authenticity, meaning, or purpose of the tradition, either to reform it and restore it, or to displace it with another which the traitor at least perceives to be better.[33]

Moreover, Irvin sees the goal of traditioning as ensuring that faith remains relevant, because "a truly irrelevant faith will soon die of its own irrelevance, and the identity of the community will pass into the arena of being a historical relic or part of the archive."[34] What is at stake for Irvin is the fact that the failure of traditioning results in alienation from tradition—"tradition no longer belonging to us but being alien to us, set over against us, mediating a past which is not our own."

> They [i.e., the times we find ourselves more distanced, more alienated from the past that "is not our own"] are the moments when we hear ourselves or others saying that the traditional language no longer speaks to us, that the tradition appears to be empty of meaning or vitality for us. In these situations the past becomes other for us, heteronomous in a manner that closes off our relationship to it, and the dead become just that – merely the dead, no longer our saints or ancestors or companions. Traditions become artifacts relegated to museums where their vitality is lost even if their remains continue to be studied.[35]

What Irvin has described surely applies to my friend and his discomfiture with the ancestor veneration ritual in the Lunar New Year liturgy and to the increasing number of US-born Vietnamese who are no longer identifying with either their elders' Vietnamese national parishes or inculturated Vietnamese liturgies, which have more in common with pre-1975 Vietnam than contemporary United States society.

Many Latino/a theologians view traditioning as an important aspect of Latino/a theology that enables theology to be rooted in *lo cotidiano*, that is, "the daily."[36] For example, in the context of Latino/a pastoral ministry, Carmen Nanko-Fernández observes that traditioning is an ongoing process that not

---

33. Irvin, *Christian Histories*, 41.
34. Ibid., 41.
35. Ibid., 42.
36. The issue of traditioning is discussed at length in *Futuring Our Past*, ed. Espín and Macy.

only occurs "in the daily and is integral to the process of constructing identity, personally and collectively," but also requires "a habit of learning how to read across contexts in order to avoid absolutizing or universalizing the particular."[37] Orlando Espín sees traditioning as a cultural, human activity that facilitates "the transmission of Christianity across generations and across cultural boundaries" within daily human life.[38] Noting that "the ordinary traditioners of Christianity are ordinary Christians," he asserts that *"whatever is traditioned (the tradition or contents of Christianity) is shaped, selected, presented, and received according to the social position, gender, cultural, and so forth, of those who ordinarily transmit Christianity as well as of those who ordinarily listen to the gospel and accept it across generations and across cultural boundaries."*[39]

In a similar vein, Gary Riebe-Estrella focuses on the process of traditioning as constitutive of tradition itself, such that "there is a mutual interaction between what is handed on and the handing on, in such a way that each influences the other."[40] He suggests that "the very reification of tradition as consisting of some *thing* that is handed on is based on an inappropriate metaphor or at least on one that obscures the interrelationship of content and process and, therefore, of the nature of tradition itself."[41] He makes the case for traditioning as the *contextualization* of tradition in the world and life experiences of the recipients. As far as he is concerned, "what is handed on is never an *already out there now* thing; rather, it is always human meaning as constructed within the specific and unique context of the human knower and his or her community."[42]

III. Liturgical Traditioning

From the foregoing discussion, we are able to see that the process of traditioning is based upon the premise that tradition is not fixed and static but rather dynamic, always changing, and deeply contextual. More importantly, liturgical traditioning questions simplistic and uncritical reproductions of the past, rejecting all attempts at fossilizing or archaizing the present in a state of stasis, as well as challenging any notion that liturgical inculturation seeks to root liturgy within a cultural framework that is ahistorical, atemporal, and independent of

---

37. Nanko-Fernández, "Traditioning latinamente."
38. Orlando O. Espín, "Traditioning," 2.
39. Ibid., 15, emphasis in the original.
40. Gary Riebe-Estrella, "Tradition as Conversation," 141.
41. Ibid., 141.
42. Ibid., 144.

sociocultural changes. Instead, traditioning entails critical reflections about a community's present liturgical worship. By going beyond mere replication of historical precedents, liturgical traditioning pursues strategic, dynamic, creative, and contextualized interpretations that seek to retell, reinterpret, and add nuance to liturgical worship within new layers of meaningfulness that address the concerns of the present context. It mediates between historical precedents and current concerns, thereby endeavoring to create a coherent liturgical worship that unites the rich legacy of tradition with contemporary needs and challenges.

In other words, liturgical traditioning is dynamic and flexible. It is open to life realities, as well as to healthy renewal and change that are integral to a community's social location and context, while remaining "in conversation with the past." Rather than looking for a single normative and essentialistic meaning in cultural traditions and heritage, liturgical traditioning seeks hybridized and multilayered meaningfulness, embodying and integrating both difference and consensus, past and present, precedent and innovation, authority and creativity, thereby facilitating the articulation of new meanings for the present and future. As a result, liturgical worship is constantly being renegotiated and renewed for all Asian American Catholics, immigrant and American born, bi/multiracial and adoptee.

I see liturgical traditioning as enabling Asian American liturgies to mediate contradictions that arise from the multiple subjectivities that Asian Americans constantly negotiate in their daily lives as they grapple with fragmented selves and mixed allegiances to many places, spaces, persons, and groups, all of which generate intersecting subjectivities, hybridities, and heterogeneous identifications. In addition, traditioning provides the impetus for Asian American liturgies to be dynamic, situational, and strategic, differentiating between elements as well as privileging the faith development of a new generation of faithful.

More importantly, traditioning reminds us that traditions do evolve and change in response to new contexts. Returning to the two examples of liturgical inculturation that were raised in the beginning of this essay, my friend is certainly justified in asking why one should romanticize the role of ancestors in Chinese American culture and religiosity or essentialize it without considering the fact that future generations of US-born Chinese Americans, bi/multiracial Chinese Americans, Chinese adoptees, and so forth, will have vastly different takes on ancestor veneration, affecting ancestor veneration in the Chinese New Year Eucharist. While my friend and I agree on the special significance of the Lunar New Year for Chinese Americans and that having a liturgical celebration of this important feast is similar to celebrating Thanksgiving Day with a Eucharist in the United States, perhaps the highlight of this feast day could be something other than ancestor veneration, with its baggage of Confucian patriarchy, misogyny, patrilineal focus, and so on. Perhaps other aspects of the Lunar New Year celebration—for example, forgiveness of past transgressions at the start of the New Year, generosity and kindness toward others—could be emphasized. Similarly, the Vietnamese American Catholic community would have to acknowledge the fact that the day will come when Vietnamese American Catholic churches will have to celebrate their liturgies in English, compose new hymns in English, create new rituals, and in general respond to the needs of the 1.5-generation and US-born Vietnamese American Catholics, many of whom will be bi/multiracial and probably not conversant in the Vietnamese language.

Hence, liturgical traditioning enables contemporary Asian American liturgies to transcend the biological and cultural essentialism of early Asian American attempts at liturgical inculturation to address the concerns and aspirations of immigrant and US-born, bi/multiracial and adoptee Asian Americans. Through the process of traditioning, Asian American liturgies are able to engage in, nuance, and redefine theologies in a creative, strategic, flexible, and innovative manner to empower Asian Americans in their effective engagement with the joys and pathos of the postmodern conditions of their daily living, helping them to engage the world around them where they are, at worst, shunned or rendered invisible for being out of line with the majority or, at best, reluctantly tolerated for being different.

12

Soundings from the Liturgical Ecumene: Liturgical Migration, Christian Mission, and Mutual Conversions

Charles E. Farhadian

I. Christianity on the Move

The challenge of thinking about liturgies in migration lies not in cataloging the diversity of liturgical actions and objects worldwide, as though we are engaging in a form of liturgical tourism. The challenge is to illuminate the developing side of liturgy specifically within the context of globalization. In our globalizing world, we need to understand the dynamics of the movement of the Spirit, a Spirit always on the move, albeit elusively so. At the same time, Christianity is a religion, bound by the kinds of institutional constraints that limit all world religions. How does a faith in the Spirit, who by nature is on the move, balance itself with its institutional life? Liturgy is of paramount importance here, because to be church, one must have liturgy. As the Jesuits of the sixteenth century noted in their conceptualization of the *missio Dei*, God is a sending God, and the mission of the church is to be sent into the world to redeem the world. Apostleship was then, as mission is now, a global concept.

Today the church spans the globe, and Christianity is the world's largest religion, with over 2.3 billion adherents. The topic of liturgy in migration is a fascinating one because it encompasses issues that are of ultimate importance to the church and to contemporary scholarship on the church in the world. Whereas earlier paradigms presented in the middle and late twentieth century celebrated the diversity of Christian communities, as though they were disparate worshiping assemblies disconnected from other assemblies worldwide, a new paradigm is emerging that takes the interconnections between churches quite seriously, not because of the recognition that Christianity is the largest religion in the world, or even that it exhibits immense diversity, but rather because our world has been so deeply affected by the forces of globalization.

Globalization and Liturgy

An important feature of this new paradigm is the recognition of global interdependence. In the words of the religious demographer Todd Johnson, "The global reality of the Christian faith is no longer about 'faithful replication' of the European model, but increasing local cultural expression into the larger world community of saints as the result of increasing various movements of people, ideology, and technology."[1] The sociologist Robert Wuthnow has noted that the "challenge of globalization is to rethink how nations and the subunits of nations—corporations, nongovernmental organizations, churches, and individual citizens—have become interdependent."[2] In the church, globalization has encouraged efficiency and standardization. There is pressure to reduce our time in worship to a swift sixty minutes.

The church is, after all, an organically connected Body of Christ. The church is one, but immensely diverse, and its interconnectedness is complex. Globalization involves what Anthony Giddens has called "time-space distanciation," that is, the shrinking of time and space. The collapsing of time and space is enabled in part through various kinds of symbolic tokens, such as money, that provide media of exchange with standard values that are interchangeable across a plurality of contexts. Along with the use of symbolic tokens are expert systems that bracket time and space through deploying modes of technical knowledge independent of practitioners and clients. Such expert systems are embodied in the roles of medical doctors, therapists, technicians, engineers, and, I would suggest, pastors, priests, and other leaders of liturgical performance.[3]

---

1. Todd M. Johnson and Sandra S. Kim, "The Changing Demographics of World Christianity," paper presented to the World Christianity Group at the annual meeting of the American Academy of Religion, Washington, DC, November 2006.

2. Robert Wuthnow, *Boundless Faith: The Global Outreach of American Churches* (Berkeley, CA: University of California Press, 2009), 61.

3. Anthony Giddens, *Modernity and Self-Identity: Self and Society in the Late Modern Age* (Stanford, CA: Stanford University Press, 1991), 18.

Whereas earlier paradigms of world Christianity traced their historical trajectories worldwide and then underscored the unique features of local Christianities, I want to draw our attention to the interconnections among communities of faith. Liturgy is the domain of divine activity. With globalization has come the compression of time and space, so the theme of interdependency is a crucial one for our time. There is a close connection between liturgy and globalization, since liturgy is, in Frank Senn's words, "nothing less than a way of doing the world."[4]

II. *Soundings from the Liturgical Ecumene*

Several features of the developing side of liturgy mark the church's expansion across cultural and linguistic frontiers within the context of globalization. The following features are of particular importance for the subject matter at hand.

A. Standardizing

There seems to be an increase of a liturgical monoculture worldwide, reflected in the increasing standardization of liturgical actions, contents, and objects. Throughout much of history Christian missionaries introduced the liturgical practices and preferences that they themselves found meaningful to new communities of faith located across boundaries of culture and language. These liturgies functioned as the models for new ritual actions interpreted in a wide variety of ways by local Christians. Yet these liturgies did not stand alone as isolated rituals; they traveled on the pathways laid down by the forces of globalization, of the history of the church, and of colonialism. These are the massive transcultural networks on whose pathways circulate liturgical knowledge, preferences, practices, and objects, yet unevenly and unpredictably.

While variations exist on the ground, such as the translation of hymns into indigenous languages, were we to travel to congregations around the world, we would recognize similar features of liturgy from church to church, particularly within the same denomination. The overall pattern remains fairly intact as a particular denomination extends itself across the world. Liturgical practices are increasingly taking on shapes and sounds that make them appear universal, whether in regard to musical styles—instruments, rhythms, melodies—creedal

---

4. Frank C. Senn, *New Creation: A Liturgical Worldview* (Minneapolis: Augsburg Fortress, 2000), 8; also quoted in John D. Witvliet, "Series Preface," in Charles E. Farhadian, *Christian Worship Worldwide* (Grand Rapids, MI: Eerdmans, 2007), xvi.

formulas, architecture, theology, preaching styles, authority structures, ritual objects, the celebration of the sacraments, or even the use of time itself. In this sense, liturgies seem to follow the same pattern as other globalized items and ideas, products and technologies that function as standardized products with a common name and uniform features. Whether they be iPods, Coca-Cola cans, or Gillette razors, these products convey ideas, values, and preferences that can shape the identity and social prestige of those who possess them. Similarly, much the same pattern is developing for liturgies across various cultures worldwide. It seems that as soon as communities get electricity, they lay down their indigenous instruments—including the melodies and rhythms carried by those instruments—and power up guitars, bass, and keyboards to express their worship. Often young people may be playing their indigenous instruments and singing local melodies, even on the way to church, but leave those instruments and melodies outside the doors of the church since those instruments and melodies are not considered Christian. Part of the challenge, then, is theological; that is, it concerns the relationship between art, Gospel, and culture.

Example: liturgical monoculture among Papuans. While there are countless examples of the development of a liturgical monoculture worldwide, I want to introduce observations I have made about evangelical churches in Papua (Indonesia). Papua makes an appropriate case study because it is an immensely diverse region with nearly three hundred language groups, and at the same time it is an example of multiethnicity that becomes unified within the parameters of a common liturgy. Papua is located on the western half of the massive island of New Guinea. With hundreds of ethnicities, the island is home to Roman Catholic, mainline Protestant, evangelical, and Pentecostal churches. In the late 1960s, the Indonesian government annexed this half of the island, resulting in the ongoing struggle of many Papuans for political independence. Currently, the population of Papua is roughly two million—half are Papuans who overwhelmingly describe themselves as some form of Christian, and half are off-islanders, mostly Muslim Javanese and Sumatrans. There has been ongoing tension between Papuans and the Indonesian authorities because Papuans have lost control of many of their natural resources to multinational corporations. Furthermore, Papuan local histories and cultures have been marginalized by a national educational curriculum that seeks to draw Papuans into the historical narrative of the Indonesian nation-state.[5]

---

5. See Charles E. Farhadian, *Christianity, Islam, and Nationalism in Indonesia* (New York: Routledge, 2005).

Evangelical faith missions to Papua entered the region just before the Second World War when American missionaries commenced their work among highland tribal groups. The task of these missionaries was twofold: to save souls and to plant churches. The churches they started introduced liturgical styles based on a Western (i.e., American) evangelical model, with centrality of the preached Word, constrained body movements out of respect for God, male leadership, and hymnals filled with local translations of many of the hymns, melodies, and rhythms found in the States. Moreover, liturgies were performed within the confines of a newly delimited space, a church building, set apart from the public sphere by its walls, roof, and fences. Yet if high numbers of adherents is a marker of success, then evangelical churches in Papua have been quite successful. The well over three hundred thousand evangelical Papuans in Papua make up a significant percentage of the overall population in the region. In fact, if today you were to ask evangelical Papuans, many would say that Christianity is their traditional religion. Like most churches in the West, these American-style evangelical churches have created a sacred space that is discontinuous with their mundane, worldly surroundings.

A new discourse has been introduced that undergirds the separation between Spirit and matter, seen throughout the liturgies and homilies of these churches, as well as a new way of seeing the self—as sinner.[6] As remote villages gain access to generators that provide a near constant flow of electricity, these churches quickly adopt modern Western instruments to play Western hymnody translated into the Indonesian language. Furthermore, members of these evangelical Papuan churches orient themselves toward the national capital, Jakarta, and frequently toward international denominational headquarters based in the United States, Australia, or Canada. Global Christians are being created as church discourse includes announcements of events and prayer concerns of brothers and sisters in the same evangelical denomination located across the island, the nation, and the world. Church posters displayed in liturgical spaces feature logos of denominations whose church headquarters are located off-island. Denominational symbols adorn the shirts of young people, encouraging them to identify with one another and with their expansive denomination. Transnational church bodies are helping to define the liturgical actions and the language of local evangelical churches.

---

6. For an investigation of similar topics on the other side of the national boundary, in Papua New Guinea, see Joel Robbins, *Becoming Sinners: Christianity and Moral Torment in a Papua New Guinea Society* (Berkeley, CA: University of California Press, 2004).

Western guests, both pastors and speakers, frequent these churches, providing face-to-face fellowship between international representatives and local believers. Guests represent an international face to the local church, and their sermons reflect the psychological categories and rhetorical styles popular in evangelical churches in the West; for instance, a few years ago a series of sermons was preached by an international guest on the topic "Five Steps to Receiving the Holy Spirit." The Papuan elite were disturbed that Western missionaries, who had access to international denominational networks, allowed such a topic in a region that has a complex view of the spiritual world.

Standardizing features of evangelical liturgies can be generally described as follows: Songs are sung from hymnals, and the liturgy includes congregational responsive reading and corporate recitation of Christian creedal statements, such as the doxology and the Apostle's Creed. However, the music is led by a band consisting of electric guitar, electric bass, drums, and keyboard. Bodily movement is limited to hand clapping, as members worship standing in place.[7] Central to the liturgical pattern introduced by evangelical missions to Papua is the preaching of the Word of God from a pulpit in front of a crowd sitting quietly either on the floor or on chairs, thus condensing the authority of spiritual knowledge to one person. These are practices that evangelicals around the world would recognize as similar to their own traditions.

B. Proliferating

A second feature of the developing side of liturgy under conditions of globalization is the proliferation of liturgies. Although there appears to be increasing homogeneity of liturgical styles, actions, and preferences throughout the church worldwide, there seems to be, at the same time, a burgeoning of diverse liturgical expressions. Ironically, it is the standardization of liturgy, and its circulation across boundaries of culture and language, that appears to strengthen local diversity. We are witnessing a flourishing of liturgical heterogeneity. What is interesting about these new developments is that liturgical innovations have often sprung as distinct movements out of mission-initiated churches.

Example: Evangelicals in Papua. Let us return to our reflections on the church in Papua. The liturgical monoculture that has developed in Papua stands in stark contrast to the ways that Papuans have traditionally practiced their religions. Traditionally, Papuan religious rituals were practiced in the public sphere, usually in

---

7. Farhadian, *Christianity, Islam, and Nationalism in Indonesia*, 122.

a village center for all to see. Blood sacrifice of pigs was accompanied by vigorous dancing and singing in public rather than in a limited, physical structure. In traditional Papuan villages religious knowledge was confined to the village big-men, whose attainment of big-man status was based in part on their ability to tell stories and share knowledge from spatially remote regions, such as villages located beyond the mountain range. Big-men also collected cowrie shells and other valuable trade items from afar, bringing them back to their own villages to be admired by fellow villagers. In their traditional environs big-men would be publicly questioned by those they addressed, which motivated them to increase their knowledge about the religious and secular realms. For instance, during a public speech delivered by the big-man, members of the audience would typically engage him directly, testing and approving his knowledge. During religious occasions in their traditional environs, members of the audience would directly engage the speaker, peppering him with questions: "What kinds of animals do they have over that mountain ridge," or more recently, "How should we vote in the upcoming election?" Today, off-island church leaders, visiting pastors, and even local pastors who have travelled more widely than their predecessors function as the new big-men or big-women, their high status achieved not by acquiring stories and objects from over the mountain, but because they are now a part of a global network of church leaders who have obtained knowledge, such as formal education, and objects from places as remote as New York City, Canberra, and Amsterdam. Despite the seemingly overwhelming popularity of the evangelical traditions in Papua, new churches animated by innovative liturgies have been emerging in the past few years. Motivated by what many perceive to be the evangelical churches' disconnection with Papuan culture, these are broadly defined as renewal movements. One such gathering is the Glory Hut, a charismatic-Pentecostal assembly consisting mostly of ex-evangelical Papuans and off islanders. The leaders of the Glory Hut desire a new way to express Papuan Christianity, one not based solely on North Atlantic liturgical styles, and they blend many liturgical styles to create a meaningful experience of worship for as many ethnically diverse parishioners as possible. Liturgy in the Glory Hut can be described as a blending of innovation and inherited liturgical actions and objects that is not absolutely discontinuous with its evangelical predecessors. Unlike the traditional or evangelical models, however, women are given a prominent role in the services. This church provides an alternative liturgical reconfiguration that is growing in popularity in many urban centers on the island.

What makes the liturgy in these indigenous Papuan Pentecostal assemblies distinct from that practiced among the Papuan Evangelicals? First, women have an equal share in liturgical leadership. While in the evangelical churches women are not allowed to preach—in fact, evangelical seminaries have few female students—women have equal access to knowledge and the sharing of that knowledge in these Pentecostal assemblies. Explaining why she left an evangelical church and joined the Glory Hut, a Papuan woman explained that "women are considered not to have value in the typical [evangelical] city church. . . . If you are not a pastor you cannot preach. . . . At our church [the Glory Hut] the men and women are equal when serving the church."[8] The question of who possesses religious knowledge, and who is able to distribute that knowledge in a gathered assembly, is answered differently by evangelical Papuans and Pentecostal Papuans. In Pentecostal assemblies like the Glory Hut, women are able to engage the congregation directly rather than simply through song or dance. Evangelical communities limit women's participation in the liturgy to reading Scripture, singing in the choir, and arranging the church decorations.

Second, musical styles distinguish the Glory Hut from evangelical churches. Evangelical churches in Papua sing mostly translations of Western hymns, which are collected in books. One message this sends to parishioners is that a significant source of spiritual knowledge comes from the text, which is portable, translatable, and immutable. Not surprisingly, then, Papuan Pentecostal assemblies have no hymnals or booklets. Rather, words are projected on a screen in front of the assembly, usually by way of an overhead projector. Musically, the Glory Hut employs styles, rhythms, and melodies from North America, the West Indies, Asia, and Melanesia, moving effortlessly from one style to another. In any given worship service the Glory Hut pumps out musical adaptations, put to Christian lyrics, from the American Chicano band Los Lobos, the Irish rock band U2, and the Jamaican reggae of Bob Marley, along with a combination of Indonesian and Papuan tribal songs. Liturgical dancing in the Glory Hut also exhibits a high degree of hybridity, with female liturgical dancers waving long colorful streamers, incorporating the dance steps of their highland villages.

Third, the worship language is relativized in these Pentecostal assemblies. The language used in worship at the Glory Hut is mostly Indonesian, but the stylized prayer, animated by charismatic energy, creates a soundscape much different from the use of language in evangelical churches. With parishioners from a wide variety of Papuan tribal contexts, off-islanders from other islands of Indonesia, such as Java and Sumatra, and even a few Western expatriate families, there is a broadening of the use of language, where parishioners pray

---

8. See ibid., 114.

charismatically and extemporaneously together. Parishioners can pray in a known language or in the language of the Spirit (glossolalia). The Glory Hut represents just one movement that has emerged from the mission-initiated churches in Papua. These sorts of new Christian movements are emerging all over the world, and liturgy is the arena in which significant changes take place.

Example: African Initiated Churches. If statisticians are correct, in the near future Africa will have the largest number of Christians on any continent in the world. In 1900, there were approximately nine million African Christians; it is estimated that in 2025 there will be 633 million Christians in Africa. The Pew Forum on Religion and Public Life notes that 147 million African Christians are in "renewal" movements, which are broadly Pentecostal and charismatic, but the new movements of Christianity in Africa are much broader than the Pentecostal-charismatic label would suggest, and the massive growth of the church in Africa is owing to African agency. Most of the growth of the church in Africa is among the African Initiated Churches (AICs). In the early twentieth century the AICs reflected new forms of worship that incorporated traditional African beliefs and practices. AICs have proliferated in the areas where Protestant missions have been most active, particularly in western Africa, southern Africa, Congo, and Kenya. Ogbu Kalu suggests that there are two distinctive aspects of emergent African Christianity, namely, "a strain of black nationalism and a tendency towards Charismatic Spirituality and expression."[9]

Most scholars suggest there are four main divisions of the AICs. First are the African Initiated Ethiopian churches, which were started in the 1880s by Africans wanting their own church. These Ethiopian churches focus on the authority of black people, thus distancing themselves from white rule. The churches were formed as a reaction to the white missionary conquest of African people. "Ethiopianism" promotes power and identity through use of the Gospel and is heavily critical of colonial Christianity. Consequently, ancient Egypt, Nubia, and Ethiopia are valorized as ideal places of the golden age of African civilization.

Second, "Spirit-type" or Zionist churches, which broke away from the mission-initiated churches, emphasize the "prophet healing power" of their leaders and focus on their messianic nature. They broke off from the historic churches because people started having dreams and visions as a source of

---

9. Ogbu U. Kalu. "Christianity in Western Africa, 1910–2010," in *Atlas of Global Christianity*, ed. Todd M. Johnson and Kenneth R. Ross (Edinburgh: Edinburgh University Press, 2009), 130.

knowledge. These churches communicate with the Spirit world directly and recognize the reality of evil spirits, which many missionaries rejected. Spirit-type adherents believe that the Holy Spirit is stronger than any medicine given by a medical doctor, so they provide a Christian way of dealing with evil spirits, disease, and mental illness, preventing traditional Africans from bankrupting themselves by spending money for magic medicine. Their liturgies are human-divine encounters carried out less through formal sacraments than through the immediacy of the Spirit's direct action among the assembly. During worship, members of the assembly surround suffering individuals with prayer and love, seeking to heal sufferers. These churches are also more open to ancestor veneration. Members wear uniforms, usually white robes or military khakis. These Spirit-type churches are the largest branch of the AICs. Examples include Simon Kimbangu's Kimbanguist Church, Isaiah Shembe's Zulu Nazareth Church, and the Aladura and Harrist churches.

Third, the Pentecostal-charismatic churches arrived in the 1980s, primarily in urban centers in Africa. Most of these are English-speaking congregations that range from small house churches to megachurches, such as the various Assemblies of God churches in Africa (e.g., Zimbabwe Assemblies of God). Congregations of this Pentecostal stripe usually consist of members from mission-initiated churches and Spirit-type churches. African Pentecostal churches usually have strong liturgical, historical, and theological connections with Western Pentecostal denominations, and a steady stream of North American Pentecostal preachers frequents their pulpits. These churches represent the fastest growing part of the church in Africa. Separating themselves from the Western mission-initiated historic churches, AICs represent an assimilation of Christianity into African lifeways. While the AICs are quite diverse within themselves, they are, in the words of Dana Robert and Inus Daneel, "the most 'authentic' form of African Christianity."[10] Worship among the AICs emphasizes singing, dancing, body movement, and the power of the Spirit to heal mind, body, and soul, with a strong emphasis on the overall well-being of parishioners. Liturgies stress ethical and pneumatic elements of the Gospel, in line with traditional African religious sensibilities. Liturgical objects consist of traditional religious symbols from local cultures, and the focus is on how God provides solutions to immediate problems, such as witchcraft, sickness, and existential crises.

---

10. Dana L. Robert and M. L. Daneel, "Worship among Apostles and Zionists in Southern Africa," in *Christian Worship Worldwide*, ed. Charles E. Farhadian (Grand Rapids, MI: Eerdmans, 2007), 43–70, here 45.

On Sundays in Zimbabwe, a hymn acknowledges the power of Prophet Samuel Mutendi. Serving as an invitation to come and see how both Jesus and Mutendi can heal, the appeal is made, "Come to Zion City and be healed":

> Come and see what Jesus does,
> Come and see what Mutendi here performs,
> Come and look from the East
> You from the West, come and observe what Zion does.
> You who are sick, to Zion City for treatment come,
> Come and see!
> You with epilepsy, come and be healed,
> Come and see what Jesus does.
> The other day we were with him [the prophet Mutendi],
> Last night we were in his sight,
> Last year we were with him
> Even today he's with us.
> Come and see what Zion does![11]

African diversity does not stop at the borders of Africa. Because of the influx of African Christian immigrant groups into the North Atlantic region beginning in the 1960s, the proliferation of liturgical styles transcends geographic boundaries. Afe Adogame reports that new African religious movements in Europe, started primarily by students, businesspersons, and members of the diplomatic community, have expanded rapidly in the past three decades. Adogame's list of new African churches in European soil includes the following: branches of the Church of the Lord-Aladura (CLA), 1964; the Cherubim and Seraphim (C&S), 1965; and the Celestial Church of Christ (CCC), 1967.[12] Other Aladura churches are the Christ Apostolic Church (CAC) and the Evangelical Church of Yahweh (ECY), the Redeemed Christian Church of God (RCCG), the Deeper Christian Life Ministry (DCLM), and the Church of Pentecost International (CPI). This list does not include several of the African-led Pentecostal churches in Europe, such as Christian Church Outreach Mission International (CCOMI) in Hamburg, Kingsway International Christian Centre (KICC) in London, the Born-Again Christ Healing Church International in

---

11. Ibid., 44–45; quoted originally in M. L. Daneel, *Old and New in Southern Shona Independent Churches*, vol. 2: *Church Growth* (The Hague, Netherlands: Mouton, 1974), 201.

12. Afe Adogame, "Globalization and African New Religious Movements in Europe," in *Interpreting Contemporary Christianity: Global Processes and Local Identities*, ed. Ogbu U. Kalu and Alaine Low (Grand Rapids, MI: Eerdmans, 2008), 301–2.

London, and the True Teachings of Christ Temple in the Netherlands. Adogame argues that the multiplication of African immigrant churches in Europe is linked to a high rate of schisms owing to "personality clashes, leadership preferences, and socio-ethnic and economic factors."[13]

What sense can we make of the relationship between the standardizing and proliferating features of liturgy within the context of globalization? Robert Wuthnow points out in his study of the global impact of US churches that local diversity, ironically, is strengthened by globalization. Wuthnow notes research done on the proliferation of Starbucks coffee houses, an apparently hegemonic company since it operates about 30 percent of all coffee houses in the United States: researchers found that Starbucks actually reinforced local diversity by creating a market for coffee consumption—a market to be fulfilled by independent coffee houses.[14] Worldwide, a similar pattern seems to exist of both increasing liturgical uniformity and increasing liturgical diversity at the same time and in the same places.

The proliferation of liturgies is connected to the ways in which they are contextualized. That is to say, a vertical dimension of liturgies embeds liturgy as a movement within a local community, a dynamic described variously as contextualization, conversion, assimilation, or transformation. The embedding relates to the vertical nature of liturgy, which provides new insights on local realities, the nature of the self, community, the land, and the Divine, and it provides guidance in the here and now, making the particular, the local "situatedness," the final destination of meaning-making and liturgical innovation. The embedding mechanisms of liturgy lead to change, but this change is based on a particular culture's own terms, using its own system of symbols as the basis for revelation.

C. Disembedding

A third major feature of liturgy under conditions of globalization is that liturgies function as disembedding devices that leverage the assembly out of their local liturgical context and into a more globalized world. One aspect of this disembedding movement is a kind of "externalization of meaning," to borrow the words of Ulf Hannerz, whereby new experiences and new modes of thinking are made public and "shareable" across distance.[15] Through the modes of externalization, meaning is made accessible to public realms and can therefore be distributed across the globe. A second aspect of the disembedding

---

13. Ibid., 303.
14. Wuthnow, *Boundless Faith*, 76.
15. Ulf Hannerz, *Cultural Complexity: Studies in the Social Organization of Meaning* (New York: Columbia University Press, 1992), 8.

feature of liturgies is related to the externalization of meaning; that is, liturgies communicate directionality. While this is present under both local and global conditions, the scope and particular nature of directionality under global conditions distinguish global liturgies from local liturgies. These focus more on God and the local community by using the religious and cultural resources of the local community, whereas global liturgies lift assemblies out of their situation and give them access to a global world. Global liturgies externalize meaning, making it public and transportable across the dimensions of time and space and across social and cultural contexts. Third, the disembedding features of liturgy are transported by abstract systems considered valid regardless of the context. Abstract systems, according to Anthony Giddens, consist of expert systems and symbolic tokens that are interchangeable across a plurality of contexts.[16] These abstract systems have the potential not only to re-create but also to reorient our lives in significant ways. Their strength lies in their ability to present global abstractions that appeal to local communities. Global liturgies shrink time and space, emptying out local content and replacing it with new material from abroad. Much as in the past when maps and clocks were able to bracket space and time, making them portable, today's global liturgies are shaped by liturgical calendars, hymnals, architectural styles, and even modern technology that can dislodge the practices of local liturgy, replacing or augmenting them with those originating from spatially and temporally remote locations. New interconnections and interdependencies are created, acting as sinews connecting disparate communities into the one Body of Christ worldwide, where transnational liturgies influence local liturgical distinctiveness.

Many elements of liturgy consist of disembedding features. First, pastors and missionaries can function as representatives of expert systems, if only because of the expert status that the church confers on them. These professionals represent an abstract system of knowledge, authority, and power, usually gained in spatially remote regions such as denominational seminaries and universities. Parishioners are encouraged to trust these nonlocal experts who embody the worldwide church. Likewise, when visiting pastors, priests, or missionaries lead worship services, church conferences, or other teaching or ministerial activities, they represent more than themselves—they embody expert knowledge. Second, the Bible itself can function as an abstract system. As the Word of God to all people in time and space, it represents an authority over worshiping communities, despite its diverse interpretations. As the

---

16. See Giddens, *Modernity and Self-Identity*, 18.

missiologist Andrew Walls and others have pointed out, a common feature of the Christian church throughout its history is the acceptance of the Bible as God's Word. This is experienced most immediately in the context of liturgy. Were we to gather up all the Christians in the world, what would unify them would be not a common liturgy but perhaps their desire to be shaped by the biblical witness. As biblical stories are integrated into liturgies worldwide, they provide vehicles for new self-understandings and reorientations across cultures. Third, even the name of God can be understood as, in the language of Anthony Giddens, a "symbolic token," an authority connecting people together across domains of space and time. Under conditions of globalization and migration, it appears that the names of God appear to be becoming fewer. While God's authority remains, local names for God are disappearing in liturgical performances as people migrate from hinterland to urban centers. We seem to see a similar pattern: Christian missionaries replaced the names of ancient deities with that of the Christian God, combining them with liturgical performances such as baptism and Eucharist, thus having an impact on local identity. The first conversion, if you will, is toward a new understanding of the community in relationship to the biblical God. But that is only the first conversion. The second conversion occurs during times of social mobility, when rural people move to larger towns and cities that are home to linguistic plurality. In liturgical contexts of metropolitan centers, the local names for God have all but disappeared. Some examples will help to illustrate the features described above.

Examples: from Peru and Indonesia. The Aguaruna people of the Peruvian Amazon refer to God as "Apajui" in their local villages, but as Aguaruna migrate to Lima and other major urban centers of Latin America, "Apajui" no longer carries the same communal meaning, and it is dropped entirely from urban liturgies. The community has shifted and so has the name of God, "Apajui" becoming "Dios" in the liturgical orbit of Lima's worshiping communities. The children and grandchildren of the Aguaruna may not even learn the name Apajui after their migration to the city.

In North Sulawesi, Indonesia, "by replacing the names of ancient deities with that of the Christian God, ministers have successfully combined baptism with a pre-Minahasa form of ritual cleansing, and have thus asserted a specifically 'Minahasa' identity."[17] Prior to the entrance of mission Christianity, the

---

17. Barbara Watson Andaya, "Christianity in Southeast Asia: Similarity and Difference in a Culturally Diverse Region," in *Introducing World Christianity*, ed. Charles Farhadian (Oxford: Blackwell, 2012), 120.

people of Minahasa referred to God as "Empung." Today, Minahasans who move to Jakarta, the nation's capital, use "Allah" to refer to God. This translation, which occurs in liturgy itself, is never a smooth process. Prior to the arrival of mission Christianity in the highlands of Papua, the Walak people used the name "Walkarige," "Creator of creators," to refer to God. The first missionaries actually tried using the term "God," in English, to refer to the biblical God, but after the Walak discovered what the missionaries were talking about, they said, "Oh, we already have a name for that being—'Walkarige.'" After the Indonesian annexation of Papua in the early 1960s, Western missionaries used the Indonesian translation of the Bible and therefore introduced a new name for God, "Allah." Today, Walak are familiar with the name "Allah," but their local liturgies employ the name "Walkarige," which is effective in village liturgies but not in urban liturgies. The same holds true for the other tribal groups in the highlands of Papua; whether Yali, Dani, Walak, or Me, they use the local name for God in their village liturgies. However, when they move to larger towns, where they enter multiethnic assemblies, in the liturgies they employ the name "Allah," which, of course, is Arabic.

Even the use of "Allah" is not free from controversy. In 2009, conservative Muslims in Malaysia decried the Malaysian Christian use of "Allah" in their liturgies and Bibles, arguing that the term belongs exclusively to Muslims. The debate about the use of the word "Allah" pitted the Malaysian government and conservative Muslim groups against the Malaysian High Court. In January of 2010, some churches were set ablaze in Kuala Lumpur in response to the Malaysian High Court's decision to strike down a three-year ban on non-Muslims using the word "Allah" in their liturgies and Bibles. The High Court of Malaysia determined that the word "Allah" was not exclusive to Muslims. This incident reminds us that the liturgical use of the name of God has immediate social and political implications in ways we might initially overlook.

Do the Yoruba maintain their use of the name "Olodumare" (God) when they migrate to New York City? Do the Masaai forget the name "Engai" (God) when they move to Nairobi? While to my knowledge there are no statistics on the demise of the local names for God in liturgies worldwide, it does appear that there has been a dramatic decrease in the number of names people use to refer to God because of increasing urbanization and the cosmopolitan nature of liturgies. The old names are descriptive of God's character and people's experience with God. Liturgical decision makers will have to ask themselves what is lost when the particular names of God are erased or forgotten.

What are we to make of the embedding and disembedding features of the developing side of liturgy? Whereas the embedding elements of liturgies run the risk of a kind of liturgical narcissism, being directed exclusively toward one's own people or community, their strength is that they can deepen an assembly's understanding of itself and its immediate surroundings since they serve as pointers to the Creator God who promises forgiveness and reconciliation.

Likewise, disembedding elements of liturgy have both positive and negative features. On the one hand, new kinship networks are created by sharing standardized liturgies across temporal and spatial domains; they help Christian worshipers to understand and experience the Body of Christ as an organic unity. On the other hand, the disembedding features can influence disproportionally the ways people worship in their local contexts, as liturgical performances and objects that are imported from afar serve to recast the liturgical celebration in a wider scope more dependent on globalizing forces.

D. Liturgical Itineraries in a Globalized World

The standardizing, proliferating, and disembedding features of the developing side of liturgy do not emerge without significant negotiations in the cultural, social, and theological domains. In this sense liturgies worldwide can be seen as itineraries that encounter one another locally and globally in complicated ways, leading liturgical travelers into new spatial and temporal realities. As itineraries, the flow of liturgies worldwide is marked by unevenness and stagnation, since they are disrupted, curtailed, reshaped, and/or promoted in their encounters with globalizing forces. Negotiations toward embedding and disembedding come with some degree of tension, in part because of competing liturgical itineraries, which in the context of globalization make liturgical negotiation a complicated process. Virtually every liturgical decision is an example of these encounters among standardizing, proliferating, and disembedding features. And the outcome of these encounters is unpredictable.

Example: Vedanayagam Sastri. In India, Vedanayagam Sastri (1774–1864) was a famous writer and poet, with over 500 lyrics and 130 books to his credit.[18] Born during the British Raj in South Asia, Vedanayagam was from a Roman Catholic family of the upper-caste Vellalars. A highly educated young man, Vedanayagam was deeply influenced by the New Testament and the German missionary Rev. C. F. Schwartz, who encouraged him to embrace Protestant-

---

18. See Indira Viswanathan Peterson, "*Bethlehem Kuravanci* of Vedanayaka Sastri of Tanjore: The Cultural Discourses of an Early-Nineteenth Century Tamil Christian Poem," in *Christians, Cultural Interactions, and India's Religious Traditions*, ed. Judith M. Brown and Robert Eric Frykenberg (Grand Rapids, MI: Eerdmans, 2002), 9–36.

ism, which he did at the age of twelve. Known for his fearless convictions and bright mind, Vedanayagam studied at the Lutheran Seminary in Tranquebar, where he studied the Bible translation of Bartholomew Ziegenbalg, the first Protestant missionary to India. He later received several titles, such as "Poet King of Illuminating Knowledge," "The Molder of the Scriptures," and "Poet King Who Trumpets the Gospel." Vedanayagam developed a talent for writing poetry, short stories, and plays, injecting Christianity into Tamil linguistic and cultural forms, and employing Hindu dramatic structure, seeking to convey Gospel truth in ways that would be meaningful to his Tamil audiences. One of his most famous liturgical dramas is called the *Bethlehem Kuravanci*; it is in form a Tamil drama, *Kuravanci*, with particular indigenous Tamil characters transformed into the church, faith, fishers of men, and the devil. The *Bethlehem Kuravanci* was popular among Tamil people. In 1830, Protestant missionaries from England of the Society for Propagation of the Gospel were granted permission to preach in British-controlled regions of India. When they arrived they were offended by the contextualization of Vedanayagam's work, particularly his liturgical dramas. The Tamilization of the Gospel caused a great stir among British missionaries who argued that the *Bethlehem Kuravanci* was an illegitimate way to present the Gospel to Tamils. The missionary L. P. Haubroe insisted that Christian Tamils should all sit together and share common meals, thus opposing caste distinctions, but Tamil Christians followed caste separation, insisting that social mingling be restricted because of saliva and pollution prohibitions. Vedanayagam defended caste distinctions in the worshiping assembly, arguing that there were classes in Europe, and that among Tamils it was unnatural to mix classes. Vedanayagam's liturgical dramas were so heavily criticized by Protestant missionaries that the second generation of Protestant missionaries strongly disapproved of his Christianized Tamil liturgies. Believing them to be pagan and showy—since, for instance, the missionaries prohibited the use of lots of flowers—the missionaries excommunicated Vedanayagam, seeking to remove Tamil music and songs from the church.

Example: He Qi. During China's Cultural Revolution (1966–76), a young man by the name of He Qi, a naturally gifted artist, and his family were relocated out of his city of birth and into a rural environment to do manual labor. During the day he worked, but at night he sketched pictures. After winning a local painting competition to see who could best paint Chairman Mao's image, He Qi recognized that he could perhaps free himself from daily labor if he continued to paint and won more competitions. One day he discovered an image by Raphael, *Madonna and Child*, from the Italian Renaissance. In the context of massive social and economic unrest throughout China, He Qi was drawn to the child's peaceful expression. As he worked to reproduce the *Madonna and Child*, He Qi wondered who that child was and why he looked so peaceful and at rest. He discovered that the child was Jesus Christ and eventually came to believe in him. He Qi later developed his own style of painting, which he hoped would communicate themes in the life of Christ and the Christian faith to a Chinese audience. Recasting Christianity into Chinese expressions, He Qi has sought to change what he calls the "foreign image" of Christianity in China through his art, which he hopes churches will use in their liturgical spaces. He Qi was the first mainland Chinese to earn a PhD in religious art after the Cultural Revolution, studying at the Hamburg Art Institute in Germany. He was a professor at Nanjing Union Theological Seminary for many years and has received numerous accolades. According to the *Far Eastern Economic Review*, He Qi "ranks as arguably China's most internationally sought after contemporary Christian artist." Yet He Qi's work is seldom accepted by Chinese pastors as Christian art for liturgical use. For instance, he tells that when a Chinese pastor asked if He Qi could create a painting for his church, He Qi agreed and offered to create a painting based on his own style. But the pastor responded, "No, we want Christian art." Because of the overwhelming acceptance of Western, and particularly Renaissance, art as the standard of worship, He Qi's work is not readily accepted as a legitimate form of art for use in church. Today, He Qi's art has become quite popular and can be seen on book covers, posters, and in art exhibits worldwide, but it remains fairly insignificant in the liturgical spaces of Chinese churches.

III. Conclusion

In the global context, liturgical itineraries can be at significant odds. For one, there is unpredictable feedback—for example, through reverse flow from the metropole and through push back. The liturgical innovations of Vedanayagam in India and He Qi in China were curtailed as the two tried to refashion Christian liturgical forms into local Indian and Chinese ways, respectively. Despite the fact that there is growing willingness to privilege liturgical productions originating from spatially remote locations, sometimes displacing local criteria for belonging, new liturgical expressions are reversing the dominant flow from center to periphery. The liturgical metropole is becoming more diverse, for instance, as liturgical spaces are opening up, redefining the physical boundaries of worship. This opening of worship space alone may have an impact on the missionary identity of the church as it becomes more connected with its immediate surroundings.

A question underlies this essay: What is the cost of decontextualizing liturgical items and transporting them across cultural and linguistic boundaries? And what are the benefits? What is unfolding in the realm of liturgical developments is of international scope. I imagine that the future of liturgy will be marked by increasing mutual appreciation, and incomprehension, as categories of liturgical performances, practices, and explanations are celebrated and misunderstood on all sides. Even a shared liturgy, possible because of increased networking worldwide, can generate new understanding and new confusion, but joint worship can also underscore the differences inherent in liturgical traditions. For example, consider an immigrant congregation in the West worshiping with a different church, as happened when an African migrant church in Cologne shared worship with its German hosts. An African leader of an African migrant church in Cologne described the event:

> Members of the host local German church were in attendance in their numbers. As prayers were enacted during the "altar call," a German woman alongside some Africans fell flat on the nave of the church. Members of the African Pentecostal congregation recognized and interpreted this phenomenon as the action and visible manifestation of the Holy Spirit. However, visiting Germans, whose pastor swung instantaneously and dashed to his office where he called the attention of the city ambulance service, understood this differently. All attempts to restrain him and to explain the actual situation proved abortive. Although the emergency doctors who rushed the woman to the hospital ended their examination without any negative results, yet this singular event had strained the relationship between the African and German congregations respectively.[19]

The religious worldviews and cultural backgrounds of the Africans and Germans created an obstacle to mutual understanding; they gave rise to different interpretations, thus, in Afe Adogame's words, "reinforcing a kind of locality."[20] No wonder that the celebration of the Lord's Supper, which draws the community of believers together, transports parishioners in two directions at once: the universal, transcultural feature of Christian faith, shared universally by the Christian faithful around the world, and the particular flesh-and-blood immediacy of our local conditions, which bind us in time and space to each other and our common Lord.

---

19. Adogame, "Globalization and African New Religious Movements in Europe," 314–15.
20. Ibid., 315.

13
Liturgical Migrations into Cyberspace: Theological Reflections

Stefan Böntert

The internet and its social effects have been discussed and researched quite extensively by now.[1] While earlier scholarship may have spoken glowingly of a "mythical" internet,[2] a more realistic approach has now replaced such lyrical formulations.[3] A broad consensus in the sociology of media holds that the internet entails pronounced changes in the understanding of the world and of reality as it develops entirely new social entities, so that traditional conceptions of community, relationality, and communication are put to the test. Because the internet represents such a transformative cultural dynamic, it ranks among the most far-reaching

---

Translated from the German by Stephen McCarthy.

1. This essay builds upon my previous publications on the subject, especially *Gottesdienste im Internet: Perspektiven eines Dialogs von Internet und Liturgie* (Stuttgart: Kohlhammer, 2005); "Jenseits aller Kirchenbänke—Gottesdienst zwischen medialer Zivilisation und kirchlicher Grundgestalt," *Liturgisches Jahrbuch* 57 (2007): 39–60; "E-Prayer und Andacht per Mausklick: Christliche Gottesdienste im Internet—Zerrbild eines Ideals oder Teilstück einer nötigen Inkulturation?" in *Religion und Medien: Vom Kultbild zum Internetritual*, ed. Jamal Malik, Jörg Rüpke, and Theresa Wobbe, Vorlesungen des Interdisziplinären Forums Religion der Universität Erfurt 4 (Münster: Aschendorff, 2007), 165–79, 239–41.

2. *Mythos Internet*, ed. Stefan Münker and Alexander Roesler (Frankfurt am Main: Suhrkamp, 1997).

3. Heidi A. Campbell has recently mapped the scholarly trajectory in the English-speaking world in her essay "Understanding the Relationship between Religion Online and Offline in a Networked Society," *Journal of the American Academy of Religion* 80 (2012): 64–93.

innovations in history. The outbreak of the so-called Arab Spring in 2010, for example, revealed how the internet can help lay low regimes that seemed solidly entrenched. Online social networks, cultivated on Facebook and similar sites, have demonstrably contributed to profound social change.

Today online networks influence political decisions, decide economic choices, and shape public opinion in unprecedented ways. In the private sphere the web has become an integral part of daily life. This obviously applies in the first place to "digital natives," that is, the younger generation that has been reared in a media culture since birth. But the so-called "digital immigrants" have also set aside their reservations and are increasingly enlarging their social networks on the internet. Although the relationships found in such internet communities are still relatively unstable, their importance for daily life is now sufficiently documented by empirical investigations.[4] These developments confirm the thesis of the sociologist Niklas Luhmann that the media are closely bound up with people's consciousness, experiences, and actions, which is why "one might also say that the media keeps society attentive."[5] It is not surprising that this development has not always met with approval. Critical engagement with the problems and dangers of the online medium are as old as the medium itself, and such critical engagement has taken place within as well as outside of theological discourse.[6]

I. The Internet: A Social, Religious, and Liturgical Medium

To begin with, the internet constitutes a medium of information and communication; as such, it can easily take on the role of a religious medium, and of a liturgical medium as well.[7] Whoever presses beyond news portals and church-maintained web sites into the deep, noninstitutional, more private internet scene encounters organizations that play with religious semantics or explicitly conceive of themselves as religious. This online religious world is as diverse as it is hard to map, since it is both fluid and boundless. As the law of supply and demand rules the economic sphere, so ever-newer religious associations are

---

4. Ibid.

5. Niklas Luhmann, *Die Realität der Massenmedien* (Opladen: Westdeutscher Verlag, 1996), 47; English translation: *The Reality of the Mass Media*, trans. Kathleen Cross, Cultural Memory in the Present (Stanford, CA: Stanford University Press, 2000).

6. See, for example, Richard R. Gaillardetz, *Transforming Our Days: Spirituality, Community and Liturgy in a Technological Culture* (New York: Crossroad, 2000), and more recently, Klaus Müller, *Endlich unsterblich: Zwischen Körperkult und Cyberworld* (Kevelaer: Butzon und Bercker, 2011).

7. See the findings published in the journal *Online: Heidelberg Journal of Religions on the Internet* at http://online.uni-hd.de, last accessed on 24 February 2012.

coming into being online, profoundly individual and customized. That some providers appear expressly as alternatives to Christian churches is no accident. Hardly any of these providers offer links to concrete ecclesial institutions or even to the traditions of individual religious congregations. Contemporary scholarship, in searching for ways to theorize this phenomenon, speaks of a new form of inculturation or of the internet as a religiously charged space, as a missionary tool, as a means of shaping religious identity and practice, as a spiritual network, and as a cultic sphere.[8]

Better known and easier to classify are the many web sites managed by large religious communities. In the Christian sphere nearly every church and group now has a presence online, from the Vatican to various Eastern churches, from evangelical megachurches to small parishes. The range of uses is diverse: congregations present their activities online,[9] allowing people to inform themselves about their church's structure or to review news of their programs; complete orders of service and homilies are made available; points of faith are amusingly conveyed; experts offer their insights in pastoral chats; and forums and communities invite an exchange of questions regarding religious belief and practice.

If appearances are to be trusted, the church's online presence rests upon the two pillars of information and communication. The contemporary conception of the church's online presence is, for the most part, pastorally oriented, intending to make the spreading of the faith more effective and appealing, maintaining contact with the faithful, and widening access to the church for those who are seeking it.[10] Foundational church documents posted online function along similar lines: they offer information and utilize the internet to publicize widely the basics of Christian faith. At the same time, religious communities for the most part are not uncritically euphoric about the possibilities of the internet. Notwithstanding all the advantages offered by this new medium, the church is also aware of potential ethical and pedagogical problems and considers its responsibility carefully.[11]

---

8. More on all of these in a recent issue of the Yale Divinity School magazine, *Reflections*, titled *iBelieve: Facing the New Media Explosion*, 98/2 (2011). See also Heidi Campbell, "Spiritualizing the Internet: Uncovering Discourses and Narratives of Religious Internet Usage," *Online: Heidelberg Journal of Religions on the Internet* 1/1 (2005), 5, http://online.uni-hd.de, last accessed on 24 February 2012.

9. See Stefan Böntert, *Verkündet es von den Dächern: Neue Medien und Pfarrgemeinde* (Stuttgart: Katholisches Bibelwerk, 2002), 26–39.

10. See Böntert, *Gottesdienste im Internet*, 58–71.

11. See, for example, the recent document from the German bishops, *Virtualität und Inszenierung: Unterwegs in der digitalen Mediengesellschaft; Ein medienethisches Impulspapier*, Die deutschen Bischöfe Publizistische Kommission 35 (Bonn: Deutsche Bischofskonferenz, 2011).

That said, most churches are involved in a process of media transformation; they are fashioning the process and are a part of it. These developments are no great surprise, but the horizon of possibilities grows wider when we take into account the innumerable migrations of liturgical materials online.

II. Liturgy Online

To begin with, there is a rather familiar format, namely, the broadcast of liturgical celebrations over the internet. When parishes or religious orders make their worship services available online, they are carrying on a tradition well established in the twentieth century, namely, live broadcasts over radio and television. Alongside such online broadcasts are the countless internet portals that provide individual building blocks for liturgical celebrations. Texts of church services already celebrated can be found online, along with, for example, homilies. Other sites offer complete orders of service, or Scripture verses for contemplation, or literature for baptisms, weddings, memorials, and burials. Foundational Christian prayers are available online, as is a wealth of set prayers from which to select texts for specific needs. Such prayers are often presented online together with meditative images and music. Aides for the preparation of liturgical celebrations are also available on the web and grow in number as each Sunday passes.

Beyond the online presence of liturgy from within "bricks and mortar" churches are liturgical elements designed exclusively for online application. This phenomenon raises questions for many since the migration of elements of Christian liturgy into cyberspace leaves behind the need for a concrete, assembled congregation in a church building. Indeed, some liturgical celebrations can now be found only on the web. They are anchored in electronically generated space and realized with multimedia technology.[12] As the internet has become a liturgical space, the church building has lost its uniqueness in light of these new online communities. In some cases, churches themselves have championed this move, while other web pages offering liturgical celebrations are the product of individual initiative. A few examples will illustrate how such liturgical elements function. The most common formats are web devotions, click-through meditations, and online prayer forums. In the German-speaking

---

12. For some reflections on the experience of such liturgical celebrations by a pastor whose congregation, Koinonia Congregational Church, gathers online only (in the virtual reality world of Second Life), see Kimberly Knight, "Sacred Space in Cyberspace," *Reflections* 96/2 (2009): 43–46.

world, for example, web sites such as www.gebetsanliegen.de, www.kirche.
funama.de, and www.bigpray.de serve a young target audience interested in
online practices of prayer and meditation. The Catholic diocese of Münster
has a site, www.kirchensite.de, on which prayer requests can be posted. In the
English-speaking world, www.cyberchurch.org and www.cyberchurch.co.za
are some leading examples. The Methodist Church in Great Britain sponsors
"the world's first 3D online church" at http://churchoffools.com, and the Anglican diocese of Oxford has worked on the construction of an online church
at www.i-church.org since 2004. The individual projects employ all the multimedia possibilities that the internet offers: chats, film, text, audio files, and
slideshows. Strikingly, most of the projects fall back on traditional liturgical
forms, carrying online pieces of the familiar canon of rites, customs, and subjects of liturgical celebrations. Thus, one can visit a virtual church building that
is an architecturally typical, traditionally ordered ecclesial space, with an altar,
a cross, pews, candles, flower arrangements, a Bible laid out to leaf through,
and even a bell in the steeple (at www.gebetsanliegen.de). The central ritual
to which the user is invited derives from a familiar context: personal prayer
requests can be inscribed in a book, and virtual candles can be lit. In projects
that leave traditional forms behind, the action follows a video clip or computer
game with Christian content and portions for prayer.

Putting aside the question of the access rates these different projects garner,
one can distinguish two different types of the online presence of liturgical
elements and rituals. The first type is internet meditations that are envisioned
not as a communal activity but rather as an individual spiritual act. As a rule,
these meditations are made up of short clips of texts, images, and sounds,
which are posted on a site and can readily be called up again and again. These
meditations typically revolve around questions of life and faith, often from fresh
and sometimes surprising angles; they might also suggest practical advice in
particular situations of need. Some of these meditations follow a fixed schema,
while others offer choices. There is no possibility of establishing contact with
other users during the meditation. A second type is online liturgical elements
that consciously employ the interactivity of the internet. Users are able to connect with others online, either immediately through chats or delayed through
e-mail. Here users are potentially incorporated into a community with others.
A virtual prayer bulletin board, for example, typically follows this principle.

How should these projects be regarded? How should they be evaluated
theologically? Are they simply a reflection of the contemporary fascination
with new technologies? Can people perform rites authentically online? Are
these extractions from traditional liturgical life benign, or do they violate core

principles of liturgical life, maybe as a desperate response to dwindling congregations? Has liturgy become a helpless victim of a widespread overestimation of the power of media? Will a liturgical rite be alterable online according to each person's disposition? Or are these phenomena an authentic expression of a liturgy that takes its changing cultural and medial context seriously? These questions illustrate that far more is at stake than pastoral strategies alone or using the internet to further the church's mission of being among the people.

III. *Theological Reflections on the Online Presence of Liturgy*

The following reflections do not seek an immediate yes or no to the question of the possibility or impossibility of online liturgical celebrations. Rather, my reflections attempt to locate such celebrations in a larger theological context. My thesis is this: Through the interactive structure of the internet new forms of sociality have arisen that are of fundamental importance for contemporary lived life. Theologically, these forms of sociality can be appreciated as sites in which the church takes shape and becomes concrete for people. In other words, the internet not only projects an image of the church online for informational purposes but is also a space in which church happens. It is therefore possible, under certain conditions, to engage in liturgical actions in internet communities.

Assessing individual existing online projects theologically is beyond the scope of the present essay. We must keep in mind, however, that some such projects operate idiosyncratically and create conditions whose theological profile may prove to be problematic. It is therefore an urgent task to reflect on how the power of the internet, in relation to religious ritual, can be grasped theologically. Just as importantly, we have to think through how the church positions itself in relation to this subject, or we will surrender this terrain to self-appointed online liturgists and missionaries.

A. Liturgy and Media Technology—a Brief Look Back

Liturgy in the world of media technology is not a new discovery of "Generation @." The subject surfaced with broadcasts of worship services via radio and television.[13] Such broadcasts are so commonplace today that it is hard to imag-

---

13. For theological reflections on TV broadcasts of worship services, see, for example, Beate Gilles, *Durch das Auge der Kamera: Eine liturgietheologische Untersuchung zur Übertragung von Gottesdiensten im Fernsehen* (Münster: Lit, 2001); and Birgit Jeggle-Merz, "Gottesdienst und mediale Übertragung," in *Gottesdienst der Kirche: Handbuch der Liturgiewissenschaft*, 2:2:

ine that they were once theologically controversial. In the German-speaking world, for example, a fierce debate arose over whether liturgical celebrations and media technology should be brought together at all. The discussion focused on how liturgical participation could be conceived when practiced in front of a radio or a television screen rather than in a church. A sharp line was drawn between the broadcasting of a liturgy and the liturgical celebration itself, with participation via the medium of a broadcast classified as deficient. The central argument hinged on the asymmetrical communication potential between radio or television and the liturgy itself, and especially the disproportion between sender and receiver in broadcasts, which disabled the active participation of those coparticipating via an electronic device. The root of the skepticism was the conviction that all coparticipants in a liturgical celebration had to be physically present and actively taking part—something that was not possible through the medium of radio and TV broadcasts. Consequently, broadcasts of worship services were understood to be solely pastoral: they were to give people a possibility of participating in worship in some way when owing to personal difficulties (i.e., sickness, infirmity, etc.) they could not participate in the liturgy in the church itself.

As the practice of broadcasting liturgical celebrations developed, the debate also moved forward. The pronounced difference seen between the liturgical participants on the one hand and the receivers in front of their radios or TVs on the other hand dissolved. Yet the task remained of identifying and naming what allowed those observing a celebration via broadcast a significant part in the liturgy. This was achieved by broadening the notion of participation and by emphasizing its spiritual dimension. In order to delineate the different types of participation, the term "intentional participant" was introduced: "Intentional participation is more than an inner act of piety. It encompassed in the first place the foundational desire of appropriation, which was constituted at the level of intention in the bodily and visible domain but could not be realized there."[14] With this step the importance of the actual liturgical celebration was maintained, while the fact that some people were experiencing it as coparticipants via a broadcast was also appreciated. In this view, the broadcast was no longer seen as dividing the congregation in the church and the coparticipants before their television screens. Instead, there was in a sense a "correlation between the

---

Theologie des Gottesdienstes, ed. Martin Klöckener, Angelus A. Häußling, and Reinhold Meßner (Regensburg: Pustet, 2008), 455–90.

14. Ambrosius Karl Ruf, *Die Fernsehübertragung der Heiligen Messe* (Frankfurt am Main: Knecht, 1961), 65.

liturgy's congregation and its television viewers, who are spiritually present, and not merely yielding to an illusory fiction, but are actually included in God's sacrament."[15] One might summarize this theological conviction as saying that participation in a liturgy is not linked exclusively to being in a specific place but is above all a relational event in which God and human beings are joined, as participants are joined to each other.

B. Sketching a Theology of Liturgical Participation Online

A look at this earlier debate is instructive because the debate assumed a specific model of communication, namely, a communication flow running in one direction only, from a sender to receivers. Yet when considering the internet, another model is called for, that of an interactive medium that transcends the one-way communication of radio and television. The possibility of multidirectional communication is foundational to the internet, after all, and with this possibility, entirely different conditions are available that call for further theological reflection. In what follows, I highlight four theological lines of argument that substantiate my claim that internet liturgical life is not a distortion but rather a responsible development and updating of liturgical life as hitherto known.

First, I note the ecclesiological possibilities opened up by an appreciation of the web's interactivity. The Second Vatican Council emphasized the identity of the church as an "assembly."[16] It is in this assembly—that is, in the lived, embodied, enacted gathering of the faithful—that ecclesial communion is constituted and confirmed. The foundational impulse for the gathering of the assembly is the salvific turning of God toward humanity, which the assembly witnesses in the texts of Scripture and in the redemptive and loving works of Jesus. God transforms the history of humankind into an overarching salvific history in which God brings about new life-giving relationships between human beings.

Yet a comprehensive, consistent, and unified practice of gathering the ecclesial assembly is not available in the New Testament or in the subsequent history of the church, just as there continue to be different emphases in ecclesiological explorations in contemporary theology. The assembly of the faithful has always been understood in different ways, and new conceptions continue to emerge, often shaped in conversation with changing social and cultural contexts. The assembly's location and format vary. "Assembly" is a relational concept and

---

15. Michael Böhnke, "Welche Art von Teilnahme ist einem Zuschauer einer Fernsehübertragung von Gottesdiensten möglich?" *Liturgisches Jahrbuch* 37 (1987): 3–16, here 10f.

16. See Vatican II's Dogmatic Constitution on the Church, nos. 8, 9, 28, et al.

cannot be limited to specific forms or places. Moreover, the identity of the church is rooted not merely in set forms but also in the continuing openness to God's own always-new presence and relational power. The constant search for adequate practices of gathering, in ever-changing sociocultural contexts, therefore belongs to the theological heart of the ecclesial assembly. This vision paves the way to explore the vast range of lived lives and forms of communication—including those online—and to ask how these diverse forms of gathering and of community can be read theologically. Maybe these forms also constitute an "assembly," theologically speaking. The contemporary diversity of sites and forms of communication should not slip through the church's net—for ecclesiological reasons, not only pastoral ones. Jürgen Werbick suggests how these sites too can be seen as places of assembly called forth by God: "Wherever the Word that sounds in the God hermeneutic of Jesus Christ is allowed to enter the processes of understanding that are constitutive of human relationality, wherever these processes themselves are claimed for a God hermeneutic, there church planting takes place as God's invitation takes root; or, less metaphorically, a 'project' of gathering to understand the Word takes place in order to find a fitting possible answer to it in always changing contexts."[17]

Thus, my thesis is as follow: The forms of sociality that arise online can be opened up for what assembly means in a theological sense, that is, as a relational encounter in the redemptive presence of Jesus Christ and of human beings with one another. The internet does not only offer information about ecclesial communion; rather, a community formed by coming together online, and grounded in the shared experience of having been claimed by God, contains the potential for community with God to come about online. The process of interaction online serves not only as an informational tool but also as a resonant and expressive medium of ecclesial communion. From these theological presuppositions, at least four arguments follow that support liturgical presence and actions online.

1. Christian Liturgy Is an Assembly of All Who Celebrate, without Distinction between Active and Passive Celebration

Assembling for worship has always been one of the foundational practices of the church's life, even if the gathered assembly has taken different forms throughout history. The primary impulse for all who gather lies in God's own turning toward human beings; everything else emerges in response to this

---

17. Jürgen Werbick, *Den Glauben verantworten: Eine Fundamentaltheologie* (Freiburg im Breisgau: Herder, 2000), 801.

gracious initiative of God. A range of practices, local customs, and traditions mark past and present ways of gathering as an ecclesial assembly. Neither the term "liturgy" nor the term "church" applies to a single form, but each refers to a wide range of variations. Where people allow themselves to be called by God, gather together, and come into relationship with one another, there a liturgical assembly arises. The precise site of the assembly plays a minor role, since "it is not the place or the building that makes a gathering an ecclesial assembly, but rather the intention of those who have gathered and the words and actions of the one who is at the heart of the assembly and guides it."[18] If we take this statement seriously, a liturgical assembly will always have to be open to new locations in which it can gather. New locations where people meet and build community—like those that form on the internet, in which exchange with one another is possible—may then become liturgical sites.

Binding together all the coparticipants in the act of worship, the Second Vatican Council emphasized the importance of *participatio actuosa*, the active participation of all.[19] A liturgical form was sought in which all present would share in the liturgical celebration in a variety of roles. This emphasis came to be at the heart of criticism leveled against worship services broadcast on TV: coparticipants before a television screen were seen as passive recipients, unable to be fully active in the liturgical celebration. But with the advent of the internet, multidirectional communication is a given. Internet users are not passive receivers but are in contact with others with whom they reciprocate. In contradistinction to television, all participants can be directly involved with a liturgical celebration service online and can be drawn in. "Active participation" is thus possible. The earlier concern about the passive and remote position of a coparticipant before a television screen loses its ground.

2. Christian Liturgy Is Both an Ecclesially Ordered and an Open Project

Liturgy is an embodied symbol system comprising many individual elements, all of which are interwoven with multilayered processes of cultural formation and reception. Liturgical forms are not isolated, closed, or static entities but rather interdependent with and shaped by their contexts. That is to say, liturgies are not timeless and dislocated rituals that can survive independent of their cultural, anthropological, historical, and technological environments. The identity of Christian liturgy is connected to its integrative power. Whether

---

18. Walter Kirchschläger, "Die liturgische Versammlung: Eine neutestamentliche Bestandsaufnahme," *Heiliger Dienst* 52 (1998): 11–24, here 13.
19. See Vatican II's Constitution on the Sacred Liturgy, no. 14.

liturgy can bring changing spiritualities, cultural transformations, and biographical processes of individuals into relationship with the content of Christian faith determines its relevance. Every liturgical celebration therefore remains dependent on signs, symbols, speech, and other forms of expression that the participants can grasp and to which they can assent. Liturgical signs and symbols can only release their active power when their intelligibility is assured. Otherwise, liturgy becomes an enclave, a ghetto. When its message is not decipherable, its symbolic forms of expression have to be rethought and, if necessary, changed. Specific symbolic forms, therefore—which are always dependent on specific times, cultures, and locations (and their individual forms)—cannot simply be equated with the very meaning of the liturgy. As much as ecclesially established and ordered liturgical forms may be plausible, the task remains to make sure that the world of the liturgy and the worlds in which human beings live converse with each other. The ongoing search for appropriate liturgical forms belongs to the heart of Christian liturgy. Liturgy is by its very nature an open, ongoing project, bearing within itself openness toward ever-new forms of expression, including those generated by technological advances and new media. The internet has to be included in such liturgical openness toward new forms.

3. Reforms Are Always an Inherent Part of Christian Liturgy

The third point builds on the first two and focuses them on the fact that liturgical celebrations themselves always call forth further reform. The history of Christian liturgy provides ample evidence that changes, revisions, reforms, and updating of liturgical life are not the exception but the norm. In ever-new movements of renewal and reform, the outer form of the liturgy is and will continue to be changed, adjusted, and developed. All reforms mirror broader developments and new orientations and thereby witness to the intricate relationship between liturgical life and the human condition. The task of maintaining this intricate relationship is an ongoing one. That this is not an afterthought but rather constitutive of ecclesial life is evident in the programmatic opening of Vatican II's Constitution on the Sacred Liturgy: "The sacred council has set out to impart an ever-increasing vigor to the Christian lives of the faithful; *to adapt more closely to the needs of our age those institutions which are subject to change*; to encourage whatever can promote the union of all who believe in Christ; to strengthen whatever serves to call all of humanity into the church's fold."[20]

20. Constitution on the Sacred Liturgy, in *Vatican Council II: Constitutions, Decrees, Declarations*, ed. Austin Flannery (Northport, NY: Costello, 1996), no. 1, p. 117; emphasis mine.

This principle—which moves away from a dominantly conservative or protective adherence to traditional forms—opens up the possibility of a responsible search for appropriate liturgical symbols and forms on the internet. Naturally, this is not an immediate, positive judgment on the formal and theological qualities of all liturgical celebrations online. Some earlier examples of such celebrations certainly exhibited a range of problems in both form and content, not least because they tended to oversimplify. What is at stake here, rather, is the possibility of a peaceful coexistence of online liturgies with the larger historical liturgical life of the church, a coexistence in which liturgies in cyberspace can stand next to the offline liturgical life in which they continue to be rooted.

Directives and guidelines will have to be formulated by the church regarding the quality and forms of online liturgies. The first step may lie in discerning which new technology-driven possibilities are appropriate for liturgical celebrations in the contemporary world. The second step is to develop criteria to assess the almost overwhelming diversity of liturgical expressions online, to inquire into their correspondence with the fundamentals of the Christian faith, and, where needed, to correct these expressions online. In both tasks the core issue is the negotiation between past and present, between tradition and innovation. Liturgical tradition and contemporary technological innovation are not two different options; rather, the two must be held together if Christian liturgy is not to ossify.

4. *Signa Sensibilia*[21] *Are a Crucial Dimension of Liturgical Life, Yet One That Is Significantly Reduced Online*

Exploring rituals online holds its own fascination, yet these rituals also quickly become contested terrain when compared with traditional forms of liturgical life. The problem is particularly evident whenever liturgical rituals, symbols, and actions involve the physical presence of a congregation. Liturgy lives in sensory, embodied forms; it engages human beings in their bodily senses and derives much of its power precisely from this. If a liturgical celebration is to open up space for an encounter between God and human beings, then this encounter cannot but include the whole of the human person. Even if embodiment does not capture the entirety of the human person, it is nevertheless the way in which human beings live their personhood. The encounter with God thus involves not only spiritual attentiveness, an inner turning, but also outward expressions that stand in close union with the inner attitude. Such

---

21. Constitution on the Sacred Liturgy: "symbols perceptible by the senses," ibid., no. 7, p. 121.

outward expressions in worship might be the acts of listening, seeing, smelling, tasting, and walking together. It is at this point that a problem arises for the internet, in that medial communication proceeds largely without physical components. The communication is virtual. Most forms of embodied expression therefore disappear in online rituals. At the same time, this is no reason simply to deny the importance and relevance of these spiritual encounters. We cannot discount the spiritual power of these rituals and the fact that they are indeed often experienced as liturgical celebrations. As such, online liturgies are relevant even if they may not involve embodiment in the way liturgical anthropology has hitherto conceived of it. Obviously, one should not underestimate the virtual nature of online liturgies, yet insisting that the internet promotes obliviousness of the body also misses the mark. After all, without a body to access the internet, there is no virtual life to be had. And the technical requirements for accessing the internet are all consistently subject to the laws of space and time. Materiality thus is an integral part even of technological mediality. Emphasizing the liturgical importance of *signa sensibilia* should therefore not lead us to exclude online liturgies from consideration of what counts as liturgy. Rather, a thoughtful and constructive engagement is called for, as well as an exploration of the internet's ecclesial and liturgical potential.

IV. Areas of Future Growth and Exploration

Without seeking to foretell the future, we can find clear indications of an ongoing diversification of the internet's liturgical culture. Its diversity will intensify, and its allure will in all likelihood increase. All indications suggest that such diversification is taking place in liturgical life both online and offline[22]—and this presents a challenge to the church's liturgy. What I have sketched above as a liturgical-theological vision needs to be developed further in order to engage in the much-needed intentional dialogue between liturgics and the internet. In this essay, I have offered an initial foray into the realm of ecclesial internet presence, with a twin focus on both praxis orientation and the grounding of all ecclesial praxis in the Christian *kerygma*. What conclusions can be drawn for Christian praxis? Where might boundaries have to be established? The following two questions help to concretize this inquiry: Can one absolve online?[23]

---

22. See Gerard Lukken, *Rituals in Abundance: Critical Reflections on the Place, Form and Identity of Christian Ritual in Our Culture* (Dudley, MA: Peeters, 2005).

23. A private and (probably) not entirely serious homepage offers "confessions" online; see www.beichte.de.

Can the Eucharist and other sacraments be carried out online? Using terms such as "liturgy" and "sacrament" in the context of cyberspace suggests that we are pondering nothing but a simple introduction of established liturgical forms and practices into a new medium, but as contemporary practices of liturgy on the internet make clear, we are not confronted with an online copy of an offline rite. The task is not to package traditional liturgical celebrations in the attractive technology of our times. This would amount to an attempt to reduce the internet to its practical use for pastoral purposes, thereby obliterating the specific opportunities that accompany every distinct mode of communication. Rather, the internet calls for a creative liturgical spirit and requires the development of new liturgical forms.[24] This implies neither a relativizing nor a distancing from established forms. Rather, the decisive challenge, as I perceive it, is to find liturgical expressions compatible with the technical possibilities of the internet and to engage and harvest their potential.

Certainly, the path is narrow on this search for the appropriate interface between liturgy and internet and invariably leads to border crossings. The intersection is a risky one; possible misunderstandings abound. Accordingly, a good number of critics consider liturgy and the internet quite incompatible or even conceive of liturgy as opposed to the growing influence of the media.[25] Michael Belzer's advice is helpful here: "Ecclesial content online needs liturgical elements, and these must be developed based on the specific nature of the internet. It is advisable, in an early phase of such development, not to draw the boundaries of the permissible too narrowly, thereby robbing the spirit of this new, virtual community of its creative breath."[26]

However, even if the Christian churches developed theologically grounded liturgical elements on the basis of the internet's unique possibilities, we should not set our expectations too high. Such online liturgies would not be a cure-all for the churches' contemporary problems, such as the loss of membership or even the loss of faith. These problems will not be solved simply by relocating an old message to a new medium in the hope that this might increase its

---

24. See my *Gottesdienste im Internet*, 297–304.

25. See Craig A. Baron, "Sacraments 'Really Save' in Disneyland: Reconciling Bodies in Virtual Reality," *Questions Liturgiques/Studies in Liturgy* 86 (2005): 284–305; Klaus Müller, "Wechsel und Verkettung: Medienphilosophische Grenzziehungen in Sachen Liturgie," in *"Das sei euer vernünftiger Gottesdienst" (Röm 12,1): Liturgiewissenschaft und Philosophie im Dialog*, ed. Stephen Winter (Regensburg: Friedrich Pustet, 2006), 264–82.

26. Michael Belzer, *Internetseelsorge: Der Leitfaden für die Praxis* (Stuttgart: Katholisches Bibelwerk, 2004), 162f.

attractiveness. Furthermore, it remains to be seen whether an internet user in front of a screen would take the plunge from cyberspace into a worship service at a parish church. To encourage such an expectation overlooks the plurality of online religious life, in which Christian ritual forms exist among many others. On the other hand, I also do not share the fear that basic liturgical forms are about to be relativized or replaced by the communication forms and social processes of the internet. The latter do not provide an alternative to the historically developed liturgy. Whether congregants assemble in a church building or online will not, in the future, become irrelevant. At the same time, we should not all too quickly reject the internet's potential but rather engage in the—unquestionably challenging yet also intriguing—process of testing Christian liturgical identity and new rituals in electronic contexts.

My central thesis here is this: Christian rituals online can supplement and expand established liturgical forms but cannot replace them. This claim does not imply any final decision about specific online rituals or web sites, but it does open a door for an expansion of liturgical forms beyond the established liturgical order, an expansion through which God's salvation can become accessible through new symbolic elements.[27] I note that in such a claim liturgical fundamentals such as spatial presence and embodiment are not simply consigned to oblivion, as some critics might assume.

As risky as online liturgy might be, it also has advantages. Developments of new liturgical elements online create an explicit witness against religious indifference—an indifference that is alive and well both online and offline. Investing in the internet's ritual capital opens up the possibility of representing Christian faith and symbols under the new conditions of an online medial-aesthetic space. This possibility is of course predicated on a clearly recognizable Christian identity of online rites. Strongly individualistic tendencies in most internet communities remain problematic here. The church can counteract such tendencies by supporting interactive rites online that appeal to individual life situations while also challenging their isolation. Individual spiritualities and ecclesial involvement are not alternatives. Both must find their home in a liturgy that is at the same time a celebration of shared faith and also an open invitation to every seeker. In practice, therefore, online forms that allow for contact between users should be supported. Such contact can be deepened by offering regular meetings online at specific spiritual sites. Finally, the connections between internet liturgical forms and established ecclesial forms offline

---

27. I develop this thesis in greater detail in my *Gottesdienste im Internet*, 225–47.

must remain recognizable. Fundamental liturgical principles, as explicated, for example, in the Constitution on the Sacred Liturgy of Vatican II, remain valid even in cyberspace. No matter how much one wants to encourage a spirit of liturgical exploration and innovation, the Bible as the Word of God, prayer as humanity's response to the Word of God, and the ecclesial grounding of all liturgical life are conditions sine qua non. Abandoning these would lead to a religious patchwork identity and an elevation of the internet to a cryptoreligious status.

The church, in the confession and celebration of its faith on the journey through time, has always been shaped by the challenges of the signs of the times in which it lived. These challenges typically cannot be solved either by radical separation or by total assimilation and immersion. The church's enduring place is "in between"—in the space between the "sanctification of human beings" and the "glorification of God,"[28] in between the "celebration of faith" and the "meaning of one's life,"[29] in the constant movement of seeking, from which the church cannot absent itself without denying its own identity. The German liturgical scholar Angelus A. Häußling describes it thus:

> The subject matter of liturgics has ceased to be an intraecclesial reality. Just as the church opened its doors toward the world and sought to find its place in the world in which human beings find themselves, turning its attention from churchgoing Christians alone to human beings as such, thereby thinking toward all who—created by God, saved by Christ, and called by the Spirit—potentially belong to the community of faith, so too the subject matter of liturgics is no longer simply the praying church alone. . . . Rather, the subject matter of liturgics is now . . . the human person.[30]

Some will disagree. They will perceive the existence of a plurality of liturgical expressions, in different spaces and under different forms, as a threat and as a watering down of the church's established liturgical life or even of the Christian *kerygma*. A few recent Vatican communiqués have regrettably

---

28. Vatican II's Dogmatic Constitution on the Church, no. 10.

29. Benedikt Kranemann, "Glaubensfeier und Lebensdeutung. Zur missionarischen Dimension des Kirchenjahres," in *Die missionarische Dimension der Liturgie: Gott feiern in nachchristlicher Gesellschaft*, vol. 1, ed. Klemens Richter and Franz-Peter Tebartz van Elst (Stuttgart: Katholisches Bibelwerk, 1998), 70–83.

30. Angelus A. Häußling, "Liturgiewissenschaftliche Aufgabenfelder vor uns," in *Christliche Identität aus der Liturgie: Theologische und historische Studien zum Gottesdienst der Kirche*, ed. Martin Klöckener et al. (Münster: Aschendorff, 1997), 321–33, here 326f.

conveyed this impression—as if uniformity were the most important principle of liturgical life. More hopeful here is a scenario that the sociologist Hans Joas suggests: "Pluralism does not weaken faith. . . . In fact, it can, under certain conditions, strengthen it."[31]

Liturgical practice is moving toward a far greater diversity than has hitherto been familiar. The end point should be a thoughtful, balanced view of the new media technologies, able to appreciate that an encounter with God can be ritually mediated online. Neither a euphoric adoption of the still-emerging world of electronic media, in a manner that ultimately expresses only the church's sense of helplessness, nor an anxious distancing, which is just as hopeless, are adequate responses to a religiously pluriform medium like the internet. As the pastoral theologian Thomas Böhm has argued, "using tools of social communication and the participation of the church in the media are necessary on the one hand. On the other hand, this engagement must not simply happen instrumentally and functionally but rather must lead—as a process of inculturation—the media and also the church to a better self-understanding. Within this framework, neither ecclesial abstinence from the media, in response to its sometimes questionable forms, nor unconditional enthusiasm, fueled by the evident power of the media, is theologically defensible."[32]

This path will entail strain and conflict, convincing solutions, and missteps. The way forward, however, lies neither in a backward-focused model of ritual uniformity nor in the quick adoption of every media fad. The most important task at this point is to foster and develop forms of Christian liturgy and spirituality *in* as well as *for* the contemporary world in which we live.[33] The internet is an intriguing and powerful site for responding to this task, as long as its power is not permitted to generate crippling fear. In times of reorientation, fear is never a good advisor.

---

31. Hans Joas, "Glaube und Moral im Zeitalter der Kontingenz," in his *Braucht der Mensch Religion? Über Erfahrungen der Selbsttranszendenz* (Freiburg in Breisgau: Herder, 2004), 32–49, here 45; English translation: *Do We Need Religion? On the Experience of Transcendence*, trans. Alex Skinner (Boulder, CO: Paradigm, 2008).

32. Thomas H. Böhm, *Religion durch Medien: Kirche in den Medien und die "Medienreligion": Eine problemorientierte Analyse und Leitlinien einer theologischen Hermeneutik*, Praktische Theologie 76 (Stuttgart: Kohlhammer, 2005), 314.

33. See Bryan D. Spinks, *The Worship Mall: Contemporary Responses to Contemporary Culture*, Alcuin Club Collections 85 (London: SPCK, 2011), 183–211, esp. 211.

Contributors

Teresa Berger is professor of liturgical studies at the Yale Institute of Sacred Music (ISM) and Yale Divinity School. She holds doctorates in both liturgical studies and systematic theology. Her publications include *Fragments of Real Presence* (2005), *Gender Differences and the Making of Liturgical History* (2011), and a volume of essays based on the 2008 ISM liturgy conference, *The Spirit in Worship—Worship in the Spirit*, which she coedited with Bryan D. Spinks (2009).

Kazimierz Bem currently serves as pastor of First Church in Marlborough (Congregational) United Church of Christ, in Massachusetts. He graduated from law school in Poland and received his PhD in international law from the Vrije Universiteit in Amsterdam, the Netherlands. Bem obtained his master of divinity (2010) and master of sacred theology (2012) from Yale Divinity School. His research interests center around the history of the Polish Reformed Church.

Stefan Böntert is professor of liturgical studies at the Catholic Theological Faculty of the University of Bochum, Germany. One of his particular research interests is the intersection between liturgy and the new media. His publications include *Gottesdienst im Internet: Perspektiven eines Dialogs zwischen Internet und Liturgie* (2005) and, most recently, *Friedlicher Kreuzzug und fromme Pilger: Liturgiehistorische Studien zur Heilig-Land-Wallfahrt im Spiegel deutschsprachiger Pilgerberichte des späten 19. Jahrhunderts* (2012).

Mary K. Farag is a doctoral student in the ancient Christianity program at Yale University's Religious Studies Department. She completed a master's degree in liturgical studies at Yale Divinity School in 2009 and has published essays on the history of eucharistic prayers in *Studia Liturgica* and *Le Muséon*.

Charles E. Farhadian is associate professor of world religions and Christian mission at Westmont College, Santa Barbara, California. His publications include *Christianity, Islam, and Nationalism in Indonesia* (2007), *Christian Worship Worldwide: Expanding Horizons, Deepening Practices* (2007), *The Testimony Project: Papua* (2007), and, most recently, *Introducing World Christianity* (2012).

Raúl Gómez-Ruiz, SDS, is a priest of the Society of the Divine Savior (Salvatorians) and formerly served as vice president for academic affairs, director of intellectual formation, and professor of systematic studies at Sacred Heart School of Theology in Hales Corners, Wisconsin. He now serves as director of accreditation and institutional evaluation for the Association of Theological Schools in the United States and Canada, Commission on Accrediting, in Pittsburgh, Pennsylvania. He earned a doctorate in liturgical studies from the Catholic University of America (Washington, DC) and is the author of the award-winning *Mozarabs, Hispanics, and the Cross* (2007) and of *Quinceañera: Order of the Blessing on the Fifteenth Birthday* and *Quinceañera: La bendición al cumplir los quince años* (both 2010).

Kostis Kourelis is assistant professor of art history at Franklin and Marshall College in Lancaster, Pennsylvania. An architectural historian and archaeologist of the medieval Mediterranean, he holds a PhD in art and archaeology of the Mediterranean world from the University of Pennsylvania. His special research interests include urbanism, historic preservation, landscape archaeology, and architectural theory. Among Kourelis's publications is a special issue of *The International Journal of Historical Archaeology* (14/2 [2010]), titled *The Abandoned Countryside: (Re)Settlement in the Archaeological Narrative of Post-Classical Greece*, which he coedited with William R. Caraher.

Clemens Leonhard is professor of liturgical studies at the Catholic Theological Faculty of the University of Münster, Germany. In 2011–12 he was a fellow at the Institute for Advanced Study at Wissenschaftskolleg in Berlin. His publications include *The Jewish Pesach and the Origins of the Christian Easter: Open Questions in Current Research* (2006) and a volume of essays coedited with Albert Gerhards, *Jewish and Christian Liturgy and Worship: New Insights into Its History and Interaction* (2007).

Vasileios Marinis is assistant professor of Christian art and architecture at the Yale Institute of Sacred Music and Yale Divinity School. His research focuses on the art and architecture of early Christianity and the Middle Ages. Marinis has published on a variety of topics ranging from early Christian tunics decorated with New Testament scenes to medieval tombs and Byzantine nuns. During his year (2011–12) as a member at the Institute for Advanced Study in Princeton, he completed a monograph on the interaction of architecture and ritual in the medieval churches of Constantinople.

Anne McGowan received a PhD in theology with a concentration in liturgical studies from the University of Notre Dame in 2011. Her dissertation, "In Search of the Spirit: The Epiclesis in Early Eucharistic Praying and Contemporary Western Liturgical Reforms," explored the historical and theological influence of the eucharistic epiclesis on the shape and content of the current eucharistic rites of several major Western churches. She spent the 2011–12 academic year as a postdoctoral associate in liturgical studies at the Yale Institute of Sacred Music in New Haven, Connecticut.

Gisela Muschiol is professor of medieval and modern church history at the Catholic Faculty of the University of Bonn, Germany. Her particular research interests are the history of religious orders in the Middle Ages and women's and gender history. Muschiol is the author of *Famula Dei: Zur Liturgie in merowingischen Frauenklöstern* (1994) and *Das Bistum Münster*, coauthored with Wilhelm Damberg (2005), and the editor of *Katholikinnen und Moderne* (2003).

Kay Kaufman Shelemay is the G. Gordon Watts Professor of Music and a professor of African and African American studies at Harvard University. An ethnomusicologist who has carried out fieldwork in Ethiopia and its diaspora, in Israel, and within the United States, she is a past president of the Society for Ethnomusicology and a member of the American Academy of Arts and Sciences and the American Academy for Jewish Research. Her publications include *Ethiopian Christian Liturgical Chant*, vols. 1–3 (1993, 1994, 1997); *Let Jasmine Rain Down: Song and Remembrance among Syrian Jews* (1998); *Soundscapes: Exploring Music in a Changing World* (2001, 2006); and *Creating the Ethiopian Diaspora*, a special double issue of the journal *Diaspora* (2011), coedited with Steven Kaplan.

Jonathan Y. Tan is senior lecturer in the study of religion and liturgical studies at Australian Catholic University's School of Theology in Strathfield, Australia.

He holds a PhD in religion and culture from the Catholic University of America (Washington, DC) and an MA in liturgical studies from the Graduate Theological Union. He is the author of *Introducing Asian American Theologies* (2008) and sixty essays, articles, and book chapters on a wide range of theological issues.

Karen B. Westerfield Tucker is professor of worship at the Boston University School of Theology and a presbyter in the United Methodist Church. She is the author of *American Methodist Worship* (2001) and coeditor of *The Oxford History of Christian Worship* (2006). A former president of the international and ecumenical Societas Liturgica, she has been the editor-in-chief of the society's journal, *Studia Liturgica*, since 2004. She is serving as the cosecretary of the international dialogue between the World Methodist Council and the Roman Catholic Church for the years 2011–16.

Graham Ward is the Regius Professor of Divinity at the University of Oxford and former head of the School of Arts, Histories and Cultures at the University of Manchester. Among his books are *Cities of God* (2000), *Cultural Transformation and Religious Practice* (2005), *True Religion* (2003), *Christ and Culture* (2005), and *The Politics of Discipleship* (2009). He edits three book series: Christian Theology in Context (Oxford University Press), Illuminations (Blackwell), and Studies in Theology and Political Culture (Continuum).

Index

active participation, 288
Adogame, Afe, 269–70, 277
afikoman, 20, 22
African Initiated Churches (AICs), 267–68
   in Ethiopia, 267
   Pentecostal-charismatic, 268
   Zionist, 267–68
Agenda of 1637, 125–30
Ahmad b. Ibrahim al-Gazi, 231
Alba, Richard, xiin5
Alemahyehu, Gabriel, 234, 235
Allchin, A. M., 198n72
Álvarez Martínez, Francisco, 215n18
Ameling, Walter, 23n6, 24n9, 27n16
Anagnostou, Yiorgos, 171
Anaphora of Basil, Egyptian, 203–7
   epiclesis, 204–7
Anaphora of St. James, 194, 196n62
Andaya, Barbara Watson, 272n17
Anderson, Benedict, 6
Andrewes, Lancelot, 191
Apostolic Constitutions, 56–59, 62–63, 194, 196n62, 203n86
Aquinas, Thomas, St., 14
Archbishop Athenagoras, 158
Archbishop Iakovos, 159
Archbishop Michael, 159, 160, 162
Arellano, A., 210n3

Arellano García, Mario, 222
Arian controversy, 60, 108n44, 120
Aristotle, 13–14
Arnhard, Carl von, 44n8, 46
Arranz, Miguel, 44n9
Asad, Talal, 8–9
Ashkenazi Jews, 20
Asian American heterogeneity, 244
   1.5 generation, 243
   adoptees, 250
   biracial, 249
   Catholics, 243–57
   Chinese, 245, 248, 256–57
   hapa-haole, 249
   hybridity, 243–46
   Vietnamese, 245–46, 254, 257
assembly, church as, 286–88
Assmann, Jan, 210, 219–21
Augustine, St., 1n1, 13–14
Avadah Zarah, 23n7

Badger, George Percy, 191
Baldovin, John, 222–23, 224
baptism, 37, 201–2
Barcelona Anaphora, 32n29
Baron, Craig A., 292n25
Barral I Altet, Xavier, 211n5
Barth, Karl, 13–14
Basil of Caesarea, 44

Baudrillard, Jean, 6
Baumstark, Anton, 181n6
Beauduin, Lambert, 190
Bell, Catherine, 246
belonging, xviii, 1–16
   evolutionary, 14
   and liturgy, 12–14
   virtual, 6–12
Belzer, Michael, 292
Benedictines, 84–85, 89
Benjamin, Walter, 15, 253
berakhot, 30
Bergjan, Silke-Petra, 54–55
Bessarion, Cardinal, 185n19
Bethlehem Kuravanci, 275
Bible, 272–73, 294
   Genesis 1:27, 13–14
   Exodus 2:1-22, 250
   Exodus 12, 26, 27
   Exodus 15, 47
   Exodus 17, 47
   Deuteronomy 8:10, 31n27
   Deuteronomy 16, 27
   3 Reigns 18, 47
   4 Kings 2, 47
   Psalm 75:8 (LXX), 46
   Jeremiah 5:22, 57
   Matthew 7:6, 32n30
   Luke 1:38, 1–2
   John 19:34, 2
   John 19:36, 25
   Acts 2:1-4+38, 201
   1 Corinthians 5:7, 25
   1 Corinthians 11, 33n32
   1 Corinthians 12:12, 6n16
   1 Corinthians 14:15, 152
   Philippians 2:7, 52
   see also the chart on page 64
Bibles, Polish, 123, 124, 127–28, 130
Binns, John, 180n5
Birhanu, Tsehai, 233, 234, 235–36, 238–39

birkat hamazon, 29–34, 41
blessings after meals, 29–34, 41
Böhm, Thomas, 295
Böhnke, Michael, 286n15
Bollandists, 196
Bollmann, Anne, 87n11
Book of Common Prayer, 133, 193–94, 202, 204–7
Book of Common Worship, 204–7
Boulay, A. du, 43n2, 46
Bouley, Allan, 30n24
Bousset, Wilhelm, 57n33
Boyarin, Daniel, 19, 21, 25
Bradshaw, Paul F., xv–xvi, 29n23, 37n42, 38, 45n10, 196n61
Brandis, Wolfgang, 89n18
bread and water, 37–38
Brent, Alan, 39n48
Brethren, Polish, 104–9, 114–19
Brettell, Caroline B., xiin5
Brightman, Frank, 192n45, 194n56, 197
Brock, Sebastian, 44n9, 61n49
Buchinger, Harald, 36n37
Budge, E. A. Wallis, 45–46, 230n2
Bursfeld and Windesheim Congregations, 85, 88–89, 92–100
Busch, Johannes, 85, 97
Byzantinization, 200, 203
Byzantine baptismal water-blessing, 44
Byzantine Orthodox churches, 186
Byzantine tradition, 162, 164, 167

Caeremoniale Bursfeldensis, 88n16, 96
Calvin, John, 104, 105
Calvinists, 105, 107–8, 118, 119, 123, 127
Campbell, Heidi A., 279n3, 281n8
Campese, Gioacchino, xiiin9
Cañizares Llovera, Antonio, 215n18
Carey, Joseph, 251n18
Carillo Morales, Enrique, Don, 211–13
Castells, Manuel, 7n18

Castles, Stephen, xin3
Castoriadis, Cornelius, 6n11
catechisms, Polish, 120–21
catechesis, 15
Catholics,
  1.5 generation, 243
  Asian American, 243–57
  Polish, 101–2, 115, 120, 129
Cavanaugh, William T., xiii
Certeau, Michel de, 6
Chan, Simon, 252–53
Charlemagne, xvii
chrismation formula, 200–203
Christ, prayers addressed to, 60–61, 63
Christendom, medieval, 9
Christianity, 259–60
  in Africa, 267–70
  in China, 275–76
  in India, 274–75
  in Indonesia, 272–73
  in Malaysia, 273
  in Papua, 262–67, 273
  in Peru, 272
Christology, 60, 62
Chrysippus, 53
church, 1
  as assembly, 288
Church of England, 132–35, 136
Ciallella, Pietro, xiiin9
Cistercians, 84–85, 89
Clinton, Fynes, 190n39
codices
  Barberini gr. 336, 43, 45, 192
  British Museum, add. 14, 494, 43
collegia, 21–22, 27n16, 28, 34, 41
"A Common Eucharistic Prayer," 187–88, 191, 205–7
Common Worship, 204, 205–7
Compain, Alice, 145, 147n38
Concilium, xiii
confirmation (sacrament), 200–207
Congar, Yves, 251

convents of nuns, 83–100
  Ebstorf Abbey, 92, 94–95
  Heideklöster, 89
  Lüne Abbey, 92, 95–97
  Medingen convent, 92, 99–100
  Schönensteinbach Abbey, 87
  Wienhausen convent, 92, 97–99
Conybeare, Frederick C., 43n1, 45, 197
Coquin, René-Georges, 45n11
Córdoba, Francisco de Sales, 210n3
Cosin, John, 191
Council of Florence, 185, 186
Council of Trent, 193n51
Couturier, Paul, 190
Cranmer, Thomas, 193
creation, 49–51, 58–59
Cristea, Hans-Joachim, 60n46, 61n48
Crosby, Fanny, 144
cross, the, 210, 225–26; *see also* Lignum
  Crucis, Stations of the Cross
Cruz, Gemma Talud, xiii
cultural change, xv
Cuming, Geoffrey J., 191, 203n86
cyberspace, 279–95
Cyprian, 38–40, 41

Damasio, Antonio, 11
Daneel, Marthinus L., 268
Daniélou, Jean, 45n11
Davalos, Karen Mary, 224n45
Davie, Grace, 2–3, 4
Debord, Guy, 6
Degler-Spengler, Brigitte, 84n3
Deleuze, Gilles, 6, 10
Denysenko, Nicholas E., 44n9
Derg, 232, 233
devotio moderna, 85
diaspora
  Ethiopian, 233, 235–42
  Jewish, 27, 28n19, 29, 41
Didache, 29–33
Didascalia, 28

304 Index

Didymus the Blind, 55n29
Diels, Herman, 53n21
"digital immigrants," 280
"digital natives," 280
Dijk, Mathilde van, 85n5
Diogenes Laertius, 53–54
disembedding, 14–15, 270–74
Dominican Observance, 84, 87–92, 100
Doraisamy, Theodore R., 141n25
Dura Europos fragment, 30–31, 33

Easter, 20, 26–29, 41
  Quartodeciman, 28, 41
Eastern Christian worship
  liturgical texts, 191–98
  liturgical units, 199–207
  westward migration of, 181
East-West liturgical exchange, 179–208
Edrei, Arye, 24n8, 27
Egeria, 185, 223
Ehrenschwendtner, Marie-Luise, 86n8
El Greco, 210
Elizondo, Virgilio, 216n20, 219
embodiment, 9–11, 290–91
enclosure, 83, 85–86
Engberding, Hieronymus, 44n9
epiclesis, 52, 61–62, 63, 204–7
Epiphany prayers, 43–46, 57–59
Espín, Orlando, 252–55
Ethiopian liturgy, 229–42
  liturgical mission, 235–37
Ethiopian Orthodox Church, 229–42
  architecture, 238
  Cathedral Office, 232
  diaspora, 233, 235–38, 240–42
  forced migration, 231, 232–33
  history, 230–33
  Hymnary, 232, 236
  Mass, 231–32
  Synaxary, 230
Eucharist, 32n29, 33, 34–40
eucharistic prayers, 59, 203–7

Eugenides, Jeffery, 171
Eusebius of Caesarea, 54–55
Every, George, 195–96
evolution, liturgical, xv
excarnation, 9–10

Facebook, 280
fasting, 28
Felbecker, Sabine, 225n46
Fellowship of St. Alban and St. Sergius, 189
Felten, Franz J., 84nn2–3
Férotin, Marius, 211n8
Fiaccadori, Gianfranco, 230n1
Fiensy, David A., 57n32
Fine, Steven, 30n25
Forma (Kraiński), 111–12, 126
Forma ac Ratio (Łaski), 107–8, 111–12, 120, 121, 123, 126, 127, 129
Fortescue, Adrian, 180, 181
Foskett, Mary, 249, 250
Foucault, Michel, 8
four elements, seasons, etc., 50, 56, 57, 58
Freckmann, Anje, 85n4
Frere, Walter, 190n39
Frey, Jean-Baptiste, 23n6

Gaillardetz, Richard R., 280n6
Galen, 56
Gan, Mary, 144
García-Villoslada, Ricardo, 213n14
Ge'ez syllabary, 231
"Generation @," 284
Gerhards, Albert, 60n44
Giddens, Anthony, 260, 271, 272
Giles, Charles, 140–41
Gilles, Beate, 284n13
globalization, 10, 15, 259–62, 270–74
Glory Hut, 265–67
Glykon Zeuxianos Aelianus, 22–25, 40
Gnosticism, 10

God
　ineffability of, 51–52
　names for, 272
　providence of, 53–59
Goizueta, Robert, 225–26
Goldbeck, Fabian, 39n48
Goleman, Daniel, 11
González Martín, Marcelo, 214n16
Good Friday, 20, 210
Gorsky, Jonathan, 25n12
Grabe, Johannes, 197
grace after meals, 29–34, 41
Gracia, Jorge J. E., 218n21
"Great art Thou," 43–82
　editions, 45–46
　phraseology, 49–53
　structure, 46–49
　terminology, 53–56
　texts, 43–44, 63, 65–82
Greco-Roman symposia, 35–40
Greek Orthodox architecture, 163–75
Greek Orthodox Church in America, 155–75
Greek Orthodox churches
　Annunciation, Lancaster, PA, 170, 175
　Annunciation, Milwaukee, 172
　Los Angeles, Cathedral, 173
　Saint George, Philadelphia, 167–70, 174
Greek Orthodox liturgy
　Divine Liturgy, 159–60
　Hesperinos, 160, 162
　hymns, 160–61, 162
　language in, 158–61
　Orthros, 160, 162
　practices, 161
　use of organ, 163
　weddings, 163
　Western practices, 162–63
Grillmeier, Aloys, 60–61
Grimes, Ronald L., 216n19

Grisbrooke, W. Jardine, 197n66
Grodzicki, Adam, 115n90
Groody, Daniel G., xin2, xiiin9, xiiin11

Hahn (Nordlingen), Joseph, 20
Haile Selassie I, Emperor, 232
Hall, Stuart G., 197n68
Hammer, Elke-Ursel, 85n4
Hammond, Charles, 197
Handel, George Frederick, 134n4
Hannerz, Ulf, 270
hapa-haole, 249
Harland, Philip, 23, 25
Harnack, Adolf, 37
Härtel, Helmut, 92n35
Harvey, David, 4n5
Hatchett, Marion J., 206n92
Haubroe, L. P., 275
Häußling, Angelus A., 294
Haviland, John, 168
He, Qi, 275–76
Hegel, Georg W. F., 3
Heldman, Marilyn, 238n8
Hellenistic terminology, 49, 53–56, 62
heretics and heresies, 10, 21
Hispanics, 209–27
Hitchcock, Richard, 210n1
Hobbes, Thomas, 13
Hobsbawm, Eric, 246–47
Hoelzl, Michael, 3n3
Hofmeister, Philipp, 94n37
Hollifield, James F., xiin5
Holy Spirit as Gift, 201
Hussites, 186
hybridity, 243–46
hymnody, 133–34, 142–50, 160–61, 162, 232, 236, 261
　in Papua, 263, 266
　in Zimbabwe, 269

incarnation, 52, 59, 62
inculturation, liturgical, 247–48, 281

Index

India, 274–75
"intentional participation," 285
internet, 279–95
   Christian websites, 281–82
   embodiment on, 290–91
   the Eucharist online, 292
   as interactive, 283, 286–88
   as a liturgical medium, 282–84
   as a liturgical space, 282–83, 288
   meditations on, 283
   rituals on, 290–91
   sacraments on, 292
Irvin, Dale, 252, 253–54

Jacob of Edessa, 44
Jaintner, Klaus, 95n43
Jameson, Frederic, 4n5
Jasper, R. C. D., 203n86
Jeffery, Peter, 231n5
Jeggle-Merz, Birgit, 284n13
Jesuits, 259
Jesus, death, 25–29
Jewish Diaspora, 27, 28n19, 29, 41
Jewish Halakha, 20
Joas, Hans, 295
Johnson, Mark, 11
Johnson, Maxwell E., 45n10, 202n83
Johnson, Todd, 260
Jubilees 22, 31n27
Justin Martyr, 32n29, 36–38, 40, 41

Kalu, Ogbu U., 267
Kant, Immanuel, 3
Kaplan, Steven, 233n6
Karstensen, Angela, 99n64
Kavanagh, Aidan, 200n78, 201–2
Keay, Simon J., 222
Keen, Ralph, 195–96
Kelm, Elfriede, 88n15
Kendrick, Graham, 12
Kerr, Fergus, 15
Khmer songs, 147–50

Khouri-Sarkis, G., 43n2, 46
Kim, Sandra S., 260n1
Kimbrough, S T, Jr., 145n36, 146, 148–49
Kirchschläger, Walter, 288n18
Knight, Kimberly, 282n12
Kochlewski, Piotr, 128
Kohwagner-Nikolai, Tanja, 96nn51–52
Kopecek, Thomas A., 60nn42–43
Kourelis, Kostis, 168n42
Kraft, Claudia, xviin22
Kraiński, Krzysztof, 109–15, 117
Kranemann, Benedikt, 294n29
Krowicki, Marcin, 103, 105

Lähnemann, Henrike, 86n8 et al.
Lakoff, George, 11
Lampe, John Frederick, 134n4
Lara, Jaime, 223nn40–41
Łaski, Jan, 104, 106–8, 111–12, 120, 126
Last Supper, 37, 38n47, 40, 41
Lathbury, Mary, 144
Latinos, 254
LeDoux, Joseph E., 11
Lee, Jesse, 143n32
Leonhard, Karen I., xiin5
Lesser, Bertram, 85n5
Lesser Poland Reformed Church, 104–15, 117
Leszczyński, Andrzej, 114
Letter of Barnabas, 29n21
Levebvre, Solange, xiiin8
Levine, Donald N., 240–42
Lignum Crucis, 211–12, 214–16, 221–22, 225
Lim, Swee Hong, 144–47, 152
Lingas, Alexander, 161n25
Linneborn, Johannes, 85n4
Lipgens, Walter, 196n60
"liquid church," 10, 15
Lithuanian Reformed Church, 107, 119–30

liturgical development, xv–xvii
  disembedding in, 270–74
  monoculture in, 261
  in Papua, 262–64
  proliferation in, 264, 270
  standardization in, 261–62
  women's roles, 265–66
  in worship language, 266–70
liturgical migration, xiv–xvii
liturgical reform, 289
liturgical texts, migration of, 191–98
liturgical units, 199–207
liturgy, 1, 12–14, 288–95
  online, 290–93
Liturgy in Migration (ISM conference), xiv, xxi–xxiii
Liturgy of St. Basil, 194
Liturgy of St. John Chrysostom, 193–94
Liturgy of the Word, 34–40
Lord's Supper, 277
  Methodist practice, 137, 140
  Reformed, 101–2, 106–9, 112, 121, 123, 124, 126
Lowe, Kevin, 136n9 et al.
Lowe, Lisa, 244n2
Luhmann, Niklas, 280
Lukken, Gerard, 291n22
Lunar New Year liturgy, 245, 254
Lutheran Book of Worship, 202
Lutheranism, 102, 110, 113, 118

Mabillon, Jean, 196
Mager, Inge, 85n4
Maltzew, Alexios von, 46n16
Mam (Mom), Barnabas, 147
Mao, Vinna, 145
Mar Thoma Syrian Church, 184
Marcus Aurelius, 54
Marinis, Vasileios, 163n32
Marrassini, Paolo, 231n3
Marx, Karl, 3
Mary, Virgin, 1–2, 238

Masaai, 273
Masqal, 241
Mass, medieval, 37
Matovina, Timothy M., 216n20
Maurists, 196
McGowan, Andrew, 36n40, 37, 38
McGowan, Anne, 61n49
McLean, A. J., 43n1
McManus, Frederick R., 193n51
Mecham, June L., 97n54
media, 6–7
Melito of Sardis, St., 26–29, 41
Melkite Catholics, 190
Melville, Gert, 85n6
Mendels, Doron, 24n8, 27
Mengistu Haile Mariam, 233
Meßner, Reinhard, 32n28, 35n36, 38n44
Mestre Sanchis, Antonio, 214n15
Methodism
  in Cambodia, 135–36, 139, 142, 145, 152, 153
  and the Church of England, 132–35, 136
  in London, 131–32
  and migration, 153–54
  missionizing period, 134
  in Singapore, 136, 138–39, 141–42, 144–45, 150, 151–52, 153
  three generations, 134–36, 153–54
  worship practices, 131–54
Methodism, characteristics of
  assembly space, 133, 140–42
  formal and informal worship, 136–40
  hymns and songs, 133, 142–50
  prayer styles, 134, 150–53
Methodist Episcopal Church, 134, 136–51
Metzger, Marcel, 60n42
Meyer, Hans Bernhard, 34n35
Meyer, Johannes, 89–92
Meyer, Stephenie, 12

migrating nuns, 83–100
migration, xxii
   Greek, 164
   Jewish/Christian, 19–42
migration conferences, xiiin14
migration of liturgical units, 199–207
migration studies, xii–xiii
Mikołajewski, Daniel, 118
Milbank, John, 15
Miller, Mark J., xin3
missions, Christian, 259–61, 263
Mitchell, Leonel L., 206n92
Mitchell, Nathan D., xv
Moreau, F. X., 212n9
Moses, 250
Moskos, Charles, 155n1, 159
Mostow, Jonathan, 10n24
Mozarabs, 209
Müller, Klaus, 280n6, 292n25
Musonius, Andrzej, 129
Mutendi, Samuel, Prophet, 269
Muth, Franz-Christoph, 231n4

Nanko-Fernández, Carmen, 252, 254–55
Nelson, Robert S., 166n38
Nichols, Aidan, 192n47
Nietzsche, Friedrich Wilhelm, 3–4, 13
Nolte, Ernst, 92n35
Non-Jurors, 187
Nordlingen, *see* Hahn
North, Frank Mason, 144
Nutton, Vivian, 56n31

"observance," 85
Old, Hughes Oliphant, 192n49, 193
Oldham, William F., 138–39
Oleśnicki, Mikołaj, 101, 103
Olwig, Karen Fog, xiiin7
O'Regan, Cyril, 10
Origen, 36
Origenists, 60

Orla convocation, 125–27, 128, 130
Orthodox Church
   Byzantine, 186
   Eastern, 180
   Ethiopian, 229–42
   Greek, 155–75
Orthodox Vespers, 179
Orthodoxy, Western Rite, 184
Orzechowski, Stanisław, 102
Oxford Movement, 191, 196

Padilla, Elaine, xiii
Palmer, William, 191
Papua (Indonesia)
   evangelical churches in, 263–67
   liturgical monoculture in, 262–64
   Pentecostal assemblies in, 265–67
Park, Kyeyoung, 243n1
Parro, Sixto Ramón, 210n3
participation, liturgical, 11, 284–86
pasos, 213–16
Passover, *see* Pesach
Patriarch Bartholomew, 189n32
Patriarch Jeremias II, 186
Paul VI, Pope, 200–201
Pelikan, Jaroslav, 251–52
Peñalver, Ignacio Gallego, 210n3
penitential practices, 223–24
Perales, Jorge, 213n13
Pesach, 20, 25–29, 41
Peterson, Indira Viswanathan, 274n18
Petkunas, Darius, 103, 107n37, 109, 121, 126, 129
Phan, Peter, xiii, xvin21
Philo, 54
Pickstock, Catherine, 15
Pliny, 29n21
Plum, Anne-Madeleine, 210n10
Plüss, Caroline, xiiin6
Poland, 101–30
   Greater, 104, 114, 115
   Lesser, 101–15

Polish Reformed liturgy, 101–30
Polycrates, 28n19
Porter, H. Boone, 207n93
postbaptismal anointing, 201–2
Pott, Thomas, 161n27, 208
prayer books, 95, 97–98, 99
prayer for the sanctification of water, see "Great art Thou"
prayer addressed to Christ, 60–61, 63
processions, 209–27; see also Stations of the Cross
  Good Friday, 211–27
  Mozarab, 209–16
Proclus of Cyprus, 44
proliferation, 264–70
Protestant reformers, 101–30, 181
Providence (*pronoia*), 53–59
Przyjemska, Barbara Leszczyńska, 114, 118
Puniet, P. de, 44n4
Putnam, Robert D., 4

rabbinic prayers, 29–32
radio broadcasts, 282, 284–86
Radziwiłł, Janusz, 125, 130
Radziwiłł, Jerzy, 121
Radziwiłł, Krzysztof II, 123, 124, 128, 129
Radziwiłł, Mikołaj, 107, 119–20
Rattray, Thomas, 197–98
Rawls, John, 13
reform of female convents, 83–100
  Bursfeld and Windesheim, 85, 88–89, 92
  Dominican, 84, 87–92
  enclosure, 83, 85–86
  liturgical, 83–84, 86–88, 90–100
  of prayer books, 95, 97–98, 99
  works of art, 96–99
  written evidence of, 86–88
Reformation, 35, 181, 192–93, 195
  in Lithuania, 119–30
  in Poland, 101–30

Reformed Church
  Brethren, 104–9, 114–19
  Lesser Poland, 104–15, 117
  Lithuanian, 107, 119–30
  Lublin, 110–13
religion, 1
remix culture, 251
Riebe-Estrella, Gary, 252, 255
Rietz, Henry Morisada, 249, 250
Riggert, Ida-Christine, 89n18
ritual migration, 19–42
rituals, 19, 22–23
Robbins, Joel, 263n6
Robert, Dana, 268
Roberts, Charles LeVerne, 151n53
Roman Catholic Church, 181, 190, 195, 200–207, 205–27
  in Poland, 101–2, 115, 120, 129
Roman Missal, 203–7
Rome, 22
rootlessness, 10
Rosenpläntner, Johannes, 88n15
Rosenstock-Huessy, Eugen, 253
Rousseau, Olivier, 180, 181
Ruf, Ambrosius Karl, 285n14
Rumbaut, Rubén G., 243n1
Runciman, Steven, 186–87
Russian Orthodox refugees, 190
Rytter, Mikkel, xiiin7

Saller, Richard P., 39n48
salutationes, 39–40
Sam (Som), Sarin, 145–49
San Antonio, Texas, 209–10, 216–18, 225, 227
San Francisco, Saint Mary's Cathedral, 245
Sarnicki, Stanisław, 106
Sastri, Vedanayagam, 274–75, 276
Sauer, Christine, 88n13
Sauget, J.-M., 43n1
Schäfer, Peter, 19n1

Scheepsma, Wybren, 85n5
Scheidt, Hubert, 44n9
Schlotheuber, Eva, 89n17
Schmemann, Alexander, 160
Schmidt, Albert, 88n16
Schmidt, Marianne, 99n64
Schmitt, Sigrid, 86n7
Schopenhauer, Arthur, 3
Schreiter, Robert, xvin20
Schulz, Hans-Joachim, 161n26
Schwartz, C. F., 274
Schwesternbücher, 87
Scripture, liturgical reading of, 34–40
secularization, 2–5, 9–10
Seder Pesach, 20
Sefer Yosif Omez, 20
Senior, Donald, xvin21
Senn, Frank, 261
Septuagint, 27
Severus of Antioch, 44
"Sex and Religion in Migration", xiv n14
Seyoum, Moges, 232–33, 236, 237, 240
Shellabear, W. G., 144
Shenoute of Atripe, 60–61
signa sensibilia, 290–91
Słupecki, Feliks, 111n61, 114
Sng, Bobby E. K., 139n17
Sobornost, 189
societas, 1, 13–14
Spinks, Bryan D., xxiin23, 12, 15, 182n7, 183n12, 197n66, 199n75, 200, 295n33
Stancaro, Francesco, 101–3, 107
Starbucks, 270
Stations of the Cross, 98, 217–19, 221, 224–25
Steinke, Barbara, 90n28
Stephens, Edward, 197
Stern, Sacha, 24n8
Stinger, Charles L., 185
Stoics, 53–56
Sunday, 29n21, 36

"Sunday School Songs," 234, 239
Susin, Luiz Carlos, xiiin8
Swainson, Charles Anthony, 194n56, 197
Sylvius, Jakub, 101–2, 103, 105
symposia, 26, 28, 33, 35–40

Taft, Robert F., xvn16, 61, 161nn26–27, 182–83, 199
Talley, Thomas J., 45n10
tapestries, 96–97, 99
Taylor, Charles, 4–5, 6n11, 9, 14
telecommunications, 5
television broadcasts, 282, 284–86, 288
Tertullian, 38
Thali, Johanna, 95n42
Theodore of Mopsuestia, 33n31
Theodoret of Cyrus, 55
theology, 1–2, 9
Theophilus of Antioch, 54
Thirkield, Wilbur P., 151n53
Thoburn, James M., 138–39, 141
Thraede, Klaus, 29n21
Tiefensee, Eberhard, xviin22
Tilley, Terrence, 247
Tillich, Paul, 246
Tobias, Alexander, 20n2
Told, Silas, 131–34, 136, 150
Toledo, Spain, 209–16, 223, 225, 227
Torah, 28, 34n34
Toruń Synod, 110
tradition, 15, 246–48, 251–52
traditioning, 244, 251–57
tradition-maintenance, 244, 251
transience, 7–9
Trinity, 1
Turner, C. H., 60n42
Turnowski, Symeon, 116, 117
Tweed, Thomas A., xxiin23
Tworek, Stanisław, 116n93, 129

Uffmann, Heike, 86nn7–9
Unitarians, 108, 120–21, 122

United Methodist Church, 136n10

VanderKam, James C., 31n27
Vatican, xiin4
Vatican Council II, 153, 166, 172, 190, 206, 289, 294
  active participation, 288
  church as assembly, 286–88
Venantius Fortunatus, 212n10
Via Crucis, 98, 217–19, 221, 224–25
Vilnius synod, 122–23
virtual belonging, 6–12
Vladimir, Prince of Kiev, 179

Wagner, Georg, 60n42
Wahlde, Urban C. von, 27n16
Walker, Mary Alemu, 238
Walls, Andrew, 272
Wang, Ignatius, Bishop, 245
Ward, Pete, 10, 15
Weber, Max, 14
Węgierski, Tomasz, 125–26, 128
Wegmann, Susanne, 98n59
Weilandt, Gerhard, 88n14
Werbick, Jürgen, 287
Wesley, Charles, 133–34, 142–44, 145–47
Wesley, John, 131–33, 135, 136–37, 142–44, 150, 154
West, Fritz, 181n6

Western postbaptismal anointings, 201–2
Western Rite Orthodoxy, 184
White, James F., 136n11
Willing, Antje, 87n10
Wilms, Hieronymus, 89n17
Windesheim Congregation, 85
wine, 38
Winkler, Gabriele, 61n49, 189n32
Winston-Allen, Anne, 87n10
Wittekind, Susanne, 98n61
Włodawa convocation, 127–28
Woolfenden, Gregory, 184n15
Wright, Frank Lloyd, 166, 171–72
Wuthnow, Robert, 260, 270
Wybrew, Hugh, 161n26

Ximénez de Cisneros, Francisco, 211

Yamada, Frank M., 248–49, 250
Yared, St., 230, 232
Yoruba, 273
Young, Carlton R., 134n4, 145n36
Yuval, Israel, 19–21, 22, 41

Zacjusz, Szymon, 119–20
Zernov, Nicolas and Militza, 187, 189
Zheltov, Mikhail, 32n29
Zwingli, Ulrich, 102–3
Zygrowiusz, Jan, 122–23

www.ingramcontent.com/pod-product-compliance
Lightning Source LLC
Chambersburg PA
CBHW051935290426
44110CB00015B/1982